Crooked on the Stretcher Board
Ch'ats'ą' Vizhit Teech'iriikii

Collected Essays on Gwich'in History, Language, and Folk Culture

by Craig Mishler

with Kenneth Drizhuu Frank

IPI

ISBN 978-9-884732-2-0

Source Acknowledgments
The following essays appear here by written permission of the copyright holders. Photograph acknowledgments reside in the photo captions.

Missionaries in Collision: Anglicans and Oblates Among the Gwich'in, 1861-1865 (Chapter One) was previously published in Arctic 43(2):121-126, ©1990.
Anthropology on the Rocks: Portraits of the Gwich'in by Interior Alaskan Field Geologists (Chapter 2) first appeared in The Alaska Journal of Anthropology 16(1):1-20, ©2018.
John Fredson: A Biographical Sketch, 1896-1945 (Chapter Three) first appeared in the volume, John Fredson Edward Sapir Hàa Googwandak/Stories Told by John Fredson to Edward Sapir. Pp. 10-20. Ed. by Jane McGary. Fairbanks: Alaska Native Language Center. ©1982.
The Story of Tľyaa: The Alaska-Yukon Boundary Survey of 1911-1912 (Chapter 5) was previously published by the Yukon Historical and Museums Association in Proceedings of the Borderlands History Conference, ©1989.
He Said, They Say: the Uses of Reporting Speech in Gwich'in and Other Native American Languages (Chapter Eight) was originally titled, He Said, They Say: the Uses of Reporting Speech in Native American Folk Narrative and was published in Fabula: Journal of Folktale Studies 22(3-4):239-249, ©1981.
That's a Rubbaboo': Slavey Jargon in a Nineteenth Century Subarctic Speech Community (Chapter Ten) first appeared in The Journal of Creole and Pidgin Languages 23(2):264-287, ©2008.
Telling About Bear: A Northern Dene Men's Riddle Tradition (Chapter Twelve) was first published in The Journal of American Folklore 97(383):61-68, ©1984.
Gwich'in Fiddlers and Gwich'in Dancers: An Alternative Musical Standard (Chapter Eighteen) was originally published in Fiddler Magazine 6(2):4-7, ©1999.

IPI Press
Post Office Box 212
Hanover, New Hampshire 03755

Distributed by Oxbow Books and Casemate Publishers

Contents

Foreword

It is a great honor to be asked to write a foreward for Craig Mishler and Kenneth Drizhuu Frank's new book, *Crooked on the Stretcher Board' Ch'ats'ą' Vizhit Teech'iriikii: Collected Essays on Gwich'in History, Language and Folk Culture.* I have long admired works by both authors. In taking on the position of Curator of the Oral History Program at the University of Alaska (UAF) over a decade ago, it was with great delight I discovered that many of Mishler and Frank's recordings were in our collection. What a privilege it is to be the steward of such culturally important recordings. And, as an Associate Professor, one of the classes I teach on a bi-annual basis in the Department of Anthropology at UAF, is on the history and cultures of Northern Dené peoples in Alaska and Northern Canada. In doing so, I always assign several of the essays in this volume to my students to read.

I first came across Dr. Mishler's seminal 1993 work, *The Crooked Stovepipe: Athapaskan Fiddle Music and Square Dancing in the Northeast Alaska and Northwest Canada* in 1999 when I was a graduate student interviewing elders in the Gwich'in communities in the Northwest Territories in Canada. Upon reading *The Crooked Stovepipe* I was in awe at the meticulous research Mishler had done to uncover the original roots of the music and dances which were from Britain, especially from the Orkney men who had come to the Northwest Territories in Canada as part of the Hudson's Bay Company workforce. Mishler also delved into other influences in the book such as those from French Canadians and gold rush prospectors from the American South. He detailed the ways in which the Gwich'in people had taken these newly introduced art forms and shaped and molded them into their own distinctive fiddling tunes, unique bowing techniques, and dancing.

What fascinated me about the book was not only the short biographies of the various fiddlers included in the book, but Mishler's detailed historical analysis in order to frame the present-day music and dance. This historical context was crucial in understanding present day festivities in the Gwich'in communities. I was also impressed with how Mishler wove his field observations and narratives from the interviews he conducted into the seamless story he was telling. Subsequent to The Crooked Stovepipe, Mishler has gone on to publish eight other books, many of which feature the Gwich'in.

To my great delight, Craig and Kenneth and Allan Hayton were speaking at an Alaska Native Language Center Colloquium at UAF about Vasaagihdzak's Scarf, Gwich'in Caribou Anatomy and Verbal Art in October 2014. This was the first opportunity to meet each of these scholars. It was a fantastic colloquium where the panel members, using artifacts and slides, discussed the close links between Gwich'in linguistic and material culture. It was an excellent opportunity to be in this learning environment with these talented teachers, each bringing their own expertise to the subject at hand.

For readers unfamiliar with Frank's accomplishments, they are many. A member of the Ch'itsyaa clan with Gwich'in as his first language, Frank is an interviewer, transcriber, translator, research associate, Gwich'in language instructor, and Gwich'in language curriculum developer. He is also a teacher of traditional games, tools, drum making, and songs. He has published several scholarly publications and penned several professional papers in collaboration with Mishler. The work presented here in this impressive volume is enriched by Frank's cultural knowledge, expertise, and willingness to teach others about his culture.

I am sure others will join me in the pleasure of seeing some of Mishler and Frank's best work related to Gwich'in history, folk culture and language collected and placed here in one volume. The book is laid out into four thematic sections which can be read in the sequence presented or randomly depending on the reader's interest.

The first section deals with Gwich'in history and the biographies of two notable Gwich'in men, John Fredson and Elijah John. The essay "Missionaries in Collision" is an absolute must read for those seeking to understand the Christianization of the Gwich'in area and it is one that I assign as a reading to my students and to scholars who inquire about good historical articles about the early missionization of the Gwich'in.

The second section of the book is dedicated to topics around the Gwich'in language but again framed within historical contexts. Of note for example, Frank and Mishler trace the radical transformation of names and kinship relations that occurred quickly after the introduction of Anglo-American missionization and education. Despite the fact that many traditional names and kin terms were suppressed by colonizing forces, the essay ends on a positive note of their re-establishment which gives rise to a person's ethnicity, social identity, and belonging. Continuing in this vein, another essay is on Mishler's observances of contemporary naming ceremonies. This essay is enhanced by Kenneth's deep cultural knowledge. The piece again drives home the point that a contemporary naming ceremony is not only a way for a person to affirm their Indigenous identity, lay claim to their Native language, but that there is also a spiritual connection between individuals and families.

The third section of the book has within it four essays devoted to folklore and folklife. They are a must read for any anthropology student or Gwich'in scholar. As a folklorist, Mishler delves into one of the Northern Dené men's riddles, "Telling About Bear," which evolved from a proto-Athabaskan belief and behavior template. Other highlights include a recent cycle of tall tales about a man named Sam Peter, a look at the tradition of making lobsticks, and a traditional card game called Mizhur.

The fourth and final section is devoted to Gwich'in rituals and festivals. From a discussion of the historical to contemporary New Year celebrations, to Northern Dené Gatherings, the reader learns about the historical roots of these two celebrations. We finally come to an essay on

Gwich'in fiddlers and dancers which summarizes key concepts from The Crooked Stovepipe. Readers who have not read the book will find it an informative introduction to Gwich'in fiddling and dancing.

The final two essays both deal with remembering loved ones. In "Tr'igwitil" Mishler traces the historical path of memorial potlatches up to the present day, and in "Tsuk'ǫǫ Tee'itree Haa" he relies on his fieldnotes and reflects on his journey to the Tsuk'ǫǫ village site in 1997 to tend the graves of loved ones and pay tribute to them. It is a read that tugs at the heartstrings. From this ethnographic journey to record historical sites, Mishler discovers that it is not just physical archaeological sites that are important to cultural heritage; but is also the oral tradition, the oral history, the very stories of the memories of the people themselves that is important to pass along to the next generation.

Time never stands still and lives are not frozen in time. The resiliency and politically savviness of the Gwich'in people to protect their homeland in contemporary life brings readers up-to-date in Mishler's afterword where he reflects on the massive changes he has witnessed in the various Gwich'in villages from his first introduction to them in 1972 to today. The appendices are highly useful to students and scholars for the understanding of the labyrinth of kinship terms, the variants of the -nyaa verb, and the Gwich'in Fiddle Music Discography brings us back full circle to Mishler's original work, The Crooked Stovepipe.

Mishler's decades of commitment, his long affiliation with the Gwich'in communities, and his research collaborations with Kenneth Frank and other Gwich'in knowledge keepers are abundantly evident throughout the text. This book clearly is written with the inspiration, tutelage, language, cultural expertise, and teaching experience of Frank, with whom Mishler has been a research and writing partner since the mid-1990s. It is from their several scholarly publications and professional papers that these essays were born. Mishler and Frank's unique, meticulously researched, pleasant writing style, and their ability to inform the reader about the historical context of the subjects at hand, make their work so important.

Events today can only be understood and appreciated with historical knowledge and within their cultural context, and this book is successful in completing these tasks. With annotations at the end of each essay, and a bevy of references cited, students, scholars, Gwich'in and non-Gwich'in alike, as well as anyone interested in the subject at hand, have a plethora of further readings to consider.

This incredible volume of essays by Mishler and Frank are essential for those who are interested in Gwich'in history, folk culture, and language on both the American and Canadian sides of the border. Educators at all levels will find this volume a great asset as the essays are concise and will easily fit into a curriculum that speaks to the array of subjects covered in this book. This is a book that should be in every library, every Gwich'in community, and be part of the curriculum in Gwich'in linguistic studies, Native Studies, and Northern Studies in higher learning institutions.

Leslie McCartney
Associate Professor,
Curator of Oral History,
University of Alaska Fairbanks

Co-author with Gwich'in Tribal Council of *Our Whole Gwich'in Way of Life Has Changed / Gwich'in K'yuu Gwiidandài' Tthak Ejuk Gòonlih Stories from the People of the Land* (2020).

Acknowledgements

In addition to my longtime research and writing partner Kenneth Frank, I would also like to thank many others over the years who have helped me write these essays and have given me helpful comments. I'm extremely grateful for having the opportunity to work with Allan Hayton, who has kept me in tune with Gwich'in language revitalization efforts. Allan works quietly behind the scenes to write grants that promote and preserve not just Gwich'in but all Alaskan Dene languages. Allan was key to helping me write the Afterward by identifying which Alaskan schools, which communities, and which teachers are still active in teaching Gwich'in.

Acknowledgements specific to each paper are included at the end of those papers. At this time I would also like to acknowledge the many fluent Gwich'in translators who have assisted me over the past fifty years, several of whom have now passed on—Judy Erick, Moses Paul Gabriel, Edward John, Lillian Garnett, Allan Hayton, Ruth Carroll, Hishinlai Peter, Katherine Peter, Kenneth Frank, Jerry Frank, Mary Rose Gamboa, Hannah P. Solomon, Mardow Solomon, Sarah James, Lincoln Tritt, Bill Stevens, Trimble Gilbert, and Nena Russell.

Most of all, I am indebted to the Frank family. Over four generations, starting with my first visit to Johnny and Sarah Frank at Gold Camp, they have individually and collectively led me to understand their language and culture in so many ways. Mary and Hamel Frank, especially, took me in to their home in the early 1970s and helped me define my research goals. Their warmth and hospitality are unmatched. Little did I know that when I walked through their door for the first time that I was walking through the door of the whole Gwich'in nation. With their help, I was able to build friendship networks that have sustained me for my entire career. It was through Mary and Hamel that I met their son Kenneth and his siblings, and it's all because of them that I returned again and again to learn more, to write more.

I want to extend a special heartfelt thanks too, to Kenneth's wife, Caroline Tritt-Frank, who from time to time has assisted Kenneth with her expert opinion on difficult words, and to their daughter Crystal, who continues to amaze us all with her command of the language. I'm indebted to Crystal for sharing her photos and for allowing me to unwrap and reveal her wonderful collection of Gwich'in names. Her ongoing friendship, along with that of her sister Tisheena, is a special gift.

I truly appreciate all the hard work of Leslie McCartney for peer reviewing a draft of this book and for providing a great wealth of constructive comments for its improvement, especially from her Canadian perspective. As a result of her close reading, this is a much better book. Leslie has worked with the Gwich'in for many, many years and continues to do so with extraordinary grace, empathy, and scholarly rigor. We are indeed privileged to have her write the Foreword.

I've been blessed during my work with the Gwich'in to receive numerous grants that have made numerous research projects and publications possible. These grants have come from the National Park Service, the National Science Foundation, the National Endowment for the Humanities, the American Philosophical Society, and the Alaska Humanities Forum.

I owe a special debt of gratitude to Peter Mittenthal, our independent publisher whose enthusiasm and professionalism for making scholarly books look bright and beautiful prevails once again. Peter is a great friend of the indigenous peoples of the Arctic.

Finally, I owe a lifetime of gratitude to my lovely wife Barbara, my steadfast companion and sounding board over the many years I've been doing research and writing on the Gwich'in. She has always embraced and welcomed my Gwich'in friends and many others into our home and greeted them all with endless courtesy and good cheer.

Introduction

The Journey

My first journey to Gwich'in country began while I was teaching English composition and literature at Anchorage Community College in the late 1960s and early 1970s. It soon became obvious to me that there were no courses at all offered in the field of Alaska Native studies, and I decided to apply for a National Endowment for the Humanities grant to take a year's sabbatical. It was my intention to help develop a curriculum or a course that would appeal to Alaska Native students.

At this time I was learning about the importance of folklore and oral traditions and about documenting those traditions. I was also developing a college course called "Alaskan Folklore." While waiting for the grant proposal to be reviewed, I read in the Anchorage newspaper that there would be a talk and workshop on Alaska Native Languages at Alaska Methodist University (now Alaska Pacific University) taught by Dr. Michael Krauss and his companion linguist Jeff Leer. This was in the spring of 1972.

At the end of the workshop, I asked Dr. Krauss if he could recommend a good place to go off the road system where lots of people still speak one of the Interior Dene languages, and he suggested I try the Gwich'in area. In fact, he said that coming summer Dick Mueller, a Wycliffe Bible translator, was going to be teaching a class in Gwich'in literacy at the University of Alaska in Fairbanks using a new orthography.

Krauss then put me in touch with Mueller, who kindly allowed me to sit in on the class. When the NEH grant finally came through, I traveled to Fairbanks and attended classes there for two or three weeks. Through Dick Mueller's class I became familiar with Gwich'in phonology, lexicon, and grammar, and I interacted and made friends with several of the other students who spoke the language fluently, especially Moses Paul Gabriel from Chalkyitsik.

When I asked about a place to rent for the summer, Mueller put me in touch with Bill Pfisterer, a school teacher in Fort Yukon who went on to edit two worthy books of Gwich'in stories, *Shandaa: In My Lifetime (Herbert, 1982) and K'aiiroondak: Behind the Willows* (Martin, 1993). I never did meet Pfisterer in person but briefly corresponded with him and arranged to rent his house. I took my wife Barbara and little daughter Molly with me to live there for the summer. We flew to Fort Yukon on Wien Airlines in June, 1972, and I immediately began to network with members of the local Native community.

Lacking transportation, I walked on foot everywhere, asked for referrals, and cautiously began making audio recordings on my Sony TCM-5000 cassette tape recorder. Behind Pfisterer's house was another house occupied by the Alaska Rural Community Action Program. I met its director, Donald Peter, who offered to let me use his ¾" video tape recorder, and with that I was able to record visual performances of stories and songs from a few elders, namely the fiddler Charlie Peter and the storyteller Stanley Luke. While out walking one day I also met up with our neighbor Dan Frank, the son of Johnny and Sarah Frank. I knew about Johnny Frank being a famous storyteller from reading Robert McKennan's book, *The Chandalar Kutchin* (1965). So I quickly made friends with Dan, who told me his parents were still alive and living in log cabins at a remote place called Gold Camp, way out in the bush north of the village of Venetie.

At the end of that summer I returned to the Palmer area, where we had a log house out in the Matanuska Valley. In the early fall, on a leave of absence from teaching, at the age of thirty, I decided to pay a visit to Moses Paul Gabriel in Chalkyitsik, who put me up in his home and introduced me to Rev. David Salmon, Daniel John, Richard Martin, Bella Francis, and Moses Peter, all major tradition bearers. Moses, a fluent speaker of Gwich'in, became my first Gwich'in translator, transcriber, and collaborator.

After winter set in, I made plans to go to Gold Camp. In early November of 1972, I flew to Venetie and made inquiries there about finding transportation to Gold Camp. Johnny and Sarah's grandson, Stanley Frank, along with Christopher Johnson, agreed to take me up on a toboggan (dachan vał) pulled by a snow machine. Robert Frank accompanied us half way to his trapping camp. It was a strenuous and exciting trip, and the full story is told in my Introduction to *Neerihiinjìk: We Traveled from Place to Place: The Gwich'in Stories of Johnny and Sarah Frank* (2001). I didn't know it at the time, but that toboggan ride changed my life.

From 1976 to 1981, I enrolled in graduate school at the University of Texas at Austin, where I eventually was granted a doctorate degree in folklore and anthropology. I lost touch with most of my Gwich'in friends during those years but was eager to return to Alaska field work and to teaching at Anchorage Community College. However, because of my interests and training at Texas, I began teaching cultural anthropology at the University of Alaska at Anchorage and then in 1982 decided to accept a position in the archaeology survey and oral history program at the Alaska Division of Geological and Geophysical Surveys. After the Exxon Valdez oil spill in 1989, I took a position as a subsistence resource specialist with the Alaska Department of Fish and Game. During these years and well into my retirement, I kept returning to the villages, feeling especially drawn to the community of Venetie.

The Contents and the Title

The present book contains ethnographic samples of Gwich'in folk culture, taken from my personal experience visiting and observing the Gwich'in over a period of fifty years. They are amazing, resilient people whose very survival has created a compelling story. Over these many years I've had the privilege to visit many communities in the Gwich'in Nation, including Birch Creek, Circle, Chalkyitsik, Fort Yukon, Venetie, Arctic Village, Beaver, Old Crow, Fort McPherson, Tsiigehtshik, and Inuvik, as well as some truly remote places such as Tąįh tr'oo'ee, Tsuk'ǫǫ, K'ahtsik (Fish Camp), the upper K'aii'eechu'njik (aka the East Fork of the Chandalar River) and the upper Ch'oonjik (Porcupine River) above Old Crow. All of these communities and wild natural areas have informed and shaped my perspective (Fig. 0.1).

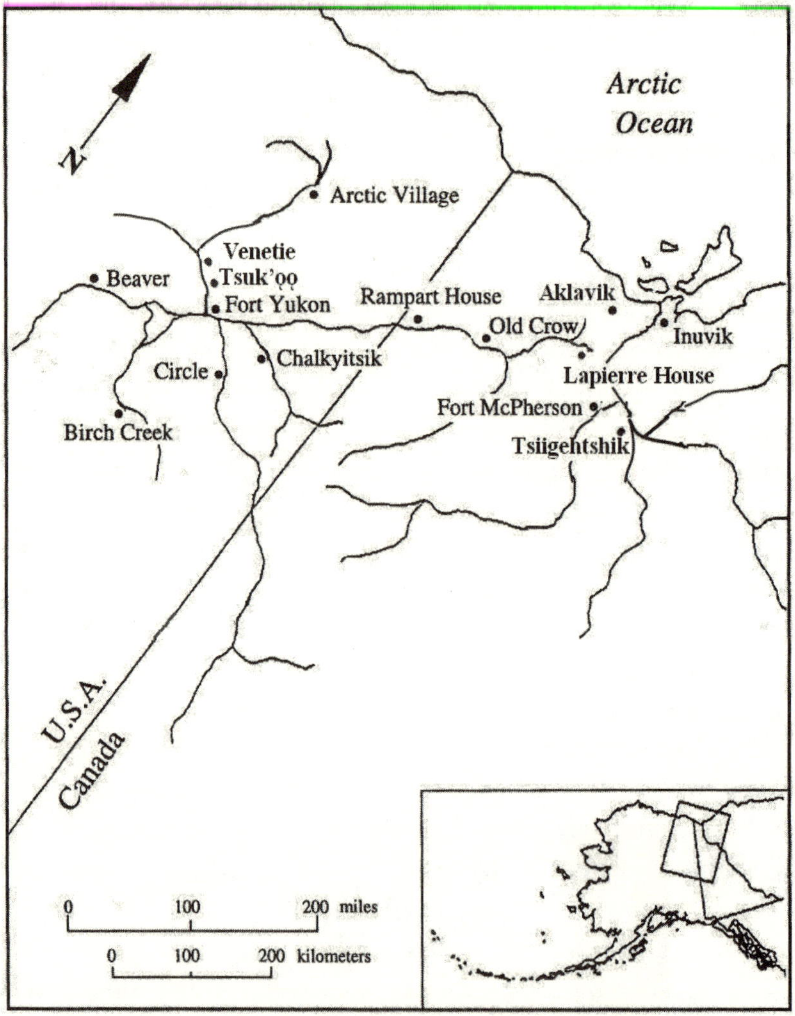

Figure 0.1. Gwich'in communities in northeast Alaska, the Yukon, and the Northwest.

The present book is topically selective, a sampler divided into four thematic sections: History and Biography, Language, Folklore and Folklife, and Rituals and Festivals. The twenty selected pieces, both old and new, are not arranged in chronological order and actually can be read in any sequence, depending on the reader's interests. In other words, they may be read and enjoyed in the moment regardless of when they were written or what they are about. Starting with 'He Said, They Say' in 1981, a fair number of the papers have been published in academic journals, where they have not been easily accessible except to journal subscribers and researchers in large university libraries.

The cover title of this volume, *Crooked on the Stretcher Board*, comes from the translation of Sarah Frank's poetic nickname for her great granddaughter Crystal Frank, Ch'ats'ą' Vizhit Teech'iriikii. Crystal received this humorous name because Sarah didn't feel that Crystal's parents (Kenneth and Caroline) were raising her correctly. Rather than criticize them directly, she picked a well-chosen metaphor as a name for Crystal. For the uninitiated, a stretcher board is a tapered piece of plain thin wood (Fig. 0.2). The stretcher board allows fur trappers to stretch and dry their pelts prior to selling them or sewing them into handmade articles of clothing. A pelt is placed on the stretcher board inside out with the fur side down, thereby allowing the skin membrane on the outside to dry. If an animal's pelt is not mounted correctly on the board, it sits askew, on an angle. Stretcher boards are made in different sizes for muskrats, beaver, marten, mink, weasels, foxes, wolverines, and wolves.

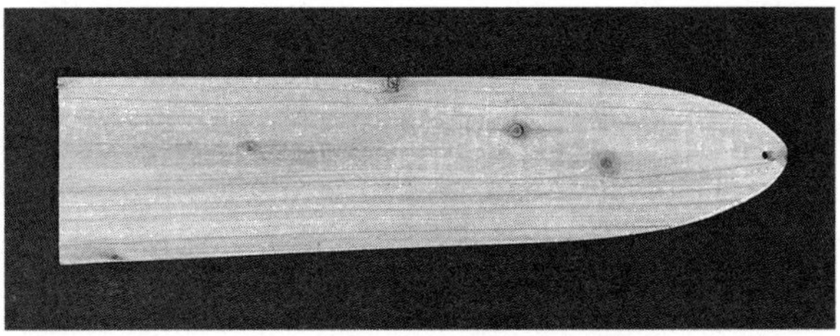

Figure 0.2. Commercially made stretcher board, about the size for fox or muskrat. Photo by Craig Mishler.

Like many other Gwich'in of her generation, Crystal actually has multiple Gwich'in names, a semiotic phenomenon explored in more detail in Chapter 6. *Crooked on the Stretcher Board* was also chosen because of the linguistic importance of personal names and because it playfully resonates well with the title of my first book, *The Crooked Stovepipe: Athapaskan Indian Fiddling and Square Dancing in Northeast Alaska and Northwest Canada* (Mishler, 1993). It also ties nicely into elder Kenny Thomas's moral philosophy of "Living by the Straight Board," of not talking about people behind their backs, or telling lies about each other (Thomas 2005:237-241).

The Goals

Each essay, in the words of Roy Wagner in *The Invention of Culture* (2016), makes parts of Gwich'in folk culture "visible" to those living outside of the homeland and outside of the culture. But each essay also makes parts of that culture freshly visible and accessible to those living inside the culture, where certain distinct practices, customs, beliefs, ingrained understandings, texts, and patterns of speech have diminished or faded from view since my work began in 1972. I trust that younger Gwich'in can benefit from such observations. As an additional resource, my field recordings have been donated to the Alaska Native Language Archive (ANLA) at the University of Alaska Fairbanks and to the University of Alaska Consortium Library Archive in Anchorage (Mishler 2023). I'm also pleased to announce that a good portion of my Gwich'in language recordings have now been digitized and are freely available for listening to online (see https://www.uaf.edu/anla/).

Historically, the Gwich'in have largely been marginalized and left out of the American mainstream. We see evidence of that in the state and federal management of fish and wildlife, in the imposition of the international border (Chapter 5), in the era of forcibly sending children away to secondary boarding schools, and in the heavily colonialized Alaska primary school system that still exists today (see Hirshberg, Cost, and Alexander, 2023). Gwich'in history is hard to romanticize.

To that extent, field documentation of the language and its associated folk culture is vital. While I certainly don't pretend to represent the Gwich'in, I do hope that what I write is of special interest to them. Certainly the loss of fluent Gwich'in speakers since I first came around in the early 1970s has resulted in profound cultural loss, for these older speakers have not been replaced. At this writing there is no one fluent in the language under the age of forty. Gwich'in, like all languages, continues to change and evolve. Even the name of the language itself has evolved during my lifetime from Loucheux to Kutchin to Gwich'in and most recently, to Dinjii Zhuu K'yaa.

As I now reread and revise this present family of papers, they rekindle in me some of the original joy and excitement which first led me to their writing. As a family of papers, they now stand together and live together. For me, they were each breakthrough discoveries, dynamic and transformative, that enhanced and multiplied my understanding of human creativity and generations of oral tradition in remote rural Alaska. The papers, taken collectively, provide a deep look and multiple points of entry into Gwich'in daily life as I saw it and knew it over five decades. The topics of these papers were both implicitly and explicitly shared by elders who, even after passing on, continue to be sources of vitality and wellsprings of knowledge. The ones who taught me magically invited me to become a part of their past. More than that, they showed me a different way of being in the world.

One major paper not included here is the lengthy ethnohistoric essay I co-authored with the late Ernest S. Burch, Jr., "*The Di'hąįį Gwich'in: Mystery People of Northern Alaska*" (Burch and Mishler 1995). For those who have not yet seen it, "The Di'hąįį Gwich'in" collaboration with Tiger Burch remains easily accessible through *Arctic Anthropology*, a major research journal. Also missing is a follow-up paper, "*Collaborating with the Tiger: the Evolution of an Essay*" (Mishler 2012). It's my feeling now that the extended length of these two papers makes them largely a standalone effort, and to have included them here might have pre-empted some of my hitherto unpublished papers which until now have only been shared orally at academic meetings: namely chapters 5-7, 9, 11, 13-17, and 19-20.

As a longtime Alaskan, most of my field work has been in Gwich'in communities on the Alaskan side of the international border. Travel to the Canadian side has proven to be more difficult and more expensive. For a few years Air North provided a route for international flights, but today Alaskans must drive the Alaska Highway to Whitehorse, overnight at a hotel, and then fly on Air North to Old Crow, Fort McPherson, and Inuvik. As noted in Chapter 2, "The Story of Tł'yaa", the international boundary, created by non-Native governmental entities in the late nineteenth century, injected an artificial colonial barrier to game hunting, social interaction, and freedom of movement. These limitations have been partially addressed and partially overcome in modern times by the political unity of the Gwich'in Steering Committee, the Gwich'in Council International, the International Porcupine Caribou Board, and the blossoming of bi-annual Gwich'in Gatherings on both sides of the border (Chapter 17). Occasionally Gwich'in still travel by motor boat across the border between Fort Yukon and Old Crow, but it's a long slow trip over many hundreds of miles, and every year gasoline gets more and more expensive.

I would also like to add a note about the exploratory nature of this volume. I don't pretend to provide a comprehensive treatment of Gwich'in lifeways, which are far too complex for one book. I have included very little about Gwich'in material culture, for example, even though I have a substantial collection of women's beadwork and greatly admire their meticulous sewing skills. I confess too that the papers are piecemeal, yet at the same time they are also symbolic of the Gwich'in ethnographic landscape and the result of my ongoing folkloristic curiosity. I trust that they are topics most readers can connect with because they are rooted in what I have seen and heard and where I have been.

For over five decades I have been lucky to stand at the intersection of many facets of Gwich'in culture. One by one these topics fell into my lap, creating new reflexive spaces and opportunities for documentation, for conservation. This happened as I gradually extended my local friendships to an inclusive network of individuals, families, and communities. As an ongoing witness, I feel that I have a responsibility to convey the wonderment I felt as I left my calling card at many doors.

The Collaboration

These essays are largely written from an etic point of view, although Kenneth Drizhuu Frank has reduced my social distance by teaching me to embrace his deeply emic perspective on a wide range of topics. He is such a source of inspiration that I asked him to be the co-author of four of the present essays. While he may not have directly written sections of the other papers, his authorial voice is strongly felt throughout. While he was physically punished in school for speaking Gwich'in as a child, Kenneth stayed close to his grandparents and survived to become a most amazing, knowledgeable, and fluent messenger from previous generations. He is quick to correct me when I am mistaken and keeps me humble.

To take just one example, for years I wrote the name of the Gwich'in card game known to me as "Mazhur," but a couple of years ago when we discussed the paper, Kenneth was insistent that it should be spelled "Mizhur." And so I made the tiny but important phonemic correction (see Chapter 14). Even in the writing of papers in this volume which do not show his direct co-authorship, Kenneth was nearly always my close oral collaborator and consultant. His breath and fingerprints are virtually on every page.

One of our biggest projects was enabled by a grant from the National Park Service to the Native Village of Venetie Tribal Government in the late 1990s. This grant allowed us to conduct field surveys of numerous historic and cemetery sites on the Venetie Reserve. Our efforts were centered on the communities of Venetie and Arctic Village and included two riverboat trips. An account of the first boat trip is detailed in Chapter 20, when I traveled with elders in early June, 1997, from Venetie to the old village of Tsuk'ǫǫ, and the second trip occurred when we traveled in Kenneth's 20-foot river boat from Arctic Village to the limits of navigation on the upper K'aiieech'uunjik (the East Fork of the

Chandalar River) in late August and early September, 1998. We were joined on that trip by elder Trimble Gilbert and Wilbert Kendi, a visitor from Fort McPherson (see Fig. 0.3 in photographic signature). When the grant ran out, we placed all the original site descriptions, place names, and narrative reports from these trips with the tribal government offices in Venetie.

Kenneth is truly my lucky penny. Heads up, he keeps coming back to work with me again and again whenever I need him. And then there is the magic of his singing and drumming. In 2014 he was the recipient of the Angayuqaq Oscar Kawagley Indigenous Scholar Award from the University of Alaska Fairbanks. Though we live far apart, our two families have remained close for over forty years, only a text or phone call away. For those interested in methodologies and how we work together, please see our papers, Collaborating in Gwich'in on the Web (Mishler, Frank, and Hayton, 2014) and Shriniinlii 'Fix It': the Grease Mechanics of Translating Gwich'in (Mishler and Frank, 2021).

The Reciprocity

I'm privileged to have traveled and lived among the Gwich'in, and I now have the honor and pleasure of giving back some of the great moments that were generously given to me. As I look at my own shadow, I take full responsibility for any mistakes or omissions in this volume, knowing only too well that the linguistic and ethnographic enterprise is prone to human error. But in the end this is a humanistic narrative, one which provides a glimpse at the unique Gwich'in cosmic spectrum and offers insights into their sacred spoken connections between people, places, water, and animals out on the land.

Craig Mishler
June 14, 2023

1. Missionaries In Collision:

Anglicans and Oblates among the Gwich'in, 1861-1865

It's fairly well-known that during the early years of exploration in the far North, British and French-Canadian fur traders were the first whites to arrive and settle on the frontier. Backed with substantial capital, the fur trade took priority over other kinds of sustained European contact with indigenous Athabaskan peoples such as the Gwich´in, previously known as the Kutchin or Loucheux (see Slobodin, 1981:530-532), whose homeland spreads across the Mackenzie River basin of the Northwest Territories, the northern Yukon Territory, and northeastern Alaska. It was not for many years after the major forts were built and after transportation routes were well-established that British and French missionaries followed.

The Peel's River Post (or Fort Bell), for example, later to be called Fort McPherson, was established by John Bell in 1840-1841, but the first missionaries did not arrive there until nearly two decades later. Although the Anglican Archdeacon James Hunter of the London-based Church Missionary Society made an initial scouting trip into the upper and middle Mackenzie River region and met a party of visiting Peel River Gwich'in at Fort Simpson in the fall of 1858, it was 1860 before Father Henri Grollier, the Oblate priest who started a Roman Catholic mission at Fort Resolution in 1852 and another at Fort Good Hope in 1859, made the first missionary trip to the Gwich'in living at McPherson (Hunter, 1859:237; Coudert and Le Chevalier, 1955:371). In a similar fashion, Fort Yukon, located in Gwich'in territory at the extreme outer edge of the Hudson's Bay Company interior trade network, was established by Alexander Hunter Murray in 1847 but did not receive its first missionary, the Anglican William West Kirkby, until 1861.

The fact that missionaries arrived in the region somewhat later than the traders, however, in no way diminished their tremendous power and influence over the Gwich'in. Since the impact of missionaries on aboriginal peoples in the North over the long term has arguably been more profound than that of the traders, in that missionaries intended to accomplish what Robin Fisher has called "the complete destruction of the traditional integrated Indian way of life" (1977:125), it is certainly worth our while to attempt to understand the kinds of social and psychological conflicts they generated during the early period of missionization.

Unlike the Hudson's Bay Company, which had a virtual monopoly on trade, the Anglican and Catholic Churches found themselves in a competitive free-for-all as they tried to win Indian converts. In the Mackenzie River region it seems to have started when Archdeacon Hunter butted heads with Father Grollier in 1858 over their mutual plans to set up missions at Fort Simpson (Hunter, 1859:235), but this was only a preliminary skirmish which did not directly involve the Gwich'in. When Anglicans and Oblates finally did visit Fort McPherson and Fort Yukon almost simultaneously in the early 1860s, the Gwich'in were placed in a real quandary as to where to place their spiritual allegiance. This quandary is well-illustrated by the following series of events.

On June 19, 1861, the Anglican William Kirkby, left his home at Fort Simpson and floated down the Mackenzie River and then ascended up Peel River to Fort McPherson. From Fort McPherson he proceeded on foot westward over the Richardson Mountains to Lapierre House on the Bell River, where he held services for 15-20 Indians. Traveling with him was a young Gwich'in boy named William Flett, the stepson of Orkneyman James Flett, who acted as his interpreter. From Lapierre House Kirkby floated down the Porcupine River to Fort Yukon. He arrived at the Fort on July 5, greeted by his friend James Lockhart (the Chief Trader in Charge), the American naturalist Robert Kennicott, and 500 Indians gathered there to trade (Kirkby, 1861b; Boon, 1965:39).

In making this trip Kirkby became the very first clergyman to visit the homeland of the western or Alaskan Gwich'in. After a frantic week of holding services three times a day, teaching hymns, and receiving long lines of individuals into his improvised schoolroom at the Fort (Boon, 1965:42), Kirkby claimed his influence was so great that "the medicine men renounced their craft, murderers confessed their sins, polygamists gave up their wives, mothers told of deeds of infanticide. . ., and then all begged for pardon and for grace" (Kirkby, 1861b; 1863; 1872:419).

When he left Fort Yukon a week later, Kirkby was ecstatic. However, when he arrived back at Fort McPherson on August 2nd, he was dismayed to find Father Grollier, who was attempting to convert the Gwich'in to Catholicism. Besides his earlier work at Fort Resolution, Grollier had established a mission at Fort Good Hope in 1859 and another at Fort McPherson in September, 1860, but he was not entirely welcome at McPherson. Mr. Gaudet, the Hudson's Bay Company trader there, had complained about the priest's activities the year before and offered him no assistance. Even as Grollier landed his canoe at McPherson that June, he was met by a Loucheux woman who apparently told him: "The minister is good to us; he is better than you; he gives us tobacco and tea. He has taken all your pictures and crosses out of the camps" (Quoted in Duchaussois, 1923:272-273). Grollier had wanted to visit Lapierre House and Fort Yukon, but his poor health and his inability to get supplies at McPherson forced him to return to Fort Good Hope that same August.

Earlier that summer at Fort Liard, Kirkby became disillusioned with Catholic missionaries when he learned that a priest he shared his tent with was attempting to win away his own followers. He was openly jealous of the Oblates' success in winning Indian converts, and attributed that success to their "perfect knowledge of the [Indian] language, their gaudy ceremonies, and...their untiring zeal and perseverance" (1861a; see also Kirkby, 1860). At the same time he accused them of using unscrupulous means to accomplish their purposes, including falsehoods and frauds. He also disliked their methods, claiming that they merely taught the Indians to recite prayers and did not endeavor to teach or preach to them.

According to Grollier, however, Kirkby himself was bribing those who listened to him with tobacco, and he accused Kirkby's converts of being "tobacco Christians" (Grollier, 1860). Grollier claimed that Kirkby had approached him at Fort Norman to try to work out an agreement for the good of the Indians such that they would try not to missionize the same forts. However, Grollier saw this as a ruse, thinking that Kirkby wanted to take over both Fort Norman and Fort Simpson.

The battle was on to establish ideological territories in the western subarctic. Being "reasonable" men and recognizing their limited resources, Grollier and Kirkby finally agreed to leave those Indians alone who were already praying with missionaries of the other faith--an agreement which was lacking in sincerity and was broken repeatedly. This truce was probably arranged through interpreters since although Grollier could speak at least one Indian language, he did not speak much English and Kirkby did not speak French (Hunter, 1859:236; Grollier, 1860).

Kirkby left Fort McPherson in August, 1861 and returned to spend the winter with his family at Fort Simpson. In the summer of 1862, he headed north to McPherson again, arriving there on June 13, where he prepared to make another visit to the western Gwich'in on what is now the Alaskan side of the mountains. It was certainly to Kirkby's consternation then, that Father Jean Séguin, an Oblate priest sent to replace the ailing Grollier, had moved from Fort Good Hope to Fort McPherson in April and had been preaching to the Peel River Gwich'in for over a month before Kirkby arrived (Séguin, 1862a; 1862b).

While Kirkby seems to have left no detailed accounts of events which transpired in Fort McPherson, it is instructive and worthwhile to read the letters of Father Séguin to Bishop Taché. Like Grollier, Séguin also complained that Kirkby was gaining the loyalty of the Gwich'in by bribing them with gifts of tobacco (Séguin, 1862b). When Kirkby returned to McPherson on the 13th of June, Séguin observed that some of his own followers went to see the Anglican to get some tobacco and then faithfully returned to him. According to Séguin, this made "the small man" furious.

Kirkby never admits in his journal that he gave out tobacco to the Indians, but his direct predecessor, friend, and superior, Archdeacon Hunter, clearly did give some away to the Slavey chief Grand Blanc at Fort Liard and to unnamed others at Fort Simpson where the Loucheux from Peel's River came to visit during the fall of 1858 (Hunter, 1859:237;240;265). It is also noteworthy that Kirkby's successor, Rev. Robert McDonald, made gifts of tobacco on at least one occasion to some Black River Gwich'in camped along the Porcupine River

(McDonald, 1866:April 21). Knowing that this practice was already well established in the region before Kirkby ever arrived, that it was continued after he left, and that Séguin's allegations are made repeatedly within in the context of Indian expectations, we can conclude that there probably was some real substance to this charge.

Before Kirkby arrived at McPherson in June, 1862, Séguin gave religious instruction to about 30 families of Peel River Gwich'in. Using the services of Mrs. Gaudet, the wife of the Hudson's Bay Company manager, the priest was able to translate three prayers, the Pater, the Ave, and the Credo into Gwich'in.

Most interesting is Séguin's dramatic story that:

> An Indian came to tell me that he [Kirkby] wanted to see me. I told him to answer that if he needed me, he could find me. The reply was carried back to him, and soon I saw my good little man as red as a rooster's comb. Entering, he asked what I wanted of him. I told him that he was the one asking for me, and my response embarrassed him for a minute, but finally he replied that he hadn't called for me.
>
> Then he accused me of having told the Indians not to shake his hand. I told him that he was enough of a liar to have invented this story and to show me the Indians I said it to. 'There are plenty of them', he told me.
>
> 'I only ask you for one', I replied.
>
> He went to the door and invited in an Indian from the Mackenzie River. I asked the latter where he had seen and heard me speak in this fashion. The Indian replied that he had never seen me. The little man got more and more red-faced. He then invited me to go outside and assemble the Indians so that he could read his bible and confront me before them. I replied that when he had gone to school a little bit more and understood his own bible a little better, I would see what I could do. For the moment I begged him to go back to school. He stomped with rage. He wished then to speak to the Indians who were gathered at the door, but I told them not to listen to him, that he spoke foolishly. . . .

> The Indians began to laugh when he tried to speak. . . . Thereupon, not knowing what position to take and having also some need of a little fresh air, he said that his breakfast was getting cold, that it was a long time since he left his table. Then he grabbed his little hat and left.
>
> Then he started calling all the Indians, one after the other, into his house, like a doctor receiving his patients. But he had parted with all his tobacco. Furious at not obtaining anything here, he left the day after his arrival, June 14, for Lapierre House and Fort Yukon (Séguin, 1862b).

So how did this big showdown come about? Was it simply a case of miscommunication? In contrast to Grollier, Séguin was fluent in English and, judging from his own words in the above account, must have told the Indian messenger something like, "If he needs me, he can find me," which may have been construed to mean, "Tell him to come see me." However, after reviewing the full circumstances, including the report of the Indians laughing at Kirkby, I think it's more reasonable to suppose that this theological minidrama was not the result of miscommunication between the two missionaries but that it had been deliberately staged by the Gwich'in.

I believe that the Gwich'in were so confused by the conflicting ideologies of the two missionaries that they were anxious to know what would happen when the two men met face-to-face and toe-to-toe. This confrontation between the minister and the priest was probably arranged by the Gwich'in in order to see which missionary was the most powerful. In other words, which one had the strongest medicine? As Kenneth Coates (1982:67-68) has observed, the Gwich'in of that period were well-established as middlemen between the Hudson's Bay Company and more distant tribes and were very adept at "manufacturing" competitive situations to manipulate the fur trade to their own advantage. It is equally important to realize that they did the same thing with the missionaries.

Kirkby's and Séguin's rivalry continued to build for the next few days, as Séguin decided to join Kirkby on foot with a caravan of 20 Indians to Lapierre House. Séguin arrived with Kirkby at Lapierre House on June 17, 1862, where he met the zealous Protestant, James Flett, who as post manager threatened not to give ammunition to Indians who prayed with the priest.

One night after prayers, Séguin noticed that the two chiefs in their midst began to chant loudly in Broken Slavey a pidginized phrase he wrote down as: "ctchezjekudjin, paginci sni l'aime todi, kka ts'dezjie sni l'aime clan" ('The English priest I don't love at all, but I love the tobacco very much') (Séguin, 1862a; 1862b). This curious mixture of Chipewyan, French, and Gwich'in caused Séguin much laughter and merriment and apparently prompted the embarrassed Kirkby to get a translation from Flett's son.

The historian in us all enjoys knowing something of what went through the minds of these adversaries on their arduous journey over the Richardson Mountains. Fortunately, both men kept records. Kirkby wrote that "We suffered equally in walking the mountains, but I took care not to manifest the pain and fatigue I felt that he might not rejoice over my weakness or even know it" (Kirkby, 1862). The suffering was not entirely equal, however. The party had to ford twelve rivers, four of which were waist deep, and also break trail along muddy mountainsides. Séguin admitted he was envious because Kirkby had a mosquito head net and gloves, while he had none. The bugs were so thick that they hindered his eyesight during the day and made it impossible to close his eyes at night. They bit so badly they made Séguin's head feel like a pumpkin and his fingers swelled up until they looked like sausages (Séguin 1862a; Champagne, 1943:16-17).

Séguin accused Kirkby of lying to the Gwich'in, of telling them that he, as a priest, had several wives. According to 19th century Gwich'in standards, having several wives should have elevated his status (Hardisty,

1872:312; Leechman, 1954:29; McKennan, 1965:56), but Séguin figured that Kirkby damaged his reputation so much that out of sixty Indians gathered at Lapierre House, only fifteen of them would listen to him. Specifically, he wrote that Kirkby tried to make the Indians believe that a priest resembles the devil by always keeping fire in front of him, that his candles represent the fires of hell to which he and those who pray with him must go after he dies (Séguin, 1862b). How much of this was actually said by Kirkby will never be known, but it is rather telling that five days later Kirkby went on to Fort Yukon rejoicing while Séguin returned rather discouraged to Fort McPherson.

In September, 1862, Séguin received orders from Bishop Grandin to try again to go all the way to Fort Yukon. Séguin traveled this time with Kirkby's replacement, the Reverend Robert McDonald, later to be named Archdeacon of the Yukon. McDonald, who was one-quarter Ojibway and who was fluent in Ojibway, Cree, and French, as well as English, was linguistically better prepared for working in the far North than any of his colleagues or rivals (Peake, 1975:55-56). Although McDonald had originally planned to begin work at Fort Liard, he suddenly changed his plans after he learned from Kirkby that Séguin was headed for Fort Yukon (McDonald, 1862).

At Lapierre House, Séguin faced the same old problem with the Indians all demanding tobacco. He concluded that "Pour les Loucheux, le tabac est leur Dieu" ('For the Loucheux, tobacco is their God') (Séguin, 1862d). At Fort Yukon Séguin spent a very lonesome winter and did very poorly, unable to persuade a single Indian to adopt Catholicism (Gilles-Mousseau, 1946:164-165). Totally isolated, his only friend was a man named Sanderson, a half-blood who had recently been converted to Catholicism.

At Fort Yukon Séguin was forced to live with the Hudson's Bay Company servants while McDonald was invited to share the Chief Factor's own quarters and dined as a guest at his table. McDonald also had the use of the hall of the principal building at the Fort for holding services and conducting school. Séguin bore all of this in stride, identifying his own persecution and suffering with that of Jesus Christ. He was handicapped even more by knowing only a few words of Gwich'in, while McDonald had the able services of Antoine Houle, an apostate Catholic Métis employed as an interpreter by the Company. Séguin tried to get Houle to teach him how to write Gwich'in by offering him tea, but Houle only came to him once. It seems as though Houle was instrumental in dissuading the Gwich'in from listening to Séguin. In Séguin's words, "It is not the Factor who is master of the fort. It is Antoin Hool [sic]. He alone can do what he wants to with these Indians . . ." (1862e). In spite of these setbacks, Séguin took credit for stopping the practice of female infanticide after he claimed to have discovered that every Gwich'in woman over the age of 30 had engaged in this practice at least once (Séguin, 1862c).

How well acquainted Séguin and McDonald became at Fort Yukon during the winter of 1862-1863 is not known. While they were almost certainly on speaking terms, and McDonald later considered his rival "a good man" (Wright, 1911:2), their relationship was obviously strained by the competitiveness of their missions. On June 1, just before their joint departure from Fort Yukon, McDonald observed that Séguin "has not affected anything among the Indians. However, I hope he will not return, as he may unsettle the minds of some of the Indians eventually if he does" (McDonald, 1863a).

On the very next day, June 2, Séguin was convinced that the victory was all his, thinking that McDonald would probably return to the Red River country of Manitoba from whence he came, leaving the Oblates as "undisputed masters of the battlefield" (Séguin, 1863:83). For Séguin, McDonald was "detested by the whites as much as a man can be" (Séguin, 1863:83), so much that "his fellow Protestants don't even want to go to his sermons, and his interpreter [Antoine Houle] has already told him to go to the devil more than once" (Séguin, 1863a:83).

When they reached Lapierre House, the two missionaries parted company. McDonald returned to Fort Yukon for another season, and Séguin continued on to Fort McPherson and Fort Good Hope.

Little more is heard about Séguin's work among the Gwich'in for the next two years. In the meantime McDonald solidified his influence among the western Gwich'in by staying at Fort Yukon another year, but then poor health forced him to leave from June, 1864, until September, 1865, during which time he lived at Lapierre House and Fort McPherson. During this time Séguin could have gone back to Fort Yukon and taken over the western battlefield, but Father Grollier died in Fort Good Hope on June 4, 1864, and Séguin was pretty well forced to retrench and stabilize the mission work Grollier had begun at that outpost (Coudert and Le Chevalier, 1955:376).

The Gwich'in at Fort McPherson remained very unsettled during the next two years. In the summer of 1863, McDonald heard accounts that the Indians at Peel River had visions of heaven, had been carried there, and had brought back hymns which they were singing. The Indians at Lapierre House told him that those living at Peel River had been instructed through dreams not to kill foxes and martens (McDonald, 1863b:June 23). Most of those affected were supposedly under Catholic influence, but McDonald may have mistaken the Catholic influence for a kind of syncretism which incorporated elements of Christianity and traditional Gwich'in shamanism. When McDonald encountered one Indian named Shahoo who had been communicating with heaven through dreams, the traditional medium of Gwich'in shamans (Leechman, 1950:158-159; 1952:88; McKennan, 1965:78; Slobodin, 1981:527), he told the man not to rely on his dreams but on "what God's word says" (McDonald, 1863c).

In his annual letter to his superiors in London the following year, McDonald reported that two of the Indians at Peel River were attempting to assert authority over the others, "representing themselves as commissioned by the Almighty to teach them" (1864). At the same time he also heard that Peter, one of the Chandalar River Gwich'in, had taken the gospel to proselytize the Eskimos on the Arctic Coast. These reports illustrated not only how fast Christianity was spreading but also how the Gwich'in were beginning to circumvent McDonald's own spiritual authority and leadership. In the same letter he confessed that "I am not sure of anyone being truly converted to God among the whole of them. I rather fear not" (1864).

Six months later, McDonald talked with one of the Peel River enthusiasts, a Mackenzie River Gwich'in named Tuyito [sic Tuyiti'] who had been making prophesies, receiving divine revelations, and had been instructed by God to pardon the sins of those who confessed to him and to baptize his fellow Indians:

> He expressed his inability to know who to receive as his instructor in religion, the [Anglican] minister or the Romish priest, since both profess to be commissioned by God to teach men; that the minister said the priest taught error, and that the Romish priest says the same of the minister. He said besides that the Romish priests say that it was the English people who crucified Christ (McDonald 1865:January 12).

In his typically clipped style of writing, McDonald wrote in his Fort McPherson journal for June 19, 1865 that Séguin had arrived in Fort McPherson with some Mackenzie River Indians and that he "Called on Père Séguin this forenoon" (McDonald 1865:June 19). McDonald supplies no details regarding this conversation, although on the following day he observed: "Excitement among some of the Indians with respect to who is the true teacher, the Romish priest or the minister; they are in a state of perplexity" (McDonald 1865:June 20).

Again on the 21st of June, McDonald wrote: "A proposal was today made by one of the Indians to Père Séguin that he should with me speak on the revelation God has given to man for his instruction. The priest declined it. Several Indians in consequence left him" (McDonald 1865:June 21). Again it appears that the Peel River Gwich'in were trying to arrange a public debate or a test of powers between the priest and the minister. Five days later McDonald notes that Séguin left Fort McPherson and went back to Fort Good Hope in the company of several Indian families. So while the Anglicans won the war in Fort Yukon and Fort McPherson, Séguin seems to have been considerably more successful at Fort Good Hope, where he built a church and reportedly converted over half the people there (a mixture of Gwich'in and Hare) to Catholicism.

Although Séguin did not fare well among the Gwich'in at Fort McPherson, Lapierre House, and Fort Yukon, a certain portion of his failure seems to have been linguistic. He did not seem to be able to learn Gwich'in or Broken Slavey, the lingua franca at Fort Yukon. It is ironic, however, that Kirkby had immense success without demonstrating any ability to learn Gwich'in, and that Kirkby perceived that the Oblates were all expert linguists. Kirkby may well have underestimated his own talents, for in 1862 he published a collection of hymns and prayers in Slavey stemming from his work at Fort Simpson and later on translated hymns and prayers into Chipewyan (Boon, 1965:38). To be sure, McDonald himself eventually became fluent in Gwich'in, but not until after many more years of hard study and the added benefit of marrying a Gwich'in woman, Julia Kuttug. And it must be added that McDonald not only had the advantage of Antoine Houle's translation services in Fort Yukon, but also those of Mrs. Andrew Flett at Lapierre House and of William

Flett of Fort McPherson, the young boy who first accompanied Reverend Kirkby to Fort Yukon.

In hindsight, the spiritual allegiance of both the eastern and western Gwich'in was largely won by the Anglicans, not only because they arrived first and stayed the longest but also because they were supported by the Hudson's Bay Company Protestant infrastructure, which included sympathetic bilingual interpreters and (apparently) a large supply of tobacco. It is in fact revealing that the list of contributors to the erection of the first Anglican Church at Fort Simpson included the Company's Chief Factors James Anderson, Bernard Ross, Lucas Hardisty, Alex Christie Jr., Robert Campbell, and D. Finlayson, not to mention numerous other clerks and servants (Boon, 1965:37).

However, the Anglicans also prevailed because they and their American counterparts, the Episcopalians, encouraged a Native ministry and Native lay readers. There are accounts, both early and late, indicating that several of the early Gwich'in catechists and lay readers were former shamans, men who were able to syncretize aboriginal beliefs and world views with Christian ones (Kirkby, 1861c:July 13; also 1862; McDonald, 1868:June 23; also 1875; McKennan, 1965:86-88).

The lively saga of missionaries in collision continues on into the early 1870s when Bishop Clut and Father Le Corre locked horns with Bishop Bompas at Fort Yukon. When all is said and done, however, ideology and doctrine probably had little to do with which brand of Christianity was adopted by most of the Gwich'in--their conversion was undoubtedly tied closely to the personalities of individual missionaries and the power of their rhetoric.

And while the Anglicans and Oblates have long since made their peace on the Canadian side, my own field experience demonstrates that this early history of denominational conflict effectively foreshadows the battle for Indian souls which still continues in northeast Alaska today. There is no denying that the Gwich'in as a whole are a very religious people, and the well-established American Episcopal Church, which inherited Kirkby's and McDonald's Anglican converts in Alaska, still has a large and loyal following. Yet the Episcopalians now face an ongoing challenge not only from followers of the Assembly of God and the Baptists, but also from a new nativistic religion.

I first saw this new religion emerge during an hour-long ceremony at Gwich'in Niin Tsyaa, the historic gathering of Canadian and Alaskan Gwich'in held in Arctic Village, Alaska in June, 1988, to address oil development and caribou protection in the Arctic National Wildlife Refuge. As one would expect, the Gwich'in Episcopal clergy walked out of this ceremony in silent protest, but whites were not excluded, and well over one hundred other Gwich'in stayed for the duration. Conducted primarily in English by a young Gwich'in from Old Crow, the ceremony was introduced as a purification and cleansing of the new Arctic Village community hall, but it was also clearly intended to purify and cleanse all of those in attendance.

Following a series of prayers to the Creator and the Great Spirit, a fragrant sage smudge placed inside a steel frying pan and fanned with an eagle feather was circulated around the hall. This was followed in turn by a jug of water and a large bowl of blueberries, which were sampled as symbols of the water and the land. At the very end, people were invited to bring blankets, guns, feathers, and beadwork up to the front of the hall to cleanse them in the smudge, and a number of individuals did so. Nearly overlooked, but carefully placed on the floor in front of the young leader throughout the entire ceremony, were a small lighted candle and a package of tobacco.

Acknowledgments

This paper was previously published in 1990 as "Missionaries in Collision: Anglicans and Oblates Among the Gwich'in, 1861-1865" in the journal Arctic 43(2):121-126. It was originally presented in a shortened form in a session entitled "Missionaries, Missionization, and Religious Expression" at the Alaska Anthropological Association Annual Meeting held in Fairbanks, March 26, 1988. The author wishes to extend particular thanks to Maurice Gilbert, O.M.I. for his diligent assistance in arranging accommodations and providing access to research materials housed at the Archives Deschâtelets in Ottawa. Travel was made possible by a grant from the Phillips Fund of the American Philosophical Society Library in Philadelphia.

2. Anthropology on the Rocks:

Portraits of the Gwich'in by Interior Alaskan Field Geologists, 1898-1927

Prompted by the gold rush in the last few years of the nineteenth century and the first three decades of the twentieth century, Alaska's largely unmapped Interior region began to receive regular visits from a handful of federal government field geologists. The fieldwork of these early American geologists is relatively unknown outside of the geological community but is known more indirectly as providing a host of primary sources for Donald Orth's *Dictionary of Alaska Place Names* (1971). Their collective work takes on added importance in that they preceded and professionally influenced skilled anthropologists such as Cornelius Osgood (1936) and Robert McKennan (1965), who first arrived in the

Interior and worked with the Gwich'in during the early 1930s. Frederica de Laguna was also part of their social circle.

Geologists and anthropologists have a lot in common, even if the objects of their study are radically different. Practitioners of both sciences traditionally spend large amounts of time traveling outdoors and camping in remote rural areas, have a common interest in stratigraphy, and require the recording of systematic detailed observations. These observations are recorded in field notes, sketch maps, and photographs that are analyzed and interpreted later on in reports and monographs. Before there can be any classification or theory, scientists in both disciplines must build up a database made from description. Fieldwork is at the core of such description.

Perhaps for these reasons, the Alaska Archaeological Survey, with whom I was employed during the early 1980s, was for several years nested within the Alaska Division of Geological and Geophysical Surveys. And not to be forgotten is the distinguished linguist Edward Sapir, who studied Gwich'in and other northern Dene languages from 1910 to 1925 as chief ethnologist of the Division of Anthropology in the Geological Survey of Canada. Sapir made the first sound recordings of the Gwich'in language from the young scholar John Fredson (see Mishler 1982; also Mishler, 2023: Box 6/49). Sapir's recordings, made on wax cylinders and now digitized by the Library of Congress, reside at the Archives of Traditional Music at Indiana University.

The importance of field geologists in ethnographic work among the Gwich'in is demonstrated by the fact that they were used as consultants by the anthropologists who followed in their footsteps. Robert McKennan, for example, corresponded with John Mertie, Jr., Gerald Fitzgerald, and Philip Smith and was personally briefed by Fitzgerald in Washington, D.C. before he left for Alaska to begin his work among the Gwich'in in the summer of 1933 (McKennan 1965:9; Mishler and Simeone 2006:xvi). McKennan (1933) was full of questions before he went to the field, and the letters he received back were especially influential while he was planning his solo expedition to the Chandalar and Yukon rivers. Smith and Fitzgerald (1933) gave him advice on which area he should visit, suggesting Arctic Village rather than Chandalar Lake because he would in turn find there "the most primitive of the upper Yukon natives." They also recommended he get there from Fairbanks using an airplane on floats. Mertie (1933) then gave him very specific advice about weather conditions, camping gear and clothing, food, river navigation, language, potential key respondents, mosquitoes and head lice, and more.

Field geologists were also the friendly traveling companions of other early Alaskan anthropologists, and there are at least two photographs in the United States Geological Survey (USGS) archives that attest to their camaraderie (see Figs. 2.1 and 2.2).

Figure 2.1: l to r: John Mertie Jr., Stephen Capps, Fred Moffit, Gerald Fitzgerald, and Frederica de Laguna on board the S.S. Yukon, June 2, 1935. Alaska Science Conference 15. USGS photo library, Denver.

Figure 2.2: l to r: John Mertie Jr., Harriett Osgood, E.J. Fitzgerald, Cornelius Osgood. June 8, 1937. Mertie 2385. USGS photo library, Denver.

Through personal correspondence, de Laguna once informed me that in the summer of 1935 she took a young University of Michigan geologist named A. J. Eardley with her to Prince William Sound on the Yukon voyage and spent a long afternoon with Mertie and Gerald Fitzgerald, who told her of their exciting 1927 visit to Arctic Village. Another geologist, Stephen Capps, gave her some photographs of petroglyphs from Cape Alitak on Kodiak Island and from Auke Bay near Juneau, which she later used in her publications. After they arrived in Anchorage, Mertie invited her to dinner and took her to a local radio station. "I believe all of the geologists on shipboard offered welcome advice and suggestions which improved our trip," she wrote. "I enjoyed being with them and admired their work" (de Laguna 1994).

Although the primary objectives of the geologists' field trips were to identify mineral deposits and make topographic maps of the Alaska Territory, most survey teams carried large-format cameras and were privileged to observe Alaska Native people at a key point in their early contact history. No official guidelines apparently governed the content of their photography, so visual ethnography was not something they were either trained or asked to do. Following their own personal interests, some geologists took the initiative to document the lives and culture of Alaska Natives, but there were many others who did not.

Certainly, it's the complex interface between human and natural landscapes that attracts us to the study of anthropology in Alaska today. It's a common truth that Alaska Natives are part of the land and an economic truth that they subsist largely off of it. However, we will probably never know why some Alaskan field geologists showed a strong interest in Alaska's indigenous peoples and left us with a magnificent visual and written record, while others did not photograph the Natives they encountered. Fred Moffit and John Reed, for example, were avid photographers and took hundreds of images, but they have left us with little more than panoramic shots of snow-capped mountain peaks, rock formations, rivers, lakes, and glaciers. At the same time Moffit did make important written observations of Native groups (see Pratt 1998).

Noteworthy Geologists Among The Gwich'in

In this essay, I want to discuss selected photos, letters, and field notes of three geologists who spent time in the field with the Gwich'in and assess the importance of their work to Alaskan ethnography and ethnohistory. In 1927, the Neets'it or Neets'aii Gwich'in and the Di'hąįį Gwich'in were two intermarried bands of semi-nomadic people inhabiting the Brooks Range of northeastern Alaska. They consisted of less than a dozen extended families who subsisted heavily off the Porcupine caribou herd, which migrated seasonally through the area.

When the caribou were not traveling north or south through their territory, Gwich'in families dispersed up and down the K'aii'eechų'njik (the East Fork of the Chandalar River) and its tributaries to catch fish and hunt moose and Dall sheep. They also ventured eastward toward Old

John Lake, the Koness River, and the upper Shiinjik. The Gwich'in homeland is quite vast, extending south into the Yukon Flats and across the Canadian border into the northern Yukon and Northwest Territories.

These early scientists who visited the Gwich'in were Frank Schrader, John Mertie Jr., and Gerald Fitzgerald.[1] Their photos are permanently stored at the USGS Photographic Library at the Denver Federal Center in Denver, Colorado, while their original field notes have been deposited separately in the Field Records Library at the Alaska Regional Office of the USGS on the campus of Alaska Pacific University in Anchorage.[2] In order to evaluate the full significance of these photo collections, I was obliged to visit both repositories and match up the photographs with the field notes. Not surprisingly, it turns out that the geologists' field notes provide valuable contexts for their photos.

Frank Schrader

In 1898, Frank Schrader was sent to Alaska in 1898 and assigned to accompany Captain William Abercrombie in the Copper River basin. Before he came to Alaska, Schrader earned a master of arts degree at Harvard and taught geology at Harvard in 1895-96. However, Schrader was preceded in the Copper River basin by Charles Willard Hayes (1892), who accompanied Lieutenant Frederick Schwatka down the Chitina and Copper rivers in 1891. Schrader visited the Copper River again in 1900 and 1902 and went on to write reports of Prince William Sound and the Copper River (1900b), of Cape Nome (1900) with Alfred Brooks, and of the Wrangell Mountains with Walter Mendenhall (1903a, 1903b). Schrader's specialty was minerals, and he was an expert on antimony, but he established an excellent reputation in Alaska as "the prospector's friend" (Schaller 1945).

When Schrader explored the Copper River basin in 1898, he took photographs of the "Stick Indians" living near Taral, who were undoubtedly Ahtnas, and took some rare photos of three Ahtnas at

Mentasta Lake, along with one shot of a sizable band of Upper Tanana Indians from Chisana living at Quartz Creek. Unfortunately, Schrader's field notes for 1898 are almost illegible, but we are fortunate that he also left a detailed topographic map of the Copper River showing the location of Ahtna Indian houses and settlements encountered by the expedition (1900b).

It can be argued that Schrader's most important contribution to Alaskan ethnography and ethnohistory, nevertheless, comes from his series of photographs and field notes depicting a small band of "Gens de Large" (Chandalar) Gwich'in he met in a remote part of the Brooks Range[3] on Robert Creek the following year in 1899. Schrader's Gwich'in photos have been published elsewhere (see Burch and Mishler 1995), and one of his fetching Koyukon group photos appeared in his published preliminary report (Schrader 1900: Plate LXIIIA, facing p. 458). Robert Creek is a small tributary of the Bettles River, and Schrader used it as a portage from the Teedriinjik (the North Fork of the Chandalar) to the North Fork of the Koyukuk. Schrader met Robert's band quite unexpectedly while enroute from Fort Yukon to view the gold diggings in the Upper Koyukuk. When he came upon Robert's band of 11, they were living in two dome-shaped caribou skin-covered huts which the Gwich'in call niinvyaa zhee (Fig. 3) and hunting Dall sheep.

What makes Schrader's photos and accompanying field notes most valuable is that this band was located almost 100 km west of where the Gwich'in are living today, in the very heart of the area Robert McKennan (1965) said was historically occupied by the Dih'ąįį Gwich'in. We may never know whether these people were Dih'ąįį or Neets'it Gwich'in, but we do know these are probably the earliest photos ever taken of any Gwich'in living in the Brooks Range. Schrader was sufficiently impressed by these Indians to name several landmarks after them, including Robert Creek, Phoebe Creek, and Mount Horace (Schrader 1899; 1900a; Schrader and Peters 1904).

Like most other geologists of this era, Schrader had a predilection for using English names rather than Native language names, to the extent that these English place names gradually became official, even though traditional Native place names were most likely available for the asking.[4] While Schrader kept careful field notes about his encounter with this group, they appear again as two Gens de Large River households in the 1900 U.S. census (Bureau of the Census 1900). Neither Schrader's photographs nor his experience of hiring these people to help pack his gear ever appeared in his published report of the expedition. And that explains why McKennan never knew anything about them when he wrote his seminal monograph, The Chandalar Kutchin (1965).

John Mertie, Jr.

The second geologist who worked among the Gwich'in is John Mertie Jr. Mertie (See Figs. 2.1, 2.2, and 2.4) started his distinguished career with the USGS when he was hired as a summer assistant in southeastern Colorado in 1908. He attended Johns Hopkins University in Baltimore, where he received a doctorate in geology in 1911 at the tender age of 23 (Overstreet and Chapman 1982). When he entered the USGS in a permanent full-time position that same year, Mertie requested assignment to the Alaska Division. He began his Alaskan fieldwork under the able leadership of Louis Prindle, who had been working in the Yukon-Tanana region for the previous five years and in Alaska for the previous 10 years. Mertie also served for two seasons under Fred Moffit in the Copper River region and for one additional season with George Martin in the upper Matanuska Valley before being given the authority to start leading his own expeditions in 1915. Alfred Brooks instituted a policy that any junior geologist had to work as a field assistant to a senior geologist for four full field seasons before being allowed to work independently (Mertie 1978).

Mertie's expertise, like that of Brooks, was in reconnaissance mapping and topography. Mertie had great physical strength and endurance, a quality he inherited from his father, who was a blacksmith. Unlike modern geologists, who get around comfortably in helicopters, Mertie did a lot of his Alaskan field work walking overland on foot, riding on horseback, or lining canoes up wild rivers. He began working in the Gwich'in homeland in the early 1920s, producing several technical papers (Mertie 1925, 1928, 1930).

Following Mertie's field work on the lower Shiinjik (Sheenjek River) in 1926, a plan was developed to do topographic and geologic mapping in the upper Shiinjik, Koness, and Chandalar river drainages in the summer of 1927. Fitzgerald and Fred Clark went ahead by dog team from Fairbanks to Fort Yukon in April of that year, ferrying supplies to Arctic Village that would be needed during the summer. Mertie then followed with C. A. Wheeler, ascending the Chandalar River in two Peterborough canoes. The two parties were united in Arctic Village on July 18. The full narrative of their joint adventures can be found in Mertie (1930).

In the history of Alaskan ethnography, however, John Mertie Jr. will be most remembered for Tuesday, July 19, 1927. On that day he took eleven fetching photographs. Among these are group portraits of seven Gwich'in families living in Arctic Village and then most of these families gathered together in front of the church for a community portrait (See Figs. 2.5-2.12 in photograph signature).[5] Since July 19, 1927, fell on a Tuesday, it's unlikely that the people walked over to the church on their own for a religious service. It makes sense that Mertie implored them all to gather there at a certain hour.

Taking these wonderful family portraits must have occupied him a good part of that day. The photos display absolutely no connection with the science of geology, but today they are a great gift to the people of Arctic Village and Venetie and to others deeply interested in Gwich'in tribal history and family genealogy. In his memoirs, Mertie wrote: "My camera interested them, and they were happy to pose for pictures. I took numerous photographs of family groups, copies of which I sent to them the following winter, later learning how pleased they were to see and receive them" (E. Mertie 1982:119).

While located near the intersection of caribou northern and southern migration routes, Arctic Village was attractive as a Gwich'in settlement site during the early summer months due to the abundant run of whitefish running down the creek called Vashraii K'ǫǫ (lit. 'Muddy Banks Creek'). In fact, the Gwich'in name for Arctic Village is the same name as this creek, and the village is strategically located at the confluence of Vashraii K'ǫǫ and the K'aii'eech'ųnjik (the East Fork of the Chandalar). People gathered at this location to harvest whitefish and hang them up to smoke and dry, a process that takes about five days. The dried whitefish gave them substantial provisions for hunting Dall sheep in the mountains later in the summer and also provided rations for pack dogs. These and various other species of fish were and still are available year-round.

Recent prints of Mertie's family images have been framed and are proudly on display in the John Fredson School in Venetie and in the Sarah Frank Community Hall. For outsiders they offer a wealth of information about household composition and kin groups, log house construction, trade goods, and clothing styles.

In terms of material culture, we see from the Mertie photos that each Arctic Village family had its own log house and that each house was structurally unique. Because of that, it would be hard to characterize this vernacular architecture as Gwich'in in style. The surprising uniqueness of each house probably stems from a variety of Native and non-Native influences such as cabins built by gold prospectors and fur trappers or those built by Gwich'in families in Fort Yukon. The structural uniqueness of each house is also likely the result of their being built by different builders at different times since the village was founded. One thing conspicuously missing from the photos are outhouses, but this is to be expected since they would normally be located behind or off to the side of the houses.

Since the area around Arctic Village is vegetated largely by small black spruce unsuitable for house construction, most if not all of the logs used to build the old village Mertie saw were harvested upriver or downriver, just before the church was completed in 1917. The village itself goes back to 1908, but we don't really know when the first cabins were built. Some of them were certainly there when John Fredson and Dr. Grafton Burke arrived by dog team in the company of their guide, Albert Tritt, in March, 1922 (Fredson 1982). Albert Tritt was the ordained Episcopal deacon in Arctic Village who later became the leader of a nativistic revitalization movement. McKennan was so intrigued by Tritt that he composed a special section of his ethnography around him (McKennan 1965: 86-89).

The Gwich'in may have made the transition from caribou skin huts to portable canvas wall tents of the kind used by Mertie in 1915 (see Fig. 2.4) even before they began building permanent dwellings with logs.[6] Canvas wall tents were in commercial production from at least the time of the American Civil War. And while most people in Mertie's photos appear to be standing in front of their own log houses, it is telling that Johnny and Sarah Frank posed with their family in front of the church. Since they were visiting Arctic Village from their home on the Koness River at the time, it seems highly likely that they were staying in the canvas tents shown behind the church picket fence on the left in Fig. 2.6. In 1933, McKennan found them all staying in a canvas tent in Venetie (Mishler and Simeone 2005:207).

Michael Mason (1924: 38, 77), a Scottish explorer, noted that lightweight canvas tents had replaced skin-covered "tipis" throughout the Gwich'in area he visited in the early 1920s, but he felt their log cabins, due to being so poorly ventilated, were responsible for a big surge in tuberculosis and influenza. This continues to be a health issue in rural Alaska even today, where pneumonia is still a big concern, especially in large households with children (Lindsey 2017).

Bypassing the question of whether the buildings Mertie saw in Arctic Village were well ventilated, they all seem to be well-crafted, with high-pitch sod-covered pole (Figs. 2.8 and 2.9) or sawn lumber roofs (Fig. 2.10) braced by purlins and ridge poles. The log corners are in two styles, butt and pass (Figs. 2.7 and 2.10) and Scandinavian saddle notched (Figs. 8 and 9), suggesting two distinct stylistic influences. Esias and Sarah Simon's house (Fig. 10) is largely made from whip sawn squared or flat-on-flat logs, with just three courses of round logs, while Albert and Sarah Tritt's (Fig. 2.11) is a hybrid that has flat-on-flat logs in front and round logs on the sides.

The Tritt house, the church, and the unidentified house shown in the background of Fig. 2.8 are the only ones with windows in front, but the Gabriel and Alice Peter house in the foreground has a fairly large side window with curtains. The house off in the background of Fig. 2.8 is the only one with an addition or wing attached, yet no family posed in front of it. At this time, glass was undoubtedly a scarce commodity. Window panes would have to have been transported in toboggans by dog team over rugged trails, and their fragility along with subzero temperatures would have prevented many of them from arriving intact.

Alice and Peter Gabriel's cabin (Fig. 2.8) has unpeeled logs and clay or mud chinking, while all the others are chinked with moss or not chinked at all. The gable ends of all the houses are peaked quite high, suggesting that each house had an inside upstairs sleeping loft. Half of the structures (Figs. 2.5, 2.8, 2.10, and 2.11) have barge boards on the gable ends. The others do not. Stovepipe chimneys are visible for each house in photos where the roof top is shown, and it is to be assumed that metal wood stoves to go under them were also freighted in by dog sled over winter trails. The Tritt house (Fig. 2.11) has one stovepipe chimney on top of the roof and a second one outside in front where the family is standing. The stove for this second pipe is not visible, so perhaps it is vented through the front wall. A wisp of smoke is seen emanating from the pipe.

Peter and Susan John's house (Fig. 2.12) is unique in having a fenced yard around it, similar to the one surrounding the church, and Titus and Maggie Peter's place (Fig. 2.9) is unique in having a raised platform cache standing right beside it. The Simon house (Fig. 2.10) in turn stands apart from all the others by having its entrance on the side rather than on the gable end. So other than the fact that all of the houses are constructed of logs with high gable ends and sod roofs, they really do not resemble one another very closely.

There are several items of interest attached or lying adjacent to the houses, including a white enamel bowl or dishpan (Fig. 2.7), a steel rake (Fig. 9), a steel shovel, a rifle, and a hand saw (Fig. 2.10), a lever action rifle, a single shot rifle, a gill net, some hanging steel traps (Fig. 2.11), some caribou skin dog packs, and a pair of snowshoes (Fig. 2.12). Individually, these items may not tell us all that much, but collectively they add up to a rather nice spectrum of material culture in use at the time.

Another area of interest is clothing. It's pretty obvious that no one in the community was wearing aboriginal-style Gwich'in clothing, except for Peter John in his caribou skin coat (Fig. 2.9) and Martha Tritt, who has on a beadwork-embroidered rabbit skin collar, cuffs, and belt (Fig. 2.11). One rather surprising thing is the number of men wearing suits. We see nearly all of the adult men in them, including Albert Tritt, Peter John, Titus Peter, James Gilbert, and Chief Esias, although Esias may be wearing a heavy wool coat rather than a suit jacket. And Esias alone wears a vest. Even Alice Peter (Fig. 2.8) has a suit coat on, which she may have borrowed from her husband just to stay warm or for protection from mosquitos.

Stephen Peter sports a white shirt and a tucked in necktie (Fig. 2.12); in place of neckties, some of the men are wearing neck scarves. Gilbert Joseph (Fig. 2.7) stands apart from his peers in his casual buffalo plaid jacket. Johnny Frank is shown in the community portrait with his trademark tobacco pipe and without a suit coat (see Fig. 2.5). Johnny nevertheless appears in another of Mertie's photos (#136, not shown here) with a suit coat, and in later years was frequently photographed in a suit. Peter John alone is dressed in button suspenders, while all the other men whose waists are visible have belts with metal buckles.

The variety of head-gear is also telling and reveals additional cultural borrowing. The adult men favor tall-crown pointy Stetson hats, while the women and girls all have their heads covered with scarves. Some of the older boys and young men wear flat caps, while the youngest ones have knitted wool caps. All the women and girls are wearing long dresses or blouses with skirts, and many have wool sweaters. Mosquitoes must have been very numerous that year because we see several men including James Gilbert (see Fig. 2.7), Peter John (see Figs. 2.9 and 2.12), Isaac Tritt (see Fig. 2.11), and David Frank (see Fig. 2.12) wearing head nets.

The adult women tend to wear dark colored dresses or full ankle-length skirts and blouses, while some of Chief Esias's daughters (See Fig. 2.10), favor cotton prints (calico) with sashes. Both men's and women's apparel reflect fashions in vogue elsewhere in the United States during the 1900s-1910s. In other words, they seem a little bit behind the times. The women certainly had not picked up on the shorter and more fitted skirts and pants of urban America in the late 1920s.

Men's footwear reveals an adaptive convergence between Western and aboriginal materials. Long wool socks pulled up to the knees are standard, but over the socks the men have calf-high moose skin moccasins whose bottoms are covered with low-cut rubbers. Their pants, which may well be knickers, are then tucked into their socks. When I caught up with Johnny Frank in 1972, he was still wearing this style of footwear (see photo in Mishler 2001: 15), a combination designed to keep the feet warm and dry and immune to mosquito bites. Gilbert Joseph (see Fig. 2.7), Linus Peter (see Fig. 2.9), and Abel Tritt (see Fig. 2.11), are the only ones who have L.L. Bean duck boots. The women's footwear is more difficult to discern. Peter John (see Figs. 2.9 and 2.12) and two of Chief Esias's sons are attired in kwaiitryaa ch'ok, beaded pointed toe moccasins (see Fig. 2.10), and Linus Peter has on a pair of dzir, beaded moosehide mittens, even though it's in the middle of summer. This would suggest that Mertie, in getting the families to pose, encouraged them all to don their very fanciest and most formal clothes rather than their everyday garb. An alternative interpretation, somewhat harder to argue, is that the villagers did not distinguish between Western-style formal and casual clothes and that they wore their suits and dresses for everyday use. We don't know whether they had more than one kind of attire. To be sure, their winter clothes had to be much different.

What motivated Mertie to make all these portraits is not revealed in his report or Gerald Fitzgerald's diary, but it may be because he believed that he was one of the first white men to make contact with these people in their homeland. This was far from the case, and it is hard to accept Mertie's characterization of Arctic Village as "a primitive Indian settlement" (E. Mertie, 1982:119) when many of the people he photographed were wearing suits and dresses and attending an established Protestant church. In exchange for furs, the people had acquired tea, tobacco, rifles, axes, steel pots, wood-stoves, manufactured clothing, and many other trade items from the Hudson's Bay Company post in Fort Yukon. This trade began in the late 1840s and early 1850s. After the purchase of Alaska from Russia in 1867, the Alaska Commercial Company moved in to the area, and American-made goods soon became widely available.

The Mertie photos, which show just seven family groups, probably do not reflect the entire Arctic Village community at the time, because some families still lived out on the land, especially during the summer months. Fitzgerald counted 75 people on May 15 and 12 families in residence on May 19, 1927 (see diary below), but individuals and families were coming and going every day. The number still resident may have been diminished when Mertie's group portraits were taken just two months later. In fact, the community portrait (See Fig. 2.5) includes only 38 individuals. Fitzgerald counted "22 exposures" by Mertie on July 19, of which only 11 prints seem to have survived, so it's possible that some were lost or scrapped due to bad exposures, some may have been duplicates, or some households may have simply refused to be photographed.

The demographics of the community are dynamic and not entirely transparent. By March, 1930, there were just eight households and 40 residents listed in Arctic Village (Bureau of the Census 1930). Ambrose Williams, Elijah Henry, David Frank, and Chief Christian are four of those Fitzgerald met in Arctic Village and wrote about in his 1927 diary who do not show up in the 1927 Mertie photographs, but they each had families and all but David Frank were included in the 1930 census for Christian Village.[7] The Frank family was listed as residing in Arctic Village in 1930 (Bureau of the Census 1930), but by 1935 Johnny Frank had a vision that led them to move downriver to Gold Camp about half way between Arctic Village and Venetie (Sarah Frank in Mishler, 2001: 476-477).

In an image not unlike those taken by Mertie, Robert McKennan snapped a family portrait of Elijah and Mary Henry's family standing in front of their log house in Arctic Village in 1933 (see McKennan 1965: 21). Esias Simon and his family were photographed by Mertie in Arctic Village in 1927, but they subsequently appear in the Christian Village census for 1930. This would suggest that the Simons, the Henrys, and the Williamses had houses in both communities and that they did not stay in one place but went back and forth. Yet by the time Robert McKennan flew into Arctic Village on June 27, 1933, there were only nine people around (Mishler and Simeone 2006:168).

In an oral history interview near the end of his life, Mertie said that "many of the natives [at Arctic Village] had never seen a white man. Some of them had gone to Fort Yukon during the winter and seen white men, but most of them lived right there in the village and hadn't had any contact with whites at all" (Mertie 1978). Gathering up the members of each household and orchestrating all of these group photographs was no easy task, and it is one that could not be easily be repeated today because people are always coming and going on airplanes, boats, snow machines, and ATVs. Mertie's systematic depiction of household groups, as opposed to shots of a few likable individuals, characterizes his effort as scientific and ethnographic. We also have to admire his sense of reciprocity in sending copies of the photos back to households in the community. He went out of his way to give something back.

Gerald Fitzgerald

The third geologist, one of Mertie's field colleagues, was Gerald Fitzgerald, affectionately known by the Gwich'in as "Fitz".[8] According to his obituary in the *Washington Post* (Anonymous 1981), Fitzgerald was "a specialist on reconnaissance mapping, [who] made 23 expeditions to map Alaska. He later was in charge of topographic surveys in Alaska." Fitz hired two dog teams to take him to Arctic Village in March, 1927, a full three months before Mertie arrived with his camera. Chief Esias Simon was his guide. Although Fitz apparently took no photos in Arctic Village, he did keep a daily "Date Book" or diary of his experiences, and this 253-page unpublished diary gives us a tremendous slice of daily life in Arctic Village over a three-month period, during which time he greatly endeared himself to the family of storytellers Johnny and Sarah Frank (see Fitzgerald 1927; Holloway 2014; Mishler 2001:310-

312). Many years later, for example, Sarah Frank warmly recalled that Fitzgerald complimented her on her sewing and parenting skills by saying, "There are lots of really rich people, and even though you are poor, your children are not raggedy and their skin doesn't show through their clothing, and I'm proud of you" (see original Gwich'in text and translation in Mishler 2001:450-451).

To give a flavor of what life was like in Arctic Village at this time, I offer some selected excerpts from Fitzgerald's (1927) remarkable diary. Fitzgerald's observations richly document subsistence methods, foodways, weather, health, and social events. There is very little ethnocentric bias in his voice:

> *April 22: . . .Esias [Simon's] wife [Sarah] makes a winter food of the marrow of caribou bones mixed with cooked (sinew meat) or tenderloin chopped up-- it is frozen in chunks and looks like some head cheese---It is very good---especially for a lunch on a cold day.*
>
> *May 7: . . .Soft fine snow all day. Wet. Hill's covered--Natives catch hundreds of grayling to-day---hook and spear thru the ice.*
>
> *May 15 [Sunday]: In village all day-- snowing all night-- not much furs. Lots of church to-day-- over 75 people in village now---counting children. The place needs a school. Summer school would be better May 1st to Aug 15th --Native teacher--Natives have already built a log school house, two stores, a lot of very hard work just to get a school---*
>
> *May 18: Work on field sheets---a very warm day---water running again---lots of robins. Johnny Frank comes over and tells us stories of Indian war time---strong men---brush men, etc---Raven and the light---We've got to get away from here soon or we will go bugs---nothing to do but eat---Natives do nothing today---Elijah Henry & Gilbert [Joseph] comes in to village with family---*
>
> *May 19: Powwow with Esias and Gilbert about trip to Salmon [Sheenjek] River--wants to share launch with Fred [Clark] and call it square---very warm to-day--- Chief Christian gives a "potlatch" for the village.[9] The village is full now---12 familys of from 5 to 11 each. Fred bakes bread for Esias outfit. Albert [Tritt] finishes his boat*

--a very neat job---canvass covered about 10 ft long---3 ft beam two men---

May 20: . . .Albert puts his boat in water---is going to make us a boat---Potlatch dance at Esias house---take out stove and everything---family move into tent. Several bunches of ducks flew over to-day---one bunch geese.

May 24: . . . Ambrose [William] has a potlatch today---Fred out hunting---I go--- Lots of food---Natives cooked---They are just like a bunch of children---Lot of Grayling in creek at Village. Each man potlatching serves two meals dinner and supper to the entire village---Albert [Tritt] will soon have our boat finished. Kids play until after midnight.

May 25: Danced last night until 4:30 oclock this morning---entire village turned out---Albert Tritt & Jim Christian play "phiddle" [fiddle]---Dance Virginia Reel or Rabbit dance---Red River Jig---Duck Dance---Square Dance[10]---Sleep late--- cloudy but clears up late in afternoon---water raising in river over 2 ft. to day but snow isn't going very fast---I pull out one of Chief Peter's Bicuspid molars---a rough job---Ambrose still has potlatch---Fred and I stay home and have a fine duck dinner-- -I bathe and wash clothes.

June 2: All these people use their dogs for summer packing--20 or 25 lb per dog ---Every lake is alive with fish. Grayling---white fish---pike---trout---

June 9: . . . I pull out Sarah Frank's teeth-- a bad one but she was game---treated Jim's wife, looked at Moses [Sam's] ankle and dressed Lea's [bullet] wound--- which is almost healed up---Take a bath and wash cloth[e]s---I don't believe these Natives ever take a bath---they sure don't look it.

July 4: Up early this morning---Fred bakes doughnuts and Johnie [Johnny] Frank & I get ready for games---Start playing at 12 noon a fair day---Everyone joins in the games---We have about $35.00 prize money---Jumps, races---sack races--- three legged race etc pillow fight on. Swing bar pole and climbing greased pole. Then at 4:30 a big feed---a real potlatch---afterwards a dance at Esias house--- This is a 4th the Natives of Arctic Village will never forget. I get another pair of moose skin moccasins from my pains a gold nugget from Esias.

July 5: Dogs raise hell all night---very snowy to-day---light N.E. wind---

Women of village throw another Potlatch---at Esias house---a good feed. Afterward they have a dance at Esias house that lasts until midnight---Fred and I dance once or twice. Red River Jigg and a sort of square dance the whole thing seems to be an endurance contest. Afterward they have tea

July 10-- . . . No news---all the Natives are out of food---no fresh meat and not many fish---nothing else---They expect a big caribou run in a few days---

Peter [John] and David should return from Ft. Yukon anytime now---Johnnie Frank says he saw a big fire up at first bend above village last night at midnight. Fred goes up creek with fish net.

July 19: Rain early this morning---we pack grub outfit and get ready to shove off. Fred bakes bread and doughnuts---Mr. Mertie takes pictures of the Natives---22 exposures. Mr. Mertie also has a long talk with Peter about law enforcement in the village. Sarah [Frank] sews up our sleeping bags and does Mr. Mertie's laundry---In all we have a very busy day.

August 17: The "Crabb" [Fred Clark] gets us all up at 6 a.m. because he could think of nothing more ornery to do. Esias and his family return to the village in two boats well loaded down with dried and fresh meat---mostly moose---8 moose

--12 sheep---We got some fresh meat. Make a deal to buy the biggest skin boat---2 moose skins and 2 caribou skins. Albert and Old John go back to their camps--- Old John[11] [at the age of] (95) walked in over the mountain (15 mi.) just to say good bye---

Closing Remarks

While all these photos and notes provide us with a wealth of data on material culture, they still leave unanswered some social and political questions. One of the major questions that remains concerns the Arctic Village leadership. First, who was the chief of Arctic Village in 1927? In his "Date Book" Fitzgerald refers to Chief Christian, Chief Esias, and Chief Peter and notes that on May 23 the village was planning to hold a meeting to elect a new chief. Unfortunately, he never tells about the outcome of that election.

At any rate we may like to ask, how could there be three chiefs? Judging from the number of potlatches and dances held at Esias Simon's house, it would seem highly likely that he was first chief. Today, Arctic Village and Venetie still annually elect first chiefs and second chiefs, but they also recognize "traditional chiefs", elders who command great respect but have few day-to-day obligations. These are generally lifetime appointments. But did Fitzgerald's "Chief Peter" refer to Peter Gabriel, Titus Peter, David Peter, or Peter John? Peter John, at 60 years of age and the eldest male in the Arctic Village behind Old John (Bureau of the Census 1930), may very well have been the community's traditional chief. The bigger picture is that Schrader met Robert's band of Gens de Large Gwich'in in the central Brooks Range some 28 years before Robert McKennan began his ethnography of the Chandalar Gwich'in, and Fitzgerald and Mertie arrived in Arctic Village a full six years before McKennan. However, anyone reading the official reports of their respective geological expeditions (Schrader 1900; Mertie 1930) would have no idea about the existence of Schrader's photographs, Mertie's photographs, or Fitzgerald's diary.

Mertie's deep interest in photography and in the people he met in rural Alaska set him apart from the average geologist, perhaps even from the average ethnographer. His exploratory work, like that of Frank Schrader, Alfred Brooks, Walter Mendenhall, and others who worked in remote parts of Alaska's Interior, provides unprecedented scientific coverage of northern Dene cultural history, a history that cannot be understood exclusively from the reports of early missionaries and traders, the only other professionals who wrote about them at all during the early contact period.

When joined with their corresponding field notes, the photographs of Alaskan field geologists do much to help shape our perception of what

Gwich'in life was like during the late nineteenth and early twentieth centuries. In vivid and stunning fashion, this remote tribal group in Arctic Village emerges full-blown from prehistory. These are the faces of the ancestors. And while they may look to be already fully acculturated and adapted to Western civilization, such looks are quite deceiving. Arctic Village and Venetie have long been among the last bastions for fluent speakers of the Gwich'in language, and it is in the retention of their language and subsistence lifeways that those pictured by Mertie retained their strong Native identity. We know this through a multitude of modern oral recordings. Furthermore, even though all the heads of families photographed have been identified with English Christian names and surnames, this masks the fact that they also had Gwich'in personal names, many of which we still know.

Perhaps, in getting Arctic Village residents to dress up for their portraits, Mertie gives us a view of them that is overly formal and romanticized. Other contemporary photographers of Alaska Natives such as Edward Curtis and the Lomen Brothers did much the same thing, but of course Curtis had underlying commercial and artistic motives. Thankfully, Schrader's and Mertie's visual landscapes were not limited to scenic mountains, rivers, lakes, and glaciers but included the people who inhabited them and their vernacular architecture. These richly textured human landscapes tell us many things we would never know if we depended solely on the writings and photographs of the anthropologists who followed in their footsteps.

Acknowledgments

This paper was previously published in the Alaska Journal of Anthropology 16(1):1–20 in 2018. An earlier version was presented to the Alaska Anthropological Association Annual Meeting in Anchorage, Alaska, in March, 1995. I am much indebted to the services of Jill Schneider, USGS librarian in Anchorage, and Joe McGregor, USGS photo librarian in Denver, for their help in accessing these collections. My good friend the late Hamel Frank of Venetie helped identify the individuals and families shown in the Mertie photos from Arctic Village. Also, Patricia

Aubin was kind and generous enough to share with me her father's unpublished diary. Lastly, I thank Ken Pratt and three blind peer reviewers for their insightful comments, questions, and requests on an earlier draft of this manuscript. Without their patience, encouragement, and good will, this essay would not have been possible.

Endnotes

1. There are also a few photos from other Interior Alaskan geologists such as those taken by Walter Mendenhall (1898, 1900), Alfred Brooks (1898, 1900), Frank Hess, and Louis Prindle that should prove valuable to Alaskan ethnohistory and historical archaeology.

2. One exception here is the field notes of Gerald Fitzgerald, which have been retained by his daughter, Patricia Aubin, of Gaithersburg, Maryland. The digitized photos are in the public domain and may now be easily accessed and searched for at: http://libraryphoto.cr.usgs.gov.

3. The Brooks Range was named in honor of Alfred H. Brooks, but it is a mountain range long known to the Gwich'in as Gwazhal.

4. The systematic knowledge of Gwich'in mountain, river, and lake place names in the Brooks Range around Arctic Village is fairly well-documented by Rick Caulfield (1983), using oral data provided by Gwich'in elders. In recent years, there has been an initiative by Edward Alexander of Fort Yukon to restore Gwich'in river place names to official government status. Alexander's efforts, consisting of proposals brought before the U.S. Board of Geographic Names, have largely been successful.

5. At one time listed as one of Alaska's most endangered historic buildings, this church, the Bishop Rowe Chapel, was restored to its original appearance in 2004-2005, due to the efforts of historic architect Bob Mitchell, human geographer Steven Dinero of Thomas Jefferson University, the National Park Service, and the villagers themselves. It was listed on the National Register of Historic Places as the Old Missionary Church in 1977 and is included in the Alaska Heritage Resource Survey as ARC-056. See https://npgallery.nps.gov/AssetDetail/NRIS/77001578. In 2017 I received an oral report from an Arctic Village resident that the old church has once again fallen into disrepair.

6. In Gerald Fitzgerald's diary excerpts, shown below, it is noteworthy that Chief Esias and his family moved from their log house into a tent, perhaps due to the warm summer weather. In another of Mertie's photos (Mertie 1366) not shown here, a white canvas tent sits in the background between several log houses not far from the church.

7. Ambrose William was mistakenly identified in the 1930 census for Christian Village as "Ambros Frank." Ambrose was nevertheless closely

associated with the Franks since he married Johnny and Sarah Frank's eldest daughter Lucy. Christian Village, or Zheh Gwatsal, now abandoned, is situated on the banks of the Christian River about halfway down the winter trail that once connected Arctic Village and Fort Yukon. It lies approximately 84 km (or fifty-three miles) south of Arctic Village.

8. Gerald Fitzgerald (1951) later wrote a brief history of geological surveying and mapping in Alaska.

9. The Gwich'in celebrate several kinds of feasts. The Arctic Village "potlatch" Fitzgerald writes about is called lavasdaa (< Fr. la fête), a traditional event for all village residents that develops whenever there is an abundant harvest of game by members of one household. In his May 24 diary entry Fitz says, "Each man potlatching serves two meals, dinner and supper, to the entire village." But lavasdaa is carefully distinguished from the invitational memorial potlatch and gift-giving ceremony known as tr'igwitil (see Chapter 19).

10. I and others have written elsewhere about this lively fiddle music and jig and square dance tradition, which continues unabated today in Arctic Village, Venetie, and other Gwich'in communities, including Fairbanks (see Mishler 1993, Stevens 2013).

11. Old John Vandeegwiizhįį was Sarah Frank's father and Kenneth Frank's great-grandfather. He lived for many years at Old John Lake about 13 miles east of Arctic Village, so that is probably where he walked from to wish the geologists farewell. A 1925 photograph of him wearing a dark wool suit and a clergyman's collar appears in Mishler (2001:309).

3. John Fredson: A Biographical Sketch

1896-1945

Of the many figures who have walked the stage of modern Alaskan history, perhaps none has been so distinguished in his accomplishments and yet received so little recognition for them as John Fredson.[1] As a folk and classical musician, orator, narrator, trapper, wood carver, river pilot, mechanic, carpenter, surveyor, mountaineer, soldier, teacher, and scholar, Fredson was truly one of the most gifted of twentieth century Alaskan Indians. Not only was he resourceful and diligent in virtually everything he attempted, but from an anthropological perspective, he was one of the key respondents who shaped our scientific understanding and appreciation of northern Dene languages and cultures.

Anthropological linguistics, for example, has been enriched by the discoveries made about Gwich'in and its relationship to other Dene languages by Edward Sapir when he recorded and transcribed Fredson's oral narratives in 1923.[2] Likewise, subarctic cultural anthropology has been significantly advanced since two early ethnographers, Cornelius Osgood and Robert McKennan, relied upon Fredson as their interpreter during separate field trips to Fort Yukon in the early 1930s. And from an ethnohistorical perspective, Fredson was a major agent and mediator in the acculturation process, greatly accelerating the transition of his people from a small-scale hunting and gathering society to a modern tribal government which today is one of the largest private landholders in Alaska.

Figure 3.1: Old Fred, Orzi Kui, John Fredson's father. Ernest W. Cook Collection, University of Alaska Archives, Acc. #2003-109-96.

The Boy at the Mission

Fredson was born at the headwaters of the Sheenjek (in modern orthography the Shiinjik or Khiinjik, 'Dog Salmon River'), a northern tributary to the Porcupine River in extreme northeastern Alaska, in mid-October of 1896. As the tenth child of Fred and Louise (neither of whom had an English surname), he was also to be their last, for Louise died just a few days after his delivery. According to Albert Tritt (n.d.), Fred Orzi Kui[3] (aka Old Fred) (Fig. 3.1) arrived at Arctic Village with baby John on New Year's Day, 1897. The first ten years of John's life were spent hunting, fishing, and trapping in the bush with his father, and by custom as well as by necessity, he was largely raised by his older sisters (see Smith, 1961).

In 1905, shortly after Hudson Stuck arrived at Fort Yukon to carry on mission work there for the American Episcopal Church, John was brought to Fort Yukon from Circle City by Lizzie Woods, the resident nurse, school teacher, and postmistress. Stuck had singled out John on a previous visit to the Circle Mission, writing in his journal: "The Indian boys here, with whom I formed a friendship on my last visit, received me enthusiastically especially 'John Frederick,' or Baby Bunting, as I call him from his dress of heavy rabbit skin" (Stuck, 1905).

By 1907, Lizzie Woods was acting as mother to seven children housed at the Mission in Fort Yukon, and John was one of them. Children housed there included orphans, the children of widows and widowers, and children whose parents were temporarily away hunting and trapping. With an average daily attendance of thirty-four pupils, Woods held six hours of school each day, and her senior classes studied such subjects as geography, physiology, hygiene, arithmetic, writing, and drawing.

In 1909, Lizzie praised John, now twelve years old, as "the smartest and best educated boy in our part of the country," adding that "he plans at some time to be sent to the States to finish his education, and the

Indians all hope that he will be a 'minister'" (Woods, 1909). This is the first indication we have of his precocity. By the time Clara Heinz Burke first met John at the Fort Yukon Mission in 1910, he was a fourteen-year-old boy with the Indian nickname of Zhoh Gwahtsan ('Wolf Smeller'), jokingly given him by his father after a long day on the trail when John pretended to smell a wolf as an excuse to make camp and sleep.[4] The earliest known photo of Fredson was taken about this time, while he was vice-president of Dr. Grafton Burke's boys' club.

After Clara Heinz and Grafton Burke were married and moved into the Mission to assume care of the children, young John was often given the responsibility of watching out for Clara when Hap (Grafton's nickname) and Archdeacon Stuck were off traveling. Clara recalls one incident which occurred while Hap was away in Circle, and a white man locked her in the cellar of the Mission in order to steal the doctor's supply of denatured alcohol. It was Johnny who finally heard her cries through the floorboard and came to her rescue, though afterwards the boy sat down on a chair and cried openly, "Sutchah tell me to take care of Sutrejo, and this is how I do!"[5] (C. Burke, 1961:155).

In 1911 John was sent to the new St. Mark's Episcopal Mission School in Nenana, and some of the important information about his life from this time on comes from his teacher, Laura Parmalee Adams. Mrs. Adams remembers John going off on several winter trips with Archdeacon Stuck. These trips often interrupted his studies but still taught him much and gave him the opportunity to visit virtually all of interior Alaska.

As early as 1910 John had served as Stuck's substitute interpreter at St. Stephen's Church in Fort Yukon, and his first big adventure came in the summer of that year when he accompanied the Archdeacon and Arthur Wright on board the motor launch *Pelican* to Circle and Eagle. In the summer of 1914 Stuck took John on the steamboat *Sarah* down to the mouth of the Yukon River and up to St. Michaels, where the *Pelican* had been left for the winter. Then the winter trip of 1914-15 took them by dog team from Fort Yukon to Chandalar Village (Venetie), Caro, Wiseman, Allakaket, Tanana, Lake Minchumina, Takotna, Ophir, Ruby, Tanana, and Stephen's Village. Excerpts from Stuck's journal for 1914 reveal much about his growing interest in Fredson's education:

> *October 7,* Fort Yukon: "Johnny works on the cutting of wood and goes to William Loola for an hour's Indian Bible after supper and comes to me for an hour's English afterwards."
>
> *November 21, Chandalar Village:* "Most of the day I have spent in interviews with natives, Johnny proving an efficient interpreter, and a good deal of interesting information being extracted from several old people."
>
> *November 25, enroute to Caro:* "Johnny has been reading aloud each night [from the Gospel and from a history book] and he improves."
>
> *November 28, on the trail:* "Johnny has done excellently well [mushing and handling dogs], as well as any boy I ever had, and I am much pleased with him."

In the summer of 1915 John piloted the *Pelican* for Stuck and Peter Trimble Rowe, the Episcopal Bishop of Alaska, up and down the Yukon and Koyukuk, proving to be a mechanical wizard several times when the engine broke down. The 1915 winter trip was even longer than the one in 1914, covering more than 1900 miles and lasting five months, but Stuck's notes on John during this trip are brief and infrequent.

The most memorable trip, however, took place in the early months of 1913 when Stuck led a party of mountain climbers on the first successful ascent of Denali (Mt. McKinley), the highest peak in North America at 20,320 feet in elevation. Stuck felt John was still a little too young to become part of the climbing team but gave him the responsibility of maintaining the base camp, located on Cache Creek at 4,000 feet, and of feeding the dogs. For thirty-one days John waited alone for four men who might well never have returned: Robert Tatum, Walter Harper, Hudson Stuck, and Harry Karstens ('The Seventy Mile Kid' of the Klondike). His young Koyukon partner Esias George was also part of the expedition, mushing dogs from and to the base camp from Nenana (Figure 3.2). The Archdeacon estimated that the climbing party should return to base camp in three weeks, eleven days before the actual mark.

Figure 3.2. Denali Expedition Team, 1913. L to R Robert Tatum, Esaias George, Harry Karstens, John Fredson, and Walter Harper. Photo by Hudson Stuck from The Ascent of Denali (1977, orig. 1914).

The Stuck expedition was quite successful, for it took the slightly higher South Peak instead of the North Peak taken by another party in 1910. Considering the logistics of ferrying equipment and supplies and the lack of air support to drop emergency gear or fly out the sick and injured, the Stuck ascent must be regarded today with awe, particularly since there was no loss of life, or even a close call for any of the men.

Stuck, Harper, and Fredson all kept diaries of their experiences during the expedition, and although Stuck's was promptly published in 1914 and reprinted with Harper's diary (Stuck, 1977), the fate of Fredson's is still unknown. Judging from a few short passages copied out of it by his teacher, Mrs. Adams, it appears John wrote a lot about his own climbs to shoot four Dall sheep and a caribou for dog feed, as well as about his inner delight with the spectacular sunrises and sunsets over the Alaska Range. Exercising much self-restraint, John abstained from using up the small amount of milk and sugar entrusted to him, knowing how gladly they would be welcomed by the returning climbers. And when he at last saw them all coming down the mountain, he had the good sense to put a pot of coffee on the fire before running full tilt to greet them. Overjoyed, he pulled off Stuck's backpack and put it on his own shoulders.[6] When the expedition returned to Fairbanks, one prospector was reportedly so impressed with their success that he threw a poke of gold nuggets on the table and told each member of the party to take his pick. The nuggets were later made into stickpins, and John wore his in his necktie for the rest of his life (Smith, 1961).

Returning to St. Mark's School in the fall of 1913, John continued his studies, with frequent interruptions for the above-mentioned trips with the Archdeacon, until his graduation on June 1, 1916. When he finally took the New Jersey state high school entrance examinations that spring, he was already nineteen. Yet despite his outspoken fear that "white boys will do so much better than I," John delighted everyone by scoring an amazingly high 92 (Adams, n.d.). Following in the footsteps of Stuck's other Indian boy proteges, Arthur Wright and Walter Harper, he was now ready to go Outside to Mount Hermon, a private prep school for boys near Northfield, Massachusetts.

At this juncture Reverend Betticher, the founder and principal of St. Mark's, decided that if John was going out to face the white world, he must change his name. Up until then he had been going by the name Johhny Fred, a double Christian name resembling those shared by many Gwich'in speakers today. The names suggested to him by Betticher were

"John Frederick" and "John Frederickson," but he greeted these first with silence and then with a request to think things over for a few days. When he came back he had solved his first problem in applied linguistics, saying, "I want a name that my own people can say as well as the white people. My father is called Fred, and Indians could never pronounce Frederick, much less Frederickson, so why couldn't I just be John Fredson?" (Adams, n.d.).

The new name was warmly received, and John thus avoided a surname which would have alienated him from his own people, a danger which never entered the minds of his teachers. Indeed, for all her kindness, Mrs. Adams seems to have been extremely naïve about language, as we witness her statement that "the hardest thing for [John] was to master the idioms and intricacies of our English grammar. The Indian language has very little in the way of grammar" (Adams, n.d.).

Adventuring Outside

Now a young man, Fredson headed Outside of Alaska for the first time in September, 1916. With some friends he sailed to Seattle and took a train to Chicago. Then he continued alone via the Pennsylvania Railroad to Jersey City, where he caught the ferry to New York City and joined Mrs. Adams, who had preceded him by several weeks. John's culture shock did not seem to be especially severe, though "his eyes nearly popped out of his head" when she took him to the top of the Woolworth Building, the tallest in the world at the time. His worst experience came on the subway when perfect strangers who assumed he could not understand English stared and made rude remarks. Racial prejudice became a problem again in 1919, when John accompanied Mrs. Adams on a trip to Niagara Falls, only to be stopped and questioned by U.S. Customs officers who accused him of being a "Jap" and demanded his papers. It took Mrs. Adams's testimony to convince them he was an American citizen.

John's four years at Mount Hermon were exciting and momentous. At this time, he was more interested in becoming a doctor than in pursuing the ministry, doubtless owing to the influence of Dr. Burke, who had arranged for him to tour Bellevue Hospital and witness an actual surgical procedure. But the decision as to which vocation to pursue, medicine or religion, was put in abeyance because of the World War, and John spent a short time, probably a year or less, in the U.S. Army, from which he was discharged in the spring of 1919.

On October 10, 1920, John received news by wire of the untimely death of his mentor and close friend, Hudson Stuck. This was a crushing blow to his spirits, since it was Stuck more than anyone else who recognized his potential and sponsored his formal education at Mount Hermon, paying for all his tuition, clothing, and other expenses, and encouraging him to return to work among his own people.[7]

Fredson went into a long seclusion with his grief, but the following summer he showed his classmate George Smith a carved wooden plaque, made of oak and inscribed with the words, "Dedicated to the Memory of the Beloved Archdeacon Stuck, 1863-1920." As Smith (1962) remembers it, the letter was intaglio cut and gold leafed. There was also a two-inch border of stylized oak leaves and acorns around the edge, the leaves stained slightly green and the acorns slightly brown. In all, it measured about 15 x 25 x 2½ inches and took about two weeks of steady work. The plaque was sent to be placed in St. Stephen's Church in Fort Yukon but was probably destroyed by a fire in the Mission House some years later.[8] To Smith, "it was a most beautiful thing."

This was not the first time John had done artistic wood carving. At Mount Hermon he was befriended by a kind old man who ran the carpentry shop and who let him have pieces of wood to whittle and carve on whenever he became homesick. Another plaque, closely matching Smith's description of the Stuck piece and just as delicately carved, was completed in the fall of 1918 and dedicated to Reverend William

Loola, the Gwich'in Episcopal deacon trained by Archdeacon Robert McDonald in the 1870's (Figure 3.3).

Figure 3.3: John Fredson's memorial carving honoring William Loola. St. Stephens Church, Fort Yukon, Alaska. Photo by Craig Mishler.

As a student, Fredson distinguished himself in debating and won the Joseph Allen Declamation Prize for three successive years. By the time he graduated with honors from Mount Hermon on July 26, 1921, he had become captain of the football team and president of his senior class, and had been awarded a gold medal for his music. As a member of the school orchestra, he was featured on the violin, doing a solo rendition of Handel's "Largo" at his own graduation. He demonstrated his sense of humor and his choreographic ability by teaching his classmates how to paint their faces, sing, and dance Indian-style.

John was, of course, greatly encouraged to continue on to college at the University of the South in Sewanee, Tennessee, both Stuck's and Burke's alma mater, but at the same time one of those who knew him well, John W. Wood, the Secretary of the Episcopal Church Missions in New York, was sensitive to the danger of John's becoming totally acculturated. This prompted Wood (1921) to write to Grafton Burke in Fort Yukon, saying:

> If he stays out much longer, he may be weaned away from his own life and his own people. A year or two in Alaska will help to re-establish the grip of his own life upon him. With this end in view, we are making plans to have him return to Alaska in the summer of 1921.

It's a credit to Wood's judgment that John returned to Fort Yukon before continuing on to college, for his first letter back to Wood alluded to his linguistic handicap: "It's fun to talk my own language. I blunder and stammer, but I can make myself understood. I can understand others all right" (Fredson, 1921-30). In just four years he had begun to lose his fluency in Gwich'in. Legend has it that while he was away in the States, John talked to himself in front of a mirror to practice his Gwich'in (Gary Simple, personal communication).

After arriving on board the steamboat Yukon and renewing his close affiliation with the Mission and with the labors of the Burkes, John's first task was to construct a solarium addition to the newly renamed Hudson Stuck Memorial Hospital. In Hap Burke's words, "Johnny Fredson alone has made it possible to get in the concrete foundation and the iron girders and the glass roof completed which would has [sic] cost by contract more than twice the amount" (G. Burke, 1921). At the same time, John regained his fluency in Gwich'in by acting as Hap's interpreter at the hospital; he brought Indian patients in to be treated, conducted choir practice, and supervised a boys' club named after Hudson Stuck. Hap reciprocated by paying him $50 per month and by tutoring him in physiology and anatomy for an hour or so every evening.

On Sunday evenings, John played his violin in church, accompanying Miss Dalziel, the white schoolteacher, who played the organ. Yet his interests at this time were not solely restricted to western classical and religious music, since he was also fond of old time Gwich'in fiddle dance music introduced by Orcadian, Scottish, and French-Canadian traders working for the Hudson's Bay company in the mid-nineteenth century (see Mishler, 1993)[9].

Mrs. Adams described John's fiddle tunes as "very simple and sketchy" but remarked nevertheless that he was asked by some unidentified company to put them on record. In later years he became interested in indigenous Indian songs, and his melodic transcriptions for five of these, published in The Etude (Fredson, 1929) constitute one of the earliest emically-focused ethnomusicology studies among North American Indian peoples.

On or about the first of March, 1922, John and Hap made a very slow and arduous nine day dogsled journey from Fort Yukon to Arctic Village, a distance of some 120 miles (Burke, 1923; see also McGary 1982). While Burke wrote primarily about his task of taking a bell, a wooden altar cross, altar hangings, Bibles, and prayer books for the new church at Arctic Village, Fredson by contrast told of the difficulty of the trail, of the strange, treeless landscape, of the curious theological questions posed by their guide Albert Tritt, and of the exciting social events, which included an all-night dance to jigs and other fiddle tunes, a wedding, and a baptism. Modestly, he even neglected to mention the gilded lettered sign he had made for the new church:

Bishop Rowe Chapel
Episcopal
Albert Edward Tritt, Layreader
Nutihsekh ako Ttia tsut tihsyah
['Let us go into the House of the Lord'][10]

Figure 3.4: John Fredson portrait, July 30, 1922. Ernest W. Cook Collection, University of Alaska Archives, Acc. #2003-109-180.

The Sewanee Years

In the fall of 1922 John enrolled at the University of the South in Sewanee (Fig. 3.4). There is little information about his first few years there, but in his third year, 1924, he began to suffer from eye trouble in the form of trachoma and had to drop out and return to Alaska for three years to recover. One of the most important events during these early Sewanee years, however, was Fredson's meeting with the distinguished scholar of American Indian languages, Edward Sapir. Sapir learned that Fredson was a summer counselor for boys at Camp Red Cloud, Silver

Lake, Pennsylvania, and began to work with him there. In several letters to Franz Boas, Sapir wrote about his relationship to Fredson and his discoveries about the Gwich'in language:

> *July 2, 1923*: "I have an excellent informant in John Fredson, who speaks Kutcha-Kutchin (Ft Yukon, Alaska). This dialect is very close to Petitot's Loucheux. The Loucheux-Kutchin group is the most specialized Athabaskan division I know of. There is an incredible number of consonants. . .endless nasalized vowels, more vowels than ordinarily. . .and tone differences."
>
> *July 25, 1923:* "Fortunately John Fredson is an excellent informant and knows his language quite well. The Loucheux-Kutchin group is extraordinarily specialized in phonology and has also some interesting morphological developments. . . .
>
> *August 9, 1923:* "The work is continuing nicely, though I do not get as much time out of my Indian as I would like. Several fundamental points of Athabaskan morphology and phonology are gradually becoming clearer to me, largely because Kutchin is so specialized: and allows certain traits to appear in a new and illuminating light. . . [In Boas, 1972]

Sometime during that summer, Sapir recorded about twenty of Fredson's narrative texts and songs in Gwich'in onto eighteen wax cylinders. In the year 2000 after an extensive investigation, I discovered that Sapir gave these cylinders to his colleague and friend, Mary Haas, who eventually donated them to the Archives of Traditional Music at Indiana University in Bloomington. Upon discovering the location of the wax cylinder recordings, I persuaded the ATM to convey them to the American Folklife Center at the Library of Congress so that they could be digitized and transferred to tape.

Fortunately Sapir transcribed most of the Fredson recordings and supplied literal English translations in what is still a very legible typescript stored in the Ethnology Division archives of the Canadian Museum of History in Ottawa (Fredson and Sapir, 1923).[11] Also in the Museum's collection is Sapir's photograph of Fredson taken at Camp Red Cloud. On the other hand, Sapir's five notebooks with hundreds of pages of handwritten linguistic notes from Fredson are archived at the American Philosophical Library in Philadelphia (digitized online at https://diglib.amphilsoc.org/islandora/search/Gwich%27in?type=dismax).

The importance of Fredson's texts to the student of Gwich'in verbal art and ethnohistory is immeasurable. Both autobiographical and traditional, they will endure as a landmark of comparison for all future studies in the style and structure of Gwich'in folk narrative. They are ethnographically useful for their vivid and detailed accounts of surface transportation and survival skills used in the bush, for their account of the annual cycle of social and economic events in Fort Yukon in the early 1920's, and for what they reveal of Fredson's own world view.

Of particular interest in these respects are the pieces entitled, "Fort Yukon," "A Trip to Arctic Village," "A Summer With Old Fred," and "Chief Jonas' Second Address on Hudson Stuck's Death" (see McGary 1982).

In the summer of 1925, shortly after his return to Fort Yukon to rest his eyes, Fredson found himself caught up in the aftermath of one of the devastating spring floods which periodically ravage Fort Yukon. Such flooding always produces much hardship, but this particular one was followed by a massive flu epidemic which filled the hospital and took many lives, including that of Old Fred, John's father. During this ordeal, Hap described John as "a tower of strength" who constantly packed water from the river to satisfy the thirst of the sick, interpreted at the hospital, and made daily rounds to the cabins of the sick and dying.

During the three years he took off from college to recover his eyesight, John continued working in and around the Episcopal Mission. His duties were to cut firewood, hunt for game, run the light plant generators, and help out at the hospital, principally as an interpreter.

He also found time to keep up his boys' club, which during the summer he activated into a baseball team. During the summers, too, he helped pilot Bishop Rowe's motor launch along the Yukon and its tributaries, much as he had done for Hudson Stuck a decade earlier. In the summer of 1926, the two covered 2500 miles by water. During this time, John's annual salary from the Church was $1,000, and he was on the payroll as a Bishop's Candidate for Orders.

But John soon became homesick for Sewanee. "The more I stay away from the place," he wrote in one letter, "the more I want to get back." In the fall of 1926 he moved to Nenana to help build and paint the new school dormitory, school house, and log chapel at St. Mark's. In January, when it became too cold for construction work, he ran a trapline to earn extra money to attend college. In so doing he caught enough lynx, mink, and muskrat to net $1,000. In the summer of 1927, he made an additional $1500 working as an assistant cook for the Alaska Railroad Commission in Mt. McKinley (Denali) National Park.

Fredson's return to the University of the South that fall was a great personal accomplishment, for without Hudson Stuck as his patron and without the encouragement of John Wood and Bishop Rowe, who both advised him to enter a theological seminary, he was almost entirely dependent on his own resources and motivation. "From my last trip home," he wrote to wood, "I could see that the medical aid among my people is as important as anything" (Fredson, 1921-30).

Yet after only a few weeks at Sewanee, heavy reading assignments took their toll. His eyes began to water every time he looked at a book. He visited an eye specialist in Nashville but was dissatisfied with the advice to wear glasses, something he had tried without success in 1924. He then went to see his former doctor in Memphis, Dr. Ellett, who reaffirmed the need for glasses but also recommended bi-weekly "treatments" through a local physician in Sewanee. In the days that followed, his spirits sank to an all-time low. In a fit of despair he wrote to

Margaretta Grider, one of his former Alaskan teachers: "My tuition here is paid up until Christmas, but after that since my trip to Memphis--I feel like pulling out. It seems that it will be impossible to study medicine and what I am studying now is useless" (Quoted in Grider, 1927).

Somehow, for the next three years he held on, partly by reducing his course load. His major interests were biology, English, and philosophy, and he was elected to two offices, "Critic" and "Reporter" in the Sigma Epsilon Literary Society. He addressed the entire student body once in the Sewanee Union auditorium and twice more in All Saints Chapel, and was always highly regarded and warmly received by the faculty. One anecdote recounted by Fred Drane, a fellow classmate of John's offers insight into his even-tempered disposition and self-control in moments of stress:

> Once there was a student whose greatest talent was his ability to exasperate. We three had just been talking about him when he walked in and almost immediately turned to Johnny who was studying over in the corner and got off a nasty wisecrack about Johnny. I expected the Indian to rise and slay his opponent. Johnny remained motionless except for the rising color on his neck and finally he put down his book, rose and went up to our exasperating visitor, put his hand on his shoulder and said, "George, you know you are my friend." Neither Wakefield or I could have done it. [Drane, 1955]

When John at last graduated from the University of the South with his Bachelor of Science degree in the summer of 1930, he distinguished himself as the first Dene Indian in Alaska ever to graduate from a four-year college. Yet before graduating he underwent several surgical procedures, presumably for his eyes, although he apparently had ear difficulties as well. To get through his final semester as a senior, he was forced to rely on $50 per month subsidies from his longtime friend,

Mrs. Betticher, then living in Philadelphia. The whole ordeal was a sheer triumph of the will.

After graduation, John was sorely tempted to go on to graduate school, for a Dartmouth alumnus promised to get him a scholarship so he could pursue an M.A. in teaching and English. John Wood wisely advised him against it, noting that there were no jobs available in the states for English teachers during the Depression and adding that an M.A. would do him little good in Alaska. Then John received an exciting offer to teach school at Beaver, a multi-ethnic community just fifty miles downriver from Fort Yukon. Unfortunately, the position never materialized, and John returned to Alaska that summer to work as a chain man for a surveying party near Wasilla. This was the survey for the first road between Wasilla and Willow, now paved and completed to Denali National Park and Fairbanks and known as the Parks Highway. In September, 1930, Fredson went back to Fort Yukon and was hired as clerk and assistant manager at the Northern Commercial Company store, a position he was to keep for seven years. Shortly after his arrival in Fort Yukon he also became acquainted with Jean Ribaloff, an Aleut nurse working at St. Stephen's Hospital, and the two were married within the year. Their first son, William Burke, was born just before Christmas, 1933, and two daughters, Lu and Virginia, followed in the next few years.[12]

Apart from his earliest childhood, the years between 1931 and 1937 comprise the largest segment of Fredson's life for which there are no detailed written records. He did continue with his boys' club, meeting with its forty or so members on Thursday evenings at the Mission. Two recorded events which highlight these years were his meetings with anthropologists Cornelius Osgood and Robert McKennan. Osgood, a student of Sapir's, arrived in Fort Yukon in the summer of 1932 and arranged for Fredson to be his principal assistant in eliciting ethnographic data from old-timer Charlie Crow. In his introduction to

Contributions to the Ethnography of the Kutchin Osgood paid tribute to John's helpfulness as an informant as well as an interpreter and applauded him with "sincere admiration and esteem" (1936:21).

Figure 3.5: John Fredson in Fort Yukon, 1933. Photo by Robert A. McKennan. Originally published in The Chandalar Kutchin. Calgary: Arctic Institute of North America, 1965.

In the summer of 1933 Robert McKennan flew into the Brooks Range and floated down the East Fork of the Chandalar to Venetie, gathering additional data on the culture of the Neets'it Gwich'in. In Fort Yukon he met and worked with Fredson, who introduced him to village elders and helped him conduct interviews for a period of about two weeks. In his ethnography, *The Chandalar Kutchin*, which contains a fine photo of Fredson (Fig. 3.5), McKennan had nothing but praise for him: "Keenly interested in the culture of his people, thoroughly bilingual, intelligent, and cooperative, he was both an ideal interpreter and an understanding friend" (1965:22).[13]

A Servant to His People

At last, in September, 1937, at the age of forty-one, John was able to apply his many years of education and travel to a professional career. He was hired to be the first school teacher at Venetie, a small Gwich'in-speaking village seventy miles northwest of Fort Yukon. Long-time resident Myra Robert remembered the hopeful expectations of the Venetie people:

> Jimmy Robert, my husband, went down to Fort Yukon to have a meeting with the school teacher there and urged him to build a school house at Venetie. The school teacher at Fort Yukon was trying to persuade my husband to have Venetie children attend school in Fort Yukon, but my husband pointed out what a long ways it was to go trapping if the parents were to have their kids in Fort Yukon: 200 to 300 miles away for some of them. "It's very bad," he said. Then he found out that if we had thirteen kids in the village, we could have a school, yet it turned out we had more than that. Older children were urged to go so they could be counted too. Some were fifteen years old, some were eighteen. So, as it turned out, a school was built at Venetie.
>
> And the next year, in 1937, John Fredson came to Venetie to teach. He came back from the states after graduating from the University and took a teaching position at Venetie because he was from this area. After John came back from the states, they asked him to be a preacher, but he took the position at Venetie teaching Indian kids instead. [Robert, 1980]

When the Fredsons arrived in Venetie, however, there were only two families in residence, and the entire village was overgrown with tall grass. When school started, John could report only two instead of thirteen pupils! The Bureau of Indian Affairs in Juneau was ready to close down the whole operation immediately, but Fredson begged to stay out the year: "All I wanted was to give the Natives a fair chance" (Fredson, 1938-45).

And such a fair chance it was. Families and students began to move into Venetie all that fall and winter, until the total population reached eighty-nine. Enrollment at the school quickly increased to ten students, all of them the children of Myra and Jimmy Robert. Early that fall, it turned out, food had been so scarce that the families all had to disperse in order to hunt and fish, following a centuries-old nomadic pattern. High water during the summer had made for poor fishing, snowshoe hares were scarce after an especially cold winter, the moose had moved north to escape deep snow, and the caribou had not yet arrived on their southward migration. Consequently, almost all the older school-age children were sorely needed for subsistence activities. John quickly adapted to the situation and began conducting night school for the older boys at one of the cabins.

On April 9, 1938, Fredson wrote his first Quarterly School Report, greatly inspired by his winter's progress:

> "Na-side School Na-gee Thut"--With great joy the natives of this part of the Arctic have said the above over and over since the school opened here in October. The interpretation is, "There is a school at Chandalar!" They have been wanting a school for a long time. Now they have one. They appreciate it. They are thankful.
>
> The natives are in a bad way. Game is getting less every year. Fish is not near as plentiful as it has been in the past. There is [a] little money in furs, but the quantity is getting lower every year. Everything points to harder times ahead. With education there is a chance; little hope without it. So the coming of the school is indeed a great event. When school began, a few simple questions showed that the children had no English at all, but they have improved some. Very little reading yet, but some have done well in arithmetic. All show great desire to learn.... There is no liquor

> here at all. Not a drop has come in. Cards (gambling) has been abandoned. This looks like an ideal place to do effective work. [Fredson, 1938-45]

In view of his progress and solid community support, Fredson was allowed to continue his work for another year, and then another. The three-room log school house did not even have a classroom in it, so badly was it needed for living quarters and office space by the Fredsons, and classes were held in a separate building known as "The Community Shop" where there was a Kohler electric power plant generator. Jesse Williams, one of John's students, remembers him playing "America" on his violin every morning just before class and credits Fredson's teaching with enabling her to qualify for her present position as postmistress and village health aide.

In October, 1939, John obtained a 15-watt radio transmitter for relaying messages to Fort Yukon and took on additional duties as U.S. Postmaster for the village. Later that winter, he held adult education classes and taught each person in the community how to write his or her name. He did this not simply as an academic exercise but as preparation for what was perhaps his greatest single contribution to his people, the writing and ratification by vote of a corporate charter, constitution, and by-laws for the village (U.S. Dept. of the Interior, 1940a, 1940b).

Through these initiatives, John's experience as a surveyor, and the provisions of the Indian Re-Organization Act of 1934 (amended in 1935 and 1936), Venetie and its sister community Arctic Village were able to lay claim to the Venetie Indian Reservation, a vast continuous tract of 1.8 million acres between the East Fork of the Chandalar River on the west and the Christian River on the east—one of the largest Indian reservations in the United States.[14] Clearly this land, freed from white encroachments and inholdings, has been instrumental in preserving the language of the Gwichyaa and Neets'it Gwich'in to the present day, for in none of the other Alaskan Gwich'in villages—Fort Yukon, Chalkyitsik,

Circle, Beaver, and Birch Creek--do any young children speak the language fluently.

In April, 1941, Fredson helped establish the Venetie Trading Company, an Indian-owned co-op which started out with only $300 in assets and after just two years built its net worth up to $3,000. With the new post office and store together, furs could be shipped Outside in large wholesale quantities without going through white middlemen in Fort Yukon and Fairbanks, who have always paid lower prices than the large buyers in Seattle and New York. The new Trading Company built a store and a cache in Venetie as well as a warehouse and a cabin to receive freight at Venetie Landing, where the Chandalar River empties into the Yukon. Part of the Company's financial success, according to Fredson, was its adoption of a barter system, trading off flour, tea, and sugar for firewood.

Soon a gravel bar was cleared for an air strip to allow chartered airplanes to come in. Enrollment at the school climbed to twenty-five to thirty. New cabins were built. The population of the village swelled to one hundred. By 1943 John was able to say cheerfully in a letter to Mrs. Adams that "all are better dressed and all have more to eat. And all are naturally happier" (Adams, n.d.). While the rest of the country felt the pinch of the Second World War and went on rations, Venetie prospered as never before.

Fredson was not content just to follow a normal nine-month school year. Periodically, he traveled east to Christian Village with its population of forty-two to hold several weeks of classes, or went downriver to K'ahtsik, population thirty-one, or to Kheedeehan and Choogoo, small summer fish camps, to teach school there. Meanwhile, his wife Jean taught the older girls how to cook and sew and supplied first-aid when needed. In 1944, under circumstances which still remain obscure, the Fredsons put in a request to the Bureau of Indian Affairs to be transferred to Jean's home village of Tatitlek in Prince William Sound, but no vacancy was available at the time, and their request was denied. Six months before his untimely death from pneumonia on August 22, 1945,[15] John received the following letter from George Dale, Alaska Director of Education:

> Personally, I feel that you have an opportunity to make a very worthwhile contribution to the people of Venetie and to the Indian Service by remaining there a long time. As you look back over the years you have already been there, you can certainly see many improvements in the village for which you can claim considerable credit. The school, the store, and efficient Council, improved gardening methods, and many other things, are in no small way signs of your industry and leadership. [In Fredson, 1938-45]

There could be no better eulogy, yet with characteristic modesty and piety, Fredson wrote to Mrs. Adams in 1943: "Had it not been for missionary work in Alaska, I probably would not be able to do this work for my own people, for it was the Church who found me and gave me an education. This is the fruit of their work and if there is any honor, it goes to them." (In Adams, n.d.).

Perhaps John's greatest personal honor came in the mid-1980s when the John Fredson School in Venetie, as part of the Yukon Flats School District, was built as a tribute to his life and his dedication to teaching the village students. Also, every July 5 the residents of Arctic Village and Venetie set aside July 5 to celebrate John Fredson Day with races, games, and a potlatch, expressing thanks for what he did to help establish the Venetie Reservation. In death, John Fredson was buried with his two great friends, Hudson Stuck and Grafton Burke, under the birch trees in the Indian cemetery at Fort Yukon.[16] It would be wrong to say his life was at all typical or representative of the Gwich'in living in the early twentieth century for it was an extraordinary and brilliant life, deeply rooted in the oral past and budded in the literate western world. Through him, both worlds were joined with grace and intelligence.

Acknowledgments

I wish to extend my sincere thanks to Richard Bauman, who encouraged me to write this paper, and to Américo Paredes, Michael Krauss, and Jane McGary, who proofread the draft with a close and careful eye. I am also greatly indebted to Elinor Hearn of the Episcopal Church Archives in Austin, Texas and to Trudy Mignery of the Jessie Ball DuPont Library at the University of the South in Sewanee, Tennessee without whose patience and cooperation I could never have reconstructed so many of the details in Fredson's life. Finally, I want to acknowledge the kind help of the late Jean Frank, who clarified several important factual matters regarding her marriage to Fredson.

A shortened version of this essay was presented to the Alaskan Anthropological Association Annual Meeting held in Anchorage on March 20, 1981. The current version was published with minor edits under the same title in Jane McGary, ed., John Fredson Edward Sapir Hàa Googwandak/Stories Told by John Fredson to Edward Sapir. (1982:10-20). A tip of the hat goes to Walkie Charles, Director of the Alaska Native Language Center, for granting permission to reprint.

Endnotes

1. This life history is based on a wide variety of sources, most of them in manuscript form, but supplemented also by an interview with Fredson's widow, Jean Frank, and with some of his former students and friends in the village of Venetie. It seems that two other life histories of Fredson already exist, for the late Rev. George Smith claimed to be working on one in 1962, and Clara Mackenzie of Cleveland, Ohio, has published another (Mackenzie 1985). Smith also claimed to have possession of some of Fredson's personal papers, rescued from the 1949 Fort Yukon flood, but these were apparently lost in the mails.

2. The discrepancy in spelling between the linguistic and tribal designation Kutchin and Gwich'in throughout this essay is an unavoidable outgrowth of the switch between old and new orthographies, respectively. Gwich'in is a much more accurate phonological representation, but Kutchin has a long academic tradition behind it. Dinjii Zhuu (lit. 'Small People') is actually the term which people use to refer to themselves since Gwich'in itself simply glosses as 'residents' or 'inhabitants' and may even refer, as in Chuuvęę Gwich'in, to the Arctic Coast Inuit.

3. In the years following the arrival of Anglican Church missionaries among the Alaska Gwich'in in the 1860's, most Indians were given Christian names which were used along with their Gwich'in names or as replacements for their Gwich'in names. Thus we have Fred Orzi Kui. In the next generation, masculine Christian names began to be adopted as surnames, and children began to be known by double Christian names such as Charlie Peter, Mary John, and Henry William. John Fredson's own difficulty in making this transition is discussed below, but for a fuller insider's view of Gwich'in onomastics, see Peter, 1978.

4. John's father, also known as Old Fred, came and took his son away from the Mission for occasional hunting and fishing trips, and this Wolf Smeller nickname was conferred in the course of one of these outings. It should be noted that widespread use of Gwich'in nicknames persists to the present day despite the nearly universal acceptance of English legal names. For more insight on the relationship between John and his father, see John's autobiographical account, "A Summer With Old Fred " (McGary, 1982).

5. Sutchah (shachaa in modern orthography) is a kin term of address meaning 'my younger brother,' while sutrejo could be shijyuu ('my sister') or shitr'injaa ('my wife'). Fredson uses shachaa here instead of shoondee 'my older brother', even though Burke was easily his senior, because shachaa is the generic for 'my brother'.

6. See Stuck's account of this reunion (Stuck, 1977:128; orig. 1914). Satterlee's account (n.d.) seems to be a freely interpolated and literary retelling, based on John's oral accounts to roommates at Mount Hermon.

7. Fredson sent all of Stuck's correspondence in his possession to John Wood in New York, who was planning to write a biography of Stuck. In his letter of August 31, 1921 to Wood, Fredson asked to have the letters returned, but it's not clear whether he ever got them back.

8. The Mission house in Fort Yukon burned to the ground on September 23, 1924. Though the Fredson plaque was sent to be placed in St. Stephen's Church, it's possible that it was placed in the ill-fated Mission house, which contained many of Stuck's other mementoes (Cf. G. Burke, 1925).

9. A sampling of this style of fiddle music appears on Side 2 of my edition of *Music of the Alaskan Kutchin Indians* (New York: Folkways Records, FE 4070, 1974, reissued by Smithsonian Folkways, Washington, D.C.). Included in the album is a pamphlet with brief notes on the history and performance of the dances. A much fuller account is given in my ethnography (Mishler, 1993).

10. This information is provided by Grafton Burke, 1923. A photo of Fredson standing with Albert Tritt, Chief Esaias, and Johnny Frank appears in this article on p. 173.

11. A copy of this typescript is also on file at the Alaska Native Language Archive at the University of Alaska Fairbanks.

12. William Fredson was the elected Chief of Chalkyitsik in the early 1980s. Virginia, born in 1937, died in an auto accident in Fairbanks in 1975. Lu, born in 1942, married Alaska's sole U.S. Representative, Don Young. She died in 2009.

13. According to his widow, Fredson actively collected traditional Gwich'in narratives on his own long after McKennan and Osgood left, outlining them on paper rather than recording them as full texts. These notes were lost with his other papers in the 1949 flood (Jean Frank, personal communication).

14. Ernest Gruening (1968:367) claims the Reservation was set aside for the benefit of just twenty-five Indian families. This estimate seems unduly conservative, if by families he means households rather than extended kin groups with common surnames. While the vote was unanimous, it nevertheless does seem strange that only thirty votes each were cast for the Corporate Charter and the Constitution and By-Laws. I have been told women voted as well as men, some traveling on foot from as far away as Christian Village and Arctic Village. Local signators to the documents were John Fredson, the Government Representative, and Johnny Frank, Chairman of the Election Board (see U.S. Dept. of the Interior, 1940a, 1940b).

On December 17, 1979 the federal government, under provisions spelled out by the Alaska Native Claims Settlement Act of 1971, conveyed fee simple title to the Indians, abolishing the Reservation and giving them full surface and subsurface rights to development. At the time it was the largest contiguous tract of land ever conveyed by the United States into private hands, but Fredson's name was never even mentioned in the press coverage (Abeita, 1980).

15. George Smith (1962) states that John died from infectious hepatitis, but Mrs. Adams and the anonymous obituary writer for *The Alaska Churchman* (1945), the Episcopal Church newsletter, both attribute the cause of death to a short bout of the flu complicated by pneumonia. I accept the latter view since Smith was out of touch with Fredson for many years after they graduated together from Mount Hermon and was not in Alaska at the time of Fredson's death.

16. At the request of his widow Jean, John Fredson's remains were excavated in Fort Yukon and reburied in the Venetie cemetery in 2007 with a new headstone. This disinterment created a lot of local controversy.

4. Elijah John:
A Remembrance

Elijah was perhaps the dean of the old Gwich'in storytellers in Fort Yukon during the 1970s and 1980s. This distinction emerged when I inquired about who could tell the old-time stories. We became fast friends, and over the ten years I worked with him I began to regard him like a grandfather. He was one of the first to take me in and teach me Gwich'in language and culture. I write this now to cherish his memory and honor his place in my life. His recordings are now an important resource for reclaiming the language, and although most of his stories have been translated, it's unfortunate that hardly any of them have been fully transcribed.

Elijah and I had a few deep philosophical discussions, and I remember one time asking him the question, "What do you think happens to us after we die?" I was expecting a standard Christian answer, but he surprised me by saying, "As John Fredson once said to me, 'We've been on this earth for over a million years, but we're still way too young to be asking that question.'"

With the right audience, Elijah was indeed a star performer, fully animated and schooled in the old ways. Proof of his traditionalism was his strong hatred of snow machines. He claimed they were a nuisance and they scared all the game off the trails, and said if he had a million dollars, he would buy them all up and pile them up into the Yukon River, which flowed by about a hundred yards from his front door.

Life History

Elijah said he was born on November 10, 1892, at Kii Dootin ('Large Rock in the Brush'), on the slough at the mouth of Lower Birch Creek near White Eye. He was a member of the Ch'itsyaa clan, the clan of his mother. He spent his first eighteen years there before moving to Circle. Elijah's younger brother was the fiddler and singer Silas John (see Fig. 4.1; also Mishler 1974), and his sister was the great storyteller and midwife, Myra Robert (see Fig. 4.2), both of whom I also recorded. Today the Venetie village health clinic is named after Myra. It was a remarkable family.

While living in Circle, Elijah married Mary Crow in 1910. Shortly afterwards, he went to work for a Swede named Nels Rasmussen. Rasmussen had ten head of horses and one mule and ran freight from Circle to Miller House and Circle Hot Springs. Elijah was hired as a teamster and a handyman. He worked in Circle for many years as a tinsmith and while there invented a nail puller made from the barrel of a .22 rifle. At some point he also worked for Dr. Milton Kepler in Tanana, who later on was the physician in charge of the Hudson Stuck Memorial Hospital in For Yukon.

In 1910, the same year he got married, Elijah ran a marathon in Fairbanks on the 4th of July. In that race he wore a bib with a number on his back and passed twenty-six other runners on an oval track. Suddenly after eighteen miles, he recalled, a muscle cramp forced him to pull out. The next day a man approached him and said he had bet $500 on him. "Why did you quit?" he said. "If you had won I would have given it all to you!" Back in those days, Elijah said, even $100 was really big money.

We don't know just when Elijah and his family moved to Venetie or when they left Circle, but they do show up in Circle in the 1920 U.S. Census household enumeration sheets. Something we do know is that by January, 1925, Elijah was the duly elected chief in Venetie (*Alaska Churchman* Vol. XIX No. 2, 1925), along with Ned Robert as 2nd chief.

Elijah said he and Mary had four sons and five daughters before Mary died in 1934, but the U.S. Census household sheets for Circle in 1920 and Venetie in 1930, 1940, and 1950 show a total of six sons and three daughters (Dept. of Commerce, Bureau of the Census). Of these, I briefly met his son Walter, who had had a family in Venetie and was the chief there in the early 1970s. I also became good friends with Eddie John, Walter's son and Elijah's grandson, who helped me with some Gwich'in translations.

Elijah's oldest daughter, Agnes, married the celebrated old-time fiddler Charlie Peter. Elijah's son Nels, a bachelor apparently named after Nels Rasmussen, died in Fort Yukon on July 24, 1972, while I was living there with my family for the summer. Elijah's son Titus married Julia Simon, the daughter of Esias Simon, on January 13, 1931. Another son, Daniel, was a bachelor with the Indian name Ch'akohandzee who had spent several years in jail. Daniel was a noted storyteller and singer whom I recorded in Chalkyitsik (see Mishler 1974). He died in Anchorage on

August 8, 1974 at the age of 57. Other children listed in the censuses include daughters Julia and Clara and sons Morris and Thomas (Tommy). One son, perhaps Tommy, died during World War II, and Elijah said he received a small pension from the Veterans Administration for this loss.

The 1940 U.S. census for Chandalar Village (Venetie) lists "Clara Elijah" (age 10) and "Alice Elijah" (age 8) as the adopted children of Henry and Sophie John. Since Elijah John became a widower while these girls were just toddlers, it makes sense that they were both adopted out and raised by Henry and Sophie, while Elijah raised his boys Walter and Tommy (Department of Commerce, Bureau of the Census 1940). It's unknown to me whether Henry John and Elijah John were closely related, but there must have been some connection. Daughter Clara eventually married Neil James from Birch Creek and had eight children.

In August of 1933, the anthropologist Robert McKennan met Elijah's father, Old John Deets'at (Old John Sucker Fish), and his mother Jennie living at Suko (Tsuk'ǫǫ) (see Mishler and Simeone, 2006), but this was well after Elijah had started his own family. Elijah lived in Venetie during the 1920s, 30s, and 40s, and at least part of the 1950s, where he made a living as a fur trapper. When McKennan first met Elijah, he was guiding four white prospectors in his boat enroute from Fort Yukon to Venetie. Before he left Tsuk'ǫǫ, McKennan did some anthropometric measurements of Elijah, one of dozens that he did that summer. He also took a photo of Old John Sucker Fish (McKennan 1965). When I visited Tsuk'ǫǫ in June, 1997, Ellen Henry told me that Elijah's wife Mary is buried in the cemetery there.

Elijah's trade was principally carpentry and cabinet-making, and he said he went to work as a union carpenter in 1951, working at U.S. military bases in Fairbanks, Murphy Dome, Big Delta, Eielson, and Fort Yukon. Elijah was kind of a self-taught dentist and said he had pulled twelve teeth with the special pair of pliers that he made. He started first with pulling the teeth of his own son, and his reputation grew from there.

Elijah retired in 1955 and spent most of his time after that "just fooling around," playing solitaire, entertaining his frequent visitors, and living alone, which he said gave him time to think. In fact, he had acquired a reputation for being a shrewd intellectual. The children in Venetie nicknamed him "Elijah Figger," because he was always thinking and figuring so much. Johnny Ross, the retired jailer in Fort Yukon, once said of Elijah, "He knows everything." And Hamel Frank once told me that Elijah was one of the leading dance fiddlers in Venetie in the early 1940s, along with Abraham Christian.

When I knew him, Elijah's vision was not very good, and he always wore either sunglasses or gold-rimmed prescription glasses. An eye operation in the Alaska Native Hospital in Anchorage didn't help him any, and our discussion of this gave rise to a humorous proverb he recited to his doctor: "Dachan duyee k'eejit neeratii", which he translated as "You can't make green wood out of a dead log."

When I first met Elijah in 1972 he was sitting on a wooden stool in front of his house dressed in a gray and white plaid flannel shirt and blue-billed baseball cap, dark green trousers, and high-laced work boots. On summer days, he was often outside doing chores, chatting with a friend, or just warming himself in the morning sun.

The Letters

During the years that I knew Elijah, I was living with my family in rural Alaska in the Matanuska Valley and also studying folklore in graduate school at the University of Texas in Austin. Although Elijah did have a telephone, it was pretty expensive to call long distance in those days. I wasn't able to visit Fort Yukon every year, so we started communicating with hand-written letters. Elijah wrote nine letters to me from 1975 until 1983. I suspect they were actually dictated to a young woman or two, for they were all written in cursive with a fair even hand. All of these treasured letters are now archived at the University of Alaska

Anchorage Consortium Library along with my other papers. A recently updated finding aid to this collection is available online at https://archives.consortiumlibrary.org/collections/specialcollections/hmc-1300/.

The letters I received from Elijah were generally short and cheerful, often an exchange of holiday greetings. Early on, Elijah offered to record his stories himself, if I would just send him blank cassette tapes, but for whatever reason, this never panned out. He mentioned in one letter that he had the story of Crow and Wolverine and also Frog and a man whose name he couldn't spell (probably Ch'iteehakwąįį). In October, 1977, I sent him a deck of oversized playing cards to help with his fading eyesight, and he wrote back that the cards were like magic for him and that by playing them he began to be lucky, lucky, lucky.

In 1978 Elijah requested a photo of me with my family, which I sent. Later that year I suggested he might want to find someone who could cook for him, and he responded by saying that he welcomed the idea but didn't have enough money to pay for one. Later that year he wrote again and said he lost my family picture and wanted two more copies plus another deck of cards and offered to pay for them.

There was a five year gap before his next four letters, all sent in 1983. In one letter he asked for an old age photo of himself plus another good deck of cards. When I saw him that April I noticed that his sheepskin-lined shoes were worn out, and I offered to send him a new insulated pair from Anchorage that were the same style. The first pair I bought and sent were too narrow, so he mailed them back and requested a size 9. I went back to Brewster's in Mountain View and exchanged them and sent him a size 9 pair, but they also were too small, so he sent them back again, and I exchanged them again. The third time was the charm, and he was happy with them.

In his most heartfelt letter, dated April 27, 1983, Elijah wrote: "I'm wondering when I'll be seeing you again? If I live long enough?! The reason I'm saying this is because you-n-I are quite a talker. I'm just pulling for you, meaning 'for success.' Happy April-N-Thank You. A Friend, Elijah John." In his very last letter, on May 26, 1983, he said he had two stories from Birch Creek and another one from Chandalar that he wanted to tell me, but circumstances prevented that recording from happening. Before I could see him again, Elijah died on May 27, 1985. He lived to be 93.

The Recording Sessions

It was difficult to get Elijah to perform stories because he insisted on having another older man fluent in Gwich'in there to tell them to, and it was hard to arrange for this guest ahead of time. Rather than tell stories spontaneously, Elijah always wanted to "line 'em out." This was so he could have time to rehearse each story's details in his mind for a day or two.

During the sessions I had with Elijah, I used a Sony portable cassette tape recorder model TCM-5000EV with a wired external lapel microphone. Before he started, Elijah always prepped his elder friends with a short speech about how they should be sure to ask him questions whenever he used words they didn't understand. In hindsight, these dialogues were a method of co-creating the stories. The five individual elders who sat in at various times when I recorded Elijah were Abraham Peter, Paul James (see Fig. 4.3), Neil Henry, John Kelly, and Clarence Alexander.

At the time it was my practice to pay consultants such as Elijah $5/hour as compensation. Sometimes my payments were in cash and sometimes by a mailed check. In hindsight this rate now seems extremely low, but trust me that it was fair and reasonable at the time and that I increased the rate dramatically over the years to keep pace with inflation.

Lacking such an audience during our first session, I found Elijah was willing to record his songs and discuss his family history, and in this way we became better acquainted. On this and all but one other session, he ceremoniously poured me and his other guests a cup of red or white wine in a small plastic cup before beginning. He had the reputation of being a local bootlegger, and when I questioned him about this, he said he was just helping out his friends. I noticed during my visits that he often had visitors knocking at the door, most of whom he quickly sent away.

The inside of Elijah's small Crow Town cabin, where all our recording sessions were held, was quite small, consisting of just two rooms. The table and cupboards were brightly painted in pink. Hanging on the wall were an old wooden walking cane, a rosary, a United Fund poster, a picture of Congressman Don Young and family, a large calendar, and later on, a picture of me and my family. He had a 2-burner propane stove for cooking, an oil stove for heating, and three chairs. One time when I stopped in to visit, I was almost overcome with strong fumes from the fuel oil. Elijah didn't realize it, but his oil stove was not burning efficiently, and these fumes were not healthy for him to be breathing, so I told him he needed to get someone to come in and repair it, which he did. The next time I stopped by he thanked me for warning him and said Grafton Bergman had come in and fixed it.

Elijah always sat in the chair facing the table by the front window. The older man who listened to the story sat against the back wall slightly behind him and to the left, and I was expected to sit at the end of the table next to the door on Elijah's right. In most Gwich'in houses during those days, visitors sat as close to the door as possible, either as a form of courtesy or as a discreet way of acknowledging social distance—possibly both.

For the first session, Elijah began with three songs sung back to back, standing and holding his fists clenched at his waist, moving both arms forward to the left in a lateral sawing motion. The intensity of the singing clearly exhausted him, and he had pretty much decided to call it quits when a young woman named Dorothy entered and while we were listening to the playback of the third song, he suddenly jumped to his feet and began to dance again in short quick steps, hands moving as before, strutting his stuff with pride.

When this was done, Dorothy encouraged him to sing a fourth song, "that Charlie Crow love song," which he did. (See photograph of Charlie Crow in Osgood, 1935, plate JL). Dorothy showed an exceptional interest in Elijah's talents and said he was teaching her "a whole lot of things," and it appeared she was consciously trying to learn his repertoire of stories. Still, when asked, Elijah declined to tell her the old stories without some other man present. At a second session, held only two days later, I was extremely fortunate to find Abraham Peter visiting with Elijah. Abraham, serving as more than a mere catalyst, moved his chair over to within three feet of Elijah and maintained full eye contact throughout the story. He sparkled and periodically reacted with words like Gee! and Aaha' and interjected several short comments that expanded the story without seriously interrupting it.

Then when the first story was over, Abraham took his turn and told the story of Shahnyaa Ti' and Cheeghwał Ti'. Elijah had heard this story in a slightly different form and when Abraham had finished, he took over and gave it his own way. Because of the lively interaction between them, my presence was almost completely ignored.

After Abraham and Elijah had each told a story, I asked if they had heard the story of Ool Ti'. Being a little bit curious, they consented to hear a taped version told by Martha Flett, which I had recorded a few days earlier, but the playback was soon met with dark stares at the floor, and Abraham eventually gave me an angry wave of the hand to turn it off. "That's not the way we heard it," he said. And Elijah added, "You could make a story out of that, but it's not true." They were clearly offended, and without any warning Abraham quickly gave his own rendition, which unfortunately I was not prepared to record.

The third time I recorded Elijah, Paul James was present. Paul, a man of about fifty-five, frequently ran errands and did yard work for Elijah, and on this day, he was out in back of the cabin burning trash and cutting weeds when Elijah invited him to come in. It was a gusty, overcast day and the wind blew down the Yukon and into Elijah's stovepipe with a hollow metallic ring. Elijah's performance was more restrained this time than it was when Abraham Peter was present, and the reason for this may have been due to the lack of direct eye contact and verbal interaction with Paul. The wine bottle was passed around ceremoniously, as usual, but Paul only stared at the floor and remained quiet and respectful until the end of the story, when at last he made some lengthy comments and added on some of his own endings. One of Paul's distinguishing genetic features was that his right eye had no pupil or iris and was completely white.

Elijah took advantage of this occasion to give me his version of Ool Ti', claiming to know just how the hero of the story died, an element which was left out of the taped version I had gotten from Martha Flett. It was also the session when he told, "The Woman Who Was Abandoned and Left to Freeze," one of his longest and most powerful stories. It is a masterpiece which ends with Paul James's commentary. I later shared a copy with Dell Hymes, who was completely fascinated by it and said he was interested in doing a structural analysis of it.

Elijah's fourth session with me was comprised of only one story, and the man recruited for an audience on this occasion was Neil Henry, son of Elijah Henry, one of Robert McKennan's principal sources (see photograph in McKennan, 1965, plate 7. Neil is young boy at far left.) This time, my arrival at the appointed time was delayed by about eighteen minutes, and Elijah seemed a little irritated because of it. He had a large alarm clock on the table in front of him and kept a fairly careful check of the time. He was vexed even more when shortly after he began the story I realized the microphone was missing its battery and had to ask him to start all over. Later on, a woman came to the door, and Neil stepped out and persuaded her to leave, but this was one more interruption, and all these elements compounded to make the shortest of the four. This time Elijah refused to accept any payment, but the rapport between us was still very good.

Five taped recordings I made of Elijah John and his friends have been donated to the Alaska Native Language Archive at the University of Alaska Fairbanks. The Alaska Native Language Center tape numbers are shown below in parentheses. They have now been digitized and are available for listening online by typing in Elijah John's name at: https://www.uaf.edu/anla/

The Translations

Most of Elijah's stories were translated for me by Moses Paul Gabriel and Charlotte Douthit. The way we worked together in those pre-Internet days was by using two tape recorders. The translators would play back the Gwich'in tape on one recorder for about 30 seconds, pause it, and then I would start and stop the second recorder. On the second recorder, the translator would speak the English equivalent. They were free translations, but by limiting the play back to short segments, we kept the English fairly close. Later I typed up the translations by playing back the translator's English tapes. Elijah spoke very rapidly in Gwich'in, in bursts of sentences, and his speech was also somewhat slurred, the combination of which has made it hard to transcribe his recordings. Katherine Peter later did Gwich'in transcriptions and translations of some of my recordings, which remain unpublished. See K. Peter (1974-1979).

In hindsight, Elijah John had much to offer a young thirty-year-old folklorist like me. He had mastered multiple genres: singing, storytelling, verbal arts, and beliefs and could perform them all with the help of a traditional audience. Thankfully he granted me the privilege to listen and record it all. His legacy now lives in these recordings.

Performances Recorded

First Session: August 12, 1972

1) Elijah John's life history (notes only)
2) Dachan duyee k'eejit neeratii. (Gwich'in proverb) (on ANLC1021A)

3) Gwichyaa Gwich'in sȯng (songs only on ANLC1016B)
4) Han Gwich'in song #1
5) Han Gwich'in song #2
6) Charlie Crow's love song

Second Session: August 14, 1972 (with Abraham Peter) (on ANLC1021A)

1) The story of Tł'evii Ti'
2) Shahnyaa Ti' and Cheeghwał Ti' (told by Abraham, followed by Elijah's corrections and comments). Elijah said he was just finishing the story.

Third Session: August 24, 1972 (with Paul James) (on ANLC1021A)

1) The story of Ool Ti'
2) The story of The Woman Who Was Abandoned and Left to Freeze (on ANLC1021B)

Fourth Session: October 3, 1972 (with Neil Henry) (on ANLC1017B)

1) The Story of the Cannibals of Kii Ts'ehch'ii

Fifth Session, August 19, 1976

1) The story of the first white men who descended the Porcupine River and met Gwich'in at T'eegwilnąįį
2) The Adventures of Vasaagihdzak, a story cycle

Sixth Session: August 16, 1980 (with John Kelly)

1) The Boundary Line Story (see translation in Chapter 2 above)

2) The Story of the Hudson's Bay Company Men Starving
3) Two songs

Seventh Session: April 10, 1983 (with a bubbling pot of moose meat and bacon on the gas stove)
1) The Gwich'in calendar

2) The Story of Shahnyaa Ti's father (with Clarence Alexander)
3) The story of Archdeacon Robert McDonald

Acknowledgments

I wish to thank not only Elijah John but also those friends who sat and listened to him perform, providing a vital audience for him to speak his language. These include Abraham Peter, Paul James, Neil Henry, Clarence Alexander, and John Kelly.

5. The Story of Tł'yaa:

The Alaska-Yukon Boundary Survey of 1911-1912

The Rumor

I first began working with Elijah John in 1972, a Gwich'in elder residing in Fort Yukon, Alaska, in 1972, but it was not until eight years later before he told me the Boundary Line Story (Fig. 5.1). On the evening of August 16, 1980, while I was visiting with Elijah and one of his senior Gwich'in friends, John Kelly, Elijah asked me if I had ever heard about Tł'yaa, the Boundary Line Story. I said no but expressed a strong interest in hearing it and promptly turned on my tape recorder. As translated into English later on by Moses Paul Gabriel, this is what he said:

I heard that the land would break in half, and I don't know the whole story, but I heard it from people gathering at the store at Fort Yukon who were talking about it. Jacob Flett's father, William Flett, was there when the white people were talking about the boundary, and he and the interpreter told the Indian people about it. But the way they told it, the land would break in half and float away. So the people got scared, and everybody went northeast [towards Canada].

My own grandmother said, "Let's move up," but my grandfather got mad at her. He didn't like the idea, so he said, "Aaa, it doesn't matter what happens."

Figure 5.1: Elijah John in Fort Yukon, 1972. Photo by Craig Mishler.

> They say a lot of people moved up north, but then nothing happened, and they didn't know exactly where the land would break. This is the way I heard it from my own father, from your grandfather [i.e. John Kelly's grandfather], and from Old Robert.
>
> They didn't know the white people were talking about tł'yaa, boundary line. The Indians thought the land would break in half and float away [laughs]. That's what they really thought. (John 1980)

As a word, Tł'yaa (and its close cognate, Tł'yah) has some intriguing cultural resonances. It may well be that the Gwich'in first conceived of the international boundary (Tł'yaa niint'aii, lit. 'strong rope') as a visible barrier running across the land, since the early government surveyors brushed out a separation several yards wide between the trees to reveal it, creating a new trail.[1] But the word also echoes metaphorically into the name for a popular square dance and fiddle tune Neets'ee Tł'yaa, where the intertwined arms of a circle of men and women dancers resemble a braided rope (see Mishler 1993:72-77).

Tł'yaa can also mean a whetstone, knife sharpener, or flint (Alexander and Alexander 2005:236). And it is embedded in the phrase, vadzaih tł'yaa nadąį, which describes a long line of caribou migrating single file across the landscape. In its most contemporary form, tł'yaa is used to designate a telephone cord (Simon Francis, personal communication). And quite remarkably, Tł'yah was the personal name for the Han elder, Dick Nukon, who was born in Eagle Village in 1925 and then lived with the Gwich'in in Old Crow during his final years (Ye Sa To 1989:43-45).

The Surveys

Although there were two cadastral boundary line surveys done in the Gwich'in homeland between Alaska and Canada, the first one in 1889-1891 and the second in 1911-1912, I believe it is the 1911-1912 survey that Elijah refers to in his story. Born in 1892, Elijah would have had no direct experience or memory of the first survey but would have been nineteen or twenty years old when the second one was done. At the same time, it is important to observe that several incidents which developed during the first survey must have heightened Gwich'in anxiety about the purpose and results of the second survey.

After reading the report left by the American field surveyor, J. Henry Turner (Mendenhall, McGrath, and Turner 1893; Turner 1893; see also McGrath 1893), it's easy to identify the circumstances and events which made the Gwich'in skeptical of the north-south boundary passing through the middle of their vast traditional homeland, which spreads across the Mackenzie River basin of the Northwest Territories, the northern Yukon Territory, and northeastern Alaska.

Turner was in charge of conducting the northern portion of the survey and based his camp at the place where the Porcupine River is intercepted by the 141st meridian, very close to the old village of New Rampart. In July, 1889, supplies were hauled from Fort Yukon on board the steamboat Yukon upstream to Camp Tittman, about thirty-nine miles west of the border. At that point the Yukon was forced to stop due to low water. A whale boat and a lighter boat borrowed from the Alaska Commercial Company were used to haul supplies the remaining distance, and Turner hired some of the local Gwich'in to haul these supplies.

After several close calls and injuries, things took a turn for the worse early in the season when one of the Indians who was attempting to carry a heavy towline across the river in his canoe capsized and drowned. In Turner's words, "The accident led to open hostility on the part of the natives, and but for the timely intervention of the Hudson's Bay Company's post trader, Mr. [John] Firth, the consequences might have proved serious. Several plans to murder the entire party were discussed among the hot-headed younger Indians, but the wiser counsels of older heads prevailed, and as our acquaintance with the natives progressed, their mistrust and hostility gave place to friendliness" (Mendenhall et al. 1893:190).

At this time it was discovered that Rampart House, previously thought to be on Canadian soil, was actually located thirty-three miles inside Alaska. The survey party was therefore forced to move its supplies upriver yet again, to a place called Camp Colonna at the mouth of the Sunhagun River. A log house was built for the winter, but the surveyors were irritated by frequent visits from starving Indians. At times they forcefully ejected these Indians from their camp and blamed it all on the Natives' failure to lay up food the previous summer. Apparently no thought was given to the fact that many of the Indians had neglected their fall subsistence activities in order to help the surveyors haul freight up the river.

That winter several old people died of starvation and more would have perished save for some timely assistance from Rev. Charles Wallis, the local Anglican missionary. Turner did help out by donating a case of flour and loaning out a Winchester rifle to an expert Gwich'in hunter who killed a few caribou. Eventually many of the Gwich'in at Old Rampart moved upriver to the site of the surveyors' house, which became known as New Rampart.

But in addition to starvation, the Gwich'in living at Rampart House were beset with a variety of diseases-- particularly pneumonia and tuberculosis. The doctor who was with the survey party was totally unsuccessful in treating these ailments, and several of his Indian patients died. In Turner's words, "From implicit confidence, the Natives suddenly reverted to extreme distrust and resumed the rites for curing the sick practiced by their own 'shamans'" (1893:192). Turner's opinion of the Rampart House Indians was that they were "grasping, unscrupulous, and often dishonest in [their] dealings with whites" (1893:193).

However, because the 1893 boundary survey was based on astronomical measurements and was not felt to be accurate, a second large-scale effort was deemed necessary to measure the 141st meridian by chronometer from Greenwich mean time. In the course of performing this second survey, undertaken at Rampart House between 1910 and 1913, the surveyors only adjusted the earlier line by a few yards (Lew Green, personal communication, June 3, 1989).

Nevertheless, this second border survey was also a disaster for Gwich'in-white relations. The initial visit of the second survey party to Rampart House was made by the steamboat *Vidette*, which arrived on June 22, 1910, with fifty tons of supplies including horse feed. These supplies were put into the storehouse of Dan Cadzow (Fig. 5.2), a native of Flatsville, Ontario, who had replaced John Firth as the local trader.

Figure 5.2. Dan Cadzow, fur trader at New Rampart, n.d. The General Synod Archives, Anglican Church of Canada, Isaac O. Stringer family fonds, Acc # P7517-446, Toronto.

Actual work on the new boundary survey did not commence, however, until the summer of 1911, when the surveyors returned with a huge contingent of eighty men and one hundred and fifty horses. The surveyor in charge for the United States in 1910-1913 was Thomas Riggs, Jr., while the Canadians were led by J.D. Craig. (Fig. 5.3). Although the party was greeted by a large assembly of Indians and dogs, none of the Rampart House Indians would pack freight for them because of a disagreement over the terms of pay.

Figure 5.3. Surveyors with Boundary Monument, Yukon 1911. Alaska-Canada Boundary Survey Collection. ACC #93-262-297. University of Alaska Archives, Fairbanks.

And this time, instead of TB and pneumonia, the Gwich'in at Rampart House were hit by a smallpox epidemic. By September 10, 1911, there were seventy-one cases reported (International Boundary

Commission 1918:67) and by November 11 there were eighty-nine cases (Cadzow 1911), with one death. It's still not clear how many Gwich'in died from the disease in the winter of 1911-1912, but so many were sick that a hospital was built at New Rampart, and a male nurse named Arthur Lee and a doctor (apparently E.D. Evans) arrived from Dawson. All of the Indians' cabins were fumigated and most of their clothes were burned. At the same time, compulsory vaccines were administered (Yukon Territorial Government 1912), and blankets and tents were requested from Dawson City (Anonymous, *The Dawson News* 1/31/11). An outpost of the Northwest Mounted Police was established at New Rampart that same year.

Meanwhile, all the Canadian surveyors left the area, and only a small party of eight Americans stayed through the winter in Turner's old cabin. Again, as in 1893, the Gwich'in faced starvation as well as disease, but this time they depended on Dan Cadzow's supply of staples to get through the winter. When the rest of the surveyors returned to complete the survey in the summer of 1912, no Gwich'in were around to greet them, and they must have known immediately that they were no longer welcome. After being placed on quarantine, most of the cabins at New Rampart were burned, and the entire band at New Rampart then moved up to Old Crow (Stringer 1912; Lysyk et al. 1977:163). The Gwich'in blamed the smallpox directly on the surveyors, but the surveyors did not accept responsibility and said the sickness came to Rampart House on clothing that had been shipped in from Dawson (International Boundary Commission 1918:70).

Elders still recall those times with sadness. In the early 1990s a field investigation of New Rampart was made with senior residents of Old Crow. Stephen Frost Sr. said, "Well, it was good hunting here, but earlier I said, the biggest reason for moving from here was when they put the border in. This line here separates the people on both sides. It spoiled all the trapping and hunting by law" (Frost 1993).

Hannah Netro, speaking through an interpreter, remembers that "The people, they had difficulties hunting and trapping. They shoot caribou on this side, but really they were on the American side. It made it difficult for them for that reason. They move to Old Crow where it's easier. There's more freedom for them to do whatever they need to do to survive" (Hannah Netro 1993). Although the people moved to Old Crow in 1911, they returned to New Rampart at least seasonally. Hannah recalls that there were still four or five families living there as late as 1927.

Most tellingly, elder Sarah Abel said that "The surveyors had a doctor, and we were told to move on the island. They [the people of Rampart House] now had log houses and nice caches with everything they needed, like dog harnesses and toboggans. The surveyors burnt everything down; no one was allowed near the full caches of meat, they were all moved to the island. They burnt everything down, and that's how Dan Cadzow went broke. . . ." (Abel 1993). Without the store, there was little incentive to rebuild.

The Backstory Behind the Rumor

When Elijah John's boundary line story is viewed within this historical perspective, it begins to resonate. For although the rumor of the country being sliced in two may have resulted from a simple misunderstanding, or even a bad translation, it also seems plausible that this story may have been intentionally circulated by Canadian traders to persuade those Gwich'in living on the Alaskan side to move across the border and sell their skins to Canadian fur buyers as they had in former times.

Following the American purchase of Alaska in 1867, the Hudson's Bay Company was put in a position of having to give up its near monopoly on furs trapped by the western Gwich'in (i.e. those living on the Alaskan side of the border). The Company was forced to retreat up the Porcupine River first to Old Rampart and then to Lapierre House on the Upper Porcupine, before returning back to Old Rampart. In the midst of this leap-frogging, Hutchison, Kohl, & Company, which was later bought out by the American Commercial Company in 1872, established a competing trading post in Fort Yukon. This post lasted only a few years before it was completely abandoned.

Turner, the first American boundary surveyor, wrote that the Hudson's Bay Company traders at Old Rampart experienced a sharp decline in their fur revenues prior to 1889 (Mendenhall et al 1893:194). As early as 1893 American whaling ships were beginning to trade with Eskimos off the Arctic coast, and the Gwich'in began traveling north to explore this new market for their own furs (McDonald 1893:April 20). New ships arrived every summer, and some of them even wintered over at Herschel Island (International Boundary Commission 1918:73).

Figure 5.4: Dan Cadzow's store with the winter furs of Peter Timble and Jacob Njootli (center), New Rampart. c. 1915. Alaska-Canada Album Acc. # 65-31-56. University of Alaska Archives, Fairbanks.

By 1893, just three years after the first boundary survey, the Hudson's Bay Company permanently pulled out of both Rampart House and Lapierre House (Coates 1982:70-71). I believe this pullout was prompted by strong competition from American traders, both on the Arctic coast and in Fort Yukon. After the Hudson's Bay Company left Alaska, independent Canadian traders such as Dan Cadzow were able to move in and capture a share of the lucrative Gwich'in fur trade (Fig. 5.4).

Warburton Pike, a visitor to Fort Yukon in 1893, noted that the Hudson's Bay Company stores at Rampart House and Lapierre House had closed that year because "the Yukon posts could easily undersell them, and the Indians think nothing of taking their furs 300 miles further to reach the best market" (Pike 1896:235). Pike also observed that "a storekeeper has put up new buildings a short distance from the site of the old fort [Fort Yukon], to open up a trade with the Indians of the Porcupine" (1896:235).

Seven years later, in June, 1903, Cadzow was involved in trading marten skins to Leonidas Wooden, the Episcopal minister in Fort Yukon (Dan Cadzow, 1892-1939, Box F-95, Folders 4 & 7). Wooden, who arrived in 1899 and found about one hundred Indians living there, complained that "there are no magistrates here, and no law and order. Consequently, reckless white men make this their headquarters, and drunkenness and immorality go hand in hand with religious rites" (Wooden 1900).

Cadzow apparently bought or built his first store at New Rampart around 1904, and there is evidence that he was well-established there by June, 1906, when he purchased a large order of rum, brandy, and rye whiskey from the Hudson's Bay Company. While Cadzow seems to have been an honest, churchgoing man who was married at different times to two Gwich'in women, Monica Njootli and Rachel Netro (ACR/YD, Box 38, Folder 1), he may also have been a desperate man. Like the Hudson's Bay Company, Cadzow also faced strong economic competition from the

Americans. Even Rev. Wooden was later accused of being a trader and a bootlegger (Stuck 1905).

By the time of the second boundary survey there were four commercial stores operating in Fort Yukon: Horton & Moore's, McIlroy's, Beaumont's, and Phillips's (Stringer 1909). Beaumont was perceived as especially ruthless and described as "a crazy demon-- a man opposed to everybody, and opposed by all" (Wooden 1901). During the winter of 1909-1910, Horton & Moore alone took in $12,000 worth of furs, including about 10,000 muskrat pelts (Anonymous, *The Tanana Leader,* 1910), and a 1911 photograph taken by the boundary survey party shows a stack of 14,000 muskrat pelts (see International Boundary Commission 1918:59).

That same year the Americans Harry Horton and Billy Moore put additional direct pressure on Cadzow by opening a second store just across the border from him at Old Rampart. And it seems curious that after the second boundary survey was completed, the Canadian boundary survey leader J.D. Craig sold his entire outfit not to his fellow Canadian Cadzow but to Cadzow's competitors, Horton & Moore. Craig did sell the large government warehouse at New Rampart to Cadzow, but this was ostensibly for "mission purposes" (Craig 1912).

By November, 1909, Cadzow was living in the old Anglican Mission house at New Rampart. The following year, Cadzow responded to all his competitors by building a big new store at New Rampart, where he also observed the construction of seven new cabins (Cadzow 1910). In light of Elijah John's story, one could speculate that these cabins were built by and for relocated Alaskan Gwich'in. It certainly would have been in Cadzow's own self-interest to manipulate western Gwich'in trappers into moving over to the Canadian side of the boundary, although there is no evidence to show that he personally planted the rumor about the country being sliced in two. We do know that he spoke Gwich'in, which may have given him an insider's rhetorical edge (Netro n.d.). The irony is that if Cadzow was indeed responsible for the rumor and the scare and benefited materially from it, it ultimately did him little good.

Joe Netro (1980:24) claimed that Cadzow died broke in the 1930s, but it may have been in the late 1920s. Robert Bruce remembered that the year he returned from boarding school in 1929 was the same year that Cadzow died (Bruce 1993; also Beairsto 1999). According to Netro (1980:24), who himself was a storekeeper at Old Crow, Dan Cadzow first started trapping and trading around Fort Yukon, and then went to Dawson, where he bought himself a scow to haul freight back downriver to Fort Yukon. At Fort Yukon he hired a Gwich'in crew to track the scow up the Porcupine River to New Rampart, a 260-mile trip that took sixteen days. Each year he would restock his store in this fashion, eventually switching from a scow to a small steamboat. It may have been Cadzow's own bad business decisions that drove him under. Netro says that Cadzow spent $1500 on the steamboat and then couldn't afford to pay a crew to run it. He also failed quite miserably at fox farming.

Cadzow's continued agitation over trading competition long after the boundary survey was over is well illustrated in a 1913 letter written by George Black of the Royal Canadian Mounted Police to Alfred Thompson, the M.P. commander residing at Dawson. Cadzow was so worried about losing his trade that he requested a customs agent and a policeman be sent to Rampart House. Black refused this request, or at least postponed it indefinitely, both because of the expense and difficulty of winter travel and because, in Black's words, "this agitation for customs officer at the boundary by Cadzow is not for the purpose of securing revenue for the Dominion but rather to shut out any business competition in his trading business" (Black 1913).

It's quite clear that Cadzow was so desperate for business from the Gwich'in living on the American side that he sponsored at least one big potlatch, and possibly more, inviting visitors from Arctic Village, Venetie, and Fort McPherson to attend (Hannah Netro 1993:15). Such a potlatch, held sometime between 1904 and 1929 with many local and distant bands in attendance would have been the direct historic model for modern day Gwich'in gatherings (see Chapter 17 below).

In retrospect, Elijah John's tale is not a very detailed account of what took place at Old and New Rampart in 1910-1911 because it tells us very little except that many of the Gwich'in living on the American side of the border were afraid for their lives and moved upriver to the Canadian side. Of course there are some interesting demographic implications in this resettlement, since a large number of Canadian Gwich'in moved over to the Alaskan side to trade with gold miners a decade earlier (McDonald 1900).

Elijah's story is extremely important, however, for the way it expresses the very real fear felt by the Gwich'in that their ancestral homeland would quite literally be cut in half. Certainly in 1911 there must have been widespread fear and suspicion that the second group of surveyors would bring accidents, starvation, and disease, just as their predecessors did in 1889-1890. This fear and suspicion were then confirmed by the outbreak of smallpox and the game shortage in 1911-1912. A photo taken at New Rampart around 1911-1912 shows the boundary line cut by surveyors up the ridge behind the village—a very visible scar on the land (Fig. 5.5).

Both Elijah John and John Kelly told me that when they were young they were both very much afraid of what was going to happen when the boundary was surveyed and truly felt their lives were endangered by the marking of it. After I recorded Elijah's story, he told me that after the land was cut in two, people believed the American side would float away into the ocean and everyone still living on that side would go straight to hell.

Psychologically their fear of the land being split in two was equivalent to a fear of the tribe being split in two--a First Nation split not merely into Canadians and Americans, but more shockingly still, into

Figure 5.5. New Rampart House village, c. 1911. The General Synod Archives, Anglican Church of Canada, Isaac O. Stringer family fonds, , Acc # P7517-242, Toronto.

the living and the dead. Trimble Gilbert, traditional chief of the Tanana Chiefs Conference and former chief of Arctic Village, says that "When they put the boundary line between us, we lost a lot of our relatives. We didn't even know them" (Gilbert 1989). Myra Kaye once told him that the Gwich'in people didn't really settle down in one place before the boundary line was established. Only since 1989, when the first Gwich'in Gathering was held, has there been consistent close communication between Gwich'in bands on both sides of the border.

The Boundary's Impact on the Han, Tanacross, and Upper Tanana

Because there are no hints of these fears of the country being cut in two in the written record, Gwich'in oral history plays a critical and essential role in understanding what happened and how events were perceived. The Gwich'in, of course, were not the only ones deeply affected by this new divide, since it also passed directly through the homelands of the Han, the Tanacross, and the Upper Tanana (Fig. 5.6). Kenny Thomas Sr., a Tanacross elder, explained to me how it used to be:

> Years ago, we used to, we had a lot of people in Canada. We had people in Canada. We [were] related to a lot of people over there. Long ago, before white people ever come into this country, the whole thing is just one, just like one people, until someone put a line in between us. We're no longer in Canada. They're no longer in Alaska. Us people we're still over there when they put that line in there. Their people were over here when they put that line in. So we had a lot of relatives over there. They had a lot of relatives here.
>
> CM: Do you think that was a bad thing for your people, that boundary?
>
> KT: Well, we always wondering why. Why it has to be that way? We don't understand it, why we have to be separated, you know? Them days, you know, people don't understand. Long time ago it's just like one people. We used to go over there; they used to come over here. (Thomas 2010)

As I have documented elsewhere (Mishler and Simeone 2004: 208, 236n), the Han people on the Alaska side of the border now face a tangled web of restrictive regulations for subsistence hunting that the Han living on the Canadian side are free of, and Norm Easton (2007) has examined the profound impacts of the boundary on the small band of Upper Tanana who once lived at Scottie Creek.

At the root of all this anxiety is the sobering fact that the governments of Russia and Great Britain, as remote political entities, never bothered to consult the Gwich'in, the Han, the Tanacross, or the Upper Tanana before negotiating the 141st meridian as the major portion of their mutual east-west boundary in 1825. Before the Anglo-Russian Treaty of 1825 established this boundary (Alaska Boundary Tribunal

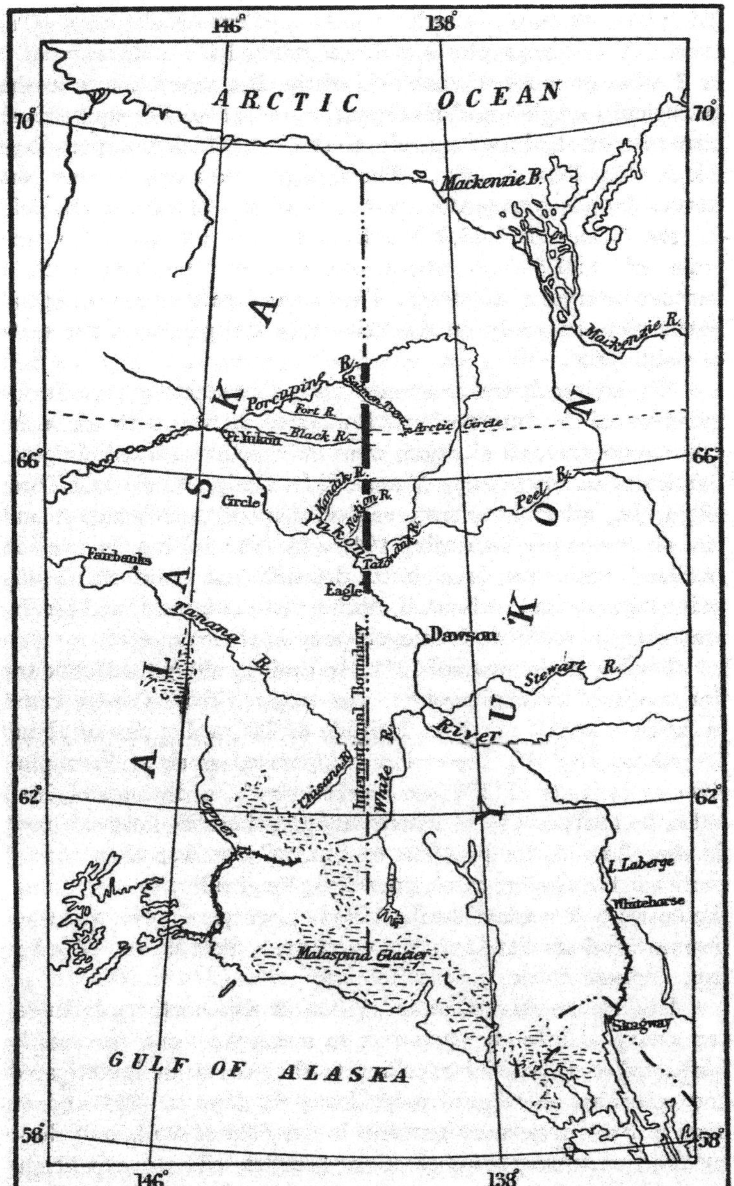

Figure 5.6. Boundary Line Map. From Cairnes 1914. Thick vertical lines indicate detailed topographic maps. New Rampart is located at the intersection of the International Boundary Line and the Porcupine River.

1903:12-16), neither the Russians nor the British had made any direct contact with the indigenous peoples whose homelands they divided. When the Americans and the Canadians renegotiated this political boundary in 1906 and marked it in 1911-1912, the land rights and subsistence needs of all these people were once again ignored. Still, clearly, they are the ones who suffered most from Tł'yaa, this arbitrary slicing up of the continent.

Thankfully, some amends have been made. Although New Rampart was abandoned in 1947, the Old Crow Vuntut Gwitchin First Nation received formal title to the Canadian side of New Rampart in 2001, and with assistance from the Yukon Ministry of Tourism, began restoring Cadzow's store and house to their original appearance (Fig. 5.7). [2] Today the historic trading posts of Rampart House and Lapierre House are jointly owned by the Yukon Government and Vuntut Gwitchin First Nation.

Figure 5.7: Dan Cadzow's house at New Rampart, just a few yards from the U.S.-Canada border. n.d. Yukon Archives #7627.

The International Border and Food Security

One of the pressing issues at the 2010 Gwich'in Gathering in Fort Yukon was cross-border food security. Subsistence food harvest by Canadian Gwich'in on the Alaska side of the border is still considered to be smuggling, and boats of meat were confiscated with the tightening of security following the violent attacks of September 11, 2001. Adding insult to injury, authorities now ask the Gwich'in to purchase and carry passports before crossing the boundary, treating them like foreign visitors in their own homeland.

The Porcupine Caribou Herd, which migrates from Alaska to Canada, and which is used by both Alaskan and Canadian Gwich'in, is governed by an international treaty signed in 1987. Although there is a Porcupine Caribou Management Board, an advisory body with representation by Canadian Gwich'in and Han, Old Crow resident Stanley Njootli Sr. observes that there is a migrating moose population which spends part of the year near the head of the Coleen and Shiinjik Rivers in Alaska, and another part of the year in the Crow Flats and the Richardson Mountains on the Canadian side. This has created another management and conservation headache, especially since there is a small plane landing strip on the Alaskan side that makes it convenient for non-Native hunters to gain easy access to these moose. And there is no governing board to manage these moose who, like the caribou, also claim dual citizenship, at least in a symbolic sense.

Still another border problem concerns the provisional agreement between the U.S. and Canada regarding the subsistence harvest of Yukon River king, silver, and chum salmon. Many of these salmon spawn in Canadian streams but pass through the United States enroute, and Alaskan Gwich'in and Alaskan Han fishermen are sometimes asked or told to stop catching fish in order to allow them to escape and spawn in Canadian streams. The Gwich'in are represented on the Yukon River Panel, which develops and implements salmon research and management programs under a 2001 international treaty, but they often balk at harvest restrictions imposed on them by the Alaska Department of Fish and Game, the official management authority in U.S. waters.

Clearly, for all these reasons, Tł'yaa has brought nothing but trouble to the Gwich'in.

Acknowledgments

This essay is based on a paper first presented at the Borderlands History Conference in Whitehorse, Y.T., June 4, 1989. An earlier version was published in paper and on microfiche by the Yukon Historical and Museums Association in Proceedings of the Borderlands History Conference 1989.

Endnotes

1. An interesting cognate for the Gwich'in "Tł'yaa niintąįį" is the Tanacross language term for the international border, Tł'uuł Tęy or 'Rope Trail'.

2. See the 2001 news story about the old border community of Rampart House posted at www.oldcrow.ca/ramp1.htm. This story also contains a photo of Dan Cadzow's weathered store as it looked very recently.

6. Oaazhrii:

Gwich'in Personal Names and Kinship Ties

with Kenneth Drizhuu Frank

Historic Names

Gwich'in personal names have undergone a radical series of transformations since historic contact was made in Alaska in the 1840s. In this paper we seek to explain the connections between Gwich'in names and Gwich'in kinship relations and explore some of the transformations these names have undergone as a result of Anglo-American missionization and education.

While we have not closely studied the changes which occurred among the eastern Gwich'in on the Canadian side of the Alaska-Canadian border, many Gwich'in names are still widely used as surnames by large families in Old Crow, Fort McPherson, Aklavik, Inuvik, and Tsiigehtshik.[1] On the Canadian side, a much larger corpus of traditional Gwich'in surnames has been preserved. The surnames Itsi, Kendi, Ḳyikavichik, Koe, Kunnizzi, Netro, Niditchi, Njootli, Neyando, Nerysoo, Teeya, Tetlitchi, Tizya, Vaneltsi, and Vittrekwaa are all in active use, although English Christian surnames such as Charlie, Francis, Peter, Elias, Robert, and Herbert are also quite prominent. The gulf of difference between Canadian and Alaskan Gwich'in surnames appears to have something to do with different contact histories and naming policies on the part of the Canadian and U.S. governments. Because most of the men who worked for the Hudson's Bay Company in the mid-19th century were originally from the Orkney Islands and several of them married Gwich'in women, the Orcadian surnames Firth and Flett have been maintained by the Canadian Gwich'in (see Clouston 1912), but only Flett has been retained in Alaska.

The first list of Alaska Gwich'in names we are aware of was that kept by Alexander Hunter Murray and his successors at Fort Yukon during the period 1849-1854 (see partial list in Table 1). Murray and his men needed these names in order to transact business and keep accounts with the trappers who brought furs into the new Hudson's Bay Company fort, which he and his men built. In this list virtually all of the Gwich'in names are men's names.

What we see in the way of patterning for these men's names is that many of them are expressive of an action or a behavior. These names are more like verbs or verb phrases than nouns. Only a few are named after animal species: e.g. Drąh ('merganser duck') and Corbeaux (<Fr. 'crow or raven'), while one is named after a physiological trait, Vakwee Chyah Ti' ('father of Big Wide Feet'). Many fathers were renamed after their first-born children using the suffix -Viti' or Ti' ('the father of'), a pattern Robert McKennan recognized as teknonymy (1965:58). It's unfortunate that Murray and his successors did not record the indigenous

names of Gwich'in women, many of whom observed this same custom by renaming themselves after their first-born daughters.

At the time of contact, and probably for a generation after that, the Gwich'in practiced teknonymy. The system worked something like this: A boy or girl was given their first Gwich'in name from their parents or grandparents while they were infants or toddlers. The entire Gwich'in name was one or two words or a short phrase, but there was nothing equivalent to a surname. To cite one historic example, a boy was named Vigwizhįį ('He's Very Wise') shortly after birth. When he grew up, acquired a wife, and his wife gave birth to a daughter, they decided to call her Shahnyaa ('He or she told me'). Vigwizhįį, to denote his new status as a father, then became known as Shahnyaa Viti' (lit. 'the father of Shahnyaa') and his Vigwizhįį birth name fell into disuse. Also, the teknonym Viti' was customarily diminished to Ti', so this man suddenly became known all over as Shahnyaa Ti', the famous trading chief of the Yukon Flats during the mid-nineteenth century (Fig. 6.1).[2] Any man who was named after his firstborn child was classified as Ch'ikil Ti'.

Figure 6.1. Shahnyaa Ti' (identified as Sinate, on right with beaded knife case, others unidentified), Chief of the Fort Yukon Indians. Schieffelin Brothers Album, 1882-1883. Wickersham State Historic Site Photograph Collection, ASL-P277-016. Alaska State Library, Juneau.

Likewise, women often took on the name of their firstborn child, using the teknonym Vahan ('the mother of'). Shijyaa Tr'oonyaa, for example, gave birth to a child she named Shoot'oo and immediately acquired new status as Shoot'oo Vahan ('the mother of Shoot'oo'). Another woman is remembered today only as Ch'adzaa Vahan ('mother of the dance'). A list of some of these old Gwich'in names has been compiled by the esteemed senior Gwich'in scholar, Katherine Peter, in a small booklet called *Deenaadai' Gwich'in Oozhri'* (1978). Another list is included in our compilation of the Frank family tree (Frank and Mishler 2001:669-679). On the Alaska side, Gwich'in surnames, save for Tritt, have now totally disappeared, and most Gwich'in personal names are now used only within families. We examine how this came to be and what it portends for the future of the language.

Christian Names: the Transition

When Anglican missionaries arrived in Fort Yukon in 1861, their first order of business was to convert the Gwich'in to Christianity and then baptize them. Since baptism meant being reborn to a new life, the early missionaries gave each convert a Christian name taken from the Bible. Some people received Old Testament names and some received them from the New Testament. Men were given names such as Elijah, Solomon, Luke, Isaac, James, Enoch, Joseph, Noah, Moses, Peter, John, Jonas, Jacob, Abraham, Gabriel, and Titus, while women received ones like Rachel, Sarah, Mary, Martha, Eunice, Eliza, Naomi, Julia, and Hannah.

An important list of Gwich'in personal names was recorded in Alaska during the early 20th century by takers of the U.S. census, who went around interviewing households in 1900, 1910, and 1920. However, it's telling that almost all of the names recorded on these census sheets are English names.[3] Gwich'in names are again conspicuous by their absence. Along with the Biblical names of the 19th century, a few secular

English names began to take hold, possibly as a result of contact with American prospectors during the gold rush. In the 1910 U.S. census, for example, we begin to see names such as Ellen, Lucy, Margaret, Annie, Agnes, and Maggie for women, and John, Henry, Charlie, Robert, Sam, Albert, Henry, and Frank for men.

During the late 19th century and for part of the early 20th century then, most of the Gwich'in, at least those who became Christians, maintained both an English Christian name and an Indian name, side by side. We still hear a lot about people such as Solomon Needachii, John Vandeegwizii, Lucy Ch'igwich'in, and Ellen Treenahtsyaa. One might think that their Gwich'in names would be retained as surnames, but that generally did not happen. With the next generation of children, namely those born during the first half of the 20th century, daughters or sons received a Christian first name, and their father's Christian name became their surname.

The phenomenon of double Christian names becomes apparent for the first time in the 1910 U.S. census. Wherever Anglican and Episcopal missionaries set up missions, we begin to encounter names such as Elijah Henry, Gabriel Peter, Peter John, and Martha James. These double Christian names are now a familiar badge of identity not only for the Gwich'in, but for most other Dene people living in Alaska's Interior.

This pattern has now prevailed for several generations, and most Alaskan Gwich'in still use these double Christian names. In the course of this process, however, some people have received redundant English names such as Frank Frank, Albert Albert, and Sam Sam. During the late nineteenth and early twentieth centuries we also see that for elder men, the word "Old" was used in front of their Christian names. Census takers recorded such names as Old Fred, Old Frank, Old John, and Old Robert. The name "Christian" was adopted as a first name and also as a surname during the early decades of the 20th century, but there are no "Christiansens" or "Christiansons."

It could be just a coincidence, but many Gwich'in women born in the mid-twentieth century and still living today have the English names of historic steamboats plying the Yukon River from St. Michael's to Dawson and Whitehorse. Such vessels as the Alice, the Anna, the Hannah, the Bella, the Clara, the Dorothy, the Fannie, the Florence, the Hannah, the Jessie, the Julia B, the Leah, the Louise, the Margaret, the Ruth, the Sarah, and the Susie, were all built during the gold rush and were seen quite frequently each summer in Gwich'in communities such as Fort Yukon and Circle (Cohen 1996:110-115). Many Indian men made a living as woodcutters for these boats, and several of the Gwich'in and Han men who knew the river well were hired as steamboat pilots. One Gwich'in man in Circle was nicknamed 'Woodchopper Joe' because of his service to these steamboats. The steamboats were very important economically, and undoubtedly their names were prestigious. The names Sarah, Hannah, and Ruth became doubly important because they were also Biblical.

One might surmise from this process that the Gwich'in had abandoned their Indian names in favor of English ones, both for first names and surnames, but this is patently not the case. The practice of using English names exclusively put a lot of stress on the Gwich'in, who began to feel a loss of their Indian identity due to the pressures exerted by missionaries and school teachers. The first time this stress became apparent was in a letter written in 1939 by school teacher John Fredson to his supervisor, Charles Hawkesworth, Assistant to the Superintendent, Office of Indian Affairs in Juneau. Fredson was the first Gwich'in to graduate from college and return to teach his own people (see Chapter 3 above).

It's essential to quote at length from Fredson's (1939) letter to illustrate the frustration that he and others felt after their names were taken from them by outside institutions. The letter begins:

Dear Mr. Hawkesworth:--

This is in regards to the question of the names of the natives here at Venetie. At first we called this place "Chandalar", but it led to so much confusion that we had to change. In like manner there is a lot of confusion of names among the people here on account of the fact that there are so many first names and so few sur-names.

For example, Enoch John. . .is known all through this section of the country as "Enook" or "Ehnook". At the stores he has been put down as "Enoch Apple", but no doubt he was baptized as "Enoch John" and the question naturally arises--"What John family?" We here know that different names apply to the one and only one person, but to the ones from the outside, it's confusing and it makes it difficult in keeping accurate records. What really happened was that in the early days when the first ministers came into the country, they naturally had difficulty in pronouncing and spelling the old names. So a lot of "Johns" appeared, and no effort has been made to change the condition.

As a result we have two Clara Johns here in school. There is a Daniel John here and another at Kachick [K'ahtsik] about 45 miles by winter trail. There is a David John at Circle and one up the Porcupine River. For a long time there were two John Franks. The John Frank here still get[s] mail for the second John Frank who has been dead these many years. And so goes the confusion.

We believe this trouble and confusion could be eliminated to some extent here at Venetie. It could easily be done using the translations of the old names. As for example, Enoch John's father was known as ----, translated, "The father of the one who dances". From this we would get, "Enoch John Dancer". Here crops up a sur-name, and it is a good one.

Then we have one John. His father, Old John, was referred to as-- "The father of the one who is pulling a load". This would give us, "Elijah John Puller."

And there is David Henry. His father was named, "The man who hunts all the time". This would make "David Henry Hunter".

> Of course there are some good surnames already and they will stay naturally. Please advise if you think it ways and worthwhile to make this addition in names for future work (Fredson 1939).

It's instructive to read Hawkesworth's reply to Fredson, which was not at all encouraging. He wrote:

> It would not be advisable to make a general revision of names at this time, since the names, for the most part, are already on record. However, as children are born into a family they might follow the custom established in other parts of Alaska, which is, the Indian name is dropped altogether, and the Christian name of the father is then used as the surname for the children.
>
> We would certainly like to maintain the Indian and Eskimo names of the native people throughout Alaska, but due to our inability to pronounce them, and also to the fact that the English language will gradually prevail wherever schools are maintained, the above procedure seems to be the most applicable method. (Hawkesworth 1939).

From this communication it's abundantly clear that the primary reason the Gwich'in were encouraged to give up their Indian names was because of the linguistic incompetence of non-Natives who resisted learning to pronounce Gwich'in words. It could be assumed that this policy was a death blow to Gwich'in naming traditions, but something else happened.

When the distinguished linguist, Edward Sapir, began working with Fredson, at a summer camp in Pennsylvania in the early 1920s, he noticed some interesting things about Gwich'in nicknames. Comparing Fredson's data on Gwich'in with what he had gathered from the Sarcee, a plains Athabaskan tribal group, Sapir observed: "A set of names recently obtained from a Kutchin Indian of Fort Yukon, Alaska [Fredson], suggests strongly that one of the most common types of Athabaskan names is the sobriquet, a name referring to some personal peculiarity, generally laughable, of the bearer and which is avoided in his presence because of its unflattering implication (Sapir 1924:116)." He added that "In Kutchin [Gwich'in] the final short unaccented vowel dropped. . . . The resulting monosyllabic adjective forms do not seem to be used entirely alone but require a preceding noun. Forms like Charlie t'cà·' "ragged Charlie," Sarah ɣo· "round, plump Sarah," and Jinny lɑ́l· "sloppy Jinny" are current today." (Sapir 1924:119).

Facing the rejection of their Indian language identity in the schools, the Gwich'in decided consciously or unconsciously to maintain their Indian names internally within the family. To this day, every Gwich'in person has a Gwich'in name. In fact, many people have several Indian names, something Sapir also recognized with the Sarcee. Some of these names are traditional names passed down from family ancestors, some are taken from animals, and others are descriptive of a child's behavior. We were fortunate to become aware of these naming patterns by compiling the Frank family tree. In the act of compilation, we came across dozens of Gwich'in names that do not appear on birth certificates or any legal documents.

Animal Names

After doing fieldwork in Arctic Village and Venetie during the early 1930s, the distinguished anthropologist Robert McKennan (1965:58) concluded that: "Chandalar Kutchin names followed no particular pattern. As a rule a child was named after an animal, an object, or some event or personal characteristic. Since any person could name a child, Chandalar Kutchin names were essentially nicknames." What McKennan did not know was that some nicknames are strongly disliked by the person they refer to, while others are gently affectionate.

Many families in Arctic Village, Venetie, and other Gwich'in communities have acquired a set of names that are variations on an animal or bird species. Moses Sam, the head of one Arctic Village family, for example, went by Moses shih ('Moses brown bear'). Shih's wife Jenny was duly called Shih shyaaghan ('old woman brown bear'), while one of his sons is Shih gii ('brown bear child') and another is Shih tsal ('little brown bear'). Another Arctic Village man was called Jim Deetrya' ('Jim Raven'). His two oldest daughters are accordingly known as Deetrya' tr'ik ('Raven woman'), while his three younger daughters are referred to as Deetrya' zhuu ('Little Raven'). Chief Christian's father went by Dinjik Choh ('Big Moose'), while the late Elijah Henry, one of Robert McKennan's principal sources on Gwich'in material culture, was called Nahtryąh ('Wolverine') because he was a restless person, always moving around (McKennan 1965; also Mishler and Simeone 2006). In similar fashion, Johnny Ross of Fort Yukon was called Vitł'ee ik zhit ts'it tsi' ('He has a porcupine tail in his pants') because he was fidgety and unable to sit still. As a child, the late Lucy Roberts of Circle was named Ch'idzin ('Green-winged teal'), and Allen Tritt, former first chief of Arctic Village, still goes by Dlak ('Tree squirrel') as well as by the nickname Allo. See Allen's photo portrait below in Chapter 20.

Not only animal names but animal body parts are used to identify individuals, providing examples of metonymy. Nena Roberts went by Nahtryah kwai' ('wolverine's foot') and Hannah Bundschuh, nee Hannah Frank, has acquired the nickname Tsuk zhrak ('marten intestines'). An early letter written by the Native minister William Loola announces the death of the daughter of William Ch'atthąįį dee (Loola 1894). Meanwhile, Hannah's younger brother, Robert Frank Sr., is known as Tsuk khyąą ('marten trap'). Ch'atthąįį dee means 'the eyes of large game animals'. In the early 1970s I recorded Daniel John, a traditional singer known as Ch'ak'ohandzee (see Mishler 1974, Mishler and Frank 2020:423). Ch'ak'ohandzee refers to the atlas bone which connects the head to the neck of a caribou or moose. In a reversal of the former Gwich'in tradition of a man being named after his first born son, David

Henry of Venetie was called David Ch'izhee ('David bone marrow'), while his son David Henry Jr. is Ch'izhee tsal ('Little bone marrow'). William Khaatryaa was named after shedding caribou hair.

The only Alaskan Gwich'in name to survive to the present day as a surname is Tritt, another animal body part. Tritt derives from ch'idrit or drit, the metatarsal or lower hind leg bone of the caribou. Drit and Drit zhuu or Drizhuu ('little metatarsal') were both sons of Shahan Dik, one of the four wives of Diitsii Giitł'uu, a legendary Di'haii Gwich'in leader. Just as the Tritt family is descended from Drit, so the Frank family is descended from Drizhuu. Even as the caribou's metatarsal has great symbolic value, it also provides the Gwich'in with materials for making skin scrapers, toys, and moccasins. The rich marrow of the metatarsal and metacarpal is also highly valued as nourishment and flavor.

Personal Characteristics

To illustrate how Gwich'in names follow personal characteristics, we have only to consider Stanley Frank's name, Stanley ghoo 'round Stanley', for his stoutness, or Jimmy Roberts, who was affectionately known as Jimmy gwat ('short Jimmy'). Abel Tritt was simply called by the adjective Zhuu ('Little') for his small stature. And Elijah John was known as Elijah Figger because he was a carpenter good at measuring and figuring (see Chapter 4). This links some present-day names to patterns found during the early contact period (Table 1).

When a team of geologists arrived in Arctic Village to do topographic surveys in 1927 (see Chapter 2 above), it's not surprising that the Gwich'in gave them all names based on their behavior and their resemblance to animals. John Mertie Jr. was called moose (dinjik) because he liked to go swimming--something the Gwich'in did not do. Gerald Fitzgerald was called sheep (divii) because his surveying took him up and down over the mountains. Fred Clark was named caribou (vadzaih) because he was so active, playing games with the children. And

C.A. Wheeler was porcupine (ts'it) because he occasionally squinted his eyes.

All of this naming and nicknaming is predicated on the ancient Gwich'in belief that animals are human and have spirits and that they are in many ways interchangeable with humans. As the elder Johnny Frank once said, "In those [early] days all the fish and all the small animals and big animals were human. And they all spoke one language, they say" (Mishler 2001:21).

While Gwich'in names may be thought of as nicknames, they are certainly much more than that. They are signs and symbols of identity, and to some degree they are fairly well-kept secrets within families and within communities. Some people are quite embarrassed by their Indian names and do not want them to be circulated or published. We have purposely withheld some of these names from this publication for that reason. The fact that they survive underground, however, is a testimony the power of tradition and the preservation of the Gwich'in language. Tł'yah, a name which translates as 'rope' or 'border', was the nickname for Han Gwich'in elder Dick Nukon, who was born in Eagle Village in 1925 and resided most of his adult life in Old Crow (Ya Sa To, 1989:43-45).

Kenneth, the junior author of this essay, has the Indian name Vandee Chuu Kwaa, meaning 'He never cries tears.'[4] It was noticed that when he was an infant he didn't cry, and this behavior was so unusual that he was quickly called that by an elder, and the name caught on with his parents and other close relatives. His father Hamel's Indian name was Vi'iidzee ndee or 'Great Horned Owl eye,' because of his excellent eyesight and marksmanship with a rifle. Ricky Frank, one of Kenneth's younger brothers, is fittingly called Vi'iidzee zhuu or 'Little Great Horned Owl,' directly after his father. This relationship of father and son is similar to that between senior and junior in non-Native circles. Some people have metaphorical names based on their relationship with other relatives. One such person is Vitsii too ('His Grandpa's cane') which stems from the fact that when this person was small he followed his grandfather around and always stayed close by his side.

Some members of the Frank family have inherited ancestral names, such as Diitsii Giitł'uu, the patriarch of the Tritt and Frank families who died in the early 19th century, or Ch'igwich'in, the name of Johnny Frank's mother which has been passed on to her great granddaughter (see Frank and Mishler 2001). Kenneth's late brother, Ron Frank named one of his sons Samson K'aiiheenjik, the legendary Gwich'in warrior, and Isaac John Jr. of Fort Yukon has acquired the name of the legendary warrior Ko'ehdan ('Without fire').

Personal Names as Place Names

Gwich'in personal names are also part of the landscape of the Gwich'in homeland (see especially Caulfield et al. 1983). In the Venetie and Arctic Village region there are several lakes named after individuals, such as Leah vavan ('Leah's lake', after Leah Druck) and David Salmon vavan ('David Salmon's lake'). The naming of places after people continues to the present day. The story of David Salmon vavan is that during the 1960s while David was living in Venetie, he always went out to this nearby lake to camp out and hunt ducks. At that time the lake had no name, so they decided to name it after him, even after he moved away. Unfortunately, this lake has dried up and no longer exists. Rev. David Salmon was once the traditional chief of the Doyon Region, a regional Native corporation, served as an ordained Episcopal priest, and was an old-time dance fiddler.

Besides lakes, many other landforms are named after people and invoke stories about people. For example, there is Old John vaddhah ('Old John's mountain') and Noah vatai ('Noah's hill'). Another hill, Gwaihshaa vatai ('Gwaihshaa's hill') recalls a man who once climbed up there hollering and looking for his wife, who had run off with another man. Some places are memorialized by the actions of individuals, such as Ambrose azhral ('Ambrose yells') after Ambrose William, or Christian teiinlir ('Christian urinated'), after Christian Tritt. Remote cabins and other structures which dot the cultural landscape are almost always named for people, such as Johnny Frank vizheh ('Johnny Frank's house'), Paul Tritt vizheh ('Paul Tritt's house'), and Dihch'i' David vatthal ('Old Man David's caribou fence'). Additional personal place names may be found in Appendix F of Mishler and Frank (2020).

Kinship Terms as Names

Kinship helps shape Gwich'in names. A well-defined Gwich'in joking relationship, for example, often exists between a boy and his father's brother. This uncle selects one of his brother's sons to be his shizhi' ('my favorite' or 'my grandson'), but he calls all his other nephews shuu ('my nephew'). Since an uncle may have several nephews, not all of whom will put up with the teasing, he tests them to see if they will accept the challenge and tease him back. Those who most enjoy the verbal duels then become shizhi'. No joking relationships exist between uncles and nephews on the mother's side, but they are well-developed between brothers-in-law and sisters-in-law.

To a very great extent, Gwich'in kinship terms of address such as shizhi' and shijuu constitute names, at least among immediate family members. Instead of calling relatives by their formal individual names, these vocative terms often serve nicely in their stead. If my mother's name is Mary, I do not call her Mary but Ne'ęę, just as an English speaking child would say, Mama or Mom. Even black bear cubs are heard to cry out, "Ne'ęę", suggesting that animals understand the language and are part of the Gwich'in kinship system. In a 2011 speech, Clarence Alexander, former chief at Fort Yukon, declared: "When I was a kid I never knew the names of my elders. It was only Shitsuu or Shitsii or Shitii or Sheek'aii"(Alexander 2011).

In Gwich'in 'my father's sister' is always addressed as shitsuu ('my grandma'), even though mother's sister is always called sheek'aii ('my aunt'). By transforming the one-generation relationship of aunt and nephew into the special two-generation relationship of grandmother and grandchild, more respect and close affection can be shown on both ends of the relationship. Vocative kin terms are thus highly important symbolic names. (see Appendix A).

Mixed bloods and half-breeds are ethnically marked by the special naming epithet Tsoo, to indicate their light-colored skin. For example, we commonly hear names of reference such as Hannah Tsoo, Bertha Tsoh, and John Tsoo. Tsoo derives from ahtsoo, 'it's yellow.' This is analogous to the traditional African-American term "yellow gal," referring to a light-skinned woman with mixed blood.[5] It's considered offensive when full-blooded Gwich'in youth use the "Tsoo" epithet as a term of address, and as such it's usually reserved for the taunting of youth by their peers, carrying the same kind of stigma as "half-breed."

A Multiplicity of Names

The Gwich'in often have multiple Native names, as well as English names, and these names establish multiple identities. For instance, Kenneth's oldest daughter has five Indian names as well as an English name, given to her by different relatives. On her birth certificate her name is Crystal Frank (see Fig. 6.2). However, one of her grandmothers, Maggie Gilbert, called her Dzehgak ('black brant'), which became the title of a book about her called *Nich'itsal Dzehgak Oozhį̨į̨* (Tritt-Frank 1989). Meanwhile, her father calls her Ch'eejii ('older sister'), while a friend of the family in Fort Yukon calls her Diti' zhyaan'ee ('Whining with our father'). Her great grandmother, Sarah Frank, had two names for her. One was Ginjik valaii ('Words ricochet off her'), and the other was Chats'ą' vizhit teech'iriikii ('Crooked on the stretcher board'). This second name is heavily metaphorical. She is figuratively named after an animal skin that has been stretched to dry but which was put on the stretcher board rather awkwardly. However, according to her father Kenneth what it means is that her parents aren't fully in control of her, that she is a bit undisciplined and "doesn't quite fit." With this name, her great grandmother provided some clever indirect humorous criticism of her parents' parenting skills.

As the Deg Xinag speaker Laverne Dementieff has said, "Something like naming is, I think, really profound to our identity and our sense of belonging and our wellness" (2021). We strongly agree and feel that in order for the Gwich'in language or any other endangered language to survive, one step which needs to be taken is to claim and repossess ancestral names. These names can be found in family genealogies, and if used daily, they become a constant reminder of each person's ethnicity and social identity. With names as conscious symbols of belonging, the legitimacy of the language in everyday public discourse can be re-established. It will no longer be hidden from the world but will be an open door invitation and a challenge to revive indigenous phonologies and semantics.

Acknowledgments

An earlier version of this essay was presented at the Second International Congress of Arctic Social Sciences, Rovaniemi, Finland, May/June, 1995.

Endnotes

1. It's noteworthy that the Gwich'in community formerly known as Arctic Red River has dropped that name and replaced it with the original Gwich'in place name, Tsiigehtshik.
2. I'm indebted to the late Elijah John of Fort Yukon for this example.
3. When village censuses were conducted by Bureau of Indian Bureau of Indian Affairs school teachers in Venetie, Arctic Village, and Fort Yukon from the 1920s through the 1960s, another large inventory of personal names was preserved. These names are in the Bureau of Indian Affairs RG 75, National Archives, Seattle.

4. Literally, Vandee Chuu Kwaa means 'Eyes without Water.' Semantically, this nickname is highly reminiscent of the Canadian Gwich'in surname Vittrekwaa ('No tears'), but there is no formal connection.

5. See for example, Huddie Ledbetter's song "Yellow Gal" on the LP recording, *Leadbelly's Last Sessions Part Four* (Smithsonian Folkways FA2942D, 1962) and the holler, "Yellow Woman's Doorbells" on the album Leadbelly (Archive of Folk Music FM-102A n.d.).

Gwich'in Names selected from the Hudson's Bay Company Fort Yukon post journals, Indian balance sheets, 1849-1854

Taken from Hudson's Bay Company Archives, Winnipeg. See Manuscripts B240/a/3 folios 28-29, B240/a/4 folios 32-33, B240/a/8 folios 22-23-24, B240/d/1 folios 24-25, B240/d/2 folios 22-23, B240/d/3 folios 24-25-26, B240/d/5 folios 27-28, and B240/d/6 folios 16-17-18. Orthographies have changed radically, and only those names which we could clearly decipher or make an educated guess at are shown here, so the list is far from complete. And as far as we know, these are all men's names, since they were the principal commercial trappers. We are indebted to Kathy Arndt for referring us to the post journals and to the late Rev. David Salmon for deciphering the name of Black River chief Vakwaiichyah Ti' from Bacanechate.

Table 1: Selected Gwich'in Names from the Hudson's Bay Company post journals at Fort Youcon, 1849 1854

Original	New Orthography	English Translation	Notes
Saveeah	Shahvyaa	'making me swim'	Fort Youcon chief
Seenazit	Sheenaazhit	'he brings it over'	
Beetsha	Vijyaa	'his partner' or 'his friend'	
Tetshanna	Deeshainyaa	'what are you saying to me?'	
Intlacko	Indlaa Choh	'he laughs big'	
Tchongquaw	Chųų Kwaa	'no water'	
Traha	Trąh	'mersanger duck'	
Betsa tee che	Veetsa Ti' Tehch'yaa	'I'm the father of Veetsa'	
Seegon athat	Tsee Gin Athat	'he pounds beaver leg'	
Tlauhsa veethe	Tł'oohsaii Viithaa	'I hit him with my left hand'	
Koo eeatee	Kwih'aa Ti'	'the father of Kwih'aa'	Elijah Henry's grandfather
Chavilte	Ch'eeghwal Ti'	'the father of foreleg radius bone'	historic chief from Old Crow
Bekethsate	Vakwaiits'at Ti'	'the father of His Toe'	
Neeleel	Neelil	'one being pulled in a sled'	
Nee leel te	Ch'eelil Ti'	'the father of one being pulled in a sled'	aka Letter Carrier (a chief)
Tlo hanley	Tł'oo hanlee	'grass coming up from the bottom'	
Natla	Natł'yaa	'braided'	
Kay sangh	K'aii tsan	'pussy willow'	
Etchee outah	Ch'iji' Oontah	'holding an animal's antlers'	Stephen Peter's grandfather
Cheet sel	Chii tsal	'little bird'	
Kay zuck	K'ehdzak	'fish spear'	
Veeta	Viidar or Viidah	'Peter'	
Nahchin	Naach'in	'twin'	
Bacanechate	Vakwaiichyah Ti'	'the father of Wide Feet'	aka Red Leggins (a chief), Fig. 3

Figure 6.3. Vakwaiichyah Ti' (Red Leggins). From Dall (1870). A visiting journalist described him as "gorgeous in a scarlet coat, with brass buttons and epaulettes" (Burlington Free Press, 1869:3). Red Leggins' death was reported about 1883 by Bishop Bompas.

7. Gwich'in Naming Ceremonies

Gwich'in personal names have undergone a radical series of transformations since historic contact was made by the Hudson's Bay Company in Alaska during the 1840s. Early Anglican missionaries gave their converts Christian names, largely taken from the Bible and conferred in baptisms, and most Gwich'in have accepted those names (see Peter 1978). Sometime in the early twentieth century, however, Gwich'in names went underground.

Contextually, Gwich'in naming ceremonies are an emergent phenomenon and stand somewhat apart from other Gwich'in rituals. Those I have witnessed in recent years include funeral ceremonies and high school and college graduation ceremonies. Funeral ceremonies, with some important variations and adaptations, have been largely shaped by the liturgy of the Anglican and Episcopal Churches, while school graduation ceremonies, also with variations, largely coincide with those initiated by non-Native high schools and universities. Several Gwich'in communities celebrate Memorial Day at the village graveyard by cleaning graves and feasting with the dead. This too has a strong Christian and western influence. Gwich'in naming ceremonies, by contrast, have no clear correlates in western Anglo tradition, and linguistically and ethnographically that makes them all the more interesting.

The first Gwich'in naming ceremony I ever witnessed and recorded was held in Fairbanks during the Athabascan Old-Time Fiddling Festival, on November 21, 1986. The name giver and presentation leader was the late Jonathon Solomon of Fort Yukon, a famous Gwich'in political leader who was honoring Katrina Frank, a young girl fiddler from Minto. Although she was not Gwich'in, Solomon gave her the Gwich'in name, Ch'ahtal Zhuu ('Little Willow Grouse'), a small bird known as a harbinger of the future. Along with the name he gave her an elegant beaded and tanned moosehide vest.

At this naming ceremony, Solomon made the following speech, referring to a personal experience he once had out in the wilderness, watching some young willow grouse learn to sing from their elders:

> And when three years ago Arthur Frank, her grandfather, asked me to name this child, I didn't know. I keep thinking about my Dad, and then all of a sudden I think about my aunt, the name came to me because she [Katrina] was sitting right under her grandfather learning how to play that little fiddle, just like Ch'ahtal Zhuu. And that's her name.
>
> And now as chief with the power in me [long pause] and to give her that name, and with that name there's a lot of power, as our Reverend [Titus] Peter told you. And it's my pleasure to give her that power because I can do this because I'm a chief in my own culture. I'd like to give her four powers. From the East, I give this child the power of peace and light. And from the

> West I give this child the power of work. And from the South it's the power of the warmth of this earth. But more power than anything else is the power of the North. I give this child the power of the North with its cold and mighty winds, gives strength and endurance to live in this country of ours.
>
> I hope my little sister will understand and use these four powers of the winds to help all the people of the world for a better place to live together. Ladies and gentlemen, I present to you Ch'ahtal Zhuu! [loud cheering and applause] (Mishler 1986)

In this ceremony Solomon is transferring some of his own power as a leader on to this young girl, Katrina Frank. The drama of bestowing her Indian name is used as a form of synergy based on his personal observation of the behavior of wild birds. Although Katrina is not his own blood relative but rather the granddaughter of his friend, Arthur Frank, he nevertheless refers to her in the speech as "my little sister" in such a way that he creates a fictive but affectionate kinship tie through the ceremony.

The second formal naming ceremony I was privileged to see was held in Venetie in 2002. The person receiving the name was the Rev. David Salmon, and the giver of the name was Kenneth Frank of Arctic Village and Venetie. Kenneth gave David the name Deets'e' (aka Deatzi), after a powerful legendary medicine man who lived in the mountains north of Arctic Village (see McKennan 1965:81). This naming ceremony was held in Venetie in conjunction with a potlatch given to honor Kenneth's wife, Caroline Tritt-Frank, who had just graduated from the University of Alaska Fairbanks with a Master's degree. Kenneth recently pointed out that when a Gwich'in name is given, an eagle feather usually goes with it, but in the case of David Salmon, he gave three eagle feathers to honor his status as a chief.

The most recent ceremony I saw, the principal subject of this essay, was held in conjunction with the biennial Gwich'in Gathering, held in Fort Yukon on Wednesday, July 21, 2010. The Gathering itself hosted

200-300 people, but this ceremony was a smaller affair attended by only about thirty to forty individuals. It was sponsored by the local elder Daisy Solomon Stevens, the younger sister of Jonathon Solomon, in order to bequeath traditional Gwich'in names on three of her grandchildren. This ceremony was held in the Community Center, used also as the school gymnasium.

This naming ceremony followed an evening meal for all those visitors in attendance at the Gathering. But not everyone who attended the meal stayed for the naming ceremony. In fact, there was a break of about forty-five minutes as gifts were brought out and arranged on a big blue tarp. The duration of the ceremony itself was about thirty minutes. This was followed by about fifteen minutes of traditional dancing and drumming and about twenty minutes of a general gift giveaway to those of us in the audience.

The elders who attended and participated in the conferring of the names included Rev. Trimble Gilbert of Arctic Village, an Episcopal priest wearing a stole (one of his formal church vestments), Simon Francis Sr., a Fort Yukon elder and traditional chief, and Kenneth Frank, from Venetie. To my knowledge, none of these elders are related to Daisy Solomon Stevens or her children or grandchildren. It was never explained just how the ceremony was organized, but Rev. Gilbert and Daisy herself seemed to take the lead roles in this communal event. Many of the insights I received about the ceremony come from my longstanding friendship and conversations with Kenneth.

Before the name was announced, Trimble put his hand on top of the head of each child and whispered to them quietly, perhaps with a prayer or a blessing. Clearly the Episcopal Church played a pivotal role in the ceremony, but this is not always the case. The two other naming ceremonies I have witnessed were decidedly more secular.

The first of the three names, K'aiiheenjik, was bestowed on Daisy's grandson Isaiah Horace. The name K'aiiheenjik was given to Daisy to give to her grandson by her grandmother, Sarah Abel of Old Crow. This happened in 1998, the year before Daisy's daughter-in-law Robbie gave birth to her grandson. It was a kind of prophecy and a gift. Even her grandson's Christian name, Isaiah, comes after an Old Testament prophet. At any rate, the name K'aiiheenjik stayed in Daisy's mind for twelve years before it was officially conferred.

In the ceremony, Daisy paid tribute to her grandmother for giving her own grandson this name, leaping four generations. The significance of this name is that K'aiiheenjik was a famous Gwich'in warrior from the upper Porcupine River area, and there is a well-known legend about him that still circulates in oral tradition. So not only was the name transferred during the ceremony, but presumably the legend that goes with the name, although this legend was not recited during the ceremony.

Also, this is not the first time K'aiiheenjik has been bestowed. Kenneth Frank's brother Ron Frank, a Gwich'in who married an Ahtna woman, also gave this name to his son, connecting it with his Christian name Samson, the strong man of the Old Testament. The point of this is that Gwich'in personal names can be and are often given without any ceremony, simply by the pronouncement of a parent or a grandparent. Most of those participating in the Fort Yukon ceremony proudly announced their own Indian names.

The second name given at the Gwich'in Gathering was to Matthew Stevens' young daughter Amara Stevens, a child just four years of age. Her new Indian name was Dee'ii Deek'it, meaning '[She takes] Our maternal uncle's place.' During the ceremony Matthew choked up as he told the story behind the name. He bestowed this name Dee'ii Deek'it on his own daughter because she was born at the same time as his own mother's brother's funeral, and he could not be present at her birth. The timing was instrumental because as Matthew tells it, his maternal uncle was none other than Jonathon Solomon. That day was July 19, 2006. Therefore, he lost someone dear and gained someone dear on the same day, and now Amara always reminds him of his lost uncle. The circle of naming then became complete. The name giver of the 1986 ceremony became the one named for in 2010.

Daisy Solomon's third grandchild, a boy about ten years of age, whose English name is Dylan Coppock, received the Gwich'in name Diitsii K'įh, meaning '[He's following] Our Grandfather's Tracks.' Like Amara, Dylan is the child of Daisy's son Matthew.

Gifts

The Gwich'in naming ceremony is full of gifts. The primary gifts are made to those who receive their Indian names. From the elders the two boys both received rifles decorated with handkerchiefs on the barrels as well as blankets, while the girl received a large doll and a blanket. All three also received an eagle feather. In addition, grandson Dylan received a special necklace from his father.

When this part was concluded, there was another round of gifting by Daisy and her son Matthew to the three elders, accompanied by speeches from Daisy, Matthew, and others. Two elders, Simon Francis and Kenneth Frank, received a dentalium shell necklace and either a rifle or shotgun with a handkerchief tied to the barrel. The third elder, Trimble Gilbert, received a dentalium shell necklace and a new chain saw.

Other people also received gifts. Some of these people were close friends and relatives of the Solomon family. Another was Crystal Frank, who flew in from Fairbanks to help her father sing. After receiving several gifts, Crystal made this speech, proudly announcing one of her own Gwich'in names, Diti' zhyaan'ee (see above Chapter 6).

When the special gifts and recipients were recognized, people in the audience received small gifts, including myself. These gifts were piled on a large blue tarp spread out on the floor of the community center and distributed by family members. Gifts I received as a guest seated in the audience included a polyester throw, a baseball cap with the embossed words "Golden Heart Native Athletics/Fairbanks, Alaska", a yellow cotton washcloth, a small tin box marked "Armitron: America's Watch" with three plastic plant leaves inside, a Ziploc bag with a piece of pilot bread and two strips of smoked salmon, a printed yellow handkerchief, a pair of brown cotton Jersey Boss work gloves, a miniature stick of Mennen Speed Stick deodorant, a small woven blue and white doily, and a small plastic bottle of Neutrogena shampoo.

Interpretation and Conclusion

According to Kenneth, Gwich'in naming is deeply-embedded in Gwich'in folklore. In the story of Wolverine and the Wolf, for example, where Wolverine marries a she-Wolf, the she-Wolf's brother names their baby Ch'ikee Vee, which is just like a thief, and this makes Wolverine mad, even though Wolverine is a well-known scavenger himself. Such a name is seen as quite humorous.

Another northern Dene group, the Tanacross people of the upper Tanana River, who are matrilineal and exogamous, also have naming ceremonies. In the fall of 2012, a middle-aged married woman in Tanacross village participated in a potlatch and gave formal gifts in order to acquire her own paternal grandmother's English name, Sarah, to bestow on her daughter. Since this middle-aged woman belongs to her mother's clan by birth, she had to give away potlatch gifts to her father and his clan to acquire the right to use the name. Her father told me that for him this was just like bringing his mother back from the grave. To this extent, personal names are not just a matter of kinship identity (one's granddaughter is treated as if she were one's mother), but constitute a kind of private property.

Kenneth says that Gwich'in naming ceremonies were formerly very traditional, but Christianity disrupted the tradition. In his words, "We have a lot of ceremonies. Ceremonies make us get stronger among ourselves. Ceremonies are what make us Gwich'in people." The irony of all this is that there is apparently no Gwich'in word for ceremony. Although funeral ceremonies go back to historic contact (see Chapter 19), naming ceremonies, like graduation ceremonies, seem relatively new on the scene. We know that many names are given to children shortly after birth by a close relative without any formal ritual. I never saw or heard of naming ceremonies while doing fieldwork in the 1970s, and I sense that many of them are newly emergent.

There is nothing in the historic record to suggest this, but I believe the Gwich'in use naming ceremonies to affirm their indigenous identity and to reclaim their Native language. Indeed, bestowing a Gwich'in name is fast becoming an act of ethnic and tribal patriotism. Giving and receiving an Indian name is also a form of spirituality, a bond of affection between individuals and families. Certain names such as K'aiiheenjik and Dee'ii Deek'it suggest a conscious process of continuous incarnation or spiritual rebirth between individuals of different generations.

In order for the Gwich'in language to survive in our accelerated digital world, one basic step which needs to be taken is to claim and repossess ancestral names. The process of preserving family names is reminiscent of the Ray Bradbury novel, *Fahrenheit 451*. There, in a future world where books have been banned, each person memorizes an entire book, and that person becomes a talking book. A similar principle holds true with traditional Native names. In a world where Native languages quickly disappearing, indigenous names are a lifelong reminder of each person's ethnicity and social identity.

Gwich'in is now classified as an endangered language, with the youngest fluent speakers in their early forties, so all the children receiving these names are essentially non-speakers of the language. Indeed, their Indian names may well be the very first Gwich'in words they ever learn, and simply repeating their names aloud during the ceremony is their only obligation. All the gifts that are purchased and given away are worth it to the families just to hear these few voiced syllables.

With traditional names as conscious symbols of belonging, the legitimacy of using the Gwich'in language in everyday discourse has been re-established. Bestowing and receiving Gwich'in personal names are thus important seeds for language retention and revival and for strengthening intergenerational kinship ties. Naming ceremonies are part of a new political movement that provides a strong and vital connection with the ancestors. To this extent, giving people traditional names is a sacred act of speech.

Acknowledgments

This paper was first presented to the Alaska Anthropological Association Annual Meeting, Seattle, Washington, March 2, 2012.

8. 'He Said, They Say':

The Uses of Reporting Speech in Gwich'in and Other Native American Languages

As early as 1930 the Russian Formalist V. N. Vološinov drew critical attention to reported speech as a literary phenomenon, defining it as "speech within speech, message within message, and at the same time also speech about speech, message about message" (1971:149). For Vološinov, the important thing about reported speech is the active relation of one message to another — namely the speech being reported and the speech doing the reporting (i.e. reporting speech). This is an important and highly useful distinction, for it allows us to see and hear reported speech as the intersection of two or more separate speech acts.

Vološinov presents an example of reported speech formulated directly and then shows us how it can be transformed by literary hands into indirect discourse. "Well done! What an achievement!" is the direct form of an utterance, while "He said that that had been done very well and was a real achievement" is the indirect. The indirect form of reported speech, he feels, is an analytical and artistic transmission, but he pays little or no attention to the subtle renderings of direct discourse.

For folklorists and other students of oral narrative this is a little disconcerting, primarily because in Native American folk narratives discourse is often formulated directly for structural reasons, and this should not preclude its analytical and artistic manipulation. Roman Jakobson, for one, has noted that certain languages such as Kwakiutl and Hopi "use particular morphological devices to denote events known to the speaker only from the testimony of others" (1971:130), and Robert Lowie has observed that "the Crow language is without any form of indirect discourse", so that the Crow speaker "has no choice in the matter. He cannot say, "They are telling me that I have not scored", but must express his meaning by, "You have not scored, they are saying" (1983:108; emphasis is Lowie's).

The generic implications of structural and stylistic features in sacred stories have been most rigorously explored by Melville Jacobs (1959; 1972), Dennis Tedlock (1972), and Dell Hymes (1975); but these studies have been largely focused on opening and closing formulas and paralinguistic features, and not on reported or reporting speech. Jacobs, for example, says of Clackamas Chinook tales, "there was evidently great strength in the stylistic demand that there be a formal beginning phrase or phrases in myth recitals" (1959:222); and Hymes, writing about Wishram texts, notes the particle '(gh)anghadix' (long ago) is a feature "generically associated with narratives of quasi-historical, legendary character, often cautionary, and with accounts of remembered times before the whites, or even times of one's own youth" (1975:65).

Hymes suggests that "myths do not need to say that they are myths" in any overt categorical fashion, for in Wishram, myths can be recognized by their immediate identification of actors and a situation and by their lack of specific place names. But this is a throwback to genre defined by content, and I would like to make the case that 'myths' do say they are 'myths' (sacred stories) in a very large number of American Indian and Eskimo languages through the coded self-conscious use of reporting speech idioms usually glossed as 'they say' or 'it is said', idioms built around impersonal pronouns. This contrasts sharply with Hymes' conclusion about the function of initial segment markers in Wishram texts, which he conjectures are not a criterion of genre so much as a criterion of formal narration, a formality he finds in legends and tales as well as myths.

In addressing the complex problem of locating formal boundaries between folk genres such as myth, folktale, legend, and memorate, it's important that we examine not simply their thematic content but also their patterned use of language, their style and texture. The rules governing narrative speech allow us as readers and as listeners to establish textual grounds for distinguishing narratives which have been fabricated solely in the narrator's imagination from those which report what he has personally experienced, those which are historically grounded, and those which have been generically codified by tradition. This is no easy task, considering the bias of many ethnographers that myths are nothing but oral fiction. Unfortunately, even when ethnic categories are taken into account, this bias persists. The term "myth" itself remains highly problematic since it was first applied to ancient Greek narratives and has been inappropriately transferred by scholars to the sacred narratives of Native Americans. Even further, the oral and literary genre labeled as 'myth' is corrupted by its journalistic use as "a falsehood or mistaken belief."

Nicholas Gubser, for example, in introducing his collection of Nunamiut Eskimo narratives, declares: "The primary concern here is 'koliaqtuq', Nunamiut ethnohistory; fiction, 'unipqaq', will be included only when informants so indicated" (1965:28). Other observers of Alaskan Arctic Eskimo oral tradition variously translate 'unipqaq' (with slight variations in orthography) as the class of "very ancient tales" relating "the experiences of very remote ancestors and mythical beings" (Rainey 1947:269), as "folktales" (Hennigh 1965:356), or as "old true stories that happened a long time ago" (Paul Monroe, quoted by Hall 1975:39). The Inuktitut lexicographer Pamela Stern observes that the language forces speakers to distinguish between what they have eye-witnessed from hearsay in order to limit speculation (2013:91). How to account for all this discrepancy and confusion?

Along with Hymes, we should like to know, "Is this an X?" and if so, "For whom?" "Why or why not?" (1975:15). Although it's true that each observer of 'unipqaq' was in this case working in a different Inuit community, it's also true that all of these communities belong to the same geographic region of Northwest Alaska and that all of the informants were speakers of closely related dialects of Iñupiaq. Unfortunately, the generic features of these 'unipqaq' cannot be tested linguistically (at least for the moment) because none of the collectors took the trouble to record texts in Iñupiaq, preferring instead to rely on the performing and reporting abilities of their English-speaking translators.

If we turn our attention to other culture areas in North America where native language texts have been collected and published, particularly in the Western Subarctic and the Northwest Coast, a formal cue to genre emerges which neatly bypasses the obvious limitations of impressionistic content-oriented definitions. This cue, 'they say', is a clausal reporting speech idiom which has approximately the same function rhetorically and semantically in a wide corpus of tale texts recorded in Gwich'in, Hän, Dogrib, Chipewyan, Koyukon, Beaver, Dena'ina, Ingalik, Kaska, Ahtna, Navajo, Chiricahua, Mescalero, and Jicarilla Apache (virtually the entire Dene family) as well as in Ojibwa, Maidu, Yuchi, Tlingit, Haida, Nootka, Kwakiutl, Crow, Aleut, Iñupiaq, and Greenlandic. The Table of Reporting Speech shown below presents the phonetic and semantic manifestations of this idiom for each language.

Part of the problem in studying Native American reporting speech is that most of the ethnographers and linguists who recorded native language texts failed to transcribe or translate the 'they say' idiom except in special interlinear literal renderings. The principal reason for this omission was no doubt its heavy redundancy. In some texts, indeed, it appears in almost every sentence. Julius Jetté even observed it "three or four times in every narrative sentence" (1909, 470) in Lower Koyukon. To outside observers this linguistic feature was undoubtedly a "distraction" from the sequence of events in the narratives, amounting to what is referred to as "noise" in communication theory (see Lindow 1974:368). Harry Hoijer's notes to Chiricahua and Mescalero Apache Texts are probably indicative of a widespread sentiment among early field workers:

> '-ná'à' is the narrative enclitic which is generally suffixed to every principal (i.e. non-subordinated) verb in myths or stories which recount events that the narrator has not personally witnessed. In order to save space and to avoid repetition, I have not translated '-ná'à' in the translations to the texts (Hoijer 1938:82).

In English, to forge a rough comparison, we are often beguiled by the phatic idiom, 'you know' and 'like', which some joke tellers employ to tedious extremes to bridge short segments of narrative action, as in this fabricated example: "The other day, you know, this Mexican went to the store, you know, and bought, you know, sixty dollars worth of tortillas, you know?"

The second reason why 'they say' idioms have been left out of free translations is probably owing to what Tedlock (1972) calls "the short story approach". A faithful translation of 'they say' in many American Indian language texts would strengthen Tedlock's argument for a dramatic-poetic rendering, one in which 'they say' figures as a steady rhythmic element which sustains two contrapuntal melodic lines (i.e. the narrated action sequence and the reported speech). Such an approach is quite compatible with the way Hymes (1977) has used initial sentence elements and verb phrases to measure lines of verse in Chinookan narrative.

One published corpus of texts in which 'they say' has been faithfully and consistently translated gives us an immediate, striking sense of the poetic. The Anglican missionary, John Chapman, renders Blind Andrew's Ingalik Athapaskan Story of a Young Man Who Was Purified From Sin with these words:

> There was once, they say, a large village where there lived two young chiefs. There they lived, they say, in a large village. Always, they say, they hunted game. And, they say, these two young men had not yet taken wives. So there, they say, they lived (Chapman 1914:50).

From a purely syntactic standpoint, this use of 'they say' is a conjunctive filler which leads away from the coherence and cohesion of the discourse. It's so free-floating that it can bob to the surface almost anywhere. Similarly, in Iñupiaq it's a particle suffixed to nouns, noun phrases, and conjunctions and therefore has the optative potential of appearing wherever nouns and conjunctions appear.

A look at my own renderings of Gwich'in texts (Mishler 2001) shows that the idiom commonly appears in a wide variety of structural environments in that language as well. Most often it's found in a sentence-final position following a verb, a direct object, or another piece of reporting speech, but it can also be found just before a sentence-final exclamation such as 'zhroo' or 'roo', immediately following the subject of a sentence, between a verb and a direct object, between two independent clauses preceding a co-ordinating conjunction or between such clauses without any conjunction, quotatively following reported speech, and at the very end of a story. In Kwakiutl, on the other hand, it seems highly restricted to a sentence-initial position, while in Haida it seems restricted to a sentence-final position.

Another syntactic dimension of 'they say' is its pronounced framing quality. Erving Goffman (1974) has drawn close attention to the verb 'to say' for its ability to generate "replayings" — that is, it enables the reader or listener to re-experience vicariously what took place in the past. These "replayings", which constitute much more than simple reports, easily become embedded in English through indirect discourse, as in the Vološinov example cited earlier, but they can also become embedded in direct discourse simultaneously on several different levels.

Four levels, in fact, can be observed in Knut Bergsland's literal translation of an Aleut text collected by Waldemar Jochelson:

> him saying/that they heard/they said/it's told:/"Raven cannot be had as husband/when there is fog,/excrements,/menstrual discharge,/food refuse/holding in his mouth when be passes above//he is not attractive" (Bergsland 1959:114).

More of this kind of foolery permeates Navajo tradition since 'žini' can mean 'he says', 'he said', 'she says', and 'she said', as well as 'they say', and such homonymy compounds the playful reduplication. In The Visionary, An Origin of the Night Chant as told by Slim Curly with the help of A. Sandoval, we find the God addressing the God boy:

> *"c'ósei!" žini, žini. "yá.!" ní, žiní.*
> "Slender one!" he said, they say. "What!" he answered, they say.
> *"šô.! nahgó.la ha.zí."', žini, žini.*
> "Look! It's over there that he spoke", he said, they say.
> (Sapir and Hoijer 1942:175).

The semantic aspect of the idiom 'they say' is less amenable to correct interpretation by non-native speakers than the syntactic aspect. Judith Espinola (1974) has raised the question of the point-of-view established by such narrative verb 'tags' as 'he said' and 'he exclaimed' in direct discourse and has come to the conclusion that such tags serve the purpose of not only identifying the speaker of the discourse but also of momentarily reminding the reader/listener of the voice of a narrator. She has also argued that the use of present tense within the dialogue "creates the momentary illusion that the speech event is occurring in the present" (1974:194).

My own perspective, however, is that 'they say' and 'it is said' operate in a radically different way from 'he said' and 'he exclaimed' in that the former terms not only shift us from the past to the present instead of from the present to the past, but they are more likely to quote actions, things, or persons than spoken words. Paradoxically then, 'they say' is reporting speech which is not reporting speech. That is, it's speech which reports, but what it reports is not usually speech.

Another semantic issue, of course, is the very indefiniteness of the pronoun 'they'. We are never told by any narrator who 'they' are, for the antecedent is always presupposed. Moses Paul Gabriel, a Gwich'in speaker and translator of my recorded texts, informs me there is a distinct difference between the meaning of 'they' in 'gwinyaa' (they say) and 'they' in 'varahnyaa' (they say about him or her). In the first idiom, 'they' can refer to anybody, but in the latter, 'they' specifically refers to Indians. To the Gwich'in then, 'varahnyaa' very nearly transforms the anonymous 'they say' into 'we say' --our people, and the same is true of 't'igwinyaa'. All three forms derive from the Gwich'in verb stem -nyaa ('say' or 'says') (see Chapter 9 below).

This is parallel with Jetté's (1909) distinction between the Koyukon use of 'mizeni' and 'tsedeni', and Günter Wagner's (1931) distinction between the Yuchi use of 'wɛgwa' or 'wɛgwadjin' for beings other than

Yuchi and 'h'˛gwa' or 'h'˛gwadjin' for beings who are Yuchi A similar indefinite use of 'they' is sometimes coded into Anglo-American proverbs such as: "They say you catch more flies with honey than with vinegar" or "They say children should be seen and not heard", but as a rule, 'they say' does not accomplish the same kind of work in English language folk narratives as it does in Native American ones.

In some respects 'they say' seems to be an appeal to tradition, but from another perspective it's the indexical sign of tradition itself—what I will call "the social voice." The Russian Formalist concept of 'strangemaking' is relevant here also, for while reported speech works towards defamiliarization and enlivened suspense, reporting speech works in quite the opposite direction, familiarizing and automatizing the discourse and restraining the individual's artistic and aesthetic impulses for the sake of maintaining group norms. Lowie tells us that reporting speech must itself exhibit restraint and that an audience listening to Crow narratives is critical of an excess in either direction:

A Crow audience, it should be noted, is likely to be critical even when listening to acknowledged masters. Thus, idiom requires a statement to end with the particle "tseruk" if the speaker is quoting what has been told rather than reporting something personally witnessed. But in the story of Scolds-the-bear and the couple he duped, White-arm was said to use this particle too frequently: you were supposed to suffix it "only when it's right" (1983:107).

If 'they say' is a narrator's simple denial of authorship or private ownership, then the idiom has a clear and useful purpose. But if, on the other hand, it's a ritualistic way for the narrator to wash his hands of all mistakes made in the act of recitation or to make himself immune to criticism directed at offensive content, then we must call into question the widely-accepted definition of performance as the assumption of responsibility before a critical audience (Bauman 1975; Hymes 1975).

Barre Toelken (1969:211) has interpreted over-reliance on 'žini' by some Navajo narrators as a kind of rhetorical apology for knowledge of the tales, yet as with the Crow, a narrator might be declared irresponsible if he or she did not use 'they say' often enough or in the appropriate slots, so it's difficult to make a tight case for this 'passing the buck' interpretation of reporting speech. The question persists, nevertheless, in my own mind because of what the late Moses Peter, a very gifted Gwich'in narrator, once said to me at the end of his account of *Wolverine and the Wolves*. He told me:

> Well, this is the end of this little short story. I hope it's good, just the way old people —five, six different old people telling me. So anything wrong with this story, well I don't make that my own way but just the way I heard it (Peter 1974).

At the time I did not think to ask Moses what he meant by 'wrong' in this context. Presumably he meant 'incorrect' or 'inaccurate', but possibly too, he was implying 'in bad taste, morally offensive'.

It's altogether conceivable that all of the texts referred to in the Table of Reporting Speech below were keyed to non-native outsiders. Missionaries such as Émile Petitot, Chapman, and even Jetté were particularly apt to be ethnocentric and critical in their reception of the Native belief system as expressed in traditional narratives, and 'they say' could well be regarded as a defensive verbal formula or frame which developed out of the contact situation, were it not for the antiquity suggested by close genetic connections between its Navajo, Denesuline, and Koyukon forms on the one hand, and its Apache and Gwich'in forms on the other.

Still, it's probably safe to say that most of the recorded texts listed in the Table were dictated for the benefit of the individual doing the collecting and not for other Natives — that is, in artificial contexts which produced interpretive reports or synopses rather than fully dramatized performances (see Hymes 1975 on "metaphrasis" and Bauman 1975 on "performance modes"). One test of this role-distancing hypothesis lies in the future field testing of the question, "Why do you say, 'they say'?" Another lies in the analysis of unelicited texts recorded by Native folklorists fluent in their own language.

But to return to our generic problem, if 'they say' is indicative only of a certain formal style of speaking, as Hymes would have it, we might expect to find it consistently in all of the texts dictated by an informant to a single collector. But this is patently not the case. Many of Peter Kalifornsky's Dena'ina narratives (1977), which he wrote down himself rather than dictated, have been classified by James Kari as 'sukdu' (traditional stories). Yet this class of stories is not evenly permeated with 'łu' (they say). Rather, 'łu' appears to be bound to a subgenre, those stories with heroic figures and localized geographic place names, akin to what folklorists usually call 'legends'. Kalifornsky's 'sukdu' with bird and animal protagonists, which folklorists would be more likely to classify on the basis of content as 'myths' or 'fables', however, bear no mention of 'łu', and there is no direct internal emphasis on their antiquity.

In John Swanton's Haida texts (1905), 'wansūga' is used discriminately, but in a fashion contrary to that found in Kalifornsky's Dena'ina texts. The animal narrative, *Tc!in Qa-idjit*, told by Richard of the Middle-Gîtî'ns is heavily larded with 'wansūga', but the *War Between the West Coast Haida and the Tlingit*, an obvious historical account coming from the same speaker, contains not a single instance of it. In my own Gwich'in collection, Daniel John's texts (John 1973) about Vasaagihdzak, a culture hero, and Shih Deetrya' Haa (Grizzly Bear and Crow) both make heavy use of 'varahnyaa' (they say about him), but his more recent and localized tall-tale-like texts about Sam Peter, someone Daniel knew personally, make no use of this idiom.

These Dena'ina, Haida, and Gwich'in examples suggest that 'they say' is in some sense a dating technique, a measure of a story's antiquity, not in any absolute or universal way but only on a culture-specific level. As a dating technique, it may help illuminate the futility of imposing Eurocentric generic terms such as 'myth' and 'legend' on Native American materials, but at the same time it can assist us in distinguishing between subgenres, especially when there is an implicit rather than an explicit emic taxonomy, as in Gwich'in, where one term, 'gwandak', encompasses all narrative genres.

Jetté's texts from the Koyukon, it must be acknowledged, reflect more of a localized difference in style and delivery than in genre. "The ever occurring forms: 'mizeni', 'tsedeni'", he writes, "are especially characteristic of the extreme lower dialect" (1909:470). Also, Pliny Earle Goddard's Jicarilla Apache texts indicate personal and perhaps generational differences exist in the way 'tc'in' is used by different narrators.

To conclude, it seems that several tasks are still in order: first, the emic testing of why 'they say' is so prevalent in the recitation (and even the writing) of Native North American folk narratives, either as performance or reportage or a mixture of both; and second, a further and much more exhaustive survey of recorded and published folk narrative texts culled from other languages, both in North America and elsewhere in the world. It certainly seems peculiar, for instance, that this idiom does not appear in Chinook, Wishram, or Zuñi, the three languages whose narrative texts have been most painstakingly scrutinized for structural and stylistic features.

For the moment, at least, we should be convinced that 'they say' is a very powerful bit of metacommunicative language, one that is often important rhythmically in the process of mythopoesis and semantically in isolating, at least for some cultures, forms resembling 'myth' and 'legend' from each other and from other narrative genres and subgenres resembling what we have been calling 'oral history' and 'memorate'. Because 'they say' openly acknowledges the process of oral transmission, its invocation may also help safeguard the narrator from charges of plagiarism or socially inappropriate speech. Finally, its omnipresence forces us to look at how much oral tradition is conservatively regulated, sanctioned, and mediated by the social voice.

TABLE OF REPORTING SPEECH

Language	Text Source	Reporting Idioms	Glosses
Aleut	Bergsland (1959)	hì·lartaza-das (plus 5 variants)	'it is told'
	Jochelson (in Bergsland)	h̲iranarí·	'it is told'
Ojibwa	Jones (1917)	kīwän	'they say'
Yuchi	Wagner (1931)	h̨̓gwa h̨̓gwadjín	'they said'
		h̨̓gɛnɛdjín	'they used to say'
Gwich'in	Mishler (2001)	gwinyaa	'they say'
		varahnyaa	'they say about him'
		t'igwinyaa	'it is said'
Beaver	Goddard (1917)	e tc'etdï	'they say'
Dcnaakk'c (Koyukon)	Jetté (1909)	tsedeni	'it is said'/'we say'
		mizeni	'we say to her/him'
Tanaina	Kalifornsky (1977)	łu	'they say'
		qdghineh	'they used to say'
Jicarilla Apache	Goddard (1911)	tc'in	'they say'
Chiricahua & Mescalero Apache	Hoijer (1938)	-na'à	'it is said'
Denesuline (Chipewyan)	Petitot (1887)	sni	'dit-on'
	Li/Scollon (1976)	sni	'they say'
Hare & Tłįcho (Dogrib)	Petitot (1887)	(e)déti hétsédi	'dit-on'
Deg Xinag (Ingalik)	Chapman (1914)	trûnĭ'	'they say'

TABLE OF REPORTING SPEECH

Language	Text Source	Reporting Idioms	Glosses
Navajo	Sapir/Hoijer (1942)	žiní	'they say'/'he says'/ 'he said'/'she says' 'she said'
		hani·h	'it is said'
		hodo·ni·d	'it was said'
Haida	Swanton (1905)	wansū'ga	'they say'
Kwakiutl	Boas/Hunt (1905)	älā' ɛlaē	'well, then it is said'
		lā'ɛlaē	'then it is said'
Crow	Lowie (1960)	-tsɛruk	'it was said'
		-tsəruk	'it is said'
Nootka	Sapir/Swadesh 1939)	-we'in	'they say'/'it is said'
Maidu	Dixon (1912)	-tsoi-	'it is said'
Kaska	Moore (1999)	gedī, géhdī, éhdī	'they say'/'they said'
Ahtna	Kari (2010)	dae' konii	'(thus) it is said'
Hän	De Reuse	hiyèh[n]ö̜ö̜, hënö̜ö̜	'they said'
Tlingit	Johnston (2016)	yú.á	'they say'
Inuit/Inuktitut	Boas (1907)	-egōq	'it is said'
		-agō(u)q	
	Rasmussen (1932)	-V+ɔ·q	'it is said'/
		-V+gɔ·q	'people say'/
		-V+rɔ·q	'they say'
Greenlandic	Holtved (1951)	7 forms, variants of Rasmussen	'it is told'

Acknowledgments

I would like to express my deep appreciation to Joel Sherzer, Richard Bauman, and Ron Scollon for reading earlier drafts of this manuscript and offering helpful suggestions and corrections for its development. An early draft of this paper was presented orally at the VIIth Congress for Folk Narrative Research at Edinburgh, Scotland in 1979. An earlier written version appeared in 1981 in the journal Fabula:Journal of Folktale Studies, Vol. 22 (3-4):239-249 and is reproduced here by permission.

9. -Nyaa, Just Saying:

The Functional and Artistic Uses of a Gwich'in Verb Stem

with Kenneth Drizhuu Frank

"It's pretty hard to live without our language. We got to have it." –Trimble Gilbert

In many Native American languages, verbs of saying are part and parcel of narration. Who says what is important, so direct reported speech and indirect reported speech are both carefully marked by the crafting of the accompanying reporting speech. In the example, "Look out!' he said", the words "Look out!" are the reported or quoted speech, and the words "he said" are the reporting speech.

In 1981 I published a paper in the European folklore journal *Fabula* called "'He Said, They Say': the Uses of Reporting Speech in Native American Folk Narrative" (Mishler 1981, revised in Chapter 7 above). In this earlier essay I essentially collected together verb stems equivalent to the English verb "they say" or "it is said" for eighteen Native American languages. I did this based on their recurrence in a variety of published scholarly texts. Since then I've added four additional languages.

A comparison of hundreds of texts showed that indigenous language verbs for "say" provide a common if not universal common denominator for understanding the voices of storytellers, particularly when the texts could be declared traditional in the generic sense that they were not based on the storyteller's personal experience or life history but had been passed down from generations of elders.

In my fifty years of fieldwork with Gwich'in speakers in northeastern Alaska and the Yukon, I've learned Gwich'in storytellers are especially conscious of distinguishing between their own words and those of their ancestors, so they are very careful not to claim traditional story ownership or appropriate their ancestors' vernacular speech. Doing so would be both disrespectful and plagiaristic. My continued fascination lies with discovering just how many forms of saying there are in Gwich'in, and how verbs of saying are cleverly doubled or tripled up to establish the quotative.

In Gwich'in, the verb stem for the English "say" or "tell" is –nyaa, pronounced –nuu in Canadian Gwich'in dialects. For example, in Old Crow Robert Bruce Jr. told us, "Aii dah gwiinzii vak'atr'anahtii goovahnuu." 'I tell them that we take good care of the blood.' (Mishler and Frank 2020:324-325).

–Nyaa is especially fascinating because of its large inflectional paradigm. I've been collecting these for many years from both oral and written sources and have discovered that even fluent speakers get them confused. One reason for this confusion is that there are so many variants and they are used almost unconsciously and unreflexively in narration. They are so common, in fact, that they often go by almost unnoticed when Gwich'in speakers are translating texts into English. To date, Kenneth and I have identified and listed well over a hundred inflections, with little doubt that there are still many, many others in print or in oral circulation that we may have missed (see Appendix B). This list illustrates the richness and complexity of the language and may help serve as a database for other Gwich'in lexical studies.

In Gwich'in storytelling these inflections are often tacked on at the end of sentences to tell us who said what. In oral traditions, of course, there are no quotation marks. Even in English the only way to signify quotation marks orally is to say "Quote" and "Unquote" and to hold up both hands with the two index and middle fingers extended. In Gwich'in, many variants of –nyaa may be understood as virtual quotation marks. And their presence in texts tells us much more than who said what.

Indexical Features

Several variant features of –nyaa attract our attention and point to contextual twists.

1. One peculiarity is that nyaa or t'inyaa all by itself usually means "he or she said." But sometimes when it appears at the end of sentences it conveys a different semantic range of meanings, something else besides saying or telling.

a) For example, Kenneth Frank says: "Aiit'ee datthak nil'aa **nyaa o'**." 'It's all butchered.' **Nyaa o'** here is just emphasizing and affirming that the butchering is done.

b) Maggie Roberts says: "Jyahts'ą' t'ee akwat dink'ee kwaa **nyaa o'**." 'You see, we didn't have any guns.' Here, nyaa o' is underscoring and emphasizing kwaa.

c) Trimble Gilbert says: "Nijin gwa'an, neerihiidal gwa'an zhoh itree ji', it'ee vizhik gwiłts'ik eenjit **t'inyaa**." The gloss is: 'Wherever you go, if you hear a wolf crying, he's howling because he's hungry.' In this context "**t'inyaa**" means he's howling instead of he's saying. Here t'inyaa is a metaphorical verb, coded to represent an animal's discourse.

2. Another interesting feature is that sometimes –nyaa signifies 'thinking' rather than speaking. A sentence final "nyaa" can refer to thought rather than speech, as in:

noihnyaa I thought
jyaa noihnyaa That's what I thought
yuunyaa he or she thought or was thinking

Such usage reminds us that when we think, we often hear our own words or the words of others in our heads. Thoughts can be made up of images, imagined sounds, or memories but are quite frequently experienced as streams of words, so it seems appropriate that inflections of –nyaa are formulated to link speaking with thinking.

3. A third indexical feature is that the -nyaa stem can be dropped altogether without affecting the meaning of the verb. The result is a kind of verbal shorthand.

A prime example of this is Kenneth Frank's statement: "Aii gwik'it **t'agwaih.**" 'That's what I'm saying.' Here **t'agwaih** is an abbreviated or truncated form of **t'agwaihnyaa.** The missing stem is understood by listeners simply by hearing the truncated prefix **t'agwaih-**. The same thing often happens with **t'ih-**, which is the shortened version of **t'ihnyaa,** as when Kenneth says "Aii geegwaldak **t'ih.**" This glosses as: 'So **I'm saying** that's what I talked about.'

4. And the reverse is also true. Speakers often drop the first syllable of the prefix **va-** when using the term **varahnyaa** 'they say'. As often as not, speakers pronounce the word as **rahnyaa,** leaving the prefix understood. Yet Gwich'in transcribers working with oral recordings always write it with the full spelling. Or yet again, Hannah P. Solomon says, "Dehch'i' naii łyaa giihiłee, nyaa." 'Elders are really fond of it, **I'm saying.**' Instead of dropping the stem -**nyaa,** Hannah drops the prefix **t'ih-** in t'ihnyaa, so '**I'm**' is understood.

5. Double plays. One of the most interesting features of –nyaa is the way it is doubled up in a sentence, a fairly common practice. Here's Kenneth talking about the changing taste of moose meat in the springtime:

"Gwiinzii vagwaandaii neelik aii, **jyaa dihnyaa t'ihnyaa.**"

'I'm saying that it begins to taste good again, **that's exactly what I'm talking about.**'

6. Or how about this rare **triple play**, when –nyaa is used three times in a sentence, as when Maggie Roberts talks about eating the maggots found in caribou nostrils.

"Gyuu chu' akaii ch'yaa," **t'igwinyaa, ginyaa, goovahnyaa**. The gloss here is:

"That maggot juice is known to be tasty," **so it's been said, they say, that's what they said to them.** It seems that nobody really wants to admit to eating maggots, or accuse someone else of eating maggots, so the identity of the person who actually said this is carefully concealed.

7. And to top them all, here is a **quadruple play**, where -nyaa seems to work almost like an echo that ricochets off the walls of a deep canyon. It's a tongue twister:

- "Diinyaa t'iinyaa noihnyaa geh'an t'ihnyaa."
- 'The reason I'm saying that is because I'm not sure what you were saying.'

Personal Names with -Nyaa

There are two good historical examples of Gwich'in personal names that contain the –nyaa verb stem:

a) **Deeshainyaa** 'What are you saying to me?' This is the name of a man who appears on Hudson's Bay Company records in Fort Yukon during the late 1840s and early 1850s. (See Chapter 6, Table 1).

b) **Shahnyaa Ti'** This is the name of the most famous 19th century Gwich'yaa Gwich'in trading chief, who had many wives. The suffix –ti' signifies 'the father of' and the gloss of his full name means 'the father of He Told Me So'. Following a system of teknonymy, Shahnyaa ('He Told Me So') was Shahnyaa Ti's first-born son, and Shahnyaa Ti' was duly renamed after him, confirming a new more prestigious social status (see also Chapter 6 above and photo). There are many folk legends about Shahnyaa Ti' (see Schneider, 1976:315-327).

Where –nyaa means something else besides saying, telling, or thinking:

1. Maggie Roberts once said: "Jyahts'ą̨' t'ee akwat dink'ee kwaa **nyaa o'**."

'You see, we didn't have any guns.' **Nyaa o'** here is underscoring, emphasizing. The final o' is essentially an exclamation mark. Or when Kenneth Frank says: "Aiit'ee datthak nil'aa **nyaa o'**."

'It's all butchered.' Again, **Nyaa o'** is emphasizing, affirming, finalizing.

2. In the words **shreenyaa** and **kǫ' nyaa**, -nyaa means 'facing towards'. Shreenyaa is the word for 'spring' but literally it means 'facing towards the sun', and kǫ' nyaa means 'facing towards the fire.'

3. **Vak'aihnyaa** is used to convey 'I'm defending him or her'.

4. **Veihnyaa** is essentially 'I'm giving him or her advice (a warning)'.

5. **Deegwaahnyaa** means 'It suddenly became quiet; you could hear a pin drop'.

Funny Stories about –Nyaa

Here are a couple of funny stories told to me by Kenneth. In the first example, Jonas John was staying with Kenneth's uncle Dan Frank, and one day in the fall time Dan told Jonas, **"Dinjik ak'ii gwinyaa."** '(They say the moose are getting pretty fat.') The next day Jonas came into the house and said the very same thing back to Dan. So Dan said, "Who said that?" and Jonas replied, **"Jyaa gwinyaa"** ("That's what they're saying'), even though he knew very well that Dan was actually the one who said it first. The statement came back full circle within twenty-four hours tagged as an oral tradition.

The second comical story goes back to when Kenneth was going to elementary school in Venetie, where one of the geography lessons was learning the names of all the states. The easiest state for him and his pals to remember was Pennsylvania. That's because in Gwich'in it sounds just like **"Pencil vaihnyaa"** 'I asked him for a pencil.'

The Song, Goodbye Shaiinyaa

Finally, my duty would not be complete if I failed to recognize that the title of one of the most famous Gwich'in folksongs, "Goodbye Shaiinyaa", includes the –nyaa verb. Glossed as 'Tell me goodbye', this love song was composed in the late 1940s by Annie Cadzow, a Gwich'in woman living in Fort Yukon who decided to leave her husband for another man. Legend has it that she confronted her husband and sang this love song directly to his face in a brazen show of defiance. I recorded the song from singer Lily Pitka in Fairbanks in 1972 (see Mishler 1974) and later heard it again from Natalie Erick in Fort Yukon (Alaska Native Language Archive ANLC1016). In Canada the song is performed as Goodbye Shaanyuu and was recently recorded by a group called The Hummingbirds, based in the Northwest Territories village of Tsiigehtshik (CBC North 2017).

Conclusions

Due to their omnipresence in storytelling, the many inflections of –nyaa or –nuu should be regarded as constant reminders of what I call "the social voice." Some of these inflections such as **gwinyaa, ginyaa, giiyahnyaa,** and **varahnyaa** persistently remind fluent listeners of the fact that the stories being told are not original, that they are traditional and have been passed down or heard from others. Stories that are fully autobiographical may not contain any instances of –nyaa unless they are used for the attribution of someone's direct speech (see for instance the texts in Stevens 2013).

Who says what is extremely important in folk tradition, so the reported speech and the reporting speech are carefully marked, and when the original speaker is either not known or simply needs to remain anonymous, the default tagline is "they say" or "it is said."

But the frequent repetition, double plays, and triple plays of –nyaa inflections in the reporting speech of folktales establish a poetic rhythm to the discourse that is not present in ordinary conversation. The easiest way to find them is by reading Gwich'in texts, where they pop up on almost every page. And most of all, their manipulation and heightening reminds us that Gwich'in speakers are constantly playing with their speech, introducing variants and shortcuts, adding little artistic twists in meaning, and poetically juggling patterns of sound on the same order as English rhyme and alliteration (Cf. Sherzer, 2002). While the many conjugations of -nyaa are to some extent predictable, they just keep on coming and never cease to surprise and amaze.

Acknowledgments

This was originally a paper presented to the Alaskan Anthropological Association Annual Meeting, Anchorage, March 22, 2018. Thanks once again to Kenneth Frank for amplifying my knowledge of this important verb and for his patience in exploring many of the variants.

10. 'That's a Rubbaboo':
Slavey Jargon in a Nineteenth Century Subarctic Speech Community

Introduction

Slavey Jargon flourished among the Gwich'in living at Hudson's Bay Company settlements in northwestern Canada and northeastern Alaska and is mentioned in a significant number of historical accounts. In this essay, I want to discuss the cultural, ethnic, and historical context of Slavey Jargon, look closely at some older and some newly found texts, and identify a few of its best-known speakers.

A number of pidgin languages developed among northern Dene peoples in the western subarctic during the nineteenth century. We know, for example, that Chinook Jargon was spoken in Alaska by the Ahtna (Cashman 1900:164; Remington 1939: passim) and by some of the middle Tanana (Mitchell 1982:73; orig. 1901-1903). Chinook Jargon was imported via direct or indirect trade contacts with peoples of the Northwest Coast, probably even before the gold rush, although it was certainly still in use during the gold rush.

On the arctic coast, a trade jargon was spoken by the Inuit living on Herschel Island and also at Point Barrow and by English-speaking American whalers and missionaries. And a variant of this ships' jargon was also in use by the Gwich'in living around Tsiigehtshik (Arctic Red River) and Fort McPherson, but it was used only in their discourse with the Inuit. The arctic explorer Vilhjamur Stefansson (1909) recorded a word list and analyzed examples of both jargons in an early essay published in the *American Anthropologist*. However, this trade jargon, including the Gwich'in variant of it, has no apparent connection with Slavey Jargon, a pidgin which was spoken throughout the Gwich'in ancestral homeland in the mid-to-late nineteenth century.

In a three-page exploratory essay, Peter Bakker (1996) distinguishes between Broken Slavey, a trade language spoken in the Mackenzie River District, and Jargon Loucheux, spoken on the Peel River and along the upper Yukon River in Alaska. Loucheux is an old French name for the Gwich'in, meaning 'squinters' or 'cockeyed'. Bakker takes this dialect distinction from the writing of nineteenth century Oblate missionary Émile Petitot (1889:292-293), who observed that Jargon au Loucheux includes words from English, Chipewyan, Loucheux, French, Cree, and Slavey, while le Jargon Esclave (i.e. Broken Slavey) includes only French, Cree, and Slavey.

This notwithstanding, Petitot records what he calls 'Jargon du Youkon' from a Scottish Ojibwe Métis and a full-blooded Ojibwe (see texts 6 and 7), classifying examples of it in a footnote as Loucheux Jargon. He also transcribes an entire conversation between a young Scotsman and a young Vantee Gwich'in man as being 'Jargon au

Loucheux,' but it is rather puzzling that this conversation is rendered entirely in French (Petitot 1889:295).

A componential analysis of the texts I have collected from Gwich'in elders (texts 8-22 below) results in something much closer to Petitot's Jargon au Loucheux than it is to Broken Slavey. The only Cree lexemes I have found are taken from Petitot's own sources (texts 6 and 7). This is what one might expect since Petitot identifies his own river guides, Peter Pelly and Saint-Pol, as 'Tchippeway' [Ojibwe]. Like Cree, Ojibwe is a member of the Algonquian language family. As represented and discussed here, however, Slavey Jargon is largely restricted to base elements and combinations of French (including traces of Michif French), Gwich'in, Chipewyan, South Slavey, and English. Gwich'in, Chipewyan, and South Slavey all belong to the Na-Dené or Athabaskan language family.

Sandy Roberts, David Salmon, and Katherine Peter, three Alaskan Gwich'in elders whom I worked with, knew something about this language and have simply called it Slavey or Slàhvíy, but I avoid this term in order to prevent confusion with North Slavey (Hare and Bear Lake dialects) and South Slavey (Dene Tha') as discrete Athabaskan languages. Ironically, there is no evidence that the Slavey people themselves, who occupy parts of northern Alberta, northeastern British Columbia, the southern Yukon, and the Northwest Territories, ever spoke anything like Broken Slavey or Slavey Jargon.

This raises the question of whether the language largely developed locally on the Peel River and the Yukon Flats or whether it was imported from elsewhere in northwest Canada by servants of the Hudson's Bay Company. Although older speakers of Gwich'in are the only ones who seem at all familiar with the jargon, it is surprising that the fifteen texts I have collected do not incorporate very many Gwich'in words. Of course these texts are little more than shards of the jargon as it was formerly spoken, but they're all we have. None of these texts, with the exception of Petitot's, are embedded in conversation or in narrative, but at least they are intact as sentences, and some reconstruction and analysis is possible.

During the 19th century, Hudson's Bay Company personnel in the western subarctic largely consisted of Scotsmen and Orkneymen, a few French-Canadians, and a very significant number of Métis, both male and female, with French-Canadian and Indian ancestors, or Scottish and Indian ancestors. The fact that Slavey Jargon incorporates elements of French, Chipewyan, Gwich'in, English, and South Slavey suggests that it was used for interethnic discourse between native speakers of those five languages.

There were, moreover, some important cultural and ethnic differences within the Métis community which influenced linguistic choice. The ethnographer Richard Slobodin (1966:158) has created a useful chart dividing the Mackenzie River Métis into two regional groups: the Red River Métis and the Northern Métis. As part of his criteria he identifies the Red River Métis in the southern region as French Catholics and the Northern Métis in the Delta area as Scotch Protestants. Many of the early fur traders at Fort McPherson, La Pierre's House, and Fort Yukon came from the Mackenzie River district and included representatives of both Métis groups, but those placed in charge of the trading posts were usually Scots or Orkneymen.

Historical Sources

The first person to document this hybrid language was the great naturalist Robert Kennicott, who spent the winter of 1860-1861 at Fort Yukon collecting bird specimens for the Smithsonian Institution. Kennicott (1942:86; orig. 1860-1861) said: "When I try to speak French, and mix English, Slavy, and Louchioux [i.e. Loucheux or Gwich'in] words with it, they tell me, 'that's a rubbaboo'. And when the Indians attempt to sing a voyaging song, the different keys and tunes make a 'rubbaboo'". A rubbaboo, he added, was also a hearty soup the voyageurs made from pemmican, flour, and a little sugar thrown into an open kettle of snow water.[1] So it seems safe to conclude the word 'rubbaboo' itself must have been an important word in Slavey Jargon. It is regrettable that most of Kennicott's texts (see 1-4 below) were not accompanied by English or French glosses, so both their origin and meaning still remain fairly inscrutable to present-day readers.

An idea of what contributed to the rise of the jargon, nevertheless, is encapsulated in Kennicott's description of the mix of passengers in the boat he rode in descending the lower Mackenzie River: "For our crew," he wrote in a letter to Lucy Hunter Baird, "we have one Eskimo, one [French] Canadian, two Youcon Louchioux [Loucheux], three Peels River Indians, one Hare Indian, the steersman is an Orkneyman, Mr. Gaudet's wife is a Cree half-breed, and I'm a Yankee—Pretty good variety!" (1860a:78). In this kaleidoscope of languages, we are prompted to ask, "How exactly did they speak to one another?" In another letter to Lucy Hunter Baird, Kennicott (1860b:95) wrote about this remarkable convergence:

> The language mostly spoken by the men (servants) at the various posts is nominally French; but such French as would if heard by Miss Lucy Hunter Baird, cause her to make a grimace . . . . The English is scarce better, from the number of queer forms and words introduced from Norwegian, Gaelic, Broad Scotch, Orkney, French, Cree, and numerous other Indian tongues. I even observe some Eskimo words commonly used.

The second visitor to write about this strange new language was Fr. Jean Séguin, an Oblate missionary who in 1862 walked across the mountains from Peel River to Lapierre House in the uneasy company of the Anglican preacher William Kirkby. One night after saying their prayers, all of the Gwich'in except for two chiefs began to shout repeatedly at Kirkby, a taunt that Séguin (Séguin 1862a) found amusing enough to document in a letter:

> *Tchéjé kudjine raguinci séni l'aime todi, kouka tsétédéji séni l'aime chan.*
> 'The English priest I don't love at all, but I love tobacco very much'.[2]

Séguin, whose first language was French, readily understood this strange jargon and laughed heartily, but claimed that Kirkby could make nothing of it and had to ask the Orkneyman trader James Flett for a translation. Since it was a fairly widespread practice for the Anglicans to distribute free tobacco to Indians as bait in order to get them to listen to their preachings and teachings (see Mishler 1990, Chapter 1), the Gwich'in used this humorous taunt to rub in the fact.

The taunt provides us with the first evidence of a Slavey Jargon text in a specific social context and provides evidence that the language was already going full tilt by the early 1860s. Speaking of his work with the Gwich'in of the Mackenzie River, Séguin (1862c) wrote:

> I had two women serving as my interpreter, one of which couldn't speak Loucheux but understood it, and with that knew a little French, and the other was a Loucheux woman who knew a little of the jargon of the country—that is to say, a kind of language made up of some Cree, Chipewyan, Slavey, French, and English. Both of them taken together made for me a good interpreter.

These two interpreters are identified respectively as Marie Gaudet, the part-Cree Métis wife of Charles-Philippe Gaudet, a French-Canadian trader from Montréal, and Mrs. Norman Lebeau, the wife of a Loucheux man (Grollier 1860; Gascon 1863).

One of Séguin's other major rivals for Indian converts, the Anglican missionary Robert McDonald, also wrote about this new jargon. Within a year of his arrival at Fort Yukon in 1863, McDonald (1863a) observed in a letter:

> It [broken Slavè] is a language which has that name perhaps from the preponderance of Slavè words in it; but it is composed of English, French, Cree, and Loucheux [Gwich'in], besides Slavè. It is a most extraordinary language in its way: the number of words in it are very limited. It is used by the officers and servants of the [Hudson's Bay] Company in their ordinary intercourse with the Indians, and it serves very well for common purposes. Most of the young men among the Indians speak it.

It is revealing to know that McDonald himself was part Ojibwe and learned to speak and write Ojibwe before he became a missionary to the Gwich'in. Over the years he studied Gwich'in and eventually became fluent in it, taking lessons from Mrs. Andrew Flett, wife of the Orkneyman in charge at Fort McPherson (Stewart 1955:303). However, in the early years after coming into the country, McDonald found that if he wanted to preach to the Gwich'in in their remote camps he had to use two interpreters. He would speak English to the first interpreter, and the first interpreter would then translate his remarks into Broken Slavey for the benefit of the second interpreter. The second interpreter would then translate the Broken Slavey into Gwich'in for everyone else.[3]

The English artist, Frederick Whymper, visiting Fort Yukon in 1867, just after it became American territory, identified what he heard people speaking there as 'broken slavee', but characterized it as 'a bastard dialect' barely suited for 'the language of common life' and completely inadequate for such things as 'the figurative language of the Bible' (Whymper 1869:226). Whymper's evaluation suggests that like other pidgins, Slavey Jargon was a simplified language, lacking in nuance or abstraction.[4]

Since Slavey Jargon was apparently not spoken anywhere else in Alaska or Northwest Canada except in select Gwich'in communities, we have to recognize that it must have been created where it was first noticed and identified in the early 1860s—that is, at Fort McPherson, Lapierre House, and Fort Yukon (see Introduction, Figure 1). There are a number of other modern-day Gwich'in communities where it may have been used but where it has never been documented: Old Crow, Aklavik, Inuvik, Tsiigehtshik, Venetie, Arctic Village, Birch Creek, and Beaver.[5] It is difficult, therefore, to imagine that Slavey Jargon predated the founding of these first three outposts of the Hudson's Bay Company. Fort McPherson (originally called Peel's River Post) was founded in 1840, Lapierre House in 1846, and Fort Yukon in 1847. The gestation period for the development of the jargon must therefore have been the period between 1840 and 1860.

As late as 1890, in his report on the Eleventh Census of the United States in Alaska, Robert Porter (1893:118) declared that the language of the Yukon River Indians "is known to the missionaries as a dialect of Tukudh, but they converse with the traders in a jargon called 'Slavey', a mixture of Canadian French and hybrid words of English, something in the nature of the 'Chinook' [jargon] of southeastern Alaska." Since Petitot observed that the jargon was still in active use during his visit to Fort Yukon in 1870, it seems safe to conclude that some form of Slavey Jargon flourished at least until the Klondike gold rush and perhaps just a few years into the early 20th century. The gold rush, with its massive influx of English speakers into the region beginning in 1886, probably provided a death blow to the jargon.

Speakers: Who spoke Slavey Jargon?

For speakers of Slavey Jargon we must look first to those who acted as interpreters between the Hudson's Bay Company and the Gwich'in. One of these interpreters, Antoine Houle [aka Hoole], was a professional servant of the Company who served for well over twenty years at Peel's River Post and at Fort Yukon. Houle, having a French-speaking father and a Métis mother, was born in 1827 and raised in a household where at least two languages were spoken. He originally came from Fort Halkett on the Liard River in what is now the southern Yukon Territory. He probably spoke South Slavey because that was the indigenous language spoken around the Liard River, although Sekani and Kaska people also frequented the area.

Antoine probably spoke French and Cree because his father, François Hoole, was French-Canadian, was fluent in Cree, and came from the Swan River District of Saskatchewan. Visiting Fort Liard, Archdeacon James Hunter (1859:240) reported that "Francis [sic] Hoole has interpreted for me and promised to do so when I ask him. He cannot speak English: I therefore speak to him in Cree, and he renders it into Siccunnee [Sekani] and the Slave language for me." Antoine's mother remains a bit more mysterious but may well have been 'la bonne femme Hoole', employed as a Hudson's Bay Company agent at Fort Liard in the 1860s and described as one of the most famous and intimidating women of the north. Élise Taupier Houle was a 'métisse française' who taught the Slavey language to Oblate missionaries. She wore skin clothes and a dagger in her belt and was known to bark out commands to Indians and whites as well (see Duchaussois 1921:348-349; Payment 2003).

At the young age of fifteen, young Antoine was given a seven-year contract and sent to Peel's River Post by the Hudson's Bay Company in 1842 for the specific purpose of learning to speak Loucheux (Gwich'in) (Lewes 1899:25-26; orig. 1842). And nineteen years later Kennicott (original emphasis, 1942:118) wrote that "Antoine speaks Kutcha Kutchin [Gwich'yaa Gwich'in] *better* than a native."

At Fort Yukon, Alexander Hunter Murray (1847-1848) called him 'a foolish boy' who was 'abominably dirty and careless' and 'dislikes work at any time'. But as he grew older Houle wielded tremendous power.

His refusal to assist Fr. Séguin in his missionary efforts changed the religious map of Alaska. Houle was an apostate Catholic and assisted only the Anglicans. Although Séguin spent the winter of 1862-1863 in Fort Yukon, he left in despair, not having made a single convert. Indeed, Séguin (1862d) complained that "as long as this wretch [Houle] remains Protestant, I believe that we can do hardly anything with the Indians . . . . It is not the Factor who is master of the fort. It is Antoin[e] Houl[e]. He alone can do what he wants with these Indians. . . ." For the next thirty years Séguin worked assiduously at Fort Good Hope and made annual visits to the Canadian Gwich'in village of Tsiigehtshik, which still has a large Catholic church.[6] However, to this day there are virtually no Roman Catholic Gwich'in in Alaska.

Houle must have learned to speak English in communicating the Orkneymen and Scots who served the Company at Peel River. And he appears to have been exposed to all of the other constituent languages found in Slavey Jargon except for Chipewyan. The naturalist William Dall (1870:110-111, 318), for example, observed that Houle translated Reverend Robert McDonald's religious services to the Indians gathered at Fort Yukon into 'broken Slavé' and also noted that "the basis of this jargon, which includes many modified French and English words, is the dialect of Liard River [i.e. South Slavey]." This provenience would seem to identify Antoine Hoole as one of the principal architects of the jargon. Houle, a most colorful character, lived in a little house behind the fort and got into trouble with McDonald for having two wives, presumably local Gwich'in women (see Mishler 1993:17). Houle died in Fort Yukon at the age of forty-one, on October 22, 1868, shortly after Dall's visit and just before Petitot arrived.

It would also appear that Marie Gaudet was Antoine Houle's stepsister, both having been raised in the Fort Halkett/Liard River area. According the biographer of Marie Gaudet, "She had relatives among the

Figure 2.3: Robert's band, a group of Gens de large (Chandalar Gwich'in) living in dome-shaped caribou skin huts on Robert Creek, an upper tributary of the Koyukuk River in July, 1899. Schrader 335. Photo by F.C. Schrader, USGS photo library, Denver.

Figure 2.4: John Mertie Jr., August 29, 1915. Mertie 421. USGS photo library, Denver.

Figure 2.5: Arctic Village community portrait in front of Bishop Rowe Episcopal Chapel, 1927. Mertie 1359. Photo by John Mertie Jr., USGS photo library, Denver.

Figure 2.7: Gilbert Joseph family. l to r: James Gilbert with his parents Maggie Divi' and Gilbert Joseph, 1927. Maggie Divi' was Johnny Frank's older sister. Mertie 1365. Photo by John Mertie Jr., USGS photo library, Denver.

Figure 2.8: Alice and Peter Gabriel family, with unidentified child, 1927. Mertie 1364. Identified by Mertie simply as "Peter and his family." Photo by John Mertie Jr., USGS photo library, Denver.

Figure 2.12: Peter and Susan John family. l to r: Peter John (Dinjii Tsik), Susan John, Madeline Peter, Leah Peter, Stephen Peter (white shirt & tie), David Peter (David Oly), possibly Moses Sam. On the fence are dog packs made from caribou skin, 1927. Mertie 1369. Photo by John Mertie Jr., USGS photo library, Denver.

Figure 2.6: Johnny and Sarah Frank family. l to r: Johnny Frank, Dina Frank, Sarah Frank, Dan Frank, Nathaniel Frank, Joseph Frank, Allan Frank, Hamel Frank, Lucy Chigwihch'in (Johnny Frank's mother), and Jessie Natthąįį, 1927. Mertie 1363. Photo by John Mertie Jr., USGS photo library, Denver.

Figure 2.9: Titus and Maggie Peter family. l to r: Peter John (with caribou skin parka), Martha Peter, Jo Ann Peter, Maggie Peter (later remarried as Maggie Gilbert), unknown boy (possibly Linus Peter), and Titus Peter, 1927. Titus Peter was the son of Peter John. Mertie 1368. Photo by John Mertie Jr., USGS photo library, Denver.

Figure 2.10: Esias and Sarah Simon family, 1927. Sarah (carrying baby), Chief Esias on right, 1927. Others unidentified but names of most children are in the 1930 census for Christian Village. Mertie 1362. Photo by John Mertie Jr., USGS photo library, Denver.

Figure 2.11: Albert and Sarah Tritt family. Front row, r to l: Albert Tritt, Sarah Tritt, Martha Tritt (James), Abel Tritt, Christian Tritt, George Tritt. Back row, r to l: Paul Tritt, Isaac Tritt (with head net), and Jessie Natthąįį, 1927. Mertie 1367. Photo by John Mertie Jr., USGS photo library, Denver.

Figure 4.3. Elijah John & Paul James (r), taken in front of Elijah's cabin in Fort Yukon on August 24, 1972. Photo by Craig Mishler.

Figure 4.2. Myra Robert in Venetie, 1973. Photo by Craig Mishler.

Figure 13.1: Moses Sam in Arctic Village, 1996. Photo by Craig Mishler.

Figure 6.2. Ch'ats'ą' Vizhit Teech'iriikii valąįį Shoh Zhuu haa. Crystal Frank and her dog Little Black Bear. Photo courtesy of Crystal Frank.

Figure 13.2: Trimble Gilbert and Kenneth Frank at K'aii Dzuu Zhit Gwitsik, 1996. Photo by Craig Mishler.

Figure 15.1. Mae Wallis in Fort Yukon, June 20, 1976. Photo by Craig Mishler.

Figure 20.2. Ellen Henry, c. 2002. Photo by Craig Mishler.

Figure 20.1. Allen Tritt, 2015. Photo by Craig Mishler.

Figure 20.3. Group photo at the Tsuk'ǫǫ village graveyard. June 11, 1997. Photo by Craig Mishler.

Figure 4.1. Craig Mishler & Silas John in Fort Yukon, 1972. Photo by Barbara Mishler.

Figure 0.3. Introduction: Historic site survey crew on the upper K'aii'eechų'njik, September, 1998. L to r: Kenneth Frank, Trimble Gilbert, Craig Mishler, Wilbert Jack Kendi. Photo by Kenneth Frank.

Slavey and Gwich'in and was fluent in Chipewyan, Slavey, and French (probably Michif French)" (Payment 2003). The Gaudets married in 1858 at Fort Resolution, then moved to Peel's River Post (renamed Fort McPherson) from 1859 to 1863, and spent most of their remaining years at Fort Good Hope. C.P. Gaudet himself was fluent in English and Inuktitut, as well as his native French-Canadian. Before he married Marie he served as postmaster at Lapierre House, and was an assistant to William Lucas Hardisty at Fort Yukon from September 19, 1853, to October 24, 1853, and again from November 25, 1853, to May 30, 1854. From these immersions he most likely learned to speak both Gwich'in and Slavey Jargon.

Perro LeNoire (also known as 'the Negro'), another young man who came to Fort Yukon with Houle, was originally from Fort Simpson, also a South Slavey community. LeNoire was hired as a fort hunter and stayed at Fort Yukon from 1847-1853, during the formative years during and right after the Fort was built. With his French surname and Indian ancestry, LeNoire is another good candidate for speaking Slavey Jargon.

But as Peter Bakker suggests in the development of Michif, Indian or Métis women married to white traders were also used as interpreters in many situations (1997:50). At Fort Yukon, three influential Métis women were present during the early years after contact. One was Anne Campbell Murray, the wife of chief trader Alexander Hunter Murray, who lived at Lapierre House from 1847-1848 and then at Fort Yukon from 1848 to 1852. Lewis Henry Morgan interviewed Anne Murray at Georgetown, Minnesota in 1861 and found out she was fluent in Prairie [Plains] Cree and was "quarter-blood Cree from Peace River, near Athapasca Lake" (Morgan 1959:114; 1997:207). Anne's mother Elizabeth McGillivray was half-Cree and presumably taught her the language, although her father Colin Campbell, a Scottish fur trader in the Northwest Company and later the Hudson's Bay Company, spoke several Indian languages (Brown 1980:99, 115; Simpson 1832). Of course she also spoke English, her husband's first language and even wrote letters in English.

In his *Systems of Consanguinity and Affinity of the Human Family*, Morgan describes Anne Murray as 'an educated and accomplished lady' (Morgan 1997:237-238). She may have also acquired some knowledge of Chipewyan since she spent part of her early teens living with her family at Fort Chipewyan (Shipley 1967:33-34).[7] Before she married, Anne spent a year among the Cree at Norway House and another two or three years attending school at the Red River settlement just north of present-day Winnipeg. If there was any early Cree influence on Slavey Jargon, it may well have come from the multilingual tongue of Anne Murray.

Mary Allen Hardisty, the wife of William Lucas Hardisty, Murray's successor at Fort Yukon from 1852 to 1860, was another Métis woman of Cree parentage. It is not clear how long after their 1857 marriage at Fort Simpson that Mary Allen remained at Fort Yukon, or indeed if she ever arrived there, since her husband announced plans to send her off to a finishing school in eastern Canada for several years (Hardisty 1857). It is interesting that even Hardisty himself had some Indian blood and contributed significantly to Morgan's database on Gwich'in kinship terms (Morgan 1997:238, 289).

Another Company servant of French descent, François Boucher, was stationed at Fort Yukon in the 1860s, and McDonald (1863b) wrote about how Mrs. Boucher helped him translate hymns and the Ten Commandments into Takudh, the Upper Porcupine River dialect of Gwich'in. Mrs. Boucher must have been fluent in English in order to translate for McDonald, and she must have been at least somewhat conversant in her husband's French. Like Houle, she was from Liard River and therefore could probably speak South Slavey, although Hoole accused her of being a poor interpreter (McDonald 1863a). However, Mrs. Boucher and her youngest son both died in 1866 during the massive scarlet fever epidemic that swept the subarctic. So in addition to Antoine

Hoole, it seems very plausible by virtue of heritage and circumstance that all three of these Métis women, Anne Murray, Mary Allen Hardisty, and Mrs. Boucher, were in an excellent social position to learn and to speak Slavey Jargon (see Brown 1983 and Peterson and Brown 1985).

Robert Kennicott (1942:85), who helped document Slavey Jargon, was also a fairly competent speaker of it. At one point he says, "I can patter after a fashion; and through any Indian who understands it, talk on ordinary topics with any of them, without any other interpreter" (original emphasis).

Ethnographic Sources

Malcolm 'Sandy' Roberts, the first person to bring Slavey Jargon to my attention, was born in or around Arctic Village in July, 1900. He was listed in the 1910 U.S. census as a ward of the Episcopal Mission in Circle, on the Yukon River, and claimed to have arrived there in 1909. Sandy said he learned to speak Slavey from his father, which would have been in the first decade of the twentieth century before he moved to the mission. Sandy's father was Robert (Ravaat) Deetreezhuu ('Little Raven'), and his mother was Sarah Chiichyaa (Mishler 2001:679).

Roberts spent part of his youth trapping around the communities of Fort Yukon, Chalkyitsik on the Black River, and Old Crow on the Porcupine River. In the late 1920s he moved back to Circle, got married, and went to work as a laborer for the Alaska Road Commission. He also did some mining, worked as a deckhand on river boats, and fathered seven children. When I met him in Circle in March, 1973, he was seventy-three, still cutting his own firewood and living with his wife Lucy in a small log cabin right on the Yukon River. He died ten years later in August, 1983, and his wife died in July, 2006.

From my conversations with him, I have the distinct impression that Sandy Roberts never really talked with anyone in Slavey but had carefully memorized favorite phrases he learned as a child from hearing his father speak it. For example, when I asked him to say, "I have five good beaver skins" in Slavey Jargon, he laughed and said he couldn't do it. However, he was the one who introduced the topic of Slavey and proceeded to give me an extended lesson in it (see texts). Roberts let me tape record a number of his traditional stories in Gwich'in over a two day period. I stayed in a small guest cabin next door to his and took most of my meals at his table. He had a robust sense of humor, enjoyed teasing me and other visitors, talked fast, and often laughed at his own jokes.

My second source, Rev. David Salmon, was a lifelong resident of the Black River. Born in Salmon Village about 1910, David was an ordained Episcopal priest and spoke fluent Gwich'in and English. For most of his adult life he lived in the community of Chalkyitsik. He was a traditional fiddler and an esteemed elder. In his final years, up until his death in October, 2007, he served as Traditional Chief for the Tanana Chiefs Conference. Unlike Sandy, however, David said he only knew a couple of Slavey words.

Katherine Peter, my third source, was a senior Gwich'in scholar with an honorary doctorate from the University of Alaska Fairbanks. Although Koyukon by birth, she was raised by Gwich'in in Fort Yukon and spent much of her young married life in the Arctic Village area. She is the principal author of *Dinjii Zhuh Ginjik Nagwan Tr'iłtsaii: the Gwich'in Junior Dictionary* (1979) and *Neets'ąįį Gwindaii: Living in the Chandalar Country* (1992). I was only able to elicit one complete sentence from Katherine in Slavey Jargon, but she was completely familiar with the French loan words still in use by Gwich'in speakers and which form the basis of many Slavey Jargon expressions (see Krauss 1983).

Structure and Make-Up

Componentially, my sampling of texts primarily shows English, Chipewyan, and Slavey nouns and pronouns joined to French verbs (5a. and 5b., 6a.), and modified by Chipewyan and Gwich'in adverbs. Others contain French nouns joined to Gwich'in verbs (text 19). Sometimes the sentences are entirely in French (modified only phonemically), or entirely in Chipewyan, raising the formal question of how to define or describe the jargon (texts 12, 13, 18, 22).

If the Gwich'in spoke Chipewyan or French without fusing them with other languages, or even with phonological alterations, were they truly speaking the jargon or simply borrowing words and phrases? Dremeaux (2003) has gone to great length to analyze the phonological shifts made in French by the Gwich'in and by speakers of other northern Athabaskan languages. She concludes that these shifts were made not by hearing French spoken directly but by hearing it filtered through Slavey Jargon. Yet several of the key traders stationed at Peel's River Post, Lapierre House, and Fort Yukon during the early contact period were French-Canadians from Québec, not Métis. These include the Hudson's Bay Company servants C.P. Gaudet and Jerome St. George (dit La Porte), as well as the influential fur trader, Moise (Moses) Mercier, who arrived in Fort Yukon in 1869 and remained there for the next five years. Moses' brother, François, was also a fur trader stationed downriver not far from present-day Tanana (see Mercier 1983).

A major puzzle is that there is no clear evidence in my own collection of ethnographic texts of Cree, purportedly one of the major source languages, and virtually no evidence of English except for the pronoun 'you'. Since Anne Murray and Mrs. Gaudet were both part-Cree, since Antoine Houle's father spoke Cree, and since both Petitot and McDonald claimed the jargon included Cree, I expected Cree words would be more evident in my own text collections. The only Cree to be found at all is embedded in texts (6) and (7), where only one word, nipaa, appears, recorded by Petitot from a full-blooded Ojibwe and a Scottish Ojibwe Métis living among the Gwich'in. And contrary to Kennicott's characterization, I have been unable to discern any Norwegian, Gaelic, broad Scotch, or Inuit language components.

Judging from most of the extant texts, if there is any matrix language for the Jargon it would almost have to be French rather than Gwich'in, Chipewyan, or Slavey. By matrix I mean that French constitutes the baseline or core to which Athabaskan languages and others have been added or substituted. This is most apparent in the Séguin and Petitot samples, texts (5)a, (5)b, (6), and (7), although predictably so since Séguin and Petitot wrote almost exclusively in their native European French. This conclusion is not nearly so apparent in the Kennicott texts (1-4), but again as Kennicott says, "the language mostly spoken by the men (servants) at the various [trading] posts is nominally French" (1860b:95). Richard Slobodin (1966:13) has described it as 'country French.'

At the same time, there are major exceptions. After reviewing all of these texts, Keren Rice (personal communication) observes that in some of the shorter samples, such as texts (2), (8), (9), and (11), the word order does not appear to be French but Athabaskan, with verbs appearing at the end of the sentence. I would add that in Parisian French, text (8) would read something like, "Comprenez-vous le Slavey?" and text (9) would probably become something like, "Ce chilak, comprend-il le Slavey?"

Origins and Uses

An analysis of the Slavey Jargon texts I collected from Gwich'in speakers along with the archival text recorded by Séguin in 1862 suggests that the language was focused on interpersonal relationships rather than commercial trade. The Roberts texts largely emphasize the social evaluation of behavior and character ('good wife' and 'foolish boy'). Indeed, there is nothing within any of these texts that refers to buying, selling, or bartering. Although Sandy Roberts or David Salmon were formerly fur trappers, they make no mention of fur or of western commodities brought in by traders except for the tobacco given to them by Anglican missionaries. Also, because there is only a little Gwich'in included in the texts, the language does not seem to be devised very well for the purposes of trade, as Slobodin (1981:529) has claimed for Broken Slavey.[8]

William Samarin (1996:320) hypothesizes that the same thing took place with Chinook Jargon, that indeed domestic relations between spouses who spoke different mother tongues rather than the necessities of trade between men provided the core social context out of which the pidgin emerged. The best observations made of Slavey Jargon's actual use was for preaching the gospel (Dall 1870) and for teasing and harassing clergymen (Séguin 1862a, 1862b; Petitot 1889) --see texts (5)a, (5)b, (6), and (7). For all these reasons, it seems inaccurate to characterize Slavey Jargon strictly as a trade jargon.

With or without Cree elements, however, I would submit that Slavey Jargon arose as an innovative way to speak across multiethnic boundaries and that it was developed and used as much by the Métis and Indian wives of fur traders as by the official post interpreters. Over the years there were several of these 'country wives' living at Fort Yukon, Lapierre House, and Fort McPherson: Anne Murray, Madame Gaudet, Mrs. Boucher, Mrs. Andrew Flett (Cahchoza), Mary Sibbiston, and Mary Allen Hardisty.

As one northern ethnographer has recently pointed out, interpreters not only provide translations but also supply introductions to people and give advice about matters of etiquette and language. In addition, they are in touch with daily events, rumors, and gossip, as well as the personal problems, illnesses, and moods of the people they are translating for (Beaudry 1997:71). Consciously or unconsciously, these translators were central figures and power brokers in the conduct of

Indian-white relations, and they received higher pay for it. They were the nodes of a small network of ethnic groups who met at trading posts and undoubtedly resolved many disputes. At Fort Yukon, traders and missionaries as well as Gwich'in trappers were almost totally dependent on their good graces. They were truly 'border people' who stood betwixt and between languages and cultures (see Szasz 1994:294).

Although Slavey Jargon is all but extinct today, I once heard the curse word 'sahlahbriy' used in a Gwich'in card game in Arctic Village, and my direct query to the speaker confirmed its meaning.[9] With the rapid movement and mixing of people through the Mackenzie River basin and the Yukon River in the 1840s and 1850s, there was little time for visitors to learn all of the new and complex languages around them. Slavey Jargon seems to have caught on because it was fairly simplified and relatively easy to learn.

Yet there is also a useful musical analogy. Elsewhere I've identified Antoine Houle as the first fiddler on the Yukon (Mishler 1993:13-18), based on his annual orders for violin strings in the Fort Yukon post accounting records. It would be hard to imagine that Houle played anything other than the rich syncretic dance music developed by the Métis of the prairies and Red River country, a music now fully accepted and performed by the Gwich'in (Mishler 1974). Incorporating both European and Native American musical styles, Métis and Gwich'in fiddlers use nonstandard tunings, foot clogging, and irregular 'crooked' phrasing, along with a dance tune repertoire consisting largely of French-Canadian jigs and Scottish reels (see Lederman 2001/2002). This fiddle music, undocumented until about forty-five years ago, also extends back to the early nineteenth century and provides a robust symbolic parallel to Slavey Jargon.

Conclusion

Slavey Jargon helped to simplify communication in a time of rapid language change and almost certainly originated among the multilingual Métis.[10] Although the Hudson's Bay Company itself was pretty hierarchical as an economic system, the polyglot forms of Slavey Jargon represent a curious inseam of linguistic democracy, suggesting that a measure of social equality was negotiated between the speakers of its diverse component tongues. Antoine Houle is perhaps the most likely progenitor, yet circumstantially it seems likely that this jargon found some of its leading proponents in Métis women married to Hudson's Bay Company traders who had daily opportunities to interact socially with the Gwich'in. Thus, Slavey Jargon should be remembered not only for its shards of borrowed phonology, morphology, and syntax, but also for the identity of its practitioners, who by virtue of their diverse ethnicities and genders, created a distinct and memorable regional speech community.

Acknowledgments

An earlier draft of this paper was first presented to the Alaska Anthropological Association Annual Meeting, March 29, 2003. An earlier draft was also published in the Journal of Creole and Pidgin Languages 23(2): 264-287 in 2008. I wish to thank the late Michael Krauss (1988) for analyzing and identifying many of the French etymologies in Sandy Roberts' Slavey Jargon lexicon. Keren Rice was instrumental in glossing many of the Chipewyan and Slave texts and contributed greatly to my thinking about the structure and make-up of the language. Peter Bakker and Anthony Grant both read the manuscript and provided numerous detailed and thoughtful suggestions for its improvement. Appropriately, the scholarship which underlies this paper is itself a kind of rubbaboo. My special gratitude goes out to the late elders Katherine Peter, Rev. David Salmon, and Sandy Roberts.

Slavey Jargon Texts [11]

I. *From unknown speakers (1860-1862, as written by Robert Kennicott)*

(1) Lacoo! nenne tsakwe zazee nazon.

No gloss provided. (Kennicott 1860a)

nenne < neni (Slave) 'you singular'

tsakwe < Cheekwaii (Gwich'in) 'Inuit'

or < ts'ékui (Chipewyan) 'woman'
or < ts'éku (Slave) 'woman'
zazee < ça c'est (French) 'that is'
or zaze (Chipewyan) 'small'
nazon < nezǫ (Slave dialect) 'he/she/it is good'

(2) SenneYu-khun curra nazic—Senne diss Anderson manatta;
Lacoo! Senne natha sa-koha manatla cooloo.
No gloss provided. (Kennicott 1860c)
senne < seni (Slave) 'I'
Yu-khun < Yukon < han (Gwich'in) 'river'
or possibly < yúkǫ́é (Slave) 'store'
curra < suré (Slave) 'truly, surely'
nazic < nizį̨į̨ (Gwich'in) 'he/she/it is good'
diss < des (Chipewyan) 'river'
manatta < manahda (Slave, Chipewyan) perhaps 'I go around on land'
[da = verb stem; one person go by land]
natha < thá (Chipewyan) or nithá (Slave) 'far, long'
sa-koha < possibly shakwai' (Gwich'in) 'my foot'
manatla < manahtla (Slave, Chipewyan) perhaps 'I go back around by land' [tla = verb stem; one person go by land]
cooloo < kúlú (Slave, Chipewyan) 'but'

(3) Et li láundy sáundy?
'which way perhaps' (Kennicott 1942:119)
et li < edli (Chipewyan, South Slavey dialect) 'where?'
(Chipewyan) edlí̧ ni (Li 1946:421)
láundy < láoni or láondi (Chipewyan, possibly Slave)
'I think, I guess'
sáundy < sóni (Slave) 'I wonder, I don't know'
or < sų̂:ni (Chipewyan)'probably, presumably' (Li 1946:421)

(4) Nazon nun Te t'an lä!
No gloss provided (Kennicott 1942:119)
Perhaps, freely, 'The land is good down that way.'
nazon < nezǫ (Slave) or nezų (Chipewyan) 'he/she/it is good'
nun < nan (Gwich'in) nen (Chipewyan) 'land, earth, ground'
te t'an < t'ee tthan (Gwich'in) 'down that way'
or dedans (French) 'inside'
lä < là (French) 'there'

II. *From unknown speakers (as written by Fr. Jean Séguin 1862)*

(5) a. Tchéjé kudjine raguinci séni l'aime todi, kouka tsétédéji séni l'aime chan.

'The English priest I don't love at all, but I love the tobacco very much'. (Séguin 1862a)

kudjine < Gwich'in (Gwich'in) 'residents, people'
raguinci < ginkhii choo (Gwich'in) 'preacher, priest'
< ginkhii (Gwich'in) lit. 'he is making a speech'
séni < seni (Slave) 'I'
l'aime < l'aime (French) 'love him'
todi < dáudí, dódî (Chipewyan, Slave) 'nothing, no'
kouka < googaa (Gwich'in) 'nevertheless, but, even so'
tsétédéji < ts'eet'it (Gwich'in) 'tobacco'
chan < chan (Gwich'in) 'again, too, also'
also possibly < chan (Chipewyan) or chǫ (Slave) or
choh (Gwich'in) 'lots, big, much'

b. c tchézje kudjin paginci séni l'aime todi, kûka tsédezjie séni l'aime chan.

'The minister I don't love at all, but I love [this] tobacco very much'. (Séguin 1862b)

III. *From M. Saint-Pol and Peter Pelly (in 1870, as written by Fr. Emile Petitot 1889: 283, 293)*[12] *French translations from Petitot. English translations from the author.*

(6) Allons, nos gens, dji dinjié jette à l'eau, après ça tikké anl'a nipaa wilili. Esdiniyé djan apiy, esdinyé djan nènè kkè bépaenda. Allons, à cette heure.

'Allons, nos gens, jetez cet homme à l'eau, puis vous l'y tuerez à coupe de fusils. Il est inutile ici, il est inutile qu'il visite le pays. Allons maintenant.'

'Let's go, folks. Throw this man [Petitot] in the water. After that you will kill him there with gun shots. He's useless right here; he's useless as he visits the whole country. Let's go now.'

dji dinjié < jii dinjii (Gwich'in) 'this man'
tikké < dink'ee (Gwich'in) 'gun'
anl'a < ąła (Chipewyan) 'together' (Li 1946:422)
nipaa < nipaha (western Cree) 'kill him'
or nipahew (western Cree) 's/he kills him/her' (Le Claire & Cardinal 1998:347)
wilily < wolé (Slave) future
or walí/walé (Chipewyan) 'should' (Cook 2004:107)
esdiniye > given the translations, this must be the 'he is useless' part
djan < chan (Gwich'in) 'again, too, also'
or possibly < jǫ (Slave) or ją (Chipewyan) 'here'
nènè < nene (Slave, Chipewyan) 'country'
kkè < k'é (Slave) 'on, to'
bépaenda < begháenda (Slave) 'he looks at, he sees'

(7) Allons, Rakρé l'a dit: ey dindjié, il faut le f. . . .à l'eau, le chien kkétinchó. Notre Père Révérend M. . ., n'est pas loin d'ici. Ey bettaoderha illè. Allons, vous autres, djugu, c'est le moment. Anl'a nipaâ.

Note: Italics are original, drawing attention to non-French words.

'Allons, le chef l'a dit: cet homme, il faut le jeter à l'eau, c'est un chien. Notre Père, le révérend M. . ., n'es pas loin. Celui-ci n'est pas nécessaire. Allons, vous autres, maintenant, c'est le moment. Tuons-le tous ensemble.'

'Let's go, the chief told him: This guy [Petitot], it's necessary to throw him in the water. He's a dog. Our Father, the Reverend M. [Robert McDonald] is not far away. This guy is not necessary. Let's go, all of you. Now's the time. Let's all kill him together.

Rakρé < khęhkwaii (Gwich'in) 'chief'
ey dindjié < aii dinjii (Gwich'in) 'this guy or this man'
ey < eyi (Slave or Chipewyan) 'that one' (Li 1946:421)
kkétinchó < possibly łąįį choo (Gwich'in) or tlįcho (Chipewyan) 'dog'
(lit. 'big dog' but commonly used for 'horse')
bettaoderha < bet'áodéʔa (Slave, probably Chipewyan) 'it's necessary'
illè < ílé or hilé (Chipewyan, Slave) negative marker
djugu < juk (Gwich'in) 'now, today'
anl'a < ąła (Chipewyan) 'together' (Li 1946:422)
nipaâ < nipaha (western Cree) 'kill him'
or nipahew (western Cree) 's/he kills him/her'
(Le Claire & Cardinal 1998:347)

IV. *From Sandy Roberts of Circle, Alaska (March 26, 1973)*
Transcription from Mishler tape recording; free translations are from Roberts.

(8) a. yuw sleɪvi koʊmbrɑh?
'Do you understand Slavey'?
yuw < you (English)
koʊmbrɑh < comprends (French) '(you) understand, know'
b. daʊdi.
'No'.
daʊdi < dáudí, dódî (Chipewyan, Slave) 'nothing, no'
Note: see above 'todi' from Séguin 1862: (5)a and (5)b.

(9) deɪnuw tʃilək sleɪvi koʊmbrɑh?
'Does that boy understand Slavey'?
tʃilək < chileku (Hare, South Slavey) or chilikwi (Chipewyan) 'boy, young man'
< chil-a-kwe (sing.); chil-a-ques (pl.) 'young man, servant' (Kennicott 1942:84,90)

(10) gənəfoʊw itsakɔɪ niyzoʊ.
'You got a good wife'.
itsakɔɪ < -ts'ą́Œkwiɛ; (Chipewyan) prefix + 'wife'
niyzoʊ < nį̨zo (Chipewyan) or nizį̨į̨ (Gwich'in) 'he/she/it is good'

(11) labar tis də minahtah.
'I'm going back upriver [in a small boat]'.
labar < le bateau or la barque (French) 'small boat'
tis < des (Chipewyan) 'river'
minahtah <minahda (Slave, Chipewyan) 'I go back'
(identity of mi not known)
Note: appears to be the same word as Kennicott's manatta in (2) above.
(12) nitłʔata dəhuw?
'When are you going back'?
nitłʔata < nahį̨da (Chipewyan)'You start back after coming'
dəhuw < ɛdláhú (Chipewyan) 'when'?
(13) vahl dəmoʊs fini.
'No more Sunday. Six o'clock'.
vahl dəmoʊs < va le dimanche (French) 'go(ing) on Sunday'
fini < finis (French) 'ended, finished'
(14) tʃilək kwɔɪ moʊriyah.
'That young man is lazy'.
tʃilək < chileku (Hare, South Slavey) or chilikwi (Chipewyan) 'boy, young man'
Note: see (9) above
(15) tʃilək kwɔɪ niyzoʊ daʊdi.
'That young man is no good'.
niyzoʊ < nezǫ (Slave, Chipewyan) or < nizį̨į̨ (Gwich'in) 'he/she/it is good'
(16) tʃilək kwɔɪ lafoʊl.
'This boy is foolish'.
lafoʊl < le fou/la folle (French) 'foolish, crazy man/woman'
(17) yuw sahlahbriy!
'You're trash'! (an insult)
yuw < you (Eng.) or vous (French)
sahlahbriy < saloperie (French) 'trash, rubbish'; also < la solapree
(French Michif)
(18) sagriy moʊdʒiy! (another insult)
sagriy < sacré (French) 'holy, sacred'
moʊdʒiy < mojee (French Michif) < maudit (French) 'cursed, damned'

V. *From David Salmon of Chalkyitsik, Alaska (March 24, 2001)*
Transcription from Mishler field notes; translations are from Salmon.

(19) la brasei

'money hunter, prospector'

La brassey < la brassée (French) 'armful or armload'

Note: In Gwich'in they say 'laraa kantii' for 'prospector' (according to the late Frank Ginnis of Fort Yukon).

laraa < l'argent (French) kantii < possibly compté (Métis French pronunciation) 'counted'

(20) leɪ kwanziy la bah.

'It's good down below [downriver]'.

leɪ < lęįį (Gwich'in) 'lots of, many' or possibly < les (French) 'the plural' (Dremeaux 2003:22)

kwanziy < gwinzii (Gwich'in) 'it's good'

la bah < là bas (French) 'over there' or possibly < le bas (French) 'lower part, bottom'

VI. *From Katherine Peter of Fairbanks, Alaska (March 27, 2003)*
Transcription from Mishler field notes. Peter's translation.

(21) lafoʊ ɪnlĩ kwaa!

'Don't be crazy'!

lafoʊ < le fou (French) 'crazy person'

ɪnlĩ kwaa < inlįį kwaa (Gwich'in) 'don't (you singular) be'
< inlin (Slave, Chipewyan) 'you (singular) are'

kwaa (Gwich'in) 'no, negative'

(22) sagriy la mard!

'holy shit'! (frustration)

la merde < (French) shit, excrement

Note: This is a variant elicited by reciting (18) above.

Endnotes

1. Another writer of this period dined on 'robbiboo' soup while traveling with a party of Swampy Crees near York Factory (see Chapters IV and IX in Ballantyne 1848).

2. See the close variant in text 5b. Katherine Peter says that if this sentence were spoken entirely in Gwich'in, it would read:

Vanoodlit ginkhii veedigwiindhan kwaa, googaa vit ts'eet'it edigwiindhan.

'We don't like the white preacher, but even so we like his tobacco.'

3. On one occasion, Rev. McDonald (1864) went to visit the Gens du Large (Chandalar River Gwich'in) and had no reliable interpreter, so he decided to

speak to them in broken Slavey and had one of the local men translate his words into Gwich'in.

4. Like Whymper, William Dall (1870:111) also complained about McDonald's reliance on "a jargon which cannot express an abstract idea."

5. Tsiigehtshik (Arctic Red River) was the site of Séguin's Oblate mission as early as 1868. Old Crow and Arctic Village were not established as villages until about 1912, and Aklavik only goes back to 1918. Inuvik is even more modern and was created as a Canadian government town in the 1950s.

6. This of course begs the question of whether sympathetic Métis interpreters were responsible for Séguin's subsequent success in winning converts at Fort Good Hope and Tsiigehtshik. For more on Oblate missionary failures in Alaska, see Champagne (1943).

7. Fort Chipewyan, Alberta, founded in 1788, was another likely cradle for contact jargons. Visiting there, the Anglican missionary William Carpenter Bompas (1867) observed that 'the most remarkable characteristic of this fort is the diversity of language.... I should be quite at loss to say which of the four is to be considered predominant. They are Chippewyan, Cree, French, and English. The Chippewyan is the vernacular of the Indians in the woods, and generally everyone who come to the Fort is traded with in that tongue. Some of them, however, understand a little Cree, and this may be called the vernacular of the Fort, and it is chiefly spoken by the children. French or English, however, is generally spoken by the adults, according as their descent is from one or the other.' For additional analysis of linguistic diversity in Fort Chipewyan see Scollon and Scollon (1979).

8. Dremeaux (2003:12, 17) re-enforces the notion of Slavey Jargon as a trade language by citing Slobodin and by noting that many of the loan words in Gwich'in are modified French names for trade goods such as tea, coffee, salt, sugar, and playing cards.

9. The deck, rules, hand play, and verbal play of this popular card game, are equivalent to another kind of jargon or rubbaboo. In this situation, the person who uttered 'sahlahbriy' was referring to low-numbered discards, or non-pointers. Mizhur, as it is known to the Gwich'in, or Bizhur, as it is known to the Han, represents a regional historic convergence between several structurally related trump games such as Triumph and Whist in England, Pinochle and Euchre in the United States, and Marjolet, Écarté, and Bésigue in France. See Chapter 14 below; also Mishler 1983; Mishler and Simeone, 2004, Appendix C.

10. I am not the first to recognize this connection. Richard Slobodin (1964:52) claims that "Métis, especially the Red River Métis, had most to do with the development of Broken Slavey." I agree in principle as far as Slavey Jargon is concerned, except that good evidence for its development and use in the Red River district is still wanting. There's some scant documentation of a Red River Métis jargon called Bungay or Bungee, but Bungay was strongly based

on English, with some Scots Gaelic and Cree, and it did not incorporate French (see Scott and Mulligan 1951).

11. Published sources I consulted for glosses of these texts include the Alexanders' Gwich'in to English Dictionary (2005), the Elfords' English-Chipewyan Dictionary (c. 1981), Laverdure's and Allard's The Michif Dictionary: Turtle Mountain Chippewa Cree (1983), LeClaire and Cardinal's Alberta Elders' Cree Dictionary (1988), and Peter's Dinjii Zhuh Ginjik Nagwan Tr'iłtsaii: Gwich'in Junior Dictionary (1979).

12. Saint-Pol, the source of text (6) was a Scottish Tchippeway [Ojibwe] Métis from the Red River area, second in charge at Lapierre House. In the summer of 1870, he escorted Petitot down the Porcupine River from Lapierre House to Fort Yukon, scorning him and ribbing him constantly. Emotionally and mentally tortured by this man, Petitot refers to him as Mephistopheles. Peter Pelly, the source of text (7) was a full-blooded Tchippeway [Ojibwe], who along with Saint-Pol, treated Petitot with scorn and contempt on the river trip from Lapierre House to Fort Yukon. Italics are Petitot's.

11. "They Haven't Found Us Yet": *Pronoun Shifts in Gwich'in Conversation*

with Kenneth Drizhuu Frank

Over the years, it's come to our attention that fluent Alaskan Gwich'in speakers grammatically shift their point of view within five primary social contexts. One is in the narration of traditional stories. Another is in situations where another person's life is in danger and their fate is uncertain. A third is when the speaker wants to make a little joke about him or her self. A fourth occurs when referring to collective kin. And a fifth often pops up when the speaker is making a personal demand. All five contexts offer discrete frameworks for discourse analysis (Goffman 1974, Gross, 2021).

While paying homage to Kenneth's distinguished grandparents, Johnny and Sarah Frank, we want to provide some text examples and suggest rhetorical reasons for why these pronoun shifts occur. English speakers occasionally run up against pronoun shifts in the editorial "we" of newspaper columnists or the royal "we" of kings and queens, but this use is fairly rare and privileged. Gwich'in speakers, by contrast, shift their pronouns in much more common and systematic ways.

Traditional Stories

Let's begin with the context of traditional stories. Just recently, in preparation for a new third edition of Johnny and Sarah Frank's book, *Neerihiinjìk: We Traveled from Place to Place* (Mishler 2001), Kenneth and I were reviewing and refining the translation of one of the most traditional Gwich'in story cycles. Each episode in the cycle is based on the adventures and misadventures of a legendary man called Ch'iteehaakwąįį.

As we were reviewing the translation made for the first two editions, published by the Alaska Native Language Center in 1995 and 2001, Kenneth noticed that surprisingly, the original translator either did not seem to notice or perhaps found it awkward to translate some of the subjective, objective, and possessive pronouns in the story accurately. This occurred both in Sarah Frank's narrative of Ch'iteehaakwąįį and also again in Johnny Frank's narrative of Ch'iteehaakwąįį. So it was not just a momentary slip of the tongue by a single storyteller but something repeated and deliberate, something intermittent yet systematic in the texture of the stories. Take these examples.

Example 1. Sarah Frank's traditional story of Ch'iteehaakwąįį and Frog (interviewed by William Schneider and Mike Holloway in Venetie, April, 1980). At one point Sarah says,

> 6.30 Diinaah'in gwiizhik,
> Dèiinch'yaa shichiindèe khìdhįį'aii ch'yaa gwįįch'in?"
> danàhnyą̀ą.

6.30 While he [Frog] was looking at us,
He told us, "Don't you look just like the one who took my hook?"

Something worth mentioning here is that Gwich'in pronouns often appear as objective case verb prefixes, as in *dii-naah'in* and *danah-nyaa.* So in our new translation, "Diinaah'in" literally means "he [frog] was looking at us," but figuratively it means "he [frog] was looking at him [*Ch'iteehaakwąįį.*]" Indeed, the original translation was "the frog looked at him." This subtle pronoun shift from "him" to "us" is further amplified by the quotative "danàhnyàą" in the next line, which glosses as 'he told us.'

Example 2. Johnny Frank's story of Ch'iteehaakwąįį and Wolverine (recorded by Kathy Alexander at Gold Camp in April, 1973), when Ch'iteehaakwąįį tries to fool Wolverine into believing that he's dead after sliding into Wolverine's trap set with a deadly sharp hook:

14.36 Zhyàa reh diinjik daa tr'iłtàa,
dzaa ch'iidàk khàriintthaii.
Ts'ą̀' reh vitsìį diinjik hàa, ts'ą̀' kwat zhyàa
tr'ìihiindii kwaa gwinyàa.
14.36 So we just purposely made *our* nose bleed,
and pretended to be hooked up this way [through the testicles].
And there's some of our nose blood on the tip [of the hook], and *we* just pretend we're limp and motionless, they say.

It's really Ch'iteehakwąįį who makes his nose bleed to fool Wolverine, but this shift from subjective third person to subjective first person plural, from "he" to "we" and from "his" to "our", is a rhetorical device used to draw listeners into the story. We expect the narrator to say "He (Ch'iteehaakwąįį) just purposely made his nose bleed."

In our view, the purpose for these embedded pronoun displacements is to artfully invite the listeners and readers of the story in to become a part of the story. The placement of the tropes appeals to our imagination. So "we", the listeners and the storyteller, gradually come to represent Ch'iteehaakwąįį, and *we suddenly become the lead character in the story.*

Lest we exaggerate, it should be said that the Ch'iteehakwąįį tale is the only story where we have found these kinds of pronoun shifts. They are not present in other folktales and legends told by Johnny and Sarah such as Vasaagihdzak, Tł'eevii Ti', Dakneehaa, Goghwaii, or Ko'ehdan, which are all told consistently in the third person. Indeed, most Gwich'in stories are told in the third person singular. One notable exception would be the cycle of Sam Peter or Sam Veet'e' stories, which are sometimes told in the first person, as if the storyteller is Sam himself (see Mishler and Frank 1998 and elsewhere in this volume).

Situations Where a Person's Life Is in Danger

It's often the case that individuals or small groups of people face life-threating situations. They may get sick or injured and go into a coma, or they may simply disappear. When they disappear out on the land or out on the water, or in the city, massive community searches are conducted to find them. These searches often go on for weeks or months. The uncertainty of their fate causes much anxiety and suffering for their families, who are looking for closure. This is why the Gwich'in keep searching for missing persons long after white people give up. According to Kenneth, "We keep searching because dead persons don't know they're dead until their bodies are found and buried."

What happens in these liminal situations is that the people who are missing or unconscious are talked about not by their name or in the third person as "he" or "she" or "they" but in the first person plural. For instance, when someone is missing or lost, people in the community will say,

> Tth'aii diigwirah'aii kwaa. They haven't found us yet.
> Or perhaps Tth'aii tr'ihiljii. Someone is still lost or missing.

In this latter case, an indefinite pronoun, "someone" is used, instead of the first person plural.

Or when someone is in a coma and may or may not live, people who know them will say something like,

> Tth'aii hakiirii'aii kwaa. We haven't woke up yet.
> Tth'aii tr'aachii. We're still sleeping.

Our impression is that these remarkable shifts to first person plural pronouns such as "we" and "us" and "our" are designed to help create empathy. By saying "we," the speaker and the audience internalize the danger and imaginatively project themselves into the life-threatening situation. In English language terms, they use these "we" pronouns to put themselves in someone else's shoes.

Humorous Jokes and Asides About Oneself

The third way that Gwich'in speakers displace pronouns is by playfully talking about themselves in the third person. In English these are known as illeisms. The muppet Elmo speaks this way on *Sesame Street* and refers to himself by name rather than "I" or "me." English speaking mothers often speak to their toddlers by objectifying themselves when they say, "Mommy has to go now." Or I (Craig) might hear my wife Barbara talking to herself. When she is frustrated at her sewing machine she often says something self-referential such as, "Barbara, you can do this."

In similar fashion, Gwich'in speakers will make little jokes by referring to themselves in the third person. Mary Frank, Kenneth's mother, for example, is famous for speaking this way. (see Fig. 11.1) Fluent speakers may announce things like,

a) Ako' heechyaa. 'Now he or she is going to sleep (to bed)', meaning "Now I'm going to sleep."

b) Ch'ihee'aa. 'He or she's going to eat.' This is readily understood by other Gwich'in speakers as "I'm going to eat."

Another example is Neeheelir ('He's going to pee'), which figuratively means, 'I'm going to pee.' A comparable phrase in English might be the euphemism, 'I'm going to see a man about a dog.' Sometimes these idioms are even created in English: 'He's coming back to Venetie' is humorously understood to mean, 'I'm coming back to Venetie.'

Collective Kin

There are just a few instances of possessive pronoun shifts which surface in collective kinship terms, making this the rarest of the four contexts. For instance, a speaker may refer to nakhwotsii nąįį (lit. 'all your ancestors'), but figuratively convey the concept of 'all our ancestors'. Or the speaker could talk about diidaazhii nąįį (lit. 'all our living relatives') when he or she actually means 'all my living relatives'. Or again, the speaker might say diik'yaa nąįį (lit. 'all our brothers and sisters') to talk about '*my* generation'.

Personal Demands

Sometimes Gwich'in speakers will make sudden unexpected demands of other speakers. These demands can often be in English, as when an elder Venetie woman recently said very abruptly to a younger man, Lawrence Roberts, "Where's my wood?" She says this because she needs firewood to heat her house. She doesn't say it politely as a request, but barks it out as a question that conceals a demand. It's not really *her* wood, at least yet, but she's expecting it right now. She would never think of saying such a thing as "Would you please bring me some of your wood?"

A second instance of personal demand was related by Kenneth when he called up an old friend who quickly said to him on the phone, "Well, where's my truck?" This elder doesn't actually own a truck at all, but he's expecting and demanding that Kenneth bring *his* truck by so he can be driven somewhere on an errand. The elder creates this fictional "my" to indicate that he not only wants but expects a ride. For Kenneth, who gave him the ride he wanted, the demanding question is somewhat humorous. Like each of the other kinds of pronoun shifts in Gwich'in, making bold demands is a deep, culturally embedded, and productive rhetorical strategy.

Conclusion

It's abundantly clear that this wide variety of Gwich'in pronominal displacements are deeply ingrained in the language. With both empathy and humor, pronoun shifts shine light on a very specialized world view. Alternating points of view from third person to first person or vice-versa are rhetorically powerful. As listeners, readers, and translators, we need to be aware of these heightened lexical moments, these compelling modes of persuasion.

That Gwich'in pronoun shifts are exceedingly old is amply demonstrated in the cycle of traditional stories told about Ch'iteehaakwąįį, artfully performed by elders such as Johnny and Sarah Frank. No one really knows just how old the Ch'iteehaakwąįį story cycle is, but it's set in a distant time where animals speak like people, a time long before the advent of white Europeans. Canadian Gwich'in elders refer to this time as the Ts'iidęįį days. The Ch'iteehaakwąįį tale, along with contexts of lives in danger and personal humor appears to have developed far back in ancient times, embedded with linguistic artifacts which underscore the rich underlying texture and resonance of Gwich'in speech play and verbal art.

Acknowledgments

This paper was originally presented to the Alaska Anthropological Association Annual Meeting March 1, 2021.

Figure 11.1 Mary Frank cutting fish at K'aii dzuu zhit gwitsik near Arctic Village, c. 1990s. Photo by Kenneth Frank.

12. Telling About Bear:

A Northern Dene Men's Riddle Tradition

Since Julius Jetté's (1913) classic collection of 110 Koyukon riddles gathered along the Yukon River in Alaska during the early part of the 20th century, a number of other Koyukon riddles have been collected (Jones and Henry 1976), as well as several from the Upper Tanana (Guédon 1974), the Ahtna (Dauenhauer 1976), the Dena'ina (Kari 1980), and the Tanacross (Mishler 1983). No riddles seem to have ever been collected from the Gwich'in despite repeated attempts by myself and others to elicit them with examples drawn from the Jetté collection and from Anglo-American tradition.

A few years ago, therefore, it came as a total surprise when I first skimmed through a copy of Katherine Peter's *Gwich'in Junior Dictionary,* to find an entry for the English word "riddle" with its Gwich'in counterpart glossed as gwizhii ideeridlii (1979:104).[1] Struck by the nearly homonymous but apparently quite coincidental resemblance between "riddle" and "-ridlii" I renewed my attempts to elicit riddles from several Gwich'in speakers, only to discover that gwizhii ideeridlii may well be the only Gwich'in riddle. Any cultural tradition with only one riddle to its credit would appear to be impoverished in this regard, were it not for the fact that there are many, many ways of posing this one riddle, and it's the creativity of this posing that lends it such a remarkable richness and complexity.

While it is true that gwizhii ideeridlii ("wisdom that is told") and its close cognate gwizhii ideegwidlii ("wisdom that is performed") have also fallen out of use over the past several decades,[2] fortunately enough is remembered about them to appreciate both how and why they were used. Such riddling stands apart from all other recorded northern Dene riddles in the following ways: by being functionally tied to a subsistence activity (the hunting of bears in their dens during the winter), by being at least partly nonverbal in form, and by being used exclusively and secretly by men.[3] Although it is known today primarily by older Gwich'in and Koyukon men, I soon learned that some older Gwich'in women also know about this riddle.[4]

The Gwich'in development of this riddle tradition is perhaps best understood in light of the explanations given to me by two Gwich'in speakers, Abel Tritt of Arctic Village, and Richard Martin, who was raised at the mouth of the Coleen River near the Canadian border. Originally delivered in Gwich'in, Tritt's (1979) commentary was later translated into English for me by Moses Paul Gabriel. It begins:

> Many years ago when the Athabaskan Indians were the only inhabitants of the interior of Alaska, hunting game and birds was the only way of surviving. Finding a grizzly in its den was one of the great things.

> Whenever a man finds a bear in its den, he goes back to the village or camp and makes it known to his friends or relatives by gestures. This is called gwizhii ideegwidlii. When you make it known verbally, it's called gwizhii ideeridlii. The reason for extreme secrecy is to keep the news from women and children because it may bring bad luck.
>
> Gwizhii ideegwidlii is used when a man finds a bear's den with a bear in it. Look it over real good and then go home. Go over to the person who lives next to you and purposely sit very close to him. When he offers you food, you ask him, "Where's the fat and grease that goes with it?" That's one way of doing gwizhii ideegwidlii.[5]
>
> When you say this to a smart man, he finds out right away. When you say these things but his mind is not on the subject, you ask him in another way, and sometimes you walk around roughly and clumsily in his house. That also is gwizhii ideegwidlii. Sometimes you enter your friend's house and walk past him, brushing against him real hard on purpose. That too is called gwizhii ideegwidlii.
>
> If a man is smart, he'll find out right away. This kind of telling and finding out about bear is known as gwizhii ideegwidlii.

Richard Martin (1983), who knew this riddle as gwizhii k'aachirigikhii ("wisdom that is asked for"), said there were many other ways of telling about bear. One time when he was still a boy, for example, his father came home and said to him, "What's that brown stuff on your cheeks?" He went to the mirror and didn't see any brown stuff on his cheeks but remembered later that black bears have brown markings around their nose and mouth, and this was his father's way of announcing the discovery of a black bear in its den.

Martin said that a man who found a bear might also pose the riddle by saying, "How come you walk around like this?" At the same time he would imitate the pigeon-toed way a bear walks. Another time he recalls a man rubbing and scratching his back up against a wooden post and then turning around to exclaim, "It looks like there's some hair left on there!" Still another way was to throw a handful of hair into an open campfire. Presumably the sight and smell of singed hair would suggest the Gwich'in custom of burning the hair off a bear skin immediately after killing it.[6]

One reason those of us who are outsiders have trouble collecting northern Dene riddles such as gwizhii ideegwidlii is that we have learned to think of riddling strictly as a pastime with humor and entertainment value, as a kind of child's play. Although gwizhii ideegwidlii, as I hope to show, does entail a high degree of verbal and nonverbal artistry, as well as wit, it strikes me as not at all entertaining and certainly has nothing to do with child's play. Its value to Gwich'in men is highly pragmatic and rests on a small cluster of traditional beliefs reinforced through traditional stories.

One such belief, as Tritt has noted, is that if women or children find out a man has discovered a bear sleeping in its den, he will have bad luck when he returns to kill it. Such a belief is not easy to explain, but my own understanding of this belief and of the riddle's logic has been advanced by reading and rereading variants of three traditional Gwich'in stories about men who went to live with female grizzlies.

In the published collection of Gwich'in stories told by John Fredson to Edward Sapir in 1923 (McGary 1982), there appears a text entitled, "The Man Who Had a Bear for His Guardian Spirit." In this text, a man and his three friends locate and attempt to kill a female bear and her mate in their den, but the man's three friends are killed by the male bear in the ensuing fight. Only the one man survives, protected by the she-bear because he has shamanistic powers and dreams to the bear as his guardian animal. The man spends the winter hiding in the she-bear's den unbeknownst to her mate and is finally allowed to return to his village on the condition that he not reveal to other men where her den is located. But several years after his release and during hard times, the man breaks his promise and leads his friends on a hunt back to her den. Betrayed and enraged, the she-bear then kills him.[7]

Two other Gwich'in tale types with relevance to gwizhii ideegwidlii have been recorded: one in Old Crow called "The Man Who Married a Bear" (Leechman 1950:159-160) and the other in Venetie called "The Woman Who Was a Bear" (McKennan 1965:144-145). What makes these two different from Fredson's narrative is that in them the man has a much more explicit sexual relationship with the she-bear, who has the ability to transform herself into a woman at will. In "The Man Who Married a Bear," which is also known to the Upper Tanana (McKennan 1959:213-214), the hunter is killed by the jealous she-bear after returning to his village and having sex with his human wife or girlfriend. In "The Woman Who Was a Bear," the man remains faithful to the she-bear and lives happily with her as his guardian and provider; but when she is in her human form, she retains some of the behavior patterns commonly associated with bears, such as a voracious appetite, awkwardness, and flopping about. Such action establishes a dramatic and thematic parallel between this tale type and gwizhii ideegwidlii, in which the hunter clues his partner or friend by miming the bear's clumsiness and roughness, acting almost like "a bull in a china shop."

The man's circumspection in avoiding any mention of the words for bear while hunting them is based on a widespread northern Dene belief shared by the Gwich'in (Cass 1959), Ahtna (Laguna 1969-70:21), Koyukon (Jones 1979:10n; Clark 1970:83; Nelson 1983:176-177,185-187), Tanana (Rooth 1971:128), Deg Hit'an (Osgood 1959:78), Slavey (MacNeish 1954:189), Tagish, Inland Tlingit, and Southern Tutchone (McClellan 1975:127). This belief is that bears can understand human speech even when physically distant from people and are greatly angered by hearing the sound of their own name. In Gwich'in the generic word for black bear is shoh, while the grizzly is shih or shih tthoo. The utterance of these words during the hunt is believed to result in antagonized, mean bears or, worse still, bears that repeatedly avoid hunters.

To counteract this, certain euphemisms are employed in place of the generic terms. "Grandpa" is one favored by the Ahtna (Laguna 1969-70:81), Dena'ina (Rooth 1971:50), and some Tagish (McClellan 1975:128), while other Tagish and Inland Tlingit prefer indefinites such as "the strong one" or "the one going around in the woods" (McClellan 1975:128). Slavey men like to refer to black bears as nakan, the name usually assigned to the brushmen who kidnap women and children and spend all winter living underground or in caves (MacNeish 1954:189). If caught out in the woods alone, some Tagish women who meet a grizzly will address it directly as "brother" in hopes that it will be reminded of the incest taboo and run away embarrassed (McClellan 1975:128). At the turn of the century Koyukon girls were taught to call a grizzly "the beast" or "the thing" (Jetté 1911:605) and today they call it "big animal" or the Koyukon equivalent of "those who are in the mountains" (Nelson 1983:185). Koyukon men are known to use circumspection even after a bear is killed and employ a wide variety of specialized allusions depending on the age, sex, and species of bear being described (1983:174). In each case, the underlying assumption, as with *gwizhii ideegwidlii*, is that bears are incapable of understanding metaphor and metonymy.

Perhaps equally fascinating is Cornelius Osgood's observation that the Deg Xinag generic term for black bear "is made safe by only the slightest shift of a sibilant" (1959:79), so that the retroflex şuš becomes harmless when palatalized as šuš (1959:171). Insofar as brown or grizzly bears are concerned, however, the Deg Hit'an feel that the generic term is even more dangerous to say than the one for black bear, and so replace it with the abstract term for "animal."

In a landmark survey of arctic and subarctic peoples, Irving Hallowell (1926) compared this profuse bear-naming synonymy among tribal groups all across Asia, northern Europe, and North America, grouping the various recorded linguistic terms into categories of: (a) descriptive periphrasis, (b) metaphorical expressions, and (c) kinship terms. He concluded that the use of such circumlocutions, coupled with a taboo on the use of specific generic terms for bear, comprised an integral trait in a vast bear ceremonial complex found throughout the northern hemisphere.

I would cautiously speculate that the reason such an elaborate synonymy has found expression in Gwich'in riddling derives from the Gwich'in hunter's suspicion that the wife of his best friend, or one of her children, might shamanistically dream to the bear and have the power to transform herself into a bear while doing so (see Slobodin 1981:527). If this is the case, she will surely warn the hibernating bear in its den of the men's plans to return and kill it, unless of course, they are extremely careful to keep their knowledge secret.[8] Since black bears (and presumably grizzlies as well) have earned quite a reputation for charging out of their dens and viciously attacking their human predators (Nelson 1983:178), hunters certainly need the element of surprise on their side.

The great importance to the Gwich'in and Koyukon of taking bears for subsistence should not be underestimated. A look at some harvest data reveals that in the summer of 1951 the men of Arctic Village shot no less than eight grizzlies (Rausch 1953:95), while in the fall of 1965, Huslia men killed a record thirty bears (Cline 1966:30). As Richard Nelson aptly noted in his seminal book on Koyukon ecology and world view, *Make Prayers to the Raven*, the taking of bears is not only an important way of bringing in food, "it is a quest for prestige and a high expression of manhood" (1983:173).

All of this leads to the inescapable conclusion that Gwich'in and Koyukon bear-telling was a very serious kind of business and, as David McAllester (1964) has observed with Comanche riddles, play and frivolity may not be the most necessary ingredients in riddling. "It is entirely within the American Indian ethos," he writes, "that their riddles are often in the context of a ritual, a dance pantomime, or a testing situation involving the supernatural. Such serious functional matters as the healing of the sick or the coming of summer may hinge on the correct answer" (1964:253).

What exactly hinges on guessing the correct answer in doing gwizhii ideegwidlii? I would say nothing less than the lives of the hunters, their very survival. Prior to the introduction of guns to the Gwich'in in the mid-19th century, grizzlies and large black bears surely stood an even chance of defending themselves successfully against humans and inevitably committed more than their fair share of mayhem. The opening and concluding episodes of John Fredson's text provide vivid testimony to this danger, and ethnographic evidence from the Neets'it Gwich'in indicates that the only effective weapons used against grizzlies prior to white contact were spears and clubs made from caribou antler, or stone adzes (Hadleigh-West 1963:141; McKennan 1965:32). But even with the advent of the modern rifle, the Neets'it Gwich'in will not attempt to kill a grizzly when hunting alone (Rausch 1953:95).

While social and economic context and world view are crucial to understanding such a riddle as gwizhii ideegwidlii, some remarks about the form and structure of the riddle are also in order. It is indeed curious that the correct answer to the riddle is nonverbal, even when the descriptive element or question part is verbalized. To guess gwizhii ideeridlii or gwizhii ideegwidlii, a man must signify that he understands the riddle by finding a pretext for getting up and leaving the house with his friend. He must not do this too suddenly or openly lest he draw attention to himself. In other words, his answer to the riddle, if verbalized at all, must be just as circumspect as the question or gesture posed to him.

This is markedly different from the structure of most Koyukon and Dena'ina riddles, whose descriptive elements arc declarative statements prefaced by a short formulaic phrase which in English amounts to

"Riddle me" or "Wait, I see something." While Gwich'in riddling uses no such formula and can be posed either as a statement or as an oblique question, a fascinating parallel exists between gwizhii ideeridlii and Jetté's Koyukon riddle #101, which is specifically concerned with hunting bears in their dens:

> Tła-dzor-karas'āna: sǫ ḳo-nirăle ōko no-rogęyar.
> Riddle me: I am looking everywhere for a lost arrow.
> Answer: Në-tselęzar-tsĕn.
> The search for a bear's den.

Part of Jetté's commentary unravels the clue contained in the riddle's descriptive segment: "One searching for a lost arrow inspects the ground carefully, moves the bushes to see under them, etc. So also does one who searches for a bear's den" (1913:647). At first glance, telling someone you're looking for a lost arrow might seem to be another creative and manly way of doing gwizhii ideeridlii.

However, a distinguishing feature about the form of the Gwich'in bear-telling riddle is that it has a descriptive element that employs the poetic device of synecdoche; that is, part of something stands for the whole of it. When the man who finds the bear is offered some food at his friend's house and asks, "Where's the fat and the grease that goes with it?", the fat and the grease figuratively represent the entire bear. In the nonverbal form of the riddle also, the hunter's rough and clumsy behavior stands for the bear's rough and clumsy behavior, and the bear's rough and clumsy behavior in turn stands for the bear itself. Sometimes metonymy may be used for posing the riddle as well. A man might say upon entering his friend's house, "Gee, I saw a lot of berries out there!" (Gilbert 1983). In this case, the bear would be associated with the food it relishes in late summer and early fall.

This is quite different, consequently, from Jetté #101, in which it is the hunter's behavior rather than the bear's that must be inferred. For this reason, even though the Koyukon and the Gwich'in are linguistic neighbors, telling your partner you were out looking for a lost arrow might not tell about bear adequately enough for a Gwich'in hunter to figure out what is going on.[9] Indeed, Koyukon riddles are largely based on personification, part-to-part, and whole-to-whole metaphors as opposed to the part-to-whole metaphors and metonymies of the Gwich'in.

What we're presented with here, at least from an ethnological perspective, is not just a synonymy but a phylogeny, a series of parallel but extremely divergent historical developments. Not only the Gwich'in and the Koyukon, but nearly every northern Dene language group has produced its own way of talking and telling about bear, apparently evolved from some proto-Dene belief and behavior template. This template has been adapted to local circumstances and slowly transformed into a wide variety of highly specialized expressive forms such as men's riddles, figurative kinship terms, phonemic distortions, abstract nouns, indefinite pronouns, songs, metaphors, and metonymies.

From an interpretive standpoint, I want to underscore the notion that gwizhii ideegwidlii maintains a very special relationship to the three traditional Gwich'in narratives discussed earlier, and particularly to the one told by John Fredson. In Fredson's text, for example, the she-bear says to the hunter, "Dinjii na'in jì' dząą sha'an gòo'ąįį shigii kwaii nąįį hàa hehshrit ndàa nihtsįį negoohihndal sheegwandak shrò' ("[Man,] if you see people here again, don't tell them about me and where my den is, where my children barely toddle along nose to tail") (McGary 1981:102-103). Of course, when he later disobeys and tells, the she-bear "hears" about it and lies in wait to kill him when he returns. Gwizhii ideegwidlii, therefore, is a pliable unit of situated speech and/or kinesic action which protects its performers against any recurrence of this story's tragic outcome.

The import of Fredson's story as a tale type circulating in tradition is accordingly manifest in every performance of the riddle, and all three of these bear stories, along with the traditional beliefs about bears who serve as guardian animals, women who can magically transform themselves into bears, and bears who understand literal human speech, are part of the same cultural logic and the same semiotic system as the riddle. The riddle itself operates synecdochically to recall and reinforce these beliefs and the collective experience invested in these three stories, almost as if it were some kind of mnemonic device.[10] By providing valuable psychological reassurance against the great risks men face in taking on one of nature's most awesome and destructive forces, gwizhii ideeridlii and gwizhii ideegwidlii illustrate how beautifully verbal and nonverbal art can articulate a belief system, promote safe subsistence hunting and biological survival, and help define a uniquely Gwich'in symbolic ecology.

Acknowledgments

Preliminary versions of this paper were presented at the Athabaskan Languages Conference in Fairbanks, Alaska on May 27, 1983, and at the XIth international Congress of Anthropological and Ethnological Sciences in Vancouver, British Columbia on August 27, 1983. It was first published in the Journal of American Folklore 97(383):61-68 (1984). I wish to thank Richard Mueller for his useful comments.

Endnotes

1. This discovery, which proved to be the tip of the iceberg, underscores the great potential that bilingual Native American language dictionaries have for advancing folkloric research.

2. Moses Gabriel. who translated Abel Tritt's commentary on the riddle, was born in 1931 and raised on the Dranjik ("Black River") near Chalkyitsik. But Mo had never heard of this tradition until I recruited him to translate Tritt's recording. Richard Nelson, moreover, in compiling his ethnography of Dranjik Gwich'in hunting and trapping practices, outlined the detailed procedures used for killing both black and grizzly bears in their dens (1973:118-122) but made no mention of any secrecy in telling about the discovery of such dens.

3. It would seem that the Koyukon variants of this bear-telling riddle rely much more heavily on verbal cues than do the Gwich'in ones. Jetté (1911:254, 605) writes of a highly secret "bear song" that Koyukon hunters jealously kept away from women, but apparently this song was intended more for the ears of

bears than other men, and Jetté heard it performed only once. I once recorded a traditional song used by the Tanana Indians at Goodpaster Village for reporting news of a bear that had either been found sleeping in its den or had just been killed in its den (Mishler 1983).

4. The extent of one woman's knowledge was conveyed to me at some length in a taped interview with Elijah John's younger sister, Myra Robert (1979), of Venetie.

5. Here a verbalized example is given by Abel Tritt even though the nonverbal term is used to describe it. It would seem that gwizhii ideegwidlii is the generic term covering both the verbal and nonverbal forms of the riddle.

6. Though no longer observed by Gwich'in hunters today, this post-mortem rite appears in the text of Joe Number Six's "The Man Who Lived With a Bear" as told to Robert McKennan (1965:144) in 1933.

7. John Fredson translated two very close variants of this same story for Cornelius Osgood (1936:162) at Fort Yukon in 1932 and for Robert McKennan (1965:144-145) at Circle in 1933.

8. While it is certainly true that men as well as women may have the bear as their guardian animal (as is clear from Fredson's text), presumably this fact would be well-known to their close friends, and such men would not be called upon to assist in killing a bear in its den.

9. The sharp phonological divergence between Gwich'in and Koyukon, a phenomenon that contributes to "the most abrupt linguistic boundary in Athabaskan" (Krauss and Gotla 1981:74) would thus appear to have an analog in the semantic structure of Gwich'in and Koyukon riddles. It's also of interest that the Koyukon primarily hunt black bears while the Gwich'in primarily hunt grizzlies.

10. This is also true of some older Koyukon riddles, in which "an allusion is made to the popular legends or to the traditional customs, which suggests the answer more plainly than any description could do" (Jetté 1913:186).

13. Sam Peter Vagwandak:
Tall Tales of a Han Hwëch'in Man

with Kenneth Drizhuu Frank

Introduction

It is to the discredit of folklorists and ethnographers that very little has been written about contemporary Native American humor. Keith Cunningham's *American Indians' Kitchen-Table Stories* (1992), a book that stands almost by itself in documenting contemporary Indian jokes, includes an intriguing chapter on "Navajo Humor." Since the Navajo are southern Dene, linguistic brothers of the Gwich'in, we sense that even though the texts of Navajo and Gwich'in jokes are radically different, their comic sensibility is very similar.

Cunningham is insightful when he says that "Navajo humor generally focuses on things at variance with what is culturally expected and accepted" (1992:154). Laughter, he maintains, helps to restore harmony and is an essential part of the Indian's world view. Another volume which examines southern Dene humor in depth is Keith Basso's classic *Portraits of "The Whiteman": Linguistic play and cultural symbols among the western Apache* (1979), a book which investigates how the Western Apache improvise comic "plays" to poke fun at white male behavior and highlight cultural differences.

A good example of traditional northern Dene humor lies in the Gwich'in custom of teasing each other about Shin. Shin are little old men who play tricks on you when you're not looking. They're usually invisible, but some elders are convinced that they're very real, what Marshall Sahlins would call "metapersons" (Sahlins 2022). So if you complain to a Gwich'in friend or family member that your pocket knife is missing, they're liable to say, "Shin naanigwii'aii?" ('Does Shin bother you?'). This is a rhetorical question without an answer, because no one wants to admit they are careless or forgetful, and very few even want to admit that Shin exist. Or should you get a sudden muscle cramp, like a Charley horse, friends will also laugh and tease you with, "Shin naanigwii'aii?" In each case the correct response is always a smile or a laugh.

In Alaska, the Gwich'in also have a traditional cycle of stories about the man Sam Peter, better known as Sam Veet'e'. Sam was a cocky and colorful Han Hwëch'in storyteller from Dawson, Yukon Territory, and Eagle Village, Alaska, who lived much of his adult life in Circle City, Alaska, a small Gwich'in community on the upper Yukon River. His lifetime spans the last half of the nineteenth century and the first half of the twentieth. Sam is the central character in a living cycle of tall tales told often in Gwich'in but also sometimes too in English. Two

Gwich'in-speaking storytellers who still tell Sam Peter tales today are Trimble Gilbert, of Arctic Village, and Kenneth Frank, of Venetie.

Back in the early 1970s I also recorded a number of Sam Peter stories from Daniel John of Venetie and Fort Yukon while he was visiting in Chalkyitsik, and from Sandy Roberts at his home in Circle (John 1973). Then in the 1990s I recorded Sam Peter stories from Moses Sam of Arctic Village and Kenneth Frank (Sam 1996). Kenneth says he heard them from Moses and from his father, Hamel Frank. So from everything we can tell, Sam Peter stories are traditionally told by Gwich'in men to other men, although there is no taboo against women hearing them.

Stylistically, there are some striking differences between performers. Daniel John, for example, told all six of his episodes in the first person, just as if Sam himself were alive and speaking. But each of the other performers we know tell the stories only in the third person. Daniel John, whose Indian name was Ch'ak'ohandzee, was born in Circle in 1917 and said that when he was a boy he used to go visit Sam Peter, and Sam would tell him to go sit on his bed, and after Sam ate he would sit down and laugh and tell him stories (Mishler 1973). So the comical Sam Peter stories that Daniel John told (see episodes 1-6 below) actually reflect a direct chain of custody. Since Daniel John heard Sam's stories first hand, he told them close to the way he heard them, while other storytellers who heard the stories second or third hand have adopted and maintained a third person point of view.

This performance matrix would put Sam Peter loosely within the classic tall tale tradition of the Munchausen, named after the German baron who told wondrous accounts about his own adventures to his companions and who later had fictional stories told about him (see Raspe 1902). The original Baron Munchausen (1720-1797), for example, bragged about killing "fifty brace of ducks, twenty widgeons, and three couple of teals" with one shot (Raspe 1902:15). Munchausen stories are autobiographical and characteristically told by a man whose eccentric personality attracts other storytellers.

Richard Dorson, in Part II of his book, *Man and Beast in American Comic Legend* (1982) addressed many of these regional tales circulating in America. Dorson identifies some well-known American Munchausens as Jim Bridger, Oregon Smith, John Darling, Gib Morgan, Len Henry, Jones Tracy, Daniel Stamps, and Hathaway Jones. All of them, like Sam Peter, told stories about hunting and fishing, and many, like Sam, lived on the frontier. In Dorson's words, the Munchausen is "a special kind of folk hero, one who acquires local renown for spinning tall tales about his own feats and in effect creates his own larger-than-life legend which other storytellers perpetuate" (Dorson 1982:77).

Carolyn Brown defines the tall tale as "a fictional story which is told in the form of personal narrative or anecdote, which challenges the listener's credulity with comic outlandishness, and which performs different social functions depending on whether it is heard as true or as fictional" (1987:11). Not knowing about Sam Peter and Gwich'in folklore, Brown classifies the tall tale as "primarily a white male form" (1987:12). We hope to show here that the Sam Peter stories feature the artistic and imaginative creation of Alaskan Indian men.

The Sam Peter Story Cycle

Altogether we have collected fifteen episodes in the Sam Peter cycle, plus two variants, but there may well be more circulating in oral tradition. For future reference, we have supplied titles. With the performers' names in parentheses, the episodes are:

1. *Sam Peter Rides a Moose to Town (Daniel John, Kenneth Frank)*
2. *Sam Peter Boxes with a Brushman (Daniel John, Kenneth Frank)*
3. *Sam Peter and the Snake (Daniel John)*

4. *Sam Peter Goes to Court (Daniel John; Kenneth Frank)*
5. *Sam Peter Falls Through the River Ice (Daniel John)*
6. *Sam Peter and the Owl (Daniel John, Kenneth Frank)*
7. *Sam Peter Tries Snaring for Lynx (Moses Sam)*
8. *Sam Peter and the Big Cats (Sandy Roberts)*
9. *Sam Peter and the Devil (Sandy Roberts)*
10. *Sam Peter's Adventures Outside of Alaska (Sandy Roberts)*
11. *Sam Peter and the King Salmon (Sandy Roberts)*
12. *Sam Peter Makes His Fortune (Trimble Gilbert, Kenneth Frank, Moses Sam)*
13. *Sam Peter Climbs a Mountain (Kenneth Frank, learned from David Salmon)*
14. *Sam Peter Mushes His Dogs to Seattle (Trimble Gilbert)*
15. *Sam Peter Ropes a Moose (Burns Frank)**

Due to space limitations, we can only share some of these stories, and only those told in English or with English language translations. There are Gwich'in texts of those told by Daniel John, for example, which may be found elsewhere, as recorded by Craig Mishler in Chalkyitsik in 1973 and transcribed by the late Gwich'in scholar, Katherine Peter (see McGary 1984: 857-872).

We start here with several of Daniel's tellings, which are unique in the sense that he tells them in the first person, although his own persona may be heard in some of the opening and closing sentences, which act as framing devices. Subsequent episodes are told by Sandy Roberts, Trimble Gilbert, Kenneth Frank, and Moses Sam.

Sam Peter Rides A Moose to Town

Told by Daniel John. Recorded by Craig Mishler in Chalkyitsik, March, 1973. Translated by Edward John.

In the past, Sam Peter tried to make people laugh and made up some stories, so I'm going to go ahead and tell about them.

Sam Peter Vagwandak

One time I was up at Dawson and wanted some moose, so I got my rifle and was walking down the creek. I saw a large group of moose approaching me, and all I had was a rifle and a knife and a moose shoulder blade [scapula]. When I rubbed the shoulder blade bone against the brush, a moose heard it and started coming towards me, and when it came near I saw the biggest moose in the whole herd approaching me, so I threw that shoulder blade away.

The big moose suddenly just kneeled over, so I dropped my rifle and jumped on its back. After I jumped on its back, I grabbed hold of its antlers and directed it towards town. And when I was close to town I got my knife out of its sheath and jabbed that moose near the heart. The moose just fell over and died right there.

After the moose died I went on ahead and skinned it and gathered up all the guts and put them in a sack. While I was packing the guts back through the village a guy came by and asked me, "Sam, how did you kill a moose so close to the village?"

But without saying anything I kept on walking home. And when I went back into the house another guy came around and said, "Somebody shot a moose close to the village."

"Ah Sam," he said, "nobody ever killed a moose that close to the village before." Then he asked me, "How did you do that?"

Then I said, "Well, you don't know Sam Peter! Whenever I want something, I get it. I always do my best and I do things that nobody else can do, so why the heck is everybody talking about it?"

Sam Peter Boxes with a Brushman

Told by Daniel John. Recorded by Craig Mishler in Chalkyitsik, March, 1973. Translated by Edward John.

This story begins about 44 miles from Circle. I had my camp there, and I realized that my food was getting pretty scarce, so I paddled back down to Circle in my canoe. When I got to Circle I got some food and walked back to camp carrying my canoe. In my camp I had a cache full of dried fish, and when evening came around I had my supper and stayed up until late, but finally I went to sleep.

I knew one of my dogs was loose, but while I was sleeping I felt someone pushing me, and I woke up, realizing something was wrong. I saw my loose dog sleeping out there, and without making any noise I untied the tent flap and peeked out.

Then I saw a brush man with an arm load of dried fish walking back into the brush. So I put on my mocassins right away, and before the brushman came back I hid under the canvas which covered the dried fish. I waited, and before long, sure enough, there he was walking back. He walked into the fish cache and started putting the dried fish on his shoulder, and while he was doing that I caught him and found out that he was really strong. He kept throwing me down, and then I realized that this brushman didn't know how to box, so I jumped up and got myself ready to box. Since he didn't know how to box, I knocked him out.

He was lying on the ground for a while, and then he woke up and found out it was me. That's when I said, "Hey brushman, I want you to go. You just get the hell out of here!" And the brushman said, "O.K. Sam," and took off. So that's the story of my friend Sam Peter. That's it.

Sam Peter Boxes with a Brushman #2

Told by Kenneth Frank. Personal communication with Craig Mishler at Gulkana, June 28, 1998 [following a family funeral].

Another time Sam Peter was walking through the woods when he came up to a brushman's campfire. We call the brushman Naa'in. Sam decided to give the brushman a boxing lesson. In those days they used to box barehanded with their underwrists up, fists clenched, and one hand outstretched in front of the other [demonstrates the John L. Sullivan pose]. So Sam gave the brushman a boxing lesson and even drew a diagram in the dirt to show him what they were going to do. And then right there the brushman beat Sam up and gave him a knockout punch.

Sam Peter and the Snake

Told by Daniel John. Recorded by Craig Mishler in Chalkyitsik, March, 1973. Translated by Moses Paul Gabriel.

I will talk about Sam Peter's story. I'm here with my friend [Craig Mishler], so I could tell about his story. He said, "I was down at Dawson. The steamer arrived and I put on my Sunday suit. I also put on a brim hat, and I boarded the steamboat. I also had a gold nugget chain on my chest. The steamboat paddled down the Yukon River, and I finally arrived at St. Michael.

Everyone there knew me. By and by, I found a hotel and entered inside. "What do you want, chief?" one white man said to me.

"Oh I'm just trying to find a place to eat. If you have some good food I would like a meal," I replied. Just then I noticed a large snake lying down on the table, so I said, "How about some of that?" So they cut some off for me. They set a plate full of food in front of me. Just as I was enjoying my meal, a certain white man came in.

"Chief, where did you get that delicious food you're eating?" he asked.

"It's that snake," I said, hinting toward the table.

He said to the waiter, "Cut off a bigger piece for me. I really would like that," he said.

So I kept on eating my meal, and this white man did likewise. The snake was alive all this time. He was lying down with his head toward the rear wall of the building. He looked at me with angry eyes because he didn't want a bigger piece cut off of him.

After we finished our meal the white man complimented me by saying, "Chief, we certainly had a fine meal." From there I left for home.

Sam Peter Falls Through the River Ice

Told by Daniel John. Recorded by Craig Mishler in Chalkyitsik, March, 1973. Translated by Moses Paul Gabriel.

This is Sam Peter's story. I wonder what place he was talking about?

One man was with me. We were walking along, and we came upon a river. This man was walking ahead of me, and he crossed the river. Although the ice was bad, he managed to go around it. Then I followed him, taking a short cut, and he spotted me.

"Aah, Sam. That ice is no good. Don't walk on it!"

But I kept right on going because I had big snowshoes on. But then as I reached the half-way point, everything just went down under me, and I fell through. The current swept me right under the ice, and at the same time I was trying to get my snowshoes off.

Glancing down, I noticed there was an opening in front of me, and as the current carried me down towards it, I touched bottom and kicked hard and got back up through the hole onto the ice. I started rolling around in the snow until I got myself covered. Then I glanced upriver and saw that my friend had a fire going, so I climbed up the bank and walked back towards him.

When I got there my friend was sitting by the fire crying. He was sitting on a spruce bough by the fire crying his eyes out. The fire was making so much noise he didn't hear me come up.

"What the hell you cry for?" I said. He turned around and was very surprised to see me. I survived from a place where ordinary people don't often survive.

"Sam, how in the world did you manage to get through all that?" he said. Then he took off all his clothes real fast and put them on me. He was drying out my clothes and was very nervous.

"Sam, how did you manage to live through that?" he asked.

I told him, "Aaa! You sure don't know Sam Peter!" So this is the story of Sam Peter. It's not long, but that's it.

Sam Peter and the Owl

Told by Daniel John. Recorded by Craig Mishler in Chalkyitsik, March, 1973. Translated by Moses Paul Gabriel.

This is another story by Sam Peter, whose Indian name was Sam Veet'e'.

One time I left Dawson carrying a gun, knife, tobacco, and matches. I just thought I'd take a little trip up that way, and I left. But to my surprise, I got lost along the way. The land seemed to be all the same to me. I had a brand new .030/.030 and had a lot of cartridges, so I started shooting. I said, "Sam Peter got lost!" and I shot, and I shot, and I shot.

I started out in different directions, but the whole land seemed to engulf me, and I just kept going in circles. Eventually I didn't know what to do.

Finally, it was getting a little dark, and as I was walking through the spruce trees there was an owl sitting up there looking down at me. He just looked at me, and I didn't know what to do. I had no cartridges left, so I couldn't shoot him, but in the meantime I was getting very hungry.

I was looking up at him, and he was looking down at me. All he was doing was keeping his eye on me, and when I started to move I noticed that his head followed me, so I walked a circle around him, and his head just kept following me.

His head turned all the way around when I went around him, so I stretched out my paces. I sped up my walking and walked around in fast circles, and I noticed his head going around and around while he was just keeping his eye on me. Then I really sped up my pace and walked around him real fast. I watched him and watched him, and his head was still turning around. Eventually, his head just rolled completely off, and his body fell dead right by me.

Then I got in front of a great big spruce tree and made something like a lean-to with spruce boughs. I plucked that owl and spread the feathers inside that place, and I cooked the heart. By then it started getting late, so I went to bed in a nice feathery place and put my coat on top of me. The next morning I got up very early and ate the owl that I cooked and started out. And then I came to the place where I was walking before, and so I followed it and came back to Dawson.

People said, "Sam, where were you? You were gone a long time."

And I said, "Well, I went out and got lost, but I managed to come back."

Sam Peter's Adventures Outside of Alaska

Told by Sandy Roberts. Recorded by Craig Mishler in Circle on August 26, 1973. Translated by Moses Paul Gabriel.

Once Sam went to the source of the Mississippi River and killed a lot of marten, altogether he got 500 marten! Then he climbed a high mountain and peeked over one edge, and there was New York City! Then he went over to the other side and peeked down, and there was Seattle!

A strange white man came up to him and said, "Sam, what are you doing in these parts? It's too dangerous. There's lots of dangerous animals around here."

But Sam kept on going until finally he came upon some kind of government house. Inside of this house there was a lot of money and large piles of gold dust in every corner. Sam's friend was there, and he had a beautiful girl in there who was just cuddling up and rubbing him with her rear end. *"Sam, why don't you be like me?"* he said.

And then the girl saw Sam and said, *"Sam, I really like you. Will you marry me?"* But before she could go any farther Sam had already disappeared out the door.

[Translator's Note: The italicized sentences were spoken in Han Hwëch'in rather than Gwich'in.]

Sam Peter and the King Salmon

Told by Sandy Roberts. Recorded by Craig Mishler in Circle, August 26, 26, 1973. Translated by Moses Paul Gabriel.

Another time Sam went up to the source of the Yukon River, and as he was walking he noticed something reddish-colored off in the distance. As he came closer, he realized there were some king salmon feeding on salmon berries.

"They saw me and made a mad dash for the river, but I clubbed them all," he said.

Whiskers here [Craig Mishler] must think I'm telling a lie, huh? That's it. No more.

Sam Peter Mushes His Dogs to Seattle

Told by Trimble Gilbert. Notes only by Craig Mishler in Arctic Village, May, 1996.

Another time Sam mushed his dogs from Dawson to Seattle, and everybody in Seattle recognized him when he walked down the street. "Hello, Mr. Sam," they all said. They treated him just like a famous person.

Sam Peter Makes His Fortune

Told by Trimble Gilbert. Notes only by Craig Mishler in Arctic Village, May, 1996.

One time Sam was walking along and he got surrounded by a bunch of wolves, so he decided to climb up a tree. When the wolves gathered around underneath the tree, he pulled out his pistol and shot a whole bunch of them. Then he took all the wolf skins into Dawson and sold them and made a lot of money.

On the way back from Dawson Sam was traveling along with his pack dogs and had all of his money stuffed inside the dog packs. But the dogs suddenly saw a moose and got excited and took off on him. When he caught up with them a couple of days later, all he could find is one dog with a $5 bill sticking out of his pack.

Sam Peter Makes His Fortune #2

Told by Kenneth Frank to Craig Mishler, 2021. Notes only.

One time Sam Veet'e' had a box of .22 shells, fifty rounds, and he was chased up a tree by a pack of wolves. So he had his .22 rifle up in the tree with him and shot the whole box of shells, killing every wolf. Fifty rounds, fifty wolves. At that time there was bounty on wolves, so he took the leg bones and collected the bounty for each wolf, and then he skinned the wolves and sold all the pelts. Somehow he made $50,000.

Sam Peter Tries Setting Snares for Lynx

Told by Moses Sam. Recorded by Craig Mishler in Arctic Village, May 29, 1996. Translated by Jerry Frank.

MS: Sam Peter was raised in the Eagle area, so he was a Han Gwich'in. Then later on he moved his family down to Circle in a boat. He lived in Circle for a long time until his old age. And then he moved all his family to Fort Yukon and then to Venetie. And then he lived in Venetie for a long time.

He did a lot of silly things. One time he was making lynx snares. As he was working on these lynx snares in his house, he found some gill net webbing, and he tied some of that onto the ends of his snares. Gee, crazy, eh? *[Translator's note: Sam should have used steel tie wire.]*

Each time he catches a lynx, the lynx would make one good jump and snap the webbing line. In one whole year of trapping he never got even one lynx. He was a relation to Ned Roberts family, and they asked him, "How come you don't kill any lynx?"

"Well, every time I get one, the lynx runs away with my snare."

And so after they found out what was happening, they showed him how to rig up his snares.

"This is how it's done," they said.

And then after that he started catching lynx. [laughs] He was a silly old man, right? A really old man, all right. He was three-quarters old and one-quarter young. Do you know what I mean?

CM: Yeah.

MS: And then when he goes out to set traps, he hitches up all his dogs, and says, "Go ahead!" When he does that he takes off ahead of the dogs, and he doesn't even look back at the dog team. He just keeps on walking, and then the toboggan gets snagged and stuck on some trees. [laughs] Without looking back he still keeps walking for a long distance, even for a whole half a day. And then finally he looks back and realizes that there's no dogs there. Now he has to turn around and go back again.

And just a little ways from where he had started out that morning, that's where he found them. [laughs] The dogs were sound asleep. So he loosened up the toboggan and started out again. That's the way they tell his story.

And so he walks all day long. He never looks back for his dog team. He just keeps on walking. And then just before the day's end, he discovers the dogs aren't there. He has to go back until he can find them. Sometimes it's really late when he comes back and finds his dogs. Crazy, eh? That's the way they tell the story of Sam Veet'e'.

Sam the Man: Biographical Discussion

It's extremely difficult to distinguish Sam Peter the man from Sam Peter the persona embodied in the stories because little is recorded about Sam's life outside of his stories. One lifelong resident of Eagle, Max Beck, claimed that Sam Peter was just a convenient name which old-timers used to hang their tall tales upon, and that in the early days there were actually several Sam Peters living in the Upper Yukon River. Beck (1997) is convinced that the Sam Peter story cycle has indeed little to do with any specific person, thinking it focuses more on a caricature.

There is undoubtedly some truth to this critique, but our research has uncovered one historical person using the name Sam Peter. This Sam is said to have been the son of Old Peter, identified as a sixty-year-old widower born in 1849 (Bureau of the Census 1910). Sam also had a sister whose married name was Sarah Walter and a brother named Paul Peter.

The Thirteenth U.S. Census taken in Eagle in 1910 lists Sam's age as thirty-nine, suggesting he was born in 1870, but the Fourteenth Census, taken in 1920, shows that Sam was still living in Eagle Village at the age of fifty-eight, suggesting he was born in 1862 (Bureau of the Census 1910; 1920). The 1940 U.S. census shows him as "Samuel Peters" living in Circle at age 75, making his birth year about 1865 (Bureau of the Census 1940).

A 1939 Bureau of Indian Affairs village census taken in Circle City by the local school teacher gives Sam's birthdate as May 24, 1864, and his birthplace as the old village at Charley Creek (i.e. the Kandik River), a former Han village. This 1939 survey also identifies Sam's mother as Belle Solomon, an eighty-five-year old woman born at Chandalar village (aka Venetie) or somewhere on the Chandalar River. If this is the case, then Sam was probably half Gwich'in and half Han.

The eight year discrepancy in these four census reports is complicated further by Episcopal Church records kept at Fort Yukon. Fort Yukon parish registers show that Sam died on October 23, 1957, at the age of one hundred fifteen, which was surely an exaggeration, for that would push the year of his birth back to 1842 (Episcopal Church 1899-1972), and make him older than his own mother and father. Nevertheless, such a statistic would be very true to the Sam Peter narrative tradition, which is centered around the improbable and fantastic. Presumably the Church was more correct in identifying Sam's death date than his birth date, so if his age as given in the 1910 U.S. census is accurate, he lived to be eighty-seven; if his age as given in the 1920 census is accurate, he lived to the ripe old age of ninety-five; and if his age in the 1939 census is correct, he lived to be ninety-three. The 1950 U.S. census shows he was still alive in Circle that year at the age of 102, which again is almost surely inaccurate (Bureau of the Census 1950).

Historically, all eight of the American Munchausens documented in Richard Dorson's tall tale study lived between 1796 and 1950, and it's important to recognize that Sam also lived squarely during this period. In any case, the remarkable and important thing is that Sam's tall tales, like his age, have long outlived him.

Sam Peter Vagwandak

Although Sam's birth date is not known with any high degree of certainty, we do know from the content of his stories that he reached manhood well before the Klondike gold rush of 1898, when he rode steamboats up and down the Yukon River and mixed socially with white prospectors of that era. Sam may very well have rubbed shoulders with American gold miners who were conversant in tall tales and apparently knew the mountainous back country very well. In 1900 Sam turned up as a guide for U.S. Army Captain Charles Farnsworth, who was trying to locate a suitable route for a telegraph line connecting Fort Egbert at Eagle City to Fort Liscum at Valdez. Sam reportedly guided Farnsworth from Eagle City as far as Kechumstuck Summit over an old Indian trail (see Webb, 1993:159).

One person who knew Sam, the late Elliot Johnson Sr., was also Han, originally from Charley Village but later on moved to Fort Yukon. Elliot, Kenneth's maternal grandfather, characterized Sam as a big heavy set man about six feet tall who told a lot of "fairy tales." Sarah Malcom (1975) of Eagle Village recalled that Sam had two wives. The first was a Han woman named Martha, who gave birth to one of Sam's sons. Indeed, Martha shows up in the 1910 U.S. census along with Sam's adopted son Elisha.

Sam's second wife, named Myra, was a Gwichyaa Gwich'in woman from Circle who, according to Sarah Malcolm, bore him three daughters, Edna, Mary Lois, and Rosa. In the 1920 U.S. census Myra is listed as thirty-four years old, twenty-four years younger than Sam, and at that time they had an infant daughter named Edna Peter and were living in the same household with Sam's stepdaughter Hannah and four stepsons, all under the age of fifteen with the surname of Nathaniel. Apparently Myra, like Sam, had an earlier marriage, and some family trees indicate that her earlier marriage was to William "David" Nathaniel. Some of these trees also give her maiden name as Solomon.

The 1939 BIA village census taken at Circle and undated Episcopal Church parish records at Fort Yukon (apparently from the late 1940s or early 1950s) show that Sam and his new family moved from Eagle Village to Circle City sometime between 1920 and 1939 (Bureau of Indian Affairs 1939). By the mid-1940s a government social worker visiting Circle noted that Sam was still receiving Old Age Assistance and was "practically helpless as a result of a crippled condition" which forced him to hobble about on two canes (Patchen 1946:7).

Irene Roberts, the daughter of Malcolm Sandy Roberts, was raised in Circle and recalls that Sam was "a kind and gentle old man who walked with a cane, became blind, and wore a hearing aid" (2011). Sandy recalled that Sam had a fish camp forty miles above Circle at the confluence of Webber Creek and the Yukon River. He would go upriver to his fish camp seated in his traditional Indian canoe or poling boat hand-propelled by "juk toh." Juk toh consists of two poles or sticks, one held in each hand, that are planted in the shallow river bottom along the shoreline, in alternating fashion. Going against the current in this fashion requires great arm strength and considerable dexterity, working with the eddies. Roberts also recalls that Sam talked about trapping on the Mississippi River and about going to Seattle, giving credence to the notion that Sam himself may have traveled and created at least some episodes of the tall tales which are attached to his name.

Roberts also remembers that Sam went around to every house in the village at Christmas and New Year's, saying "Happy Merry Christmas!" and giving out gifts. He would give Black Bull chewing tobacco to the women and tsaih (red ochre) to the men. When the senior author showed Irene transcripts of her father's Sam Peter stories, she was quite incredulous. She had never heard her father tell these tales and didn't think he would ever stoop to talking this way about the Devil.

At his death Sam was living in Circle with his daughter Mary Lois and his two stepsons, Amos and David Nathaniel. Mary Lois, also known as Lois Alexander, now deceased, once told me she had no photographs of her father because her house in Fort Yukon burned down many years ago, destroying all of her family possessions. But David Nathaniel says he has seen a photograph of Sam which belongs either to his sister Edna Nathaniel or his niece Nancy Joseph, both of whom live in Fairbanks. We have not yet had an opportunity to see this photograph.

Context and Conclusion

It may have been Sam's association with gold rush prospectors that led him to become a teller of tall tales about himself. Indeed, several episodes about Sam are set in Dawson City, where there was a big gold rush in 1896. Today Sam is fondly remembered as an "Indian comedian" whose stories are unlike anything else circulating in the Gwich'in language tradition but are reminiscent, in a fashion, of the much older Vasaagihdzak tales (see McKennan 1965 and Mishler 2001), another comic story cycle popular among the Gwich'in. Vasaagihdzak has a personality reminiscent of Sam Peter's, but Vasaagihdzak's stories are situated far in the distant past, while Sam's stories are set in recent historic times. Most Sam Peter stories are probably fifty to a hundred years old, while the Vasaagihdzak stories appear to be quite ancient, possibly originating in prehistory, and are closely connected to the robust Cree cycle of stories about Wesakechak (see Skinner 1916).

Both Vasaagihdzak and Sam Peter are smug, bumbling fools who think they are just a little smarter than the next guy, and sometimes they are, but all too often their pride goes before a fall. Most of all, they lack common sense. One difference is that Sam Peter in oral tradition is more of a showman than Vasaagihdzak, more self-conscious of his image, while Vasaagihdzak is credited with helping to make the world friendlier to humans. More importantly, however, is the matter of audience. Vasaagihdzak stories are generally told to children, to educate and amuse them, while Sam Peter stories are told to adults, often at funerals, to cheer people up when they are feeling depressed.

Many of the Sam Peter stories turn the everyday Gwich'in world upside down. For example, when Sam Peter goes to Seattle and to St. Michael he is recognized and greeted by everyone. And of course he is also famous in Dawson City. In Seattle he's the perfect inversion of the average Indian, who gets totally ignored and becomes largely invisible when visiting a big city. Or when Sam Peter encounters a snake, a creature not even found in Alaska, he does something the Gwich'in and other Alaskan Indians find very frightening and disgusting. He eats it. Inversion and the reversal of social norms follow him everywhere.

Most of the episodes in the Sam Peter cycle recall Sam's vanity, stupidity, and pretensions as a rich dandy. The central flaw in Sam's character is his pride, his large ego. The Sam Peter of oral tradition is a man who, contrary to the everyday norms of Han and Gwich'in social conduct, basks heavily in his own knowledge, prestige, and influence. In these respects he is like a modern-day Vasaagihdzak.

One unusual thing is that Sam Peter is primarily remembered in Gwich'in oral tradition when in fact he was Han and presumably spoke Han as his first language. We infer this in the translator's note to Sandy Roberts telling of Sam's Adventures Outside of Alaska (see above). Sam is still remembered fondly in his home community of Eagle Village, but the stories told about him there are much more fragmented than those we heard from Gwich'in speakers.

If the Sam Peter of the Gwich'in tall tale cycle was indeed the Sam Peter of historic record, we can speculate that his stories may have caught on in Gwich'in due to his having learned to speak Gwich'in as a second Native language or by his having learned to speak compelling English.

Upon hearing and reading Sam's stories, even in English translation, we begin to grasp the kind of personal magnetism and infectious sense of humor he must have had as a storyteller. If he was not some kind of a regional communal creation, as Max Beck believes, then he may have become a popular figure in oral tradition by creating some or all of these tall tales himself. If on the other hand he was indeed a communal creation, the living cycle of tales which carries his name has clearly been elaborated by other male tradition bearers who continue to shape and reshape our enjoyment of Alaska Gwich'in humor.

Acknowledgments

An earlier version of this paper and Kenneth's oral performance of Sam Peter stories were jointly presented to the American Folklore Society Annual Meeting in Portland, Oregon, on October 30, 1998. Thanks to the late Sandy Roberts, David Salmon, and Daniel John and also to Trimble Gilbert, Kenneth Frank, and Burns Frank for sharing their tales.

**It turns out that the episode told to us by Burns Frank is not a traditional Sam Peter story. We might even call it apocryphal. According to both Kenneth Frank and Christopher Johnson, it was actually a true story that happened to a white man named Lynn Short, who is now deceased but lived in Fort Yukon for many years. At the same time, this story has many Sam Peter story qualities: a man who thinks he's very smart gets outfoxed and ends up looking silly and stupid.*

14. Mizhur, Monsieur?
A Gwich'in Card Game

Introduction

To the Gwich'in of northeastern Alaska, playing cards, called "lagar" (< French "la carte"> have not only been a great source of entertainment since their introduction shortly after European contact during the 1840s and 1850s but have also served aesthetically as models for names and beadwork designs.[1] Although rarely seen today, diamonds and hearts were formerly incorporated into beaded moosehide mittens, purses, moccasins, knife sheaths, and rifle cases (Sloan 1982). In addition, the Gwich'in have identified two of the standard card suits with features of their own natural and cultural environment. While hearts are simply "ch'idrii"[2], a direct literal translation of the English word "heart" and spades are called "shovel", clubs are promptly recognized as "dagoo kwai'" ('ptarmigan feet') and diamonds are "ch'adhah tr'ihchoo" ('skin boats', after the shape of moose skin boats).

The Gwich'in play a wide range of card games, and in the villages of Chalkyitsik and Venetie there has always been a cabin designated as "the card house" where both young and old men gather almost daily to gamble at "Pan" (short for Panguingue, the Filipino card game) and Stud Poker.[3] There are also several children's card games with Gwich'in names such as Gasinaa, better known in English as "Stealing Bundles" and Gwich'uu, a variant of the Anglo game "Go Boom" (Morehead et. al. 1964:474-475).

Adult games include Vitsi' (lit. 'its tail') and Mizhur. While Vitsi' appears to have no obvious European or American counterpart, it's a relatively simple game both structurally and psychologically, and the same can be said for Gwich'uu. The non-gambling game of most interest and complexity and the one played with the most enthusiasm by Gwich'in adults is Mizhur. Though fading rapidly in popularity since the introduction of television in the 1970s and 1980s, Mizhur appears to be an obsolescent French card game which has been adapted and preserved in the North American subarctic, like many of the Gwich'in contact-traditional contra dances (Mishler 1993), long after its progenitors have disappeared from the European continent.

However, what seems to me more likely, is that Mizhur represents a regional historic convergence between two or more structurally related trump games such as Triumph and Partnership Whist in England, Pinochle and Euchre in the United States, and Écarté and Bezique (or Bésigue) in France, the latter being an ancestor of pinochle (see Morehead et. al. 1964:116-118, 232, 246, 361).

My hypothesis is that such a convergence took place shortly after European contact with the Gwich'in in the mid-19th century and that the significance and popularity of the game reflects the shift from a subsistence bartering economy to one based on the commercial trapping and sale of fur pelts. I shall elaborate and return to this notion after describing the mechanics of how the game is played.

The name Mizhur clearly appears to be of French derivation, (<"monsieur"), although it may have some associations with the adjective "majeur" ('major'). In the game, "Mizhur" refers specifically to the King of Hearts, while the Jack of Clubs is known as "Mizhur tsal" or "Little Mizhur." Among the Han people farther up the Yukon River at Eagle Village, the same game is known as Bizhur, which I have written about elsewhere (see Mishler and Simeone 2004: Appendix C). Like Gwich'in fiddling and square dancing (Mishler 1993), the rules for Mizhur appear to have been borrowed from Anglo-Scots or French-Canadian Métis culture sometime during the mid-to-late 19th century, but since then they have gradually evolved into something distinctive to the Gwich'in.

Just as playing card logos have been extended from the sphere of card playing into the sphere of beadwork and toponomy, so too has the word "Mizhur" been extended from the sphere of card games into the sphere of formal social greetings, where it's spoken simultaneously with a handshake between friends who have been long absent from one another. It's also spoken in this fashion between neighbors on New Year's Day. This long-established custom emulates the friendly handshake and greeting extended to the Gwich'in by French-Canadian voyageurs who traveled to Alaska with the Hudson's Bay Company during the early fur-trading era.

In this greeting context its presumed function was to recognize a man or woman in a somewhat formal manner. Despite its masculine French meaning, I've heard "Mizhur" exchanged between Gwich'in women as well as men. Such a greeting (the word plus the friendly handshake), focuses attention on the hands and has its semiotic correlative in the metaphor "a hand of cards," in which the hands are also at the locus of interaction and exchange. In Venetie, the game of Mizhur is more popular among women than men, and it's not uncommon for two games to be going on simultaneously in the same household on a warm summer afternoon.

The Players--

Mizhur is a game for four adult players; neither more nor less will suffice. These four players must sit opposite from one another to form two partnerships or sides, as in Bridge. An often-preferred partnership is two men versus two women, particularly if they are married couples, but women may also play against women. The language of discourse during play is nearly always Gwich'in.

The Deck--

A full pack of 52 cards is used but only 36 are dealt or drawn. The power rank of cards in each of the four suits is A,10,K,Q,J,9,8,7,6. This ranking is closely akin to the nineteenth century French trump games of Marjolet and Bezique (or Bésigue), except that the French games do away with the sixes (Gibson 1974:24-32). One suit, more powerful than all the others, is drawn from the pack and designated as trump or "shriitin" (lit. 'knife lying motionless'). The ace of trump is accordingly "shriitin choo" ('big trump') and the 10 of trump is "shriitin tsal" (little trump), while the non-pointer trumps (Q,J, 9, 8, 7, and 6) constitute "gii lii". The 7's are called "inglis da'ąįį" or "English axes" because the design of an English-made steel axe closely resembles the shape of the number 7. Non-trump aces and 10s are identified as "din" and face cards are "ch'inya'" ('faces').

In terms of taking tricks, the most powerful card in the deck is the King of Hearts ("Mizhur"), followed immediately by the Jack of Clubs ("Mizhur tsal"), and then the ace of trumps ("shriitin choo") and the other trumps by rank. The Queen of Hearts is "tr'injaa" ('woman') and the 9, 8, 7, and 6 non-trumps are "vatsal ch'ahaii". The smallest cards in the deck--the 5, 4, 3, and deuce--form a kitty, which is known collectively as "the Company". Jokers are not used at all. When these cards are drawn out of the Company two at a time (two cards are equal to "one dollar") to award the winners of a hand, they are referred to as "laraa" < French "l'argent" ('money'). Unlike poker chips, however, these cards have no cash value at the end of the game. They simply provide a handy means of keeping score without recourse to pen and paper.

Object of the Game--

The winner of the game is the side which captures all the "laraa" and ends up "owning the Company". The winner of each hands receives two cards from the Company, and since there is a total of sixteen cards in "the Company" at the start of the game, a full game nearly always requires a minimum of eight hands.[4]

After all the dollars or laraa is paid out of the Company, the two sides or partnerships must begin paying one another "a dollar" at a time. This continues until one side goes completely broke, which ends the game. The odds are that the "dollars" will see-saw back and forth between the two sides for a considerable length of time, and this occasionally results in a game which lasts for eight or nine hours. When Mizhur games become prolonged this way, it's quite common for substitute players to enter. Generally there are other people drifting in and out of the house, either members of the host family, or individuals stopping by to talk and watch the game. This free substitution of players allows a long game to proceed without exhaustion or tedium.

The immediate object of each hand of Mizhur is to capture tricks containing "pointers". A point is earned by a side when it captures either an ace or a 10 or when it captures the final trick of the hand. In Marjolet and Bésigue these two pointer cards, aces and 10s, are called 'brisques.' A side which manages to capture the final trick of the hand with a 10 is awarded two extra points. Normally, there are nine points in a hand, and the side which gains five of these points will earn "one dollar". If it so happens that each side captures five points, they each receive one card ("fifty cents") from the Company.

Preliminaries and the Deal--

In the evening, especially when there are visitors present, someone is liable to shout "Mizhur hatsee gooya'!" ('Let's play Mizhur!) Players then arrange themselves around a playing surface, which may vary from a large round wooden table to the corner of someone's bed. It's customary, however, to cover the playing surface with a folded tablecloth, blanket, or large towel. One person arbitrarily takes it upon himself to shuffle the cards ("nihtee tth'aak inlii" or "t'eechiirilii") and deal out three cards face down to the other players. One player is the banker or custodian for the laraa and pays out cards to the winning team at the end of each hand. The deal begins with the player immediately to the left of the dealer receiving the first card, and so on in a clockwise manner, one card at a time. When all players have received three cards, the dealer turns up one more card from the top of the deck and sticks it under the deck face up at a ninety degree angle. This turn-up card indicates which suit will be trump for the duration of the hand.

The Play--

The person directly to the left of the dealer leads first. He or she may play any card, and the opponents, as well as the dealer's partner, may also play any card, for following suit is entirely optional. Nevertheless, the highest card in the suit led takes the trick unless it's trumped or unless Mizhur or Mizhur tsal are played. Play proceeds rapidly clockwise, and the person who takes the trick becomes the one to lead off the first card for the next trick. All players draw a new card off the top of the deck after the close of each trick, with the person who captured the trick being the first to draw, and the other players drawing in clockwise order.

If someone draws or is dealt the six of trump, that person may at any time substitute the six for any higher upturned trump stuck beneath the deck. The game continues at a very fast tempo until all the cards have been drawn and those left in each player's hand have been played. Participants play their cards without hesitation, almost never taking more than a split second to deliberate which card they will play. In the final draw, the upturned trump goes to the player who draws last. Altogether, there are nine deet'ah or tricks to a hand.

At the end of the hand, the person collecting tricks for each partnership flips over the trick cards face side up in a broad fanfold and verbally counts the pointers. If successful, this person collects laraa from the Company or, if the Company is broke, from the other team. In Venetie the women quickly slip their laraa underneath a corner of the tablecloth, so no one else can tell how much or how little has been saved. In case of a lost hand, laraa is doled out from its hiding place. A sample hand is shown in Figure 1 below.

Strategy--

The end-game is often the most exciting part of the play. After all the draw cards have been taken, there are just three tricks left to be played, and these are usually the highest point-getters. Consequently, most players try to save their "pointers" and their highest trump for these final tricks. The exclamation, "Dhiit'ah" means 'I trumped it.' The exclamation "Gwit'eh" means 'I cut the bottom card without using any trump, playing the same suit as the lead off card.' Good players pay close attention to which of the highest cards have already been played, calculating which ones are left unplayed. Of course, partners try to help each other out by tossing on "pointers" when it becomes obvious or highly likely that a trick will be taken by the first partner to play. In fact, such a strategy is fundamental to a side attempting to "make bread" in the early going.

Cheating--

An important part of the game is slyly taking advantage of your opponents. Players are known to make toe kicks or nudges under the card table as prompts. They also use winks of the eye. These nonverbal gestures are made to persuade one's partner to throw down a 10 card early in the hand, so that the nudger or winker can take it with a trump card or with Mizhur or Little Mizhur.

Making Bread--

When one side manages to capture all of the first five pointers played in a given hand, they are said to "make bread" (łuuch'yaa), and a side which "makes bread" is entitled to two dollars (four cards) at the end of the hand instead of one. If there is no pointer thrown on one of the tricks in the sequence, one of the partners is likely to say, "łuuch'yaa tsį̨į̨" ('We won't make bread.') However, for a side to "make bread", it must capture five points exactly. After a side makes bread they continue playing out the hand until they lose one trick.

If someone from the opposing side throws an extra pointer on the trick which produces the fifth point, thereby making six points instead of the desired five, the result is called łuuch'yaa k'in ("burned bread"). The side earning six points will still win the hand but will not be awarded more than the usual "one dollar" and will usually receive a big laugh from their opponents. If players succeed in making bread or if they manage to "cut" or "kill" their opponents' shriitin choo (ace of trumps), they will continue to talk about it for years and rub it in whenever they see their opponents.

Variation--

One variation which I have been told about in Fort Yukon but have not personally seen proceeds as follows. After all the cards are dealt, no trump is turned up by the dealer. Instead, the player to the left of the dealer plays one card face down. This card is usually, but not necessarily, a pointer. The others do likewise, and then the dealer turns up trump. Surprise! This usually gives one side three or four points right away, and the action gets hot because the side which wins these three or four points will really be trying to "make bread" on the very next trick.

Analysis --

A key to the significance of the game lies in the fundamental linguistic metaphors which accompany the game, particularly such terms as "laraa", "the Company", and "making bread", and from the structure of the game, which involves lots of rapid giving and taking until one partnership has a monopoly on all the money. In this respect Mizhur symbolically defines the Indians' historic relationship with the Hudson's Bay Company in the mid-19th century and with the Alaska Commercial Company in the late 19th and early 20th. In its beginnings the game may well have provided a convenient way to practice handling cash without the risk of losing that cash.

Because the Hudson's Bay Company conducted nearly all its trading by barter, money came into use only after American prospectors flooded into the country during the Gold Rush era of the 1890s. It would seem that Mizhur's emphasis on money therefore reflects a fairly modern-day cash economy. According to the late Elijah John of Fort Yukon (1983) and Sarah Frank of Venetie (Mishler 2001), the Gwich'in didn't know anything about money until the gold rush at Circle in 1894. Yet since the "laraa" paid out of the Mizhur Company's kitty comes from a French loan word, and since the Hudson's Bay Company employed several French-Canadians as interpreters at Fort Yukon, it would seem that the game may well predate the arrival of the first Americans there in 1867.

There is one tantalizing piece of historic evidence that Antoine Houle, the young interpreter who helped found Fort Yukon in 1847, was engaged in playing cards with his Indian wives (Séguin 1863), in a house located just behind the Fort. Much to the consternation of Anglican missionaries and officers of the Hudson's Bay Company, Houle persisted in keeping two and sometimes three wives, following a tradition that had been well-established by powerful Gwich'in trading chiefs and medicine men. Houle was a Métis (of mixed French-Canadian and Indian blood) and was noted for his remarkable ability to speak many Indian languages, including Gwich'in, along with French, English, and presumably the pidgin jargon known as Broken Slavey or Slavey Jargon (see Chapter 10 above). In fact, the Slavey Jargon swear word, "Salabrie!" (perhaps derived from the French saloperie 'trash, rubbish') is still used by people playing the game (see the game transcript below).

Though we cannot be certain what card games Houle played with his wives and the other Indians at Fort Yukon, we can speculate that he played a leading role either in the conception of Mizhur, or in its development and popularization. Other French speakers who lived in and around Fort Yukon and may have invented or introduced the game were François Boucher, a contemporary of Houle's employed by the Hudson's Bay Company for several decades; Moses Mercier, a French-Canadian who managed the Alaska Commercial Company store at Fort Yukon from 1868 until 1874; and Joe Ladue, a French-Canadian prospector who arrived from upstate New York in 1885.

"Making bread" allows another point of entry into the semiotics of Mizhur, for flour used to make bannock was undoubtedly introduced by the Scots employed by the Hudson's Bay Company, so the association of "making bread" with a streak of exceptionally good luck in cards suggests that in the early days after contact flour for making bread was a high-prestige commodity. Today Gwich'in pan-fried bannock is still a highly popular form of bread on both sides of the border.

Another very interesting aspect of the game's structure is its emphasis on partnerships. One might expect such a popular game to mirror certain aspects of Gwich'in social structure, and it does. In playing the game two people work together and contribute points to get their dollars from the Company. The ethnographic record indicates that partnerships are also essential to maintaining the Gwich'in hunting and trapping economy. During the 1930s Robert McKennan found that a Neets'it Gwich'in man generally had one or more partners (shitł'ii) within and outside of his own band, that such partnerships were based on friendship rather than kinship, and that partners mutually supported one another in the division of large game animals (1965:63).

Another skilled ethnographer, Richard Nelson, found such partnerships highly essential to Dranjik Gwich'in trappers but noted that while partners generally share food, gear, and cabins, they run separate traplines and do not share the profits of their catch (1973:151-152). At this point, perhaps, the analogy between trapping partners and card game partners breaks down, for Mizhur partners share equally in the winnings, even though they may contribute unequally in being lucky and playing smartly to capture points.

Two-couple participation at a Mizhur table is also strongly reminiscent of the two couple set used in the Double Jig dance and the traditional bond formed between two Gwich'in couples who hunted, trapped, and lived together during the early 19th century. The arrangement of two skin tents facing each other, sharing the same fireplace is called "nihts'įį gwiwiich'įį" (see Burch and Mishler 1995; Mishler 2001). What this suggests is that beyond individual partnerships two-couple or two-household partnerships were and are also important. The Gwich'in were exposed to many new cultural forms during the early contact period, but they selected and adopted and adapted those forms which were compatible with their traditional ways of communicating. Contextualized, it becomes easier to understand why the they took more strongly to Mizhur than games such as Pinochle or Canasta.

The rapid see-saw of Company dollars in Mizhur would seem to reflect the fluctuating price paid for fur pelts form one season to another, the Indians' competition with one another, and the seemingly endless cycle of accumulating credit and debt with the Hudson's Bay Company and then, after the sale of Alaska, with the Alaska Commercial Company. Although Mizhur is certainly not gambling for high stakes, the winners take all, and the losers go home broke.

The price of fur as well as the number of animals trapped during a given season depend not upon the hard work or skill of the Indian trapper but upon remote and uncontrollable factors such as game cycles, weather conditions, or the latest fashion trends in Paris, London, and New York. Consequently, dealing across the counter with the trader or fur buyer (i.e. "the Company") is a lot like playing several hands of cards. While strategy plays a definite role, that role is certainly very limited, since it's really a matter of luck as to what cards you draw and how well you do.

Although some Gwich'in men continue to trap fur to earn a small cash income, the great days of trapping are largely over, and we may ask why Mizhur continues to be so popular socially today. The answer seems to reside within a different sphere of pleasure--an antidote to the cultural and technological hegemony represented by English language television. The card game's social emphasis on face-to-face partnerships, either through marriage or through hunting, trapping, and fishing activities, continues to sustain the Gwich'in subsistence economy. And from that perspective, playing Mizhur is an ideal but long overlooked way of revitalizing Gwich'in language and culture.

Acknowledgments

An earlier draft of this paper was presented at the American Folklore Society Annual Meeting in Nashville, Tennessee, October, 1983. I am most grateful to Johnny and Sarah Frank and the Rev. David Salmon and his wife Sarah for introducing me to Mizhur in 1972, but since then I have also benefitted greatly from the observations of Hamel Frank, Elijah John, Kenneth Frank, and Charlotte Douthit.

Endnotes

1. Old Man Alexander and his wife Maria, who appear in the 1910 U.S. Census for Fort Yukon, were better known by their Gwich'in names, Lagar Dyahchii and Lagar Shyaaghan ('Old Man Card' and 'Old Woman Card'), undoubtedly for their penchant for playing card games.

2. Ch'idrii is also the name of a mountain where Johnny and Sarah Frank had a sheep hunting camp. The river which flows by this mountain is called Ch'idriinjik ('Heart Mountain River'). See Caldwell (1981).

3. Pan is a low stakes game with an ante of only 50 cents. Since a stack of chips costs just $20, almost anyone can afford to play. Stud poker, with much higher stakes, is generally played when the village is flush with money, such as during the summer when fire-fighting crews have just been paid.

4. The only exception to this would occur if one side should "make bread" in the midst of winning all of its other hands in succession. A discussion of "making bread" follows.

Fig. 1. Sample Hand of Mizhur with East-West and North-South as Partners

Sequence	East	South	West	North	Results
North's Deal	K♠ 9♥ 8♦	K♣ 7♥ 6♥	^J♣ J♦ 7♣	A♣ Q♠ 9♣	Uptumed trump is K♦
Trick 1	9♥	6♥	7♣	9♣	East wins
Draw	*K♥	8♣	10♥	J♠	
Trick 2	K♠	8♣	10♥	J♠	East wins (1 pt)
Draw	7♦	8♠	10♠	Q♥	
Trick 3	7♦	7♥	J♦	Q♠	West wins
Draw	7♠	A♠	6♠	A♥	
Trick 4	8♦	8♠	10♠	Q♥	East wins (1 pt)
Draw	6♣	J♥	10♣	9♣	
Trick 5	7♠	A♠	6♠	A♥	South wins (2 pts)
Draw	A♦	6♦ /K♦	Q♦	8♥	South trades 6♦ for uptumed K♦
Trick 6	6♣	K♣	Q♦	8♥	West wins
Draw	9♦	6♦	10♦	Q♣	
Trick 7	9♦	J♥	^J♣	9♣	West wins
Trick 8	A♦	6♦	10♦	Q♣	East wins (2 pts)
Trick 9	*K♥	K♦	10♣	A♣	East wins (2 pts + 1 for final trick=3)

Each player receives 3 cards in the opening deal.
Final results of hand: E/W side eams 7 points and receives $1 (2 cards) from "the Company".
N/S side eams 2 points but receives no laraa

*Mazhur
^Mazhur Tsal

Pointers: A,10

Rank (after Mazhur and Mazhur Tsal):
A, 10, K, Q, J, 9, 8, 7, 6

Mizhur Dialogue Transcript (mixed Gwich'in and English)

Recorded on videotape at Kenneth and Caroline Frank's home in Arctic Village by Craig Mishler, May 22, 2000. Translated by Kenneth Frank.

Game Participants: Jimmy Roberts (J), Hannah J. Solomon (H), Florence Newman (F), and Caroline Tritt-Frank (C). Jimmy and Florence are partners; Hannah and Caroline are partners.

F: Did somebody get only two cards [from the deal]?

H: We got five [including herself and her partner C].

J: In 1959 she [F] was just a young girl hopping around. Don't make a mistake. We got only five cards. You just gave me all aces.

[H&C capture two pointers]

C: My cards are no good.

J: It's mine again [taking the trick]!

C: Ch'ah! [a Gwich'in swear word meaning "Raggedy!"] I got no trump. [She lies. The video shows she holds Big Mizhur.]

H: We win again.

J: Who cut the deck?

C: Gwit'eh. ['I cut the bottom card without trumping it.' i.e. C plays a higher card in the same suit as the lead off.]

J: My friend [F] took the Deet'ah [the trick].

C: Is he thinking about it? [referring to J. Note: When playing Mizhur you're not supposed to hesitate or think about what card you will play next.]

H: Ah shit! I threw away a little trump.

O: That's not a trump!

F: [To J] That's mine. [Hoping J will toss on a pointer.]

C: Ho! [throws down Big Mizhur]

H: We've got five points now.

J: [To H] They're taping you on video. Act goofy. [To CM] You're 30 years old.

C: In one hand I burned my own bread. [laughs] Ooh. Shriitin Choh. [the Ace of trump turned up under the deck after the deal.]

F: Why don't you say "Haa'aii" ['Thank you'] again?

C: Salabrie! [Swear word from Slavey Jargon < Fr. saloperie]

H: Oozhuu! [Gwich'in word meaning 'No good!']

C: I did something bad. Take it. Sacrifice. [laughs] When my grandpa played Mizhur he wiggled his foot under the table, but once he touched someone else's foot instead of his own partner's. [laughs]

J: [To F] Your hands are shiny just like your father's were.

F: My hands are shiny because I wash dishes.
C: I don't know what's going on here.
J: I don't think any of us know what's going on.
C: I'll just kill it with a little eight.
F: Vahalt'an. [This word refers to the noise made when slapping or thumping the card on the table.]
C: Little Mizhur, goodbye. [someone else has just played Big Mizhur]
J: [To F] I don't think we'll ever win again.
F: We've only got one dollar [of card money or laraa]!
H: [To C] We had a lot of pointers when you burned your bread.
C: But right after that hand we made bread.
H: When we cut it I thought they only had four pointers but actually they had five.
J: [Aside to CM] You're Charlie Peter's friend, right?
F: We just took two pointers.
C: [laughs] Because J burned their bread.
J: You almost burned your hands [for trying to take a trick that wasn't yours.]
C: Ninjik gwanzhį̨ kwaa! ["Don't cheat!"]
J: I cut it.
H: No pointers.
J: [To F] Hey, your glasses are just like rope.
H: I'll hit you [takes a fake punch at J].
C: I found out J cheats. We caught him in the act.
H: Who threw the 7?
J: I don't know. [eating candy, looking away]
F: Well, now we're bankrupt.

Some Terminology and Sayings:

łuuchy'aa tsį̨į̨ 'We won't get bread'
łuuch'yaa k'in 'Burned bread'
Deet'ah 'one cut or trick'
Dhiit'ah 'I cut it or trumped it' [This means that the speaker took the trick, not that they cut the deck.]
Juu nihteech'iinlii? or Juu łihteech'iinlii? 'Who shuffled and dealt the cards?'
Example: Caroline nihteech'iinlii. 'Caroline shuffled.'
Nihteech'ihihłyaa. 'I shuffled.'

15. Njah, Njoh:

Lobsticks Among the Gwich'in and Others

Introduction

It's not known exactly or even approximately when the cultural phenomenon of creating lobsticks first came into existence. A lobstick is a spruce or pine tree, physically altered with an axe to remove branches and create a simple locational landmark or establish a living tribute to some person. In the nineteenth century it was a widespread symbolic creation, known all across subarctic Canada and northern Alaska, where it was practiced by the Gwich'in, the Koyukon, the northern Tutchone, the Cree, and the Hudson's Bay Company voyageurs.

Lobsticks have been called many things through the years. In English the words top sticks, lopsticks, loptsticks, lopped sticks, may poles, and lodge poles are some of the synonyms. What I want to demonstrate here is that lobsticks are highly interesting because they are both living organisms and cultural artifacts. They have a long and distinguished history in the north, assume a variety of shapes and sizes, and continue to integrate nature and culture in an imaginative non-verbal form.

Early Accounts

The earliest historic description of lobsticks that I know of comes from the pen of the explorer and fur trader Alexander Mackenzie, who discovered them somewhere in the Mackenzie River delta, north of present-day Inuvik, on June 18, 1789, in an area that serves as part of the Gwich'in homeland but which also borders on Inuit territory. Mackenzie (1966:69) said, very briefly, "We observed a great number of trees, in different places, whose branches had been lopped off to the tops. They denote the immediate abode of the natives and probably serve for signals to direct each other to their respective winter quarters."

A second more vivid and detailed description came from the hand of Frances Simpson, the young 18-year-old wife of Governor George Simpson of the Hudson's Bay Company, as she was traveling west by canoe from Montreal with her husband. On June 25, 1830, at some place near York Factory, she was an eye-witness to the creation of a lobstick in her honor and duly recorded the event in her diary:

> the Voyageurs agreed among themselves to cut a "May Pole," or "Lopped Stick" for me; which is a tall Pine Tree, lopped of all its branches excepting those at the top, which are cut in a round bunch: it is then barked: and mine (being a memorable one) was honored with a red feather, and streamers of purple ribband tied to a poll, and fastened to the top of the Tree, so as to be seen above every other object: the surrounding trees were then cut down, in order to leave it open to the Lake. Bernard (the Guide) then presented me with a Gun, the contents of which I

> discharged against the Tree, and Mr. Miles engraved my name, and the date, on the trunk, so that my "Lopped Stick" will be conspicuous as long as it stands, among the number of those to be seen along the banks of different Lakes and Rivers (Nute 1954: 17).

What Frances Simpson tells us is that not only was the pine or spruce tree lopped of its lower branches, but that the tree was also debarked. And importantly, her name was engraved on the trunk of it, and that a ceremony took place afterwards, in which the person being recognized and honored fired a gun into the tree. It also shows that the custom of making lobsticks was already known far to the east of the Gwich'in homeland before direct historic contact.

Another person to write about lopsticks was Robert Michael Ballantyne in his book, *Hudson's Bay or Everyday Life in the Wilds of North America* (1848). In late June, 1845, Ballantyne camped for the night at one place which had lots of lopsticks and says that the person who was honored by a lopstick was also "always expected to acknowledge his sense of the honour conferred upon him by presenting the boat's crew with a pint of grog, either on the spot or at the first establishment they meet with. He is then considered as having paid for his footing, and may ever afterwards pass scot-free."

Just before he came to Alaska the naturalist Robert Kennicott (1942:59), noted on a canoe trip in 1859 that:

> It is customary for the voyageurs to make what they call a 'lob stick' or 'may pole' in honor of any gentleman who may be passengers with them, and on Cross Lake ours made one for Mr. Hubbard and myself. A tall pine, standing out on a point in the lake, was climbed by one of the voyageurs, who, with an axe, cut off all the branches, excepting a tuft at the top, thus rendering it very conspicuous. As we paddled off it was saluted with three cheers and the discharge of the guns, we of course being

> expected to acknowledge the compliment by a treat at the first opportunity.

Kennicott's lobstick was located somewhere on the voyageurs canoe route between Lake Superior and Lake Winnipeg. Other early 19th century accounts are related in Carolyn Podruchny's remarkable book, *Making the Voyageur World* (2006:134-142).

The practice of making lobsticks either spread quickly north and west as new forts were built on the Canadian frontier, or perhaps it was already there when the first voyageurs arrived, as part of an aboriginal tradition. It's still an open question as to whether the lobstick and its attendant ceremonies were part of indigenous Native American tradition, or whether northern indigenous peoples simply borrowed it from the early voyageurs.

Gwich'in Traditions

In 1861, while traveling through the Gwich'in homeland along the Porcupine River, the Anglican missionary W.W. Kirkby noted in his journal that "Coming through the Ramparts the Indians in my canoe managed to get to the top of the rocks in a favorable place to cut a 'top stick' in remembrance of my visit to the Youcon" (Kirkby 1861).

Two years later Kirkby's successor, the Rev. Robert McDonald, noted in his journal for August 14, 1863: "Encamped near Janet Barber's loptstick [somewhere above the mouth of the Sheenjek where it flows into the Porcupine River]." And then again on August 20: "Camped above Vikwatrul's loptstick today [somewhere above the mouth of North River]" (McDonald 1863). Antoine Houle, the longstanding interpreter at Fort Yukon who helped McDonald preach to the Gwich'in, was not actually Gwich'in but a Métis who spoke Gwich'in. After Houle died on October 22, 1868, McDonald duly noted his lobstick the following year (McDonald 1869).

What we don't know is who actually made these lobsticks, the Gwich'in themselves or the men working for the Hudson's Bay Company. What we do know is that they were made to honor individual Gwich'in and Métis employed by the Company. Clearly, in an age before there was much mass media, lobsticks were a way of broadcasting and conferring celebrity status on certain individuals. Such individuals may have been as distinguished as the wife of the Governor of the Hudson's Bay Company, but they may also have been important only locally, as with Vikwatrul, about whom we now know virtually nothing except his name. At any rate, it's clear that men and women and children were honored by lobsticks.

Although they were first documented by non-Native visitors to the Gwich'in homeland, explorers and missionaries, I was curious to know what the Gwich'in thought about the creation of lobsticks. My first indication that the Gwich'in themselves had a lobstick tradition came from looking at a list of place names on the Gwich'in Social and Cultural Institute web site. There we find a contemporary place called Njoh Njii'ee lit. 'Lobstick it stands'. The name refers to a specific hill in the Campbell Hills on the East Channel of the Mackenzie River, Northwest Territories. According to the *Gwich'in Place Names Atlas*:

> This name refers to a lobstick tree which once stood on a hill near the outlet of Gull Creek. According to Hyacinthe Andre people would select a tall tree standing off on its own. They would climb up the tree and cut all the branches off near the bottom of the tree, leave two branches, climb further up the tree and cut some more branches just leaving the top branches. This was a marker which indicated a good fishing place. Many years ago Hyacinthe saw such a marker at Loche Creek where there are thousands of loche in the fall... According to Tony Andre...this is a good spot for blueberries and cranberries and many people in the Delta come here to pick them. (https://atlas.gwichin.ca/index.html?module=gwichin.module.main#)

Other lobsticks helped to mark good subsistence fishing spots. One historic Njoh across from Pierre's Creek near Tsiigehtshik was purchased by Hyacinthe Andre as a gift to his wife Eliza, and one near Chìi chyah tshik marks the place where an Inuit boldly climbed up to spy on a Gwich'in camp (Heine et al. 2007: 34-35).

Making lobsticks still has currency in the Fort McPherson area. As recently as 2007, a new lobstick was made to honor the young Dutch anthropologist, Peter Loovers (2011, 2016). It seems as though the tables were turned, however, in that Loovers was instructed to create his own lobstick memorial at Bear Creek while following the instructions of his Gwich'in mentor, Johnny Charlie. According to Loovers, the task of climbing the tree and cutting the limbs proved to be hard and exhausting work, especially during cold weather.

In Alaska Gwich'in lobsticks are called Njah rather than Njoh. The Njah was meant to provide good luck to its owner. It was a gift, and it was sacred because it was meant to represent a person's life. Its lower or middle branches only were removed, and it was usually a tree growing up high on a hill, so it was easily visible to passersby. The tree was fully personified and vested with the identity of its owner.

The first person who told me about Njah was Mae Wallis in Fort Yukon (Fig. 15.1). Mae said that her own mother-in-law had a lobstick tree made for her when she was very young, and she died on the same day that a forest fire burned down her tree, even though her health was quite good at the time. Mae said that it used to be that some people wanted to have an Njah made for them so that they would know ahead of time when they would die (Wallis 1976).

Kenneth Frank (personal communication, 2006) heard that lobsticks were created when the trees were quite small because they were often dedicated to young children. The Njah was meant to represent a child's life. It was widely believed that if someone cut down such a tree, the child would also die. Kenneth adds that in addition to a lobstick, the word Njah also refers to a wedge or stone axe used for cutting down trees.

David Salmon (personal communication, 2007) of Chalkyitsik, an Episcopal priest and former traditional chief of the Doyon Region in Alaska, likewise confirmed to me that the Gwich'in believed that if the lobstick tree stayed green and healthy, the person honored by it would have a long life. But if it turned brown and died, it was an omen that the person honored by it would also die soon thereafter. This folk belief apparently goes back at least to the latter part of the nineteenth century, when an early traveler on the Lobstick River in west-central Alberta claimed that "there is an old superstition that your health and length of days will correspond to your lobstick's" (Grant 1873: 196).

Salmon remembered two lobstick trees from his youth—one in Chalkytsik and one at Salmon Village, on the Black River. The latter was known as the Stephen Englishoe Njah. Both of these trees are now gone because they burned up in a forest fire. Whatever its connection to the Hudson's Bay Company, the Gwich'in Njah certainly did not include the gun salutes and grog or whiskey drinking ceremonies of the voyageurs.

Spruce trees were used to commemorate Gwich'in deaths as well as births. Fred Hadleigh-West (1959:80), in his doctoral dissertation, learned from residents of Arctic Village that: "Honored persons might be 'buried' in spruce trees. The body was placed in two scooped out half-logs and then wrapped. The tree was then limbed to keep anything from getting to the body. After a year or so the body might be taken down and cremated." In 1933, Robert McKennan learned much of the same thing, except that the log coffin was said to be "elevated on four posts or bound to two standing trees" and "a pole bearing a carved animal figure was often erected over the grave" (1965:59-60).

Other Northern Dene Traditions

The lobstick also had some currency among the Northern Tutchone. Dan Van Bibber, a Northern Tutchone, recalls that a man named Billy Atkinson of Ross River trimmed a "lodge pole" to mark the birthplace of his brother Abe at Ross Lakes. This had to be sometime in the early 20th century, since Dan himself was born in 1913. Van Bibber heard that the tree was trimmed by climbing up and cutting off all of the limbs except for those at the top. He also says "The old people did this to mark a special spot, the turning back of their hunting areas to show they had been there, or to mark a border" (Van Bibber 1989:21).

The widespread nature of lobsticking is also attested to in Father Julius Jetté's notes on the Koyukon language, as published in the *Koyukon Athabaskan Dictionary*. The Koyukon word for a lobstick or 'lopped spruce tree' is nonododekkaadle. There is also a Koyukon place name called Nonok'edodekkaatl Denh, located sixteen miles below Nulato on the north bank of the Yukon River, which Jetté says "used to be marked by one (or several) spruce trees, of which the branches had been lopped, except a small bunch left at the top. This is often done by the Ten'a to mark certain spots, as graveyard, a village, a trail, etc. and attract the attention of passersby" (Jetté and Jones 2000:327). Yet even during Jetté's time, while he was resident in Koyukon villages from 1898-1919, he noted that this practice was "gradually being abandoned."

It may be just a coincidence, but the ongoing Lower Koyukon Stick Dance held at Kaltag and Nulato still centers around a spruce tree whose lower branches and bark have been removed and decorated with ribbons, leaving only a cluster of branches at the top. This tree, called the Hi'o, is tied to the rafters in the center of the community hall, and gifts such as wolf and wolverine skins are placed on it. I had a chance to see this tree and the dance ceremonies attendant to it in Kaltag in 1973. Former Alaska State Senator John Sackett (1972), a Koyukon, has hinted that communication with deceased relatives is achieved through the Stick, which operates like an "antenna or life line to the departed person", and Martha Demientieff (1974) says "the tree represents the person who died and the people are happy to see it because it is like they still have the dead person with them." The big difference, however, is that the Hi'o is a tree that is cut down, while the lobstick is a living tree left standing where it was found.

The lobstick also has a strong parallel in a Lower Tanana narrative related by the late Chief Peter John of Minto. In his little book, *The First Christmas Tree: Ts'eba Tthadda* (1991), Chief John tells the story of a man who befriended a Stick Man or Netr'eł'enenh, a kind of wild person who was often feared and lived apart from other Indians. Stick Men are also thought to have magic powers similar to those of a shaman. The Lower Tanana call them Netr'eł'enenh and the Gwich'in, who refer to them in English as Brush Men, call them Naa'in or Ninaa'įh (see Chapter 13, Endnote 1).

At any rate, in this story the Stick Man, who is grateful to the Indian hunter for generously sharing his caribou meat, tells him to keep his eye on a young spruce tree, adding: "When I have died, then this spruce will wither up and die" (John 1991:10). Eventually, the hunter returns to this tree to find many beads hanging from its branches, which he is encouraged to claim as a gift from the Stick Man. But one or two years later when he goes back to the tree he hears potlatch singing and finds the tree is standing dead, and then he knows right away that his Stick Man friend is dead. In this story, it would seem that the Stick Man's death presages the tree's death, rather than the other way around, as with Gwich'in belief. Also, there is no indication in this tale that any of the tree's branches were cut.

Cree Traditions

The Cree observed the lobstick tradition as well. In August, 1899, the Canadian poet Charles Mair wrote about a cliff top containing three lop-sticks at Point Brulé, along the Athabasca River in present-day Alberta. Describing a very different shape for the tree, in branches are removed only from the middle, Mair (1908:126-127) says that an alternative aesthetic prevailed:

> The Indian's lop-stick, called by the Cree piskootenusk,[1] is a sort of living talisman which he connects in some mysterious way with his own fate, and which he will often go many miles out of his direct course to visit. Even white men fall in with the fetish, and one of the three we saw was called "Lambert's lop-stick." I myself had one made for me by Gros Oreilles, the Saulteaux Chief, nearly forty years ago, in the forest east of Pointe du Chene, in what is now Manitoba. They are made by stripping a tall spruce tree of a deep ring of branches, leaving the top and bottom ones intact. The tree seems to thrive all the same, and is a very noticeable, and not infrequent, object throughout the whole Thickwood Indian country [around the Liard River].

In 1909 Agnes Deans Cameron wrote that the Cree lop off all of the branches from one section of the tree trunk except for two, which are left to represent wings. "If the lobstick is to stand a monument to a certain man or party," she says, "the names of those to be honored are written in Cree on an attached slab. We were to notice lobsticks from point to point along the rest of our journey, some of them indicating good hunting-grounds or fishing-places back from the shore, but most of them memorials of happenings on the river" (Cameron 1909).

One of the eye-witness accounts of lob-stick making, written in 1907 by the naturalist Ernest Thompson Seton (1911) says that the person being honored by the lobstick actually had a choice of which tree would be selected and that the honoree's name was duly inscribed on the trunk of the tree. The men who made the lobstick, Métis voyageurs,[2] were supposed to be rewarded with a plug of tobacco and a drink of whiskey. Seton's lobstick was created on the shores of Great Slave Lake in the Northwest Territories.

Popular Culture

Primarily articulated in the 19th and early 20th centuries, lobsticks have now entered the commercialized arena of Canadian and American popular culture. They have even been suggested as a potential symbol of Canada itself (Massie 2012). Wikipedia, for example, lists seventeen place names in Canada which contain the word Lobstick. For instance, there is the Lobstick River in Alberta, as well as an unincorporated community called Lobstick, located on the Yellowhead Highway (Route 16) directly west of Edmonton. In addition, there is a Lobstick Lodge in Jasper, Alberta and a Lobstick Bay in the Lake of the Woods in western Ontario. Lobstick Tours, based in Prince Albert, Saskatchewan, offers guided motorcoach tours to various destinations in Canada and around the world. The Waskesiu Golf Course located in Waskesiu, Saskatchewan, inside Prince Albert National Park, claims to be "The Home of the Lobstick" and is renowned for its annual Lobstick Tournament, in honor of the tree which grows on the fairway off of the first tee (Fig. 15.2). Here are the rules for Hole #1 Par 4: "The lobstick tree is straight in front of the first tee. A local rule allows you to replay your ball if it hits the lobstick tree in mid-air."[3]

And it's not simply a Canadian or Alaskan phenomenon. For example, there is a Lopstick Lodge on First Connecticut Lake in Pittsburgh, New Hampshire, noted for fly fishing and snowmobiling (see https://www.lopstick.com). Aside from place names and commercial venues, Lobstick is the name of a former interdisciplinary journal of Creative Thought, Social Commentary, Scholarly Research, and Debate that was published in Grand Prairie, Alberta. Lobsticks also serves as the title for a small book of Margaret Atwood poems. Still another book entitled, Lobsticks and Stone Cairns: Human Landmarks in the Arctic (Davis 1996) is a collection of one hundred biographical sketches honoring arctic explorers and scientists. These literary "lobsticks," akin to festschrifts, are verbal metaphors for what was once done to honor people in the north through physical landmarks visible to travelers.

Figure 15.2. Lobstick tree on the Fairway of Hole #1, Waskesiu Golf Course in Prince Albert National Park, Saskatchewan. Photo courtesy of the Waskesiu Golf Course.

Ecology

Lobstick or lopstick seem to derive from the Middle English word loppe, signifying branches or twigs. When I looked at the practice of lobsticking, and the manner in which humans have interacted with their natural world, I began to wonder about the ecology of trees. What is the effect of lobsticking on spruce and pine trees? One might guess that lobsticks may have been a death sentence for the targeted trees, but perhaps not.

Lobsticking is essentially a form of pruning. The U.S. Forest Service has some guidelines for pruning trees on its website. There are several recognized ways of pruning trees, some of which are beneficial, and some of which are detrimental to the health of a tree. Lobsticking actually follows the customary and approved practice of crown raising. "Crown raising is the practice of removing branches from the bottom of the crown of a tree to provide clearance underneath or to develop a clear stem for timber production. Also, removing lower branches on white pines can prevent blister rust. . . . After pruning, the ratio of the living crown to total tree height should be at least two-thirds (e.g., a 12 meter tree should have living branches on at least the upper 8 meters)."

There is actually considerable variation in lobsticking, judging from verbal descriptions and historic photographs. In some cases, all of the lower branches were removed, violating the 2/3 rule. But in other cases, only the middle branches were removed. Did the Gwich'in and other indigenous people harm the trees they lopped? Chances are they did shorten the lives of the trees in some cases by not following the 2/3 rule, but in the areas where they practiced crown raising, they may have actually enhanced growth, which always occurs in the crown or top of the trees. One scientific source claims that "Crown raising increases the amount of direct sunlight reaching the turf in the morning and late afternoon. It also removes the least productive branches from the tree."

In cases where trees were "barked" around the circumference, as with the Frances Simpson tree, the trees were almost certainly short-lived. Ring-barking, or girdling, as it's known to foresters, allow insects easy access to the tree and stops the flow of sap and nutrients to the upper branches. Firing bullets into the tree trunk and carving initials into the exposed wood was not a very smart conservation practice either. However, Simpson's tree is the only one documented where several such destructive practices were observed, and hers was at the hands of the voyageurs, not the Indians.

Conclusion

Lobsticks began as sacred symbols, and the creation of lobsticks by the Gwich'in, the Koyukon, the Cree, and other northern peoples was a ritual of the North. That ritual established a homology with the human life cycle of birth and death. In a sense, lobsticks provided a very literal representation for the genealogical notion of a 'family tree'. In other words, they invoked a non-western model for looking at kinship ties. They could be bought and sold and given away as gifts. They sometimes marked the location of subsistence food resources. And they embodied a spiritual world view that had a secular cross-cultural manifestation in the celebrity memorials created by the voyageurs of the Hudson's Bay Company.

Lobsticks were a truly important part of both Native and voyageur life in the nineteenth and early twentieth century. They may be considered an integral part of historic northern Dene material culture. They were practical but also highly symbolic and attendant to some important ceremonies and beliefs. While they conferred high status on selected individuals, they also modified the landscape aesthetic and served the function of marking geographic borders and trail heads, supplying place names for persons traveling along lakes and rivers.

Lobstick making, as a multi-semiotic rite of passage, may well predate the historic period in which lobsticks were first documented, and it seems to have been in full swing shortly after historic contact with Canadian First Nations. The Hudson's Bay Company voyageurs used lobstick trees as places to rest and entertain their VIP guests during laborious canoe-paddling journeys across the North. Although the traditional and sacred Dene practice of making lobsticks apparently declined around the 1920s, when roads and airplanes began to replace wilderness canoe travel, its folklore clearly lives on among the Gwich'in in the 21st century. While emerging first from indigenous material folk culture, lobsticks are now accepted as part of contemporary western Canadian popular culture, where they have become a commercial novelty for attracting tourists.

Acknowledgments

An earlier draft of this paper was presented to Alaska Anthropological Association Annual Meeting, Fairbanks, on March 16, 2007. The elders who taught me about lobsticks first-hand include David Salmon, Mae Wallis, and Kenneth Frank.

Endnotes

1. According to Maria M'Lot (2002: 87), the Cree word for a "lopstick" used as a marker is mistîkôkan.

2. One contemporary Saskatchewan artist and author, Leah Marie Dorion, regards the lobstick as an item of pride in Métis culture and history and has made at least two new lobsticks herself to help revive the tradition. See her children's book (Dorion 2014) and her compelling essay, "Recent Métis Voyageur Lobstick Pole Projects Funded by The Saskatchewan Arts Board" (www.leahdorion.ca/pdf/Lobstick%20Article.pdf), where she writes that "Building a Lobstick is a spiritual, celebratory, and a highly physical process. We used cultural practices such as making tobacco offerings, used song, and prayer in every aspect of the construction. . . ."

3. Photos of two historic lobsticks in Manitoba from the early twentieth century can be seen at: www.mhs.mb.ca/docs/pageant/14/ballantynejourney.shtml

16. Saturnalia in the Subarctic:

Gwich'in New Year's Celebrations

Arctic Village New Year's As I Saw It in 1996-1997

The Gwich'in New Year's holiday as celebrated today in northeastern Alaska and northwest Canada has historic mid-nineteenth century roots in the folklife of northern Scotland and the Orkney Islands. In this respect it's quite comparable to Gwich'in fiddling, jigging, and contra-dancing traditions, which came in with the Hudson's Bay Company during the 1840s and 1850s (Mishler 1993). However, before I discuss the Old World roots of Gwich'in New Year's festivities, I want to describe ethnographically how the holiday was celebrated when I saw it in Arctic Village twenty-five years ago. The primary fieldwork for this essay was done between December 30, 1996 and January 4, 1997, in Arctic Village, Alaska, where I visited during extreme -50°F to -60°F weather.

I should preface this description by noting that in most Alaskan Gwich'in communities local leadership consists of a First Chief, a Second Chief, and a Tribal Council. There is also the honarary title of Traditional Chief. In Arctic Village Christmas is celebrated by the village Second Chief, who cooks and hosts a farewell potlatch on Christmas day. Then the First Chief in turn cooks and hosts a farewell potlatch on New Year's day. Kenneth likes to joke that when he cooks breakfast for his family on these days, it's the only time in his life that he gets to be the Second Chief and First Chief.

The potlatch itself is simply an informal community meal featuring caribou head soup and roast turkey, and served in the midst of a square dance accompanied by live fiddle music. The Christmas and New Year's potlatches are called "farewell potlatches" because the chiefs must stand for election every January, right after the holidays. As I observed this tradition in Arctic Village, the First Chief gave his farewell potlatch starting about 1:30 a.m. on New Year's morning. In my field notes I wrote:

> The 1997 New Year's festivities in Arctic Village got underway with an Episcopal church service starting at 11 p.m. on New Year's eve. At midnight the church bells ring loudly, while villagers cheer, shoot off fireworks, and fire their guns into the air. After church the action moves to the community hall, where young children get rowdy and begin mussing each other up with handfuls of corn meal, white flour, pancake syrup, and squeeze bottles full of yellow mustard. This foolery often pits the girls against the boys, the women against the men. A big bonfire outside of the community hall provides a gathering place for teenagers and provides a beacon visible from nearly every home.

The Arctic Village tradition is that people dance all night in the community hall until at least 4 or 5 a.m. On New Year's eve in 1996-1997 I witnessed and videotaped a special jig dance in which First Chief Allen Tritt was surrounded by a circle of women and girls and took each of them in turn as his jig partners. In twenty-four years of visiting Gwich'in villages, this was the first time I ever saw this dance, and my first impression was that it was a special Chief's dance. But as I learned later, this kind of dance is done whenever the Gwich'in want to honor any individual, man or woman. This dance was not described in my earlier book, *The Crooked Stovepipe* (Mishler 1993).

After an evening of Red River jigs, contras, and square dances, the Arctic Village people go home to take a short nap only to get up early and go around house-to-house wishing each other a Happy New Year. But if anyone locks their door, the visitors will break the door down or break the lock on the door. And if anyone is found asleep in bed on New Year's morning they will grab that person, carry him or her outdoors, and toss them into a snowbank. Sometimes they do that while people are still inside their sleeping bags. Or they might throw buckets full of snow on the sleepy heads while they are still lying in bed. The Lower Tanana residents of Minto and Nenana also practice this throwing into the snow custom if the people inside a house do not get up and join the singers as they go house-to-house (see Pearce 1985:23). Another favorite prank for the Gwich'in youth in Venetie is to shoot bullet holes through the outside chimney pipes of houses as they are visited.

After being greeted by the visitors, everyone in the house puts on their jackets and joins the group as they go to the next house. When they reach the last few houses in the village, they may pick up whatever they see in the front yard and carry it inside. It might be a sled or a dog, a garbage can, or even a snow machine. In Kenneth's words:

> And sometime they put perfume on somebody, someone in the house, and sometime they put mustard on their hand, and

> they start shaking hands with another person, and sometime they put syrup on their hand, and they pat on that person's back and put syrup on it, saying, 'How you doing, buddy? Happy New Year!' And that guy will have a big piece of syrup on his back, or mustard. Then they shake hands; they sing Happy New Year! and go out.
>
> And then they get hold of the Chief. If the Chief walk in, they grab the Chief, and then everybody go outside and start throwing him up in the air, and after that they throw him in the deep snow and shower him with snow. That's the way they celebrate with the chief. Because New Year is the Chief's day to make potlatch, so New Year is the Chief's day.
>
> And then after they get through they go to the community hall to eat breakfast, but. . . the people that cook breakfast, you know, they usually board up the door, and the people that [are] coming in for breakfast have to break their way through that door to get in, and after that door is out of the way, then they could eat breakfast, you know, and shake hands, and everybody say, 'Happy New Year!' to give greeting to the people that [are] cooking breakfast (Frank 1997).

Although I traveled all the way to Arctic Village to see the house-to-house visits, I learned on New Year's eve that the house-to-house visits only take place in the core neighborhood of the community. Families living on the outskirts, such as where I was staying with the Franks, are not bothered because of the long walking distances and the extreme cold weather. I was told to listen for rifle shots to be fired and then go up to the main part of the village to observe the house-to-house visits, but by the time I arrived at 8:15 a.m. the visiting and the pranks were already over, and everyone who participated had gathered for breakfast at the community hall. Some people said the extremely cold weather of -55 degrees F forced the house-to-house visits to end prematurely.

On New Year's night I attended yet another potlatch which began about 9 or 10 p.m. This is a more elaborate potlatch than the one thrown by the First Chief and his wife in that most of the women in the village bring a dish and serve what they bring in a buffet line. After the potlatch meal there was a break of two hours before another square dance began, and this dance also continued until 4 a.m. In Old Crow it's the Christmas night feast or "Double Way" that is hosted by all of the women in the community.

On the day after New Year's I was told they used to go house-to-house to gather food for another community potlatch, and they would sing for whatever they need to make that potlatch. In Kenneth's words,

> They call that [song] K'ontee Ch'araach'aa Goochilik. K'ontee Ch'araach'aa mean 'after New Year', and if they want to make potlatch and there's no food, so they walk around house-to- house with blanket, and they sing song, and whatever they ask for, that household throw that in the blanket. And that's how they make potlatch, especially after the holiday. If you ask for meat, if you ask for fish, if you ask for tea, sugar, flour, whatever they sing about, then if they sing outside, you have to listen to them, what they're saying. And if they ask for sugar, then you throw sugar in that blanket. If they want tea, they say, they sing, "Aii lidii eejii? Aii lidii eejii? Aii lidii eejii?" ('Where's that tea?'). If they ask for sugar, then "Aii songaii eejii? Aii songaii eejii? Aii songaii eejii?" (sings 'Where's that sugar?'). And if they want meat, they say, "Aii nilii eejii?" ('Where's that meat?'). And one of my uncles was saying that after they sing it they say, "Hee'ee, hee'ee, hee" (Frank 1997).

One of these begging songs was performed on tape for me by Maggie Gilbert in Arctic Village when I interviewed her on April 21, 1973. Maggie's lyrics included lots of vocables but also the common line "Lidii eejii?" or 'Where is that tea [you've got]?' Although I remained in Arctic Village until January 4, 1997, I didn't see or hear anything about this second round of house-to-house visits to gather up food. Kenneth says this custom was discontinued some years before he was a child. One story he heard is that there was a man who jumped from his front door right into the singers' blanket, thereby volunteering himself to assist in the potlatch. This house-to-house solicitation of food has a close analogue among the Upper Tanana people in Alaska, where in Tetlin they went door-to-door with a hook, and villagers would attach donated food to the hook (Guédon, 1974).

Historic Antecedents

The Hudson's Bay Company journals for Fort Yukon from 1848-1855 do not indicate much of a New Year's celebration except for the playing of cards and checkers and a special in-house dinner for the Company servants (Murray, 1848). It was really pretty quiet and dull. Still, there's good evidence that the Gwich'in New Year's morning celebration was in full swing in Fort Yukon by the early twentieth century, when the resident Episcopal missionary Leonidas Wooden penned this account:

> I have to add that our New Year opens fully as cheering [as at Christmas]. I was entertained yesterday [January 1st, 1902] at a feast given at the chief's house. Was also tossed up and cheered by the young men, who were around with a spread moosehide gathering up contributions for their feast, to which I added a pail of lard. The N.A.T.&T. agent and the natives themselves furnished several hundred dollars' worth of provisions. The number of people shaking hands on such occasions keeps one pretty busy. (Wooden, 1902)

Just two years later, Wooden (1904) added:

> On New Year's morning the Indian men shouldered their guns and kept up a serenading fusillade from house-to-house. A great volley was fired just at the door of the mission, and then a general handshaking began. --with a chorus of "Happy New Year" and a tossing of the missioner [Wooden] in the air. Later, the women and children came, in detachments, to shake hands

> and express their greeting. New Years is the principal event with this people. On their departure to their camps, the handshaking must be repeated, accompanied this time with "Good bye."

We're also lucky to have another detailed early 20th century description of the New Year's celebration in Fort Yukon, from the words of John Fredson, who was interviewed by the linguist Edward Sapir in 1923. Fredson told Sapir:

> On this day, in the morning when it's still dark, everyone goes around from house-to-house and we all shake one another's hands, and the women even kiss each other. This morning we really don't get any sleep. On New Year's Day, just as it starts, there is really a lot of noise. There is shooting, we shout, bells ring, and dogs bark, and with all that, you'd better believe that some of us don't sleep at all. The poor cooks don't rest all night, and sweat pours out over their white aprons all night long. When it becomes daylight, we all scramble into the chief's house and grab hold of the chief. And then, after we toss him up in the air, he makes a little speech. After this we go into the cookhouse and have a morning meal. At midday, around that time, we have speeches in the church. After the speeches we go into the chief's house. And then we really have a meal, indeed meat of all kinds, fish of all kinds, and all kinds of white man's food are there" (Fredson 1982:23-24).

Fredson adds that the big feast was followed by a kind of soccer game, using a big moose skin ball stuffed with hair that players tried to kick through two stakes to score goals. Then the community would go home and change into their best clothes for an all-night dance. The dances would include Han Gwich'in dances, Inuit dances, and white people's dances accompanied by fiddles. The dancing would be repeated night after night for a week or until the village ran out of food and money. Then all the families would disperse and go back to their winter traplines. Elder Hannah P. Solomon (1985) recalled virtually the same thing from her early years.

Other Gwich'in Variants

In Fort McPherson, on the Canadian side, New Year's is celebrated today a little bit differently than it is on the Alaska side, but reminiscent of what Wooden saw in 1902-1904. In McPherson the mischief is more gender-based. The men throw baby powder on the women, and the women spray perfume on the men. On New Year's eve they build a big community bonfire. Then on New Year's morning, according to longtime resident Bertha Francis, guns are fired off, and that is a signal for the men and women to gather at the Chief's house. From there they usually split up into two groups, although in 2002 they all stayed together. Most years the men go from house-to-house at one end of the village, and the women do the same at the other end. At each house they shake hands with the occupants and say, "Happy New Year!" If anyone is slow getting up, they also pull pranks and tease them, dragging them out of bed or putting a big chunk of snow under their covers.

When the visitors arrive families are ready for them with a big pot of coffee, some bannock bread, and perhaps some dry meat. At the end of their rounds, the men's group and the women's group usually meet up at one last house and really raise a ruckus there. Then later in the day they have dog races and gather for a community feast.

In Old Crow, Yukon Territory, as in Arctic Village, there is an 11 p.m. church service on New Year's eve, followed by lots of greeting and handshaking at the church. As in Arctic Village, the foolishness and teasing with syrup and mustard between boys and girls and men against women in Old Crow starts right after church, but this is something just recently added to the tradition. At midnight in Old Crow they also shoot off their guns. Usually, but not always, there is a square dance after midnight, and in the morning they shoot their guns off again and go house-to-house greeting one another. However, according to Charlie Peter Charlie (1997), elder, old-time fiddler, and former First Chief, there is no breaking down of doors or throwing people out in the snow for sleeping in. But on New Year's night at about 6 p.m. the First Chief and his wife make a big feast for the community, featuring moose head soup, and there is always lots of food left over to take home. Then everyone returns later for a dance, and sometimes they dance all night long.

Commentary: Old World Connections

All of these pranks and rowdy behaviors, of course, have deep European roots in what the anthropologist Victor Turner has described as "rituals of status reversal" (1977:167), which go back to the ancient Roman festival of Saturnalia, when social norms were upended in December during a period of merrymaking, feasting, and gambling. During Saturnalia, for example, Roman masters served meals to their slaves. Gambling was wide-open but normally outlawed. These kinds of outrageous behaviors spread throughout Europe during medieval and modern times, and they eventually reached the Gwich'in through the Scots who worked for the Hudson's Bay Company. The Gwich'in version of status and role reversal is manifested in women kissing women, people wasting store-bought food and ammunition, homes being rudely invaded, and chiefs being mocked and insulted. All in good fun, of course.

The Gwich'in were quite selective about what they borrowed from their mid-nineteenth century white visitors, most of whom were Scottish and Orcadian employees of the Hudson's Bay Company (see Brown 1988). In the process of trading and socializing with these newcomers, the Gwich'in nevertheless accepted many of the festive northern European traditions associated with Christmas and New Year's.

From both the Scottish and Gwich'in point of view, for example, New Year's is a 'bigger' holiday than Christmas. Christmas, called Drin

Tsal (lit. 'the Little Day') by the Gwich'in, contrasts with New Year's or Drin Choh ('the Big Day'). As John Fredson said, "At Christmas there are good times, but on New Year's Day it is even better" (1982:23).

What makes an analysis of the cross-cultural diffusion tenuous and somewhat baffling, however, is the complete absence among the Gwich'in of several other well-known Scottish New Year's practices. 'First footing' visits with a lump of coal, a black bun, and a bottle of Scotch whiskey, for example, are totally missing from Gwich'in communities. And although the Scottish practice of men calling on women to secure a New Year's kiss caught on with Indians in places such as Red River (Fort Garry, Manitoba), it apparently never captured the fancy of the Canadian or Alaskan Gwich'in (MacLeod 1953:44). The closest thing to this was John Fredson's observation of women kissing women (1982:23).

Instead, it appears that the celebration of the Gwich'in New Year's is more closely related to the Gaelic *Oidhche Calluinn* known in the Scottish Highlands, western islands, and Orkney than the pagan Hogmanay traditions circulating in the Scottish Lowlands (see Bennett 1989:115-116; the web page *hogmanay.net* provides an overview of local Scottish traditions). One indication of this is the Gwich'in use of songs during house-to-house visits to collect foods for a feast a day or two after New Year's. Another is that while the Gwich'in continue to celebrate New Year's both on New Year's eve and again on New Year's day, while Lowland Scots celebrate primarily on New Year's eve.

The information I've found on Scots Gaelic traditions is fragmentary and certainly needs additional research, but the Rev. Walter Gregor described Scottish house-to-house visits on New Year's as charitable in motive: "Very often on New Year's Day companies of young men in twos, threes, and fours set out shortly after breakfast to 'thigg' for an old woman, or an old man, or an aged couple, or an invalid that might be in narrow circumstances. Carrying a sack to receive the alms of meal and a small bag for the money, they travelled over a good many miles of district of the country in which they lived. . . ." (Gregor 1881:160-161).

Another report by Ben Johnson (n.d.) says, "On the Isle of Lewis, in the Outer Hebrides, the young men and boys form themselves into opposing bands; the leader of each wears a sheep skin, while another member carries a sack. The bands move through the village from house-to-house reciting a Gaelic rhyme. The boys are given bannocks (fruit buns) for their sack before moving on to the next house."

The Orkney scholar John Firth writes "the advent of New Year's Day was heralded by the young people going from house-to-house singing the New Year's Song. . . . Some wily ones, rising early on New Year's morning, secreted . . .nettles underneath the blankets, whereupon the sleeper, on giving a morning stretch, received a severe burn on his feet coming in contact with the noxious weed" (Firth 1974:122). This practice is very reminiscent of the Gwich'in prank of throwing sleepyheads out into a snowbank or sticking chunks of snow under their bed covers.

Firth also records all the verses of the traditional Orcadian New Year's Song as sung in the parish of Firth during his childhood. This ancient song, the verses of which read like Chaucerian couplets, has lines that refer to the gathering up of eatables during house-to-house visits and contains an open threat to break down the host's door if it's not opened to welcome in the visitors (Firth 1974:123-124). Though the Gwich'in New Year's song lyrics are far different, this Orcadian song has its Gwich'in counterpart in the house-to-house visits to sing and gather up food in a blanket for a community potlatch a day or two after New Year's. Herein too lies the precedent for the Alaskan Gwich'in custom of breaking down locked doors on New Year's Day, both at private homes and at the community hall. Apparently this practice underscores the belief that no one can keep the New Year from coming in.

Another Orkney New Year's song, collected and published twelve years before Firth's book, documents the way people sang when they went house-to-house on the island of Sanday. Verses 31 and 32 of this song are almost identical to verses 19 and 20 of the Firth song: "Open the door! we maun be in,/To keep us out is surely sin./But if you dinna open the door,/We'll ding it owre upon your floor" (Johnston and Johnston 1907-08).

The shooting off of guns at midnight is well-rooted in Scottish tradition, and even the bonfire enjoyed by Arctic Village teenagers starting right after midnight is part of Scottish tradition. The custom of 'burning the Old Year out' with a giant bonfire was traditionally practiced in Wick, in the far north of Scotland (Hole 1976:38-39) and elsewhere in places such as Biggar in Lanarkshire, based on the belief that fire would ward off evil spirits for the New Year (see https://www.visitscotland.com/see-do/events/christmas-winter-festivals/hogmanay/).

In summary, what the Gwich'in appear to have preserved from the Orcadian and Scots Gaelic holiday are New Year's eve dances, shooting off guns, roaring bonfires, house-to-house visits on New Year's morning, the breaking down of locked doors, pranks to wake up and punish sleepyheads, and the enjoyment of bannock bread. Corresponding celebrations held in Old Crow and Fort McPherson, respectively, differ somewhat from those in Venetie and Arctic Village on the Alaska side, but house-to-house visits and bannock bread are mainstays there as well.

David Masaan, a Cree Indian living at York Factory, Manitoba, on the shores of Hudson's Bay, describes a traditional New Year's eve celebration in his community that is quite reminiscent of the one enjoyed by the Gwich'in:

> On New Year's eve people would travel from house-to-house using dog teams, right until midnight! During this time the church bell would be ringing and there would be shooting! The guns would be fired into the air. . . . The next morning people would go around from house-to-house shaking hands with everyone. To all the houses. (In Beardy and Coutts 1996:37).

During the Gwich'in house visits, however, social norms are inverted, especially those which respect personal and family privacy, and there is a license to do things that are not done at any other time of the year. Outlandish pranks are pulled by house guests, yet no one may get angry over these. First Chiefs, the elected leaders of the communities, can be mocked and insulted. On New Year's most people get up extremely early in the morning, even though the normal daily custom in Venetie and Arctic Village is to stay up very late and then sleep in until about 10 a.m.

Rifle and shotgun shells, which are quite expensive and highly prized for subsistence hunting, are fired off with abandon. Store-bought packaged food, such as maple syrup, mustard, flour and corn meal, all of which can be expensive and a little hard to come by during the coldest part of the winter, are openly and extravagantly wasted. This squandering of both ammunition and food (which to be clear does not include meat or fish) on New Year's eve and New Year's day is highly contrary to the Gwich'in ethic of conserving resources. They are both liminal displays of inversion and reversal, but as the late Charlie Peter Charlie (1997) once explained to me, "You have to open your heart sometimes. You can't be stingy on New Year's."

In all of this, one important thing to keep in mind is that the Gwich'in New Year is now celebrated in ways never imagined by those Scots and Orkneymen who introduced it a hundred and seventy-five years ago. At the same time, it would seem as if Gwich'in villages provide a precious glimpse and time capsule of what holiday social life might have been like in Orkney and northern Scotland in the early nineteenth century.

Acknowledgments

Earlier drafts of this essay were originally presented to the Alaska Anthropological Association Annual Meeting Whitehorse, YT on April 11, 1997, and to the American Folklore Society Annual Meeting in Austin, Texas, on October 30, 1997. I extend my appreciation to the community of Arctic Village for allowing me to welcome in the 1997 New Year as their guest.

17. Northern Dene Gatherings:

The Gwich'in And Their Neighbors

As venues for social solidarity, the elaborate funeral and memorial potlatches of old seem to have been augmented, amplified, and in some cases supplanted by the phenomenon of Gwich'in and other northern Dene summer "gatherings".[1] These gatherings, which began to emerge in the late 1980s and early 1990s, have become very popular and attract hundreds of northern Dene for outdoor camping, singing, dancing, speechmaking, games, and feasting. Each gathering is memorialized by specially made t-shirts inscribed with the name, date, and place of the event. There is also evidence that "the gathering" concept has taken root among the Cree in northern Ontario, Manitoba, and Alberta, and among the Tlingit, Haida, and Tsimshian people of Southeast Alaska.[2] In this essay I will speak to the five northern Dene gatherings I have attended since 1988 and contextualize them via historical antecedents during the early fur trade era.

In contrast to traditional northern Dene funeral and memorial potlatches, which serve some of the same social functions of bringing people together, modern Dene gatherings seem to be organized more around friendship than kinship and are generally open to non-Natives and other groups outside the host nation. And unlike funeral and memorial potlatches, northern Dene gatherings are not clan and moiety-based pay-back parties. Although there are many variations in size and protocol, one feature all gatherings have in common is that they satisfy a need for belonging and social identity. That alone makes them important. They are also notable for being drug and alcohol free. Drugs and alcohol are seen as antithetical to the spirit and purpose of Dene gatherings.

Legendary Gatherings

The legendary medicine man on the Canadian side, Yamoria, also known as the Great Lawgiver, is credited with establishing the first Dene gatherings and with teaching the sacred importance of such gatherings. Yamoria "used his voice medicine power to speak to the people" and told them, "I am going to establish a gathering place and I want everybody to go there to talk about any problems or concerns" (Blondin 2006:25). Yamoria also set up a protocol for such gatherings, saying that the Elders would take turns speaking to the people, with the purpose of teaching the people to govern themselves. These gatherings would also include whole families. "All the parents shall bring their children," Yamoria said, "so they can listen as well." In this way, the children could be prepared for a good life.

Historic Gatherings

One historical antecedent of modern day gatherings was the spring fur trading rendezvous held at Nuchalawoya, located at the confluence of the Tanana River and the Yukon River near the present village of Tanana.[3] The meaning of Nuchalawoya is 'the place where two rivers meet and mix'. This gathering was visited during the first week of June in 1866 by the Anglican missionary Archdeacon Robert McDonald (1866), who traveled there with ten canoes of Indians, including the Gwich'in chiefs Red Leggins and Shahnyaa Ti' (see above Chapter 6). They found about two hundred Indians (eighty-seven men, forty-eight women, and fifty-eight children) gathered in anticipation of meeting traders of the Russian-American Company. The tribal groups McDonald met there were the Gens de Milieu, the Tetse Gwich'in, the Kitli Gwich'in, and the Gens des Buttes (Lower Tanana).[4] McDonald did not see any Russian traders but was told that the Indians were gathered there to sell their winter's catch of fur to the Russians.

Almost exactly a year later, when William Healy Dall stopped at the village of Nuklukahyet on his way upriver to Fort Yukon on June 8, 1867, he observed "the annual dances which take place here were performed on empty stomachs" (1898:93). One of the dances he saw was performed with a circle of spectators surrounding two men stripped to the waist who held eagles' feathers in each hand and whose heads were shaven. Dall's traveling companion, Frederick Whymper, noted the elaborate welcoming ceremony and firing of guns which they received and returned upon landing at this site. He was favorably impressed that the Indians "come from all quarters" including "Co-Yukons [Koyukons], Newicarguts, Tananas, and even the Kotch-á-kutchins [Gwichyaa Gwich'in] from Fort Yukon. On some occasions," he adds, "their gatherings have numbered 600 persons" (Whymper 1868: 210).

When McDonald (1870) returned to the Nuchalawoya site again four years later, it had been transformed into an American fur trading post operated by François Mercier of Hutchinson, Kohl, and Company. McDonald recognized that the Indians assembled there represented four distinct tribal groups: the Tetse Gwich'in, the Tunun Gwich'in, the Kitlit Gwich'in, and the Tetlit Gwich'in. This time he did not mention either the Gens des Buttes or the Gens de Milieu people, but the gathering was clearly pan-tribal. McDonald went to this rendezvous once again in 1875, where he again found more than two hundred Indians.

Nuchalawoya does not seem to be mentioned again until Hudson Stuck's *Ten Thousand Miles with a Dogsled* (1914: 153), and Stuck writes as if it were already a lost tradition. Stuck recognized the old fur trading site was no longer in use, with two hundred U.S. Army soldiers stationed at nearby Fort Gibbon. This fort, which was established during the gold rush of 1899 and was not abandoned until 1923, became a commercial trading post for the miners. One historic photograph shows Indians arriving in their canoes for this gathering in 1883 (Fig. 17.1). Stuck's observations leads to the conclusion that the annual gatherings

Figure 17.1. Canoes arriving at Nuklukayet for spring rendezvous. Schieffelin Brothers Prospecting Trip album, 1882–1883. Alaska Digital Archives. Original at Alaska State Historical Library, Juneau. https://vilda.alaska.edu/digital/collection/cdmg21/id/918/rec/1

ceased sometime between 1910 and 1914. If they continued after that, they either went without journalistic notice or there was a long hiatus in between them.

The modern revival of Nuchalawoya in 1963 was predicated on cultural celebration rather than the economics of trade. It continued to be celebrated annually or semi-annually from the early 1960s into the early 1990s (Monaghan 1977) and then came back again in 2003 and 2008 but has again been suspended. The latest incarnation featured traditional dancing, games, races, potlatch feasting, and a Queen Contest. A law passed by the State legislature along with permitting regulations by the Alaska Board of Game in 1991 allows the taking of up to three moose for the Nuchalawoya Potlatch (05 AAC 092.53).

The nineteenth century origin of gathering at Tanana for a trading rendezvous is now gone, but the modern reincarnation of Nuchalawoya at the same place links it closely to the past. Events featured at the new Nuchalawoya have included foot races, bike races, a queen contest, motorboat races, a greased pole walk, arm wrestling, and tea-making (Roberts 1975). In the evening aboriginal-style Native dances and square dances accompanied by fiddle music have been very popular. Today it is commemorated by the Tanana Chiefs Conference as a place where Athabaskans came together to work for political self-determination, subsistence rights, and land rights (see http://www.tananachiefs.org/corporate/history_tcc.shtml). Comprised of representatives from forty-two communities, the TCC has become one of the largest employers in Fairbanks.

Because some of the first Hudson's Bay Company men at Fort Yukon in the 1840s and 1850s were highland Scots, it's plausible that the English term "gathering" may have been borrowed from the Scottish gatherings which became popular in northern Scotland during the early nineteenth century. The chief trader at Fort Yukon, Alexander Hunter Murray, for example, was from Argyllshire and was raised among

Scottish gatherings. Today the annual Argyllshire Gathering features stone and hammer throwing, tossing the caber, dances, foot races, games, and bagpipe competition. And the Braemar gathering in Aberdeenshire is still older, having taken root in 1832. Of course, most of these events are indigenous to Scottish culture, and although the Scottish notion of a summer festival with dancing and games provides a rough cultural template for the northern Dene festivals of today, I'm not suggesting that Scots traders introduced the idea of gatherings to the Gwich'in in the way that they introduced bannock, Scottish reels, and fiddle music. But what I am suggesting is that the Gwich'in and Han have borrowed the Scots term "gathering" to describe their own social events. Almost anywhere else in North America such large social get-togethers would be called festivals, fairs, or conventions.

To be sure, the Gwich'in have their own words for a gathering. The 1988 Gwich'in Gathering in Arctic Village was called Gwich'in Niintsyaa, which means 'where we feast', and the 1992 Gwich'in Gathering in Venetie was called Gwich'in Khelan Nihjyaa ('Gwich'in grouping together in one place'). Kenneth (2000) says that gathering places have several names in Gwich'in. Łirijil, for example, means 'where we gather' and Łineeraadal k'it means 'a place where we rendezvous (over and over again).' Kenneth says there was a traditional place on the upper Coleen River called Ga'al Tąįį ('the place where trails come together'). This location was chosen because it was equidistant for all of the Gwich'in bands to travel to. Although it was located in the heart of the Gwich'in homeland (Gwich'in nąįį gwats'ą' k'eegwaadhat, lit. 'going to where the Gwich'in are fully in charge'), the last time this place was used for gatherings was probably 100-150 years ago, perhaps during the Hudson's Bay Company years in interior Alaska, 1847-1869.

The eastern Gwichya Gwich'in on the Canadian side had their own regional gatherings, many of them held at a traditional location known as the Flats, just downriver from the modern village of Tsiigehtshik (Arctic

Red River). Tsiigehtshik is strategically located at the confluence of the Arctic Red and Mackenzie rivers. These traditional gatherings took two principal forms. One form focused on tea dancing and the playing of the Dene stick game (locally known as udzi) a gambling pastime played with great passion for days on end. These activities were shared with the Slavey who came to visit from farther up the Mackenzie River. The other form of gathering, which may be more modern, had "football" as its focus and was played by the Gwich'in with their coastal Eskimo neighbors. Apparently both types of gatherings ended in 1947 when the conclusion of steamboat traffic and the decline of the fur trade made inter-village visits less frequent (Heine et al 2007:222-232).

Modern Gatherings

The first modern-day Gwich'in Gathering, called Gwich'in Niintsyaa, was held in Arctic Village from June 8-10, 1988, and I was lucky enough to be alerted to it by Dr. Mike Holloway, a longtime friend of the Gwich'in and a leading advocate for protecting the Arctic National Wildlife Refuge (see Holloway 2014). This Gathering was ostensibly called because of the need felt by Gwich'in leaders to unite against the threat of oil field development in the Refuge. The letter of invitation, however, said the gathering was called to address the broader question of "What must we do to ensure that our language, our culture, and our way of life remain a positive option (alternative?) for our people now and generations to come?" (Tritt 1988a). The seeds of this first modern gathering, however, seem to have come from a request by the late elder, Myra "Choo" Kyikavichik, aka Myra Kaye, of Old Crow, Yukon shortly before her death.

The Gwich'in perceived that industrial development in the caribou calving grounds could easily disrupt the Porcupine caribou herd's use of its calving grounds and alter its migration routes (Tritt 1988b). Elders felt that oil exploration and drilling would not only reduce the caribou population but limit subsistence hunters' access to it. In spiritual harmony with the caribou, who gather each summer on the Arctic plain, the Gwich'in decided it was time for them to gather together as a Nation. They ignored the artificial division created by the Alaskan-Canadian border. One of the major organizers of this first modern gathering was Bob Childers, a non-Native employed as an environmental consultant by the Gwich'in Steering Committee. The Gwich'in Steering Committee emerged as the political action group lobbying Congress to protect the Refuge. Another organizer was Sarah James of Arctic Village, who travels and speaks continuously against oil exploration and development within the Refuge (see James 2005). The chief of Arctic Village at the time was Lincoln Tritt.

This first modern Gwich'in Gathering needs to be put in the historic context of other Alaska Native festivals. As Hiroko Ikuta has noticed, there were a lot of festivals launched during the 1980s because this was a time of immense political change following the Alaska Native Claims Settlement Act (ANCSA): "Through the process of negotiation for land claims and subsistence hunting rights, Alaska Native leaders sought ways to present a unified, collective image of their heritage that could empower their political autonomy" (Ikuta 2011:60). The first Camai Yup'ik Dance Festival, the first Arctic Slope Kivgik or Messenger Feast, the first Quyana Alaska, and the first Celebration for Tlingits, Haidas, and Tsimpshians in Southeast Alaska were all started during the 1980s. We could add to this list also the first Athabascan Old-Time Fiddling Festival, which the Gwich'in have participated in since its inception in 1983 (Mishler 1993:126-142).

At the first Gwich'in Gathering plane after plane arrived in Arctic Village with visitors, and tents were pitched colorfully on every hilltop. Mine was one of them. The gathering featured hours and hours of speeches by elders followed by hours and hours of dancing to fiddle music and rock n' roll played by local musicians. In between there was much feasting or lavasdaa. Caribou heads were roasted over open fires. There was a church ceremony, a smudging ceremony, and a naming ceremony. Gifts were given to honor elders and others. On June 10 a resolution was passed by the chiefs urging the United States Congress and the President to prohibit development in the calving and post-calving grounds of the Porcupine Caribou Herd and that the 10-02 area of the Arctic National Wildlife Refuge be set aside as a wilderness area. That resolution was updated in 2012.

Media coverage of the original event was pretty intensive. The Canadian Broadcast Corporation sent two film crews (Northern Native Broadcasting 1989) and *National Geographic* sent another. A reporter and a photographer came from the *Anchorage Daily News* (see Hulen 1988) along with a broadcaster for the Alaska Public Radio Network.

A second Gwich'in Gathering was also held in Arctic Village in 1990. The third was held in Venetie from June 15-21,1992 , the fourth was in Old Crow in 1994, the fifth in Fort McPherson in 1996, the sixth in Fort Yukon in 1998 (for a detailed account see Inoue 2004), the seventh in Aklavik in 2000, the eighth in Old Crow in 2002, the ninth in Beaver in 2004, and the tenth in Inuvik (called "A Gathering of Minds") in 2006. A special Gwich'in Youth Gathering was held in Arctic Village in 2001. The next biennial gathering was held in Old Crow in 2008, followed by Fort Yukon in 2010, Fort McPherson in 2012, Old Crow again in 2014, returning back to Arctic Village in 2016, and back across the border again to Tsiigehtshik in 2018. There was no gathering in 2020 due to the Covid-19 pandemic, although one was planned for Old Crow, and the Gwich'in Steering Committee staged a Virtual Gwich'in Gathering online using Zoom from September 24-26. When I attended this, there were only about fifty people present with me, and only a couple of them were Gwich'in. After a four year hiatus, in person gatherings resumed at Old Crow in 2022. One of the important symbols that has emerged from these gatherings is a bold turquoise flag featuring

Figure 17.2. Fort Yukon Gathering in July, 2010, showing octagon tent arbor and Gwich'in Nation flag design, near the Yukon River. Photo by Craig Mishler.

In addition to the first Gwich'in Gathering at Arctic Village in 1988, I participated in the 1992 Gwich'in Gathering at Venetie, the 1996 Gwich'in Gathering in Fort McPherson, the 2000 Han Gathering in Moosehide, Yukon Territory, the 2001 Spiritual Unity of the Tribes Gathering in Tanacross, the Eagle Village Han Gathering in 2004, and the Fort Yukon Gwich'in Gathering in 2010. I made video footage of all of these except the first and the third to last, along with still photos and field notes. Gatherings are difficult to document because there are so many events involving hundreds of people over several days. For the participants they amount to a kind of social marathon.

The people of Old Crow have maintained their own localized gathering every summer for several days surrounding July 1st, Canada

Day. The Gwich'in and Inuit living in the Mackenzie River delta also gather at Midway Lake west of Fort McPherson each July for a large music festival that features nightly fiddling and square dancing into the wee hours. Popular country and rock n' roll bands as well as local musicians are prominent during the afternoon and early evening.

Apparently prompted by the success of the biennial Gwich'in Gatherings, the first Han Gathering was held at Moosehide Village near Dawson City in the summer of 1993, the second one in 1994, the third in 1996, the fourth in 1998, the fifth in 2000, the sixth in 2002, and the seventh in 2004. Han Gatherings are held biannually, and in recent years have been held during the same years as Gwich'in Gatherings. Though they each attract a different audience and a different following, since 1996 the Han and Gwich'in Gatherings have been held on different weeks during the same summers so that it is possible for individuals to attend both events.

These gatherings provide an opportunity for the Alaska Han and the Canadian Han and the Alaskan Gwich'in and Canadian Gwich'in to establish stronger social and political ties, to celebrate each other's lives, and to maintain their expressive traditions. In a very real way, the gatherings transcend the artificial political boundaries imposed on them by the federal governments of Canada and the United States. The social and cultural ties maintained at summer gatherings actually mirror those formed at the Athabaskan Old Time Fiddling Festival, a major winter event held each November in Fairbanks since 1982 (see Mishler 1993). Many of the same people attend both.

Gatherings are expensive to put on, and a variety of methods have been used to finance them. The 1992 Venetie Gathering was largely supported by the sale of pull-tabs or Vegas, a form of Alaska legalized gambling. Pull-tabs, which work on the same principle as slot machines, are operated year-round by the Native Village of Venetie Tribal Government.

The 2000 Han Gathering in the old village of Moosehide, on the other hand, was supported by a $20,000 CF grant from the Community Development Fund of the Yukon Territorial Government and by the sale of raffle tickets. This gathering, which I attended, attracted well over 500 people and featured many workshops, games, and musical performances by various Native groups. Due to the enormous amount of work and expenses they entail, Han Gatherings are held every other year, but during the off years, the Han usually hold a youth culture camp at the same site. Participating in the Han Gathering of 2000 were visitors from Arctic Village, Tanacross, Northway, Tetlin, Wasilla, St. Mary's, and Anchorage, Alaska. Canadian visitors came from Haines Junction, Fort McPherson, Old Crow, Whitehorse, Victoria, and Edmonton. In 2004 I attended a much smaller Han Gathering in Eagle Village, Alaska. This gathering honored the memory of two individuals who had died the previous winter, making it similar to a memorial potlatch. It was primarily attended by the Dawson Han and featured singing, dancing, and a gift giveaway.

Southern Tutchone Gatherings began in 1996 and were held annually until the Covid pandemic. The events that take place at the Southern Tutchone Gatherings include games, races, tea boiling, bannock making, rabbit snare setting, music, dancers, a kids fair, cultural demonstrations, and local crafts persons who set up tables to sell their products. These gatherings are sponsored by three bands: Ta'an Kwach'an Council of Haines Junction, the Champagne/Aishihik First Nation, and the Kluane First Nation.

The people of Tanacross, located on the upper Tanana River, have also hosted several gatherings in recent years. Host communities, such as Tanacross, are supported by a pantribal organization known as The Spiritual Unity of the Tribes, loosely affiliated with the Baha'i faith. The principal organizers for these gatherings are urban Natives from Fairbanks and Anchorage. These gatherings seem to appeal to urban dwellers who are out of touch with their tribal identity and seek to locate themselves within a non-Christian Native American spirituality. At the Spiritual Unity of the Tribes gatherings there is a lot of ceremony and prayer to the Creator, but very little mention of Jesus. The emphasis is on sharing and healing. Workshops are held on all kinds of alternative therapies, and there are a substantial number of Native elders who speak about their life experiences under a central arbor in an open field. Underneath the arbor is a ceremonial fire that is maintained day and night for the four days of the gathering (Figs. 17.2-17.3).

Figure 17.3. Inside octagon tent arbor with fire pit. Fort Yukon, July, 2010. Photo by Craig Mishler.

The first Spiritual Unity of the Tribes Gathering was held in Saskatchewan in 1989, one year after the first modern day Gwich'in Gathering. Consequently, they are not simply for the benefit of Tanacross but for indigenous peoples everywhere, and non-Natives are always welcome. These gatherings are designed to promote spiritual unity without becoming evangelical. Their guiding principles are spiritual compassion, tolerance, and equality. So far Tanacross has hosted international gatherings in 1993, 1996, 1999, 2001, and 2003. The tripartite theme of the 2001 gathering was "Spirit, Unity, Peace." In 2003 the chosen theme was "Raven's Journey."

This was the 33rd Gathering since the inception of the gatherings in the 1980s. Since the first one in Saskatchewan, Canada, there have been other gatherings in Alaska, Russia, Australia, and the lower 48 states. Each has been unique, and each has brought spiritual growth and healing to its participants. "'Honoring the Youth' was the theme for one year's gathering. "Our young people are our future. They are the people who will inherit the world we leave to them; and they are the ones who have the chance to make this world a better place."

One of the featured activities at Tanacross gatherings are talking circles,[5] something rarely seen at Gwich'in and Han Gatherings. Talking circles are ceremonial focus groups that encourage individuals to share their life experiences with others. Some talking circles are topical, focused on alcohol and drugs, or grieving. Others are especially for men. Native Americans have used talking circles ceremonially for many centuries, and they seem to be growing in importance. A talking circle is considered very sacred because it is a form of counseling and an opportunity for singing and storytelling. Different kinds of symbols are held by the speakers during a talking circle to ensure that the person holding the symbol can hold the floor and speak without interruption. The symbol might be something like a decorated walking stick, a braid of sweet grass, an eagle feather, or a tobacco pipe. When the person who has the symbol has finished speaking, he or she passes it to someone else, usually in a clockwise direction.

The "mixed" talking circle I participated in at the Tanacross gathering in August, 2001, consisted of five women and four men. There was no advanced sign-up sheet; we just showed up at the announced time. Two other talking circles, one for veterans and one for women, were held simultaneously with ours just outside the arbor. Two women in our circle identified themselves as facilitators and explained the process. The initial round consisted of a smudging, administered by the oldest women. The smudge was a large clam shell containing a combination of dry sage, dry cedar shavings, and braided sweet grass. The second round consisted of songs, of which there were only two. The third round was a round of self-introductions, and the third round was one of stating our feelings and mood at the moment. The fourth and longest round was called the sharing round. Most individuals talked at great length in this round, revealing a wide range personal fears, anxieties, and shortcomings. They also talked about their spouses and partners and their children. The fifth round consisted of responses to what others had shared in the fourth round.

At the end, each participant was invited to take a pinch of loose tobacco and make a silent prayer. The tobacco was then deposited in the smudge and emptied into the large ceremonial fire for the whole gathering. Following this everyone stood up and held hands and prayed. After the prayer, hugs were exchanged all around and some exchanged their addresses and phone numbers.

The community of Tanacross participated in the gathering, but largely on the fringes. They were seldom seen at the ceremonial arbor, but they did provide a friendly setting for the gathering to happen in a rural road-accessible area. Tanacross villagers also provided the evening meal at the old community hall, which was followed most evenings with a dance. The Tanacross dancers and drummers performed twice during the four-day gathering. The Spiritual Unity of the Tribes gatherings also featured ceremonial sweat lodges, something usually absent from the Gwich'in and Han Gatherings. Separate sweat lodges are held for men and for women. At Tanacross they also had a "medicine wheel" made out of small stones. The medicine wheel was located next to the arbor and was explained to us as a sacred place because each stone in the wheel represented an alcohol-related death in the families of those attending the gathering.

All of the gatherings I have attended have been free of charge and open to the public, but due to their location in small rural communities, attendance has been about 90-98 per cent Native and invitations are largely by word of mouth. The one exception to this was the Han Gathering at Moosehide in 2000, where a lot of non-Native tourists came to the site each afternoon and went back upriver to Dawson City after only a few hours. Some came only for the boat ride and free evening meals.

One marked difference between Gwich'in Gatherings and Han Gatherings is that Han Gatherings are always held in the same place, at Moosehide near Dawson City, while the Gwich'in Gatherings have been held each time in a different host village throughout the Gwich'in Nation, a moveable feast. Another difference is that Gwich'in Gatherings have been politically motivated (the symbolic flag), while the Han Gatherings have not. Oratory is always prominent at Gwich'in Gatherings, with elders speaking for hours on end, but speeches at the Han Gatherings are kept short and are primarily related to the schedule of daily activities.

Even the annual Denakkanaaga Youth-Elders Conferences can be viewed as gatherings, although they are not commonly referred to as such. These popular annual early summer conferences are held in a different Interior Alaskan village each summer, so that over a decade those attending have an opportunity to visit new communities and form a network of friendships outside of their own kin groups and outside of their own villages. The first Denakkanaaga ('Our People Speak') Elders Conference was held in 1982, and the Youth Conference was added to it in 1987. While social and political issues such as alcohol, drug abuse, and subsistence are at the focus of attention, here too singing and dancing are a mainstay, and one of the primary goals is to pass on the knowledge and values of the elders to those in their teens. Male elders are usually paired with male youth and female elders with female youth.

One of the cultural forces behind northern Dene Gatherings is that of convergence, which may be defined as a centripetal coming together of people and cultures. Convergence sets the stage for the dynamic exchange and diffusion of expressive forms. While some Dene are loathe to copy another group's songs and dances, they are nevertheless impressed by what they see and what they hear, and they like to be invited to join in celebrating the traditions of other tribal groups. While convergence leads to variation and innovation, it also leads to the standardization of tradition, as individuals and groups attempt to conform to the behavioral expectations of their peers. In Gwich'in country that means everyone present needs to try the Red River jig.

To conclude, the emergence of tribal and pan-tribal gatherings, revived from the nineteenth century historic fur trading rendezvous, is very important to the Dene and worthy of cultural documentation. Indeed, the choice of the word "gathering" adds a fresh twist to the time-honored anthropological phrase "hunting and gathering" societies. It does so by highlighting their persistent sociability, love of travel, and sense of fun.

Acknowledgments

An earlier version of this essay was presented at the Alaska Anthropological Association Annual Meeting in Fairbanks, Alaska, March 22, 2001.

Endnotes

1. A side issue reflected in the title of this paper, is that it is more and more appropriate to use the term "Dene" rather than Athabaskan, Athabascan, or Athapaskan in our scholarship. It is time we start referring to these groups by their own indigenous language names rather than the ones historically imposed on them by the Cree and non-Native scholars. In this respect, the whole puzzle over whether to spell "Athabaskan" with a "p" or a "b" and a "c" or a "k" is moot if we look to appropriate emic terms such as Dene, which has been widely and wisely adopted throughout Canada.

2. Cree gatherings continue to be held. The Fisher River Cree Nation has announced that they are hosting a gathering in Manitoba between August 3-6, 2023. These gatherings have proven to be expensive. In 2007, at their twelfth National Cree Gathering at Grand Rapids, Manitoba, the tribes spent $325,000 CAD and came up $125,000 short. Tlingit, Haida, and Tsimpshian Indians of Southeast Alaska have been holding bi-annual get-togethers since 1982 sponsored by the Sealaska Heritage Foundation. These are not called gatherings but "celebrations," yet they bring all the clans together for a renewal of song, dance, and oratory traditions in much the same way as the Gwich'in and Han Gatherings. A major difference is that the Southeast Alaska celebrations are held entirely indoors because the weather is too wet for camping.

3. The gathering site known as Nuchalawoya (also known in the Koyukon language as Noochu Loghoyet and in English as Nuklukayet), as distinct from the physical confluence of the Tanana and Yukon rivers, actually moved around from year to year to a number of locations miles apart from one another, making its use as a specific place name quite confusing. See Fr. Jules Jetté's notes (Jetté and Jones 2000: 491); also de Laguna (1999: 93-94).

4. These band names are no longer in use today and the descendants of the people to whom they were ascribed are difficult to ascertain. According to Arndt (1996:198-199), the Tetse Gwich'in seem to refer to the Middle Koyukon living along the Yukon between the mouths of the Tanana and Koyukuk rivers. The bands represented at the spring trading rendezvous, therefore, included the Gwichyaa Gwich'in from the Yukon Flats (Shahnyaa Ti' and his followers), the Dranjik Gwich'in from the Black River (Red Leggins and his followers), the Middle Koyukon (Tetse Gwich'in), and the Lower Tanana (Gens des Buttes or Tunun Gwich'in). The Gens de Milieu, and Kitli or Kitlit Gwich'in have not been identified linguistically, but apparently lived somewhere downriver from Fort Yukon.

5. There are several types of Indian ceremonies widely used in North America that are gradually being introduced to the subarctic. These include Fasting, The Vision Quest, The Talking Circle, The Pipe Ceremony, The Sweet Grass Ceremony, and the Sweat Lodge Ceremony. See Mishler (1990, Chapter One in this volume), and Scott (1994). The only Gwich'in Gathering which had Talking Circles was the one at Old Crow (Stevens 1994), but Tanacross Gatherings make extensive use of them.

18. Gwich'in Fiddlers and Gwich'in Dancers:
An Alternative Musical Standard

Musical History

Gwich'in old-time fiddling and square dancing have been around for over 175 years, introduced in the 1840s by Scots, Orkneymen, and French Canadians in the employ of the Hudson's Bay Company, who established fur trading posts at Fort McPherson, NWT, and Fort Yukon, Alaska. The venerable old tunes are as robust and crooked as they come, and the dance repertoire is very conservative, consisting of various contras, large running sets known as "square dances", and step dances known as "jigs" (see Mishler 1993). During the gold rush era at the end of the 19th century, waltzes, fox trots, one steps, two steps, and schottisches were also adopted, but little has changed in the repertoire since then.

Unlike Anglo-American fiddlers, who play competitively and for cheering audiences in contests, concerts, and clubs and jam in festival parking lots, Gwich'in fiddlers in rural Alaska and Northwest Canada have only one principal venue, the square dance. Although jig dance contests have been popular among the Gwich'in since at least the early 1970s, it was not until August, 1996, at the Gathering held in Fort McPherson, NWT, that I saw my first Gwich'in fiddle contest. The elevation of one fiddler over another is generally avoided in Indian society because it breeds jealousy and conflict.

Although talented Indian fiddlers have earned a high degree of prestige as leaders in their communities, the important thing for these musicians is not competing with one another for trophies or applause or demonstrating their virtuosity with hot licks, but keeping smooth, steady time and communicating effectively and pleasurably with the dancers in front of them.

In the north, this musical communication creates a social solidarity that is essential to the social continuum we understand as tribal groups. Every two years the Gwich'in Nation has a tribal gathering to discuss political issues such as the threat of oil development on caribou calving grounds in the Arctic National Wildlife Refuge, and nightly fiddle dances ignite a fire, reminding everyone of their kinship and ethnic affiliation. The face-to-face and hand-to-hand interaction provided by the dances proves to be much more politically unifying than long speeches or sit-down feasts. As the ethnomusicologist Alan P. Merriam once said, "The anthropologist... is interested in the relationship of the dance group to other groupings in society, in how dance reflects social and cultural structure, and in the contribution of dance to the other structures which mesh with it to form society" (1974:13).

Since dancers are crucial performers in Gwich'in musical events, two key questions which arise in my mind are: 1) Who's in charge? Do the fiddlers lead the dancers or do the dancers lead the fiddlers? and 2)

How do fiddlers and dancers communicate with one another during a performance?

There are some dance-specific lines of communication between Gwich'in fiddlers and Gwich'in dancers, links between sound and movement. In certain reels such as the Handkerchief Dance (K'oonitaii Ch'adzaa), an elegant dance for two women and one man better known in the British Isles as "The Scottish Reel", dancers are expected to execute certain steps when they hear the A and then the B part of the fiddle tune, the A part being the low notes and the B part the melodic high notes. During the A part dancers are supposed to jig in place, and during the B part the women dancers are expected to do a loop figure underneath the man's arms. Fiddlers say they also simultaneously give dancers a visual cue for the beginning of the B part, "whenever the bow goes down."

In the contra dance called Eight Couple (Neekę̨ę̨ Dǫǫ), dancers also alternate between executing figures and jigging in place. The fiddlers declare that "the shuffle" played on the D and G strings goes with the jig step. And when the fiddlers shift to "the bridge", played on the E and A strings, it's a cue for the dancers to execute their figure 8's. In both the Handkerchief Dance and Eight Couple the two-part structure of the fiddle tune determines the structure of the dance.

The Management of Energy

Fiddlers have certain cues they follow to spare themselves from being fatigued by unnecessary playing. Bill Stevens of Fort Yukon and Fairbanks, for example, says that when the Red River Jig is played, a dance for just one couple on the floor at a time, it can go on almost endlessly if there are a lot of if there are a lot of participating couples. Therefore the fiddler can quit any time dancers start walking off the floor or at any time jiggers start repeating the dance with new partners. Another way to end the Red River Jig is for one of the backup musicians to announce over the microphone, "Now everybody on the floor". This effectively terminates the long sequence of one couple jigging at a time. Trimble Gilbert says that when enough couples have had an opportunity to jig, he just slows down and stops. What bothers him the most and makes him tired is when dancers appear to be shy or lazy.

What really irritates Gwich'in fiddlers (and other fiddlers as well) are situations in which too many couples line up for a contra or a square dance, all in one set. If more than five or six couples want to dance "Varandii", for example, the fiddler may hold up his outspread hand to indicate just five couples, or wave his bow and verbally order them to form a second set before starting to play. This cuts the playing time in half.

One Canadian Gwich'in fiddler, the late Alfred Francis of Fort McPherson, considered large square dances (better known to outsiders as "progressive" or "running" sets) to be an insult to fiddlers and guitar players because such dances are so long and exhausting. He preferred ten or twelve couples to a set. Still, every Canadian Gwich'in square dance I have watched over the years has included twenty-five or thirty couples. To spare the musicians and shorten the dances, Canadian dancers frequently elect two lead couples facing one another on opposite sides of the set. With two lead couples the running set or square dance can be completed in half the time, very comparable to a set of ten to twelve couples featuring just one lead couple.

Fiddlers are also able to step in and end a dance when dance leaders lose their concentration and control. I saw this happen at the Gwich'in Old-Time Fiddling Festival held in Fairbanks in November, 2015. The seventeen couples were performing Neets'ee Tł'yaa, which is something like a little square dance. Traditionally, all of the figures in this dance are done in one full sequence (see Mishler 1993: 72-77), making for a dance of about six minutes in length. And sometimes the whole sequence is repeated. But on this occasion, the dance leader and his partner decided to stretch the dance to a third iteration of the figures, and both the dancers and the musicians really began to slow down and tire. When the fiddler realized what was happening, he stopped playing right in the middle of a figure, which brought the dance to an abrupt halt and reminded the dance leader of his choreographic error.

Gwich'in square dances present a special case in that the fiddlers are involved in a lengthy pre-dance ritual. This ritual calls for the fiddler to play a square dance tune such as "Soldier's Joy" or "The Girl I Left Behind Me" to get the dancers out on the floor and lined up to dance. It usually takes seven or eight minutes of warm-up playing to get all the men out on the floor, and then another minute or so for the women to take up positions next to their partners before the dance can begin. At Midway Lake in 1991 I timed one of these dances on videotape and discovered that the warm-up to the dance actually took longer than the dance itself. The men must decide whether or not they will dance, while the women must decide who they will dance with. And sometimes after all the couples are assembled on the floor the dancers still have to negotiate which couples will be the lead couples and where they should be positioned. All this time the fiddler and guitar player must carry the burden of warming up.

Evaluations

Fiddlers are also privately critiqued by dancers and by other fiddlers. Some are characterized as playing "too fast" or "too slow". But of course "fast" and "slow" are very subjective categories. One Gwich'in fiddler I interviewed has been criticized by dancers as playing too fast, but when I asked this fiddler how he liked the playing of a certain Canadian Inuit fiddler, he in turn claimed that the named Inuit fiddler was "too fast". Uninspiring fiddlers are avoided by dancers, who "vote with their feet" and simply stay off the dance floor if they want a new fiddler. On a trip to Venetie in August, 1996, I saw a fiddler warming up for two hours in the dance hall, but the dance never happened. Some people said it was because the fiddler had no guitar player. Others said it was because no dancers showed up. Yet another dance in Arctic Village was canceled on December 30, 1996, because nobody built a fire in the community hall. In order to have a dance in the winter it's necessary to have firewood to heat the barrel stoves in the community hall, and if no one cuts wood, the musicians get the night off, and the dance doesn't happen. It's usually the chief's responsibility to provide wood for the community hall.

I was also curious to know how fiddlers are chosen for dances, since in each community there are usually at least two or three active fiddlers. Trimble Gilbert of Arctic Village says that the village first chief or the young people always call him up to ask if he will play, and if he is too tired or sick, he will call up another fiddler. "We're all just like one family," he says. "Musicians are very close to each other." They are not all *that* close, however.

Although most fiddlers like to have another musician around to give them a break, in 1992 I listened to a Venetie fiddler play for three hours while another visiting fiddler sat on stage with his fiddle case open, waiting for an invitation to play that never came. At 2 a.m. another Venetie fiddler suddenly appeared at the front door, and the performing fiddler abruptly passed his bow over to this man, whom he must have sent for by messenger. The visiting fiddler who waited so patiently with his fiddle case open could only participate as a dancer and a square dance caller. Visiting fiddlers are nevertheless in demand, especially during the Christmas holidays and during the Spring Carnivals held in late March and early April. Only the best fiddlers are invited to play on these occasions, and for their services they receive a stipend plus airfare, accommodations, and meals.

And then there are the often testy relationships between fiddlers and their guitar players. Many Gwich'in fiddlers are very picky about who will chord for them, and not just anyone who wants to sit in will do. During the 1980s I witnessed one dance in Venetie which totally collapsed because the fiddler, Jimmy Roberts, played endless warm-ups and little melodic runs and kept stopping to retune, waiting for an uninvited young guitar player to take a hint and leave. Jimmy never said anything to the guitar player, but he simply never committed himself to playing more than a few bars of a tune. After waiting patiently for an hour and a half for another guitar player to show up, Jimmy and the assembled dancers, a crowd of about 50 or 60 people, finally left the hall without having danced a single step.

Another stressful situation occurred at the Midway Lake Music Festival near Fort McPherson, N.W.T., in the summer of 1990 when a Gwich'in fiddler sat on stage and played tunes in a lackluster fashion for about forty minutes early one afternoon. During this low-energy performance not a single dancer took the floor. The chemistry was simply not there. I happened to be videotaping the performance, and when the fiddler saw me with my camcorder, he was so embarrassed that he waved at me to turn the camera off. Although this was not exactly "prime time" for dancing, those dancers who were present voted with their feet, and the fiddler and guitar player cut their performance short.

Some fiddlers say they consciously follow the dancers. The Old Crow fiddler, Allen Benjamin, says that he looks for the best couple on the floor and then follows them. He doesn't follow the ones who dance too fast or too slow. This would suggest that some fiddlers adjust their tempo to suit those who are on the dance floor, but this may only apply to the slower dances such as waltzes, two steps, and fox trots. In the contras and square dances everyone must operate at roughly the same tempo.

Fiddlers say they can play whatever they want to until they get a request from the dancers, and then they try to play what the dancers want. Many of these requests are verbal, but some of them are nonverbal. In the villages I often see the dance leaders line up in sets that dictate the next dance the fiddler must play. Since only one tune is customary and acceptable for a given dance (the dance and the tune sharing the same name), this pre-dance choreography puts the dance leaders almost completely in charge of the fiddler's repertoire. Medleys are hardly ever heard.

The exception to this rule is the square dance, which is sometimes played with a medley of tunes. Bill Stevens says he draws upon a number of different tunes for square dances, but medleys really just confuse the dancers. In the square dance the fiddler has a lot more choice in what he will play. Since the square dance consists of two or three parts, each part is played to a different tune or different medley. It's also true that four of the contras, the Virginia Reel, Varandii, Eight Couple, and the Rabbit Dance, all have similar longways sets. In this instance, the dancers must make a verbal request to the fiddler to designate which contra they wish to perform.

Until the early 1970s, the square dance caller, or K'eechigilik, played an important male leadership role, but the caller's role nearly disappeared from the dance, apparently the victim of electronic instrument amplification. However, new electronics has come to the rescue and callers such as Randall Tetlitchi of Old Crow have recently emerged with portable wireless microphones and bluetooth technology. While it's hard to hear the calls distinctly under this system, the caller's rhythmic chants are an important way of confirming square dance tempos. Today the local senior male dance leader, sometimes nicknamed Chadzaa Ti' ('father of the dance') plays a prominent role in selecting the dance sequences. This dance leader and his female partner are usually the lead couple in square dances or contras and the lead-off couple in jigs. Famous former dance leaders are the late Hamel Frank of Venetie, Horace Cadzow of Venetie, and Neil Colin of Fort McPherson. Along with Randall Tetlitchi, another active dance leader is Jeffrey John from Venetie.

Canadian Gwich'in dancers are more particular about what fiddlers play for square dances. During a three-day visit to Old Crow during the

1996 Christmas holidays, Trimble Gilbert noticed that if he tried playing square dance tunes of his own choice, the dancers would interrupt him and shout, "Other one! Other one!" Usually, they want to hear "The Devil's Dream" played for their square dances. In Alaska, however, fiddlers can play any traditional tune. What this means is that different dance communities respond differently to fiddlers, and the fiddlers must adjust their repertoires accordingly.

Musical Leadership

Fiddler Bill Stevens sees himself as the dance leader: "The dancers follow me, and the guitar players follow me. I set the beat, and I don't slow the tunes down for old timers. In fact, the old timers like to have it lively." Stevens also says "I play better for good dancers, but most of the time the dancers don't keep up with the beat. In the old days people were more physically fit from hunting, fishing, and running traplines, and because they were fit they were very light on their feet."

The late Gwich'in guitar player Walter Newman, who often played backup with Bill Stevens, agreed that even though the guitar player's duty is to strum chords and play rhythm, it's the fiddler who establishes the rhythm. The guitar player must follow the fiddler. Walter said he can play with almost anybody because he watches for two things--the fiddler's foot beat and his bow speed. Almost all Alaskan Gwich'in fiddlers play sitting down and clog their feet as they play; the feet are essential in setting the tempo. For dancing the rhythm is much more important than the melody.

The Canadian Gwich'in, however, always do things a little bit differently, even though they belong to the same nation as their Alaskan counterparts. Some Canadian Gwich'in fiddlers, such as Colin Adjun and his son Gustin, for example, play standing up. And Grafton Njootli, a guitar player from Old Crow, once pointed out to me that Alaskan Gwich'in guitar players play only half as fast as the Canadians. The

Canadians play short fast up and down strums while most Alaskans play slower with much stronger emphasis on the down strum. Grafton provided a good example of the Canadian style of guitar chording.

The issue of fiddlers leading dancers or following dancers is perhaps, in the end, a moot point, because it works both ways, and most Indian fiddlers are also avid dancers. Both groups, as co performers, must put pressure on one another in order to have a close and pleasurable exchange. Fiddlers often serve a dual role, first playing for dancers and then handing over their fiddle to another musician so they too can take to the floor. The late Paul Ben Kassi of Old Crow was regarded as one of the best jig dancers ever seen.

Upriver and Downriver: the Politics of Social Dance

In 1983 The Athabascan Fiddle Festival, an urban fiddle dance revival celebrated in Fairbanks, first brought together the Gwich'in, Koyukon, Han, and Tanana people. Socially and politically, all of these groups federated under The Tanana Chiefs Conference during the Alaska Native Land Claims Settlement Act of 1971. Originally all of the tribal groups performed together at the old Eagles Hall, and as the festival grew in size, they moved to the more spacious ballroom of the Westmark Hotel. It was initiated by the Institute of Alaska Native Art and funded by the Alaska State Council on the Arts. But then the Institute of Alaska Native Art disbanded, and the Festival fell under the direction of the Athabascan Fiddlers Association.

In about 2000, the current organizers of the Athabascan Fiddle Festival, a group from the Koyukon and Tanana area, got themselves elected to the Athabascan Fiddlers Association Board of Directors. In the Koyukon and Tanana region, known as Downriver, social dances have always featured waltzes and two-steps, which first came into the country during the Gold Rush of the 1890s. And in recent years, there have been very few fiddlers participating, so that today nearly every Downriver band consists of a couple of electric guitars, a drummer, and an electric bass player. There is not only a distinct contrast in dance styles from the Upriver community, but also a marked contrast in instrumentation.

As mentioned above, the Gwich'in and Han or Upriver musical and choreographic tradition is much older than the Downriver tradition, going back to the Hudson's Bay Company traders of the mid-nineteenth century. Gwich'in dances include jigs, contra dances, and running sets or "square dances" that were relatively unknown to the Tanana and Koyukon. These dances are quite lengthy and often take twenty to thirty minutes to perform. Nevertheless, the Athabascan Fiddle Festival organizers, headed by singer and guitarist Ann Fears, made a hard and fast rule that each band would only be allotted thirty minutes, to allow for more "equal" participation. For the Gwich'in this meant only one full traditional dance could be performed by a group before their time was up. The musicians could barely get warmed up before they had to quit, and their full repertoire of dances was effectively shut down.

Out of frustration, the Gwich'in, led by Daisy Solomon Stevens, decided to start holding their own separate dances beginning in 2006-2007, at the old National Guard Armory in south Fairbanks. This split or dance rebellion, when the Gwich'in broke away to have their own dance festival, is both politically tribal and choreographic. The Gwich'in counter-festival has also distinguished itself by offering things like moosehead stew and bannock as part of the ticket price. In 2008 Dixie Alexander replaced Daisy Solomon Stevens as the principal organizer.

The final break came when the organizers of the Athabascan Fiddle Festival refused to pay the air fare, hotel bills, and honoraria of the Gwich'in village musicians even if they played at both venues. Nearly all of the Gwich'in fiddlers and guitar players balked and boycotted the Athabascan Fiddle Festival. In response, dances for each group began to be held simultaneously on the same evenings in different venues. The Tanana and Koyukon dances have been held at the David Salmon Tribal

Hall while the Gwich'in dances have been hosted a mile away by the Morris Thompson Center.

There are still a few Gwich'in who attend the Koyukon/Tanana dances and a few Koyukon and Tanana who attend the Gwich'in dances, but for the most part they remain separate and distinct. It should be said that both venues were idle during the Covid pandemic in 2020, although a small group of Gwich'in did get together at a rented hall in Fairbanks during the 2021 Christmas holidays and once again in 2022.

Today Gwich'in square dances are to a large extent conservative predictable events. But the matching of fiddlers to guitar players and fiddlers to dancers on any given night is highly variable, and this matchup sparks the interest of both the musicians and the dancers. The complex communication paradigm between Gwich'in fiddlers, guitar players, dancers, and callers should force us to rethink generalizations about fiddlers and dancers elsewhere. In the subarctic old-time fiddling and dancing is not so much an exhibition of talent as an exchange of emotions and a political affirmation of tribal identity. And from this perspective, the fiddler is indeed a chief.

Acknowledgments

An earlier version of this essay under the title "Athabaskan Fiddlers and Athabaskan Dancers: An Alternative Musical Standard" was published in Fiddler Magazine *6(2):4-7 (1999). A special thanks and shout out to Bill Stevens for his friendship over the years and his insider perspective as a dance fiddler.*

19. Tr'igwitil: The Gwich'in Memorial Potlatch:

A Re-Awakening

"Without witnessing a death
one cannot feel that one understands
very much about a people."
Margaret Mead, *Blackberry Winter*

In this essay I want to establish the antiquity of the Gwich'in memorial potlatch celebration and trace its documentation from the early contact period to the present day, noting both its continuity and discontinuity and its deeply religious overtones. My discussion is consequently divided into an historical section and an ethnographic one. For clarification, many contemporary northern Dene people traditionally have a funeral potlatch shortly after someone's death. And then one or two years later they often hold a memorial potlatch to honor the memory of that person and give away gifts to relatives and friends of the deceased.

From the earliest days of contact with the Hudson's Bay Company in Fort Yukon during 1847-1848, the Gwich'in observed the death of their chiefs and elders with funeral potlatches that were also memorial potlatches. Whites referred to them as "feasts for the dead" or "dead dances," but the traditional Gwich'in name for them is "tr'igwitil." The earliest account of these ceremonies appears in Alexander Hunter Murray's journal for November 17-18, 1848, where he wrote that various parties of Indians were stopping in Fort Youcon on their way to a "great feast" to trade furs for tobacco. Murray notes that he personally donated some tobacco to be given away for the feast, to be held on the Porcupine River. One week later, he added that "Mr. McK [McKenzie], [Antoine] Hoole, & Perro [Le Noire] returned in the evening from the Indian feast where 13 lodges congregated. A great number of moose and deer [caribou] skins were collected to be given away as presents. They will be here with them by & by." (Murray 1848).

But what really happened to the Gwich'in memorial potlatch tradition? Although fairly detailed accounts of this tradition were published in the 1860s by other Hudson's Bay Company traders living in Fort Yukon, virtually nothing has been published about it since then (Hardisty 1867; Jones 1867). So it's now difficult to determine whether the Gwich'in memorial potlatch tradition actually died out, or whether it simply went underground and remained unnoticed by outside observers. We do know it was outlawed in Canada starting in 1884 (expanded below). Clearly the ceremony expressed a fundamental set of beliefs and values and an immanent world view that intimately connected the Gwich'in to one another, to their ancestors, and to neighboring tribal groups.

From the early traders' accounts the following traits emerge: first, the feasts for the dead were organized by invitation, usually by sending special messengers to remote villages and camps; second, they included a lot of feasting and dancing taking place over three or four days; third, they included the performance of specially composed songs in memory of the deceased; fourth, they incorporated a goodly number of games and speeches; and fifth, they featured the giving away of gifts such as beads, furs, and animal skins (marten skins in particular) by the bereaved families.

When I started visiting the Gwich'in in their villages in the early 1970s, there was never any talk about people hosting such gift-giving potlatches. As a frequent visitor to Venetie and Arctic Village during the 1970s, 1980s, and 1990s, I was only aware of community feasts hosted by individual families in their homes after a successful caribou hunt, funeral feasts held after a church service and burial, and feasts held in village graveyards on or around Memorial Day. These feasts were conducted without gifting or giveaways, lasted only a couple of hours, and were intended primarily for the benefit of locals rather than visitors from outside the community.

One of the newest and most common reasons for holding a feast or potlatch today is a young person's graduation from high school or college, including advanced degrees. Such life event potlatches may be given not only in the graduate's home village but also in cities such as Fairbanks. These potlatches do not involve widespread gift-giving as much as food-sharing in the form of a large meal for the friends and relatives of the honoree. Such meals must include a menu of traditional Native foods, such as caribou and moose meat, ducks and geese, and salmon. Several households often contribute. I attended one where roasted ground squirrels were served. These potlatches are generally held in the late May or early June, shortly after the spring graduation ceremonies.

There are several ways of talking about these small potlatches in Gwich'in. One is called "Lidii hałtsyaa", glossed as 'I'm making tea.' Or "Lidii hahtsyaa", 'Someone's making tea.' These are two instances of synecdoche, where a small part of the ceremony, the making and drinking of tea, represents hosting the whole social occasion and ceremony.[1] Another Gwich'in way of talking about a small potlatch is "Vikeech'ahałch'yaa" or 'I'm cooking (something).' Gwich'in speakers also use the word "lavasdaa" for a potlatch feast. Both lidii < le thé and lavasdaa < le festin are borrowed from French and go back historically to the voyageurs employed by the Hudson's Bay Company during the mid-nineteenth century.

We can only postulate that the Gwich'in memorial potlatch or tr'igwitil was dormant for nearly one hundred and fifty years as the result of missionary and government suppression. The first missionaries to visit the Gwich'in at Fort McPherson and Fort Yukon arrived in the late 1850s and early 1860s. The Anglican Rev. William Kirkby, for example, wrote brief accounts of Gwich'in "dead dances" without criticizing them, although he was very quick to speak out against the sins of shamanism, polygamy, and infanticide (Kirkby 1861). Kirkby wrote that "Nightly wailings follow for a time, when the nearest relative makes a feast, invites his friends, and for a week or so the dead dance is performed, and a funeral dirge sung, after which all grief for the deceased is ended" (Kirkby 1872:419; see also Boon 1965). There is nothing at all in Kirkby's account about gifting or tobacco use.

However, we know that other Anglicans worked hard to persuade the Indians to give up their memorial potlatches. In 1865, Archdeacon Robert McDonald told the Gwich'in not to grieve for their relatives who died from scarlet fever in 1865 because they were now all in heaven (McDonald 1866). And the Rev. Vincent Sim made no secret of the fact that he did not approve of the "feast for the dead" held by the neighboring Han at Fort Reliance on the Yukon River in 1883. Sim, who also worked among the Gwich'in at Rampart House and Fort Yukon, saw such feasts as evidence of "heathenism" and thought they represented an institution incompatible with Christianity (Wesbrook 1969:42).

Although they did not arrive in the Gwich'in homeland for some fourteen years after the Hudson's Bay Company set up the first trading posts, these early Christian missionaries were undoubtedly encouraged by the fur traders to suppress feasts for the dead. As trade developed, furs and beads became the primary units of exchange between whites and Natives, and concerns were expressed about how the grieving Gwich'in openly destroyed many of their material possessions.

William Hardisty, the Hudson's Bay Company clerk in charge at Fort Yukon, for instance, wrote this post journal entry on March 16, 1852: "I am sorry to hear that the Chief of the Lower Indians is very ill & not likely to live-- this will have an injurious effect on the Returns of this year-- for should he die they will undoubtedly destroy the most of their furs. They have already smashed a great quantity of Beads since he fell ill" Hardisty 1852a; also Hardisty 1855).

That same fall Hardisty wrote a letter to his superiors complaining about the effect such feasts were having on the Fort Yukon post returns. He said:

> Many of the Indians too are sick and not likely to pass over the winter, the death of several of the most influential men during summer, will I am afraid, have an injurious effect on our Returns, for as is customary among them, on the death of any of their Friends they have destroyed most of their Beads (Note the Indians proceed to the land of the outer Indians to trade. Beads are one of the chief articles of trade. Hence when they destroy their beads they have nothing to give for the furs, and of course our Returns will suffer.) (Hardisty 1852b)

And during the height of the scarlet fever epidemic of 1865, when hundreds of Gwich'in were sick and dying, Archdeacon McDonald noted that the Gwich'in were destroying their material possessions, namely guns and beads (McDonald 1865). The late Rev. David Salmon, traditional chief for the Doyon region, recalled that his father told him that his Gwich'in ancestors did indeed destroy their beads in the process of grieving for loved ones (personal communication May 21, 2004). So this perception is supported by oral tradition.[2]

Another issue is what becomes of the deceased person's belongings. Today his or her things are often put away in storage for about a year, due to the belief that the sight of these things will only increase the grief of the bereaved family. This storage includes not only the dead person's clothing, but also his or her favorite chair and bed. All are immediately removed from the house following a death. In earlier times, such items may have been cremated with the remains of the deceased. Now they are gone through by family members, sometimes after the year in storage, and any valuable items, such as knives or guns, are passed on to family members and friends, while the non-valuables, such as clothes, are burned.[3]

In all contemporary memorial potlatch traditions that I am aware of, including the Tlingit, Upper and Lower Tanana, Ahtna, and Lower Koyukon, the bereaved family saves up for a year or more and gives away most of its wealth to pay back people of the opposite moiety who helped them at the time of their loved one's death. They do this to thank those who donate food, prepare the body, build the casket, and dig the grave, and to formally end their own period of grieving. It's understood that those who receive potlatch gifts are free to do anything they want to with them immediately after the potlatch. So today, wealth is not destroyed at a memorial potlatch. It's simply redistributed.

The suppression of the Gwich'in memorial potlatch in the nineteenth century was also endorsed by Canadian government officials. In 1884, the Canadian federal government amended the Indian Act, making participation in the potlatch a misdemeanor. Although primarily created to eradicate the extravagant potlatches along the Northwest Coast, this law also took effect in the Yukon Territory and in the Northwest Territories, where many of the Gwich'in reside (McClellan 1987:222; also Cole and Chain 1990).

Kenneth Frank insists that the Gwich'in memorial potlatch is an ancient ceremony, and as evidence for that he points to the folktale known as "Loche's Potlatch" told by his grandfather Johnny Frank (see McKennan 1965). This tale was collected by Robert McKennan in Venetie during the summer of 1933.[4] The loche is a freshwater fish better known in English as burbot but better known in Gwich'in as chehłuk.

In Johnny Frank's version of the story, Loche decides to give a big potlatch for his deceased cousin. He invites other species of fish to the potlatch and gives away many gifts to them, but also keeps a few gifts for himself. These gifts may now be found in the anatomy of various species of fish, including pike (jackfish), suckers, and king salmon, as well as caribou. Some of the miniatures found in the body and skeleton of these fish and animals are: a set of moose horns, a bear's arm, a bear's leg, a knife case (the loche's tail skin), a girl's menstrual cap, and mouse pants (from a caribou hind leg tendon), among other things.

The loche's liver represents the bag of marrow grease used in potlatch games. As Kenneth heard it, his ancestors used to throw the men a bladder full of Indian ice cream, meaning grease mixed with berries. The men would make a mad scramble for the grease and tear it into little pieces. A similar thing would be done by the women, who would scramble and "fight" over a tanned moose hide, tearing it into shreds.

Each piece of the loche's anatomy represents part of Gwich'in culture or the natural world in which the Gwich'in live. The fish is an elaborated metaphor of the Gwich'in universe. According to Kenneth Frank and David Salmon, this story helps preserve the ceremony of the memorial potlatch and validates its enactment into the present day. The events in the story function as a blueprint for the potlatch ceremony. Kenneth insists that the main purpose of the Gwich'in memorial potlatch is healing. When gifts are given away to friends and relatives, he believes it makes the spirits of the dead happy.

Today, memorial potlatches in honor of the deceased are well-known observances in Southeast Alaska, among the Tlingit and Haida, and among certain interior Dene groups such as the Upper Tanana, Middle Tanana, and Lower Koyukon, neighbors to the Gwich'in. As I noted above, the Gwich'in memorial potlatch has not been documented in the continuous way that the memorial potlatches of neighboring peoples have been documented, and as someone who began visiting the Gwich'in on a regular basis in the early 1970s, I did not notice its appearance until 1999.

Judy Erick in Venetie informed me that the Solomon family made a memorial potlatch and gave away many guns and blankets in honor of the late Paul Solomon Sr. at the Gwich'in Gathering in Fort Yukon in the summer of 1998. And the following year the Rev. David Salmon made a memorial potlatch for his wife Sarah in Chalkyitsik, giving away gifts in her memory, while the Rev. Paul Tritt gave a feast in Venetie in honor of his late wife Julia, a feast that did not include any gift-giving. In 2002, Kenneth and his family made a feast and distributed gifts to honor the memory of his father and my great friend, Hamel Frank, in Venetie. These dates mark the modern revival of the Gwich'in memorial potlatch, but I don't have any clues as to why these families decided to bring back the ceremony after more than a hundred years. Perhaps it was due to their increased exposure and visits to Tanacross, Lower Tanana, and Lower Koyukon memorial potlatches.[5]

In July, 2003, I was fortunate and honored to be invited and attend a Gwich'in memorial potlatch dedicated to the memory of James and Maggie Gilbert, held in Arctic Village. James Gilbert, who died in 1998, was an Episcopal minister, and his wife Maggie, who died in 1983, was a gifted blind storyteller whom I interviewed and recorded in 1973 (Mishler 2013:67-91).

James and Maggie Gilbert's memorial potlatch was held in Arctic Village from July 17-19, 2003. I received an invitation to attend by the Rev. Trimble Gilbert, one of the three surviving children of James and Maggie, and a longtime friend. Trimble's stepbrother Kias Peter was also a sponsor, but as it turned out the principal organizer of the potlatch was Florence Newman, Trimble's younger sister.

Without going into the detail of my field notes, let me say that the following events seemed to characterize this potlatch. First, there was an ongoing feast held in the center of the village for visitors. Meals, snacks, and coffee were available all day long at the cookhouse, symbolically located in James and Maggie Gilbert's old cabin. Evening meals were served buffet style with the aid of many family members and volunteers. On the afternoon of my arrival on July 17, during a pouring rain, the only events of note were the elders gathering to sing Takudh hymns and to play Mizhur, the Gwich'in card game (see Chapter 14 above), in the cook house.[6]

As for participation, it's important to mention that not everyone living in Arctic Village attended. There were conspicuous absences by many households, and approximately half of those attending were visitors like myself, who flew in from other villages and cities. Altogether, about fifty or sixty persons participated in different elements of the potlatch. So this potlatch did not really bring together the community of Arctic Village where it was held. It constructed and recognized a different kind of community comprised of the Gilberts' extended family and numerous outsiders.

A defining event was the transport and placement on July 18 of a new engraved headstone on the grave of Mary Gilbert, who died as a two-year old infant in 1934, near K'aii dzuu zhit gwitsik ('At the mouth of little willows creek'). Mary Gilbert was the sister of Kias, Trimble, and Florence, and they wanted her to be remembered along with their parents. To honor her memory about thirty of us undertook a day-long pilgrimage upriver to her grave site.

The grave of Mary Gilbert is located about a mile back from the river, so as a group we faced a big logistical battle to move the heavy gravestone from the river to the grave site. This was accomplished by a brigade of headstone carriers and a canoe that ferried the headstone across the lake. Once we all arrived at the grave site, Takudh hymns were sung and speeches were made in English and in Gwich'in. There was much tearful emotion. The weather was sunny and hot, and the mosquitoes were very active.

The third day of the potlatch was the most intense. The ceremonies started at 1 p.m. in the village graveyard. Officiating was Mark McDonald, the Episcopal Bishop of Alaska, who wore his vestments, led prayers, and gave a sermon in the village graveyard before and after the placement of headstones and large wooden crosses on the graves of James and Maggie Gilbert. This was followed by a blessing and consecration of the log cabin where James and Maggie lived and then by a lengthy confirmation service for young people entering the church. This was in turn followed by a general communion service on the Gilbert cabin porch. A buffet dinner followed. The food served included mashed potatoes, potato salad, whitefish, salmon, moose head soup, and other native foods. One item I had never seen before in a Gwich'in meal was barbequed pork ribs, cooked over an open fire grill.

After dinner there was a giveaway. The giveaway probably represents the oldest component of the potlatch, other than the feasting. The first things given away were many pairs of yellow "monkey gloves", the kind of cotton work gloves that their father James always liked to wear. Florence reminded us that one of her father's favorite tricks was to go around the village pounding people on the shoulder. What ensued then was a sequence of mock boxing matches, initiated first by Florence and then by others, all wearing their yellow gloves. As elders got involved, there were spontaneous outbursts of laughter. I managed to record some of this foolery on video. Noteworthy here were challenges to hierarchy, including Bishop McDonald and village chief Evon Peter.

The next items given away were pouches of Red Man chewing tobacco, a favorite of Maggie Gilbert. Many of us tried "a chew" only to make faces and spit it out. Also, a few people were invited to roll cigarettes with Prince Albert brand smoking tobacco. Both the boxing and the chewing were done mimetically to remind us of the distinctive personal habits of James and Maggie. In Gwich'in there is a special verb for these kinds of actions, goorah'in (lit. 'we imitate them'). The remarkable thing is that one hundred and fifty-five years after Alexander Hunter Murray's observations in 1848, tobacco still played a central symbolic role in the Gwich'in memorial potlatch.[7]

The Gilberts' giveaway lasted for at least an hour. There were many general items, including little prayer cards (in Gwich'in), embossed books of matches, napkins, felt bookmarkers, and other small favors. I received a large coffee mug with a handprinted label fastened to it with scotch tape that said, "In Loving memory of Rev. James & Maggie Gilbert, July, 2003." Some things were given only to women, such as bundles of fabric, and only the kids got bags of candy. A few people received framed color photos of James and Maggie.

After the general distribution, individuals were recognized with special gifts. All of the elders in attendance were given hand-made blankets made out of fleece. Some people also received black T-shirts with the names of James and Maggie on the back. Florence even gave gifts to her two brothers, Trimble and Kias. Near the end of the presentations she gave away her parents' family Bible and her father's walking cane. These were very touching moments, for they were certainly among her most precious family possessions.

Florence also made a special flag presentation to chief Evon Peter. This hand-made flag had red and white stripes similar to the American flag, but in place of the fifty stars it had a Gwich'in prayer, read aloud by Caroline Tritt-Frank. And overlaying the stripes was a flock of flying geese. Florence explained that each goose represented one Gwich'in family, and the leader of the flock was the chief. On the corner of the prayer section was also a white candle representing the light provided by the elders. The flag was made by Florence, her children, and her grandchildren to be placed in the village council office. An elaborate ceramic religious statue was also presented to be placed in the Arctic Village Episcopal Church.

When the distribution was complete, Florence called for people who wanted to come up and say something. There were many thank yous and a few short speeches. After a recess of about an hour and a half, the community gathered at the community hall for a big square dance. The band consisted of Trimble Gilbert on fiddle, with two of his sons on bass and rhythm guitar. This fiddle dance was still going strong when I left it at 1:30 a.m. The end of the dance marked the end of the potlatch.

In retrospect, the only events at this potlatch congruent with those held during the early contact period were the gift-giving and the feasting. Memorial songs are no longer composed to honor the deceased, except among the Koyukon and Tanacross. Even the gifts have changed from furs and beads to blankets and small keepsakes. Certainly the liturgical elements of the Christian graveside prayer, the placing of a headstone, the youth confirmation, house blessing, and the general communion led by Bishop McDonald were never present during the early contact period and seem to have been added by the Gilbert family due to their close personal ties and devotion to the Episcopal Church. The Episcopal Church is, of course, a close sister to the Anglican Church of Canada and England, which first brought Christianity to the Gwich'in and tried to discourage the feast for the dead or tr'igwitil ceremony.

Though each new memorial potlatch must be examined and described on its own merits, the Arctic Village memorial potlatch I observed was transformed into a sanctioned religious activity, with the full authority of the American Episcopal Church behind it. Because of this, the present-day memorial potlatch has been reconfigured and bears only a slight resemblance to the "feast for the dead" observed in the early contact period. As a cultural performance, it has its own gestalt.

And it's certainly ironic that the church, one of the institutions which historically suppressed the Gwich'in memorial potlatch, has now become its strongest ally and advocate. We can only attribute this to a liberalization of church theology in the late twentieth century, coupled with its longtime policy of encouraging the Gwich'in to enter the ministry.[8]

When the esteemed Rev. David Salmon, the senior Gwich'in Episcopal priest and traditional chief of the Doyon Region, died in the fall of 2007, something very unusual occurred. With an estimated dozen other Episcopal priests in attendance, the Salmon family held a giveaway at the funeral potlatch in Chalkytsik. Kenneth Frank was invited to attend.

Kenneth says he is convinced that such community and extended family funeral potlatches only developed when airplanes became commonplace in Gwich'in villages during the late 20th century. Before that, he believes, funeral potlatches were quite small and held only for the gravediggers, coffin makers, and those who prepared the body of the deceased for burial.

Of course it's traditional among all northern Dene to give a potlatch feast right after the funeral, but with groups such as the Koyukon, Tanacross, and Upper Tanana, the memorial potlatch is always held a year or more afterwards, primarily so that the family has time to accumulate the gifts it needs to thank relatives and friends of the deceased. This wait also marks the formal grieving period. However, in this instance, with the gifts given out on the same day as the burial, the Gwich'in resumed a practice first recorded in 1848, our earliest historic account. In the words of a visiting journalist to Rev. David Salmon's 2007 funeral potlatch:

> "Once the meal was complete, a few tables were pushed aside and a large blue tarp spread out to hold potlatch presents. A parade of a dozen men and boys bearing rifles started off the giveaway ritual. The rifles were gently laid on an Indian design

blanket and piled around with practical items from toolboxes to blankets to hatchets and plastic gas cans" (Smetzer 2007).

The Episcopal church in Alaska now celebrates many diverse ideals, cultures, languages, and theological perspectives, and it has gradually made room for the revival of sacred Gwich'in traditions and beliefs. At the same time the Gwich'in are still searching to recover those first indigenous funeral and memorial traditions and order them in such a way that they can be smoothly integrated with Christian ones.

Acknowledgments

An earlier draft of this paper was presented to the International Congress of Arctic Social Sciences (ICASS IV) at Fairbanks, Alaska on May 22, 2004.

Endnotes

1. According to Kenny Thomas Sr. (personal communication), this same expression of "making tea" is also used in Tanacross for putting on a small potlatch, such as the one celebrated with children at the annual culture camp in Mansfield Village. A memorial potlatch, by contrast, is called "a big cook."

2. It was also a practice for grieving Gwich'in to singe their hair and tear up furs as well as destroy their beads. Other northern Dene groups followed suit. Lower Tanana people at Minto still talk about a man who tore up a fox skin worth over $1,000. See the video, *Hitting Sticks, Healing Hearts: A Minto Memorial Potlatch*, by Curt Madison. Manley Hot Springs: River Tracks Productions, 1992.

3. See Alan Boraas and Donita Peter, "The Role of Beggesh and Beggesha in Precontact Dena'ina Culture." *Alaska Journal of Anthropology* 6 (1&2) (2008):211-224. Boraas and Peter hypothesize that the dearth of artifacts excavated in Dena'ina Athabaskan sites is directly attributable to the belief in beggesh (lit. 'his or her scent or smell), which associates a person's belongings with an impurity that represents a danger to others. Hence these belongings are destroyed in the cremation. It seems logical to postulate something similar for the prehistoric Gwich'in and other northern Dene.

4. I recorded a closely related Gwich'in language variant from Myra Robert in Venetie in November, 1972. In Myra's version the loche is female, while in Johnny Frank's version it's male. Also, Myra says the deceased relative that Loche gave the memorial potlatch for was her own child, not her cousin, as claimed in the Johnny Frank text. Since the Gwich'in have no kinship term equivalent to "cousin", McKennan may have depended on a faulty translation for Johnny's

text. Kenneth Frank's own variant of the tale (Mishler and Frank 2020:254-255), which he likely heard from his grandfather, also says the potlatch was given in honor of Loche's dead child.

5. According to Hannah P. Solomon (Hannah Tsoh), her family was inspired to begin having funeral potlatches in Fort Yukon after visiting one for her brother-in-law, Peter Solomon, in the lower Tanana village of Minto. This was the first time she saw Native dancing at a funeral. The first modern-day Gwich'in funeral potlatch was that of Hannah's late husband, Paul Solomon Sr., who died on September 29, 1974, although his memorial potlatch did not take place until the summer of 1998. Hannah believed that the potlatch feast held immediately after a burial makes the families "feel stronger" and reduces the amount of crying and suffering. "Now everybody does it," she said. See Hannah Solomon interview on February 26, 1985, Oral History recording # H90-06-72, Elmer E. Rasmuson Library, Alaska Polar Regions Collections and Archives, University of Alaska Fairbanks. The Gwich'in do not have Native dances after a funeral, as the Lower Tanana do, but sometimes they do have a fiddle dance or a gospel sing and prayer meeting. As far as we know, the Solomon family was also the first modern day Gwich'in family in Alaska to hold a memorial potlatch.

6. Takudh is a nearly lost dialect of Gwich'in from the Upper Porcupine River region in the Yukon Territory. It's a prestigious dialect, however, since Archdeacon McDonald used it to develop literacy materials such as prayer books, hymnals, and translations of the Bible in the nineteenth century. Accompanied by formal classes, Takudh has undergone a strong revival among devout Gwich'in Episcopalians and Anglicans, and the singing of Takudh hymns remain a mainstay at all Alaskan Gwich'in funerals.

7. Tobacco did not play a role in Hamel Frank's memorial potlatch in Venetie, perhaps because he died from smoking-related lung cancer.

8. During the days of Archdeacon Robert McDonald, Rev. William Loola of Fort Yukon became an ordained deacon. Other Alaskan Gwich'in who have followed his trail include Albert Tritt, Titus Peter, Paul Tritt Sr., David Salmon (the first ordained Episcopal Native priest), James Gilbert, Trimble Gilbert, Mardow Solomon, and Mary Nathaniel.

20. Tsuk'ǫǫ Tee'itree Haa:
A Visit to the Gwich'in Homeland to Fix Up a Graveyard

Introduction

The Yukon Flats constitute a distinct bioregion in northeast Alaska extending some 10,800 square miles. or 28,500 square kilometers. Populated by a rich diversity of wildlife, the Flats have been an integral part of the homeland of the Gwich'in since well before historic contact in the 1840s. The Yukon Flats is especially noted for its shallow lakes, slow-moving streams, its abundance of moose, and rich waterfowl nesting and molting areas. Each year the Flats provide a summer home and nesting habitat for an estimated 2.1 million geese and ducks.

Perhaps because of its vast size and remoteness, only one extensive cultural resource field survey has ever been done on the Flats. Elizabeth

Andrews (1977) made a preliminary list of known sites in her *Report on the Cultural Resources of the Doyon Region,* and Rick Caulfield (1983) did some excellent work on Yukon Flats Gwich'in place names that has only recently borne fruit in the restoration of aboriginal names. Caulfield developed a series of highly useful detailed maps for the Alaska Department of Fish and Game, Division of Subsistence, for the communities of Fort Yukon, Venetie, Birch Creek, Circle, and Chalkyitsik, as well as Arctic Village.

It was not until 1983 that Dale Slaughter (1984) and Matt Ganley did a Native-assisted riverine survey of sites along the Yukon and Porcupine Rivers and Birch Creek. They located approximately forty-seven historic sites and attempted to ascend the Christian River but were turned back by trees lying across the river. To my knowledge no field surveys of sites on the Flats have been done since that time. One linguistic place name compilation, based on interviews and archival materials, has been completed by James Kari and Adeline Peter Raboff (2014), and another was done soon after (Matesi 2016). In the summer of 1997, however, I had an opportunity to visit historic sites on Marten Creek, better known as Tsuk'ǫǫ, and several others along the lower Chandalar River, better known by locals as the Ch'idriinjik.

The occasion which prompted my survey was really not a formal systematic plan based on transects but rather a spiritual pilgrimage to the old village of Tsuk'ǫǫ, a sacred place for many Gwich'in families. From the obituary of Moses Sam, who was born in Tsuk'ǫǫ, we know the site was occupied at least as far back as his birthday on May 8, 1912, and probably much longer (Sam family, 2001). Moses himself believed the village was actually two to three hundred years old.

In June, 1997, the Native Village of Venetie Tribal Government, the same entity which went to the Supreme Court over the issue of "Indian Country" was awarded a grant from the National Park Service to survey and take inventory of historic and cemetery sites on the former Venetie

Reservation, a 1.8 million acre parcel belonging to the Venetie Tribal Government since the early 1940s. Although some 14(h)1 BIA ANCSA investigations had taken place in the late 1970s and 1980s around Old John Lake, these were all done off the reservation. Due to the decision by the Venetie Tribal Government not to participate in ANCSA but to take fee simple title to their former reservation, no 14(h)1 sites were ever documented on the reserve. Our National Park Service grant (Mishler 1999) was designed to help rectify this situation.

When I began to write the grant proposal for this survey, I asked a number of middle-aged and elderly tribal members what was the most important thing we could do to preserve old sites, the nearly uniform answer was, "We need to fix up the graveyard at Tsuk'ǫǫ." Tsuk'ǫǫ ('Marten Creek') is located on the Venetie Reserve directly adjacent to the northern boundary of the Yukon Flats National Wildlife Refuge. It's also situated on an old winter trail linking Fort Yukon and Venetie.

After talking to many people, I gradually developed the impression that Tsuk'ǫǫ was an extremely important place in the early lives of these elders, many of whom were raised there, hunted, trapped, and traded for fur there during the 1940s and 50s. It was apparently abandoned in the late 1950s or early 1960s. One of the last remaining residents was Ginnis Golen, the village storekeeper, whose cabin and cache are still standing. I became interested in seeing and documenting the old village, a remote place which had not been visited by an anthropologist since Robert McKennan first hiked to it in 1933 and discovered three families in residence: the households of Andrew Roberts, Ned Roberts, and Old John Sucker Fish (see McKennan 1965:22).

McKennan stopped and visited Tsuk'ǫǫ for three days in 1933, where he met Old John Sucker Fish. See McKennan's journal description of this creek and old village by the same name (Mishler and Simeone 2006:210-213). At the time of our visit there were still some caches and log cabins standing. The community graveyard lies about 1/4 mile away from the village on top of a small hill. At one time Jacob Flett, Daniel Roberts, and Henry John also had log cabins here. Another cabin was shared by Elijah John and Steven Fredson. Beaver dams often block the creek just below the village.

Moses Sam told me a story about the old Tsuk'ǫǫ village site on May 29, 1996. Moses lived there from 1912-1925, until he was thirteen years old. Additional stories about the site were recorded by Judy Erick and myself from elders Ellen Henry, Mary Frank, Mary Simple, Daniel Flett, and Abraham Henry Sr.

The Pilgrimage

Even though the grant funds arrived at the tribal office too late to outfit our party, we decided to go ahead anyway because it was felt that the trip's success depended on the presence of high water, which can only be assured in early June. Although it's possible to hike to Tsuk'ǫǫ from Venetie in half a day, in order to take camping gear, cooking pots, food, and graveyard cleaning tools, we needed access by river boat. Fortunately, the village store, owned by the Tribal Government, provided us with $500 in credit on groceries, and the Venetie Village Council supplied gas for the boats. The initial group of about twenty-seven participants included one person from Arctic Village (Chief Allen Tritt, Figure 1) and the rest all from Venetie, ranging from six years of age to eighty-four (Ellen Henry, Figure 2). The group took along chain saws, axes, and a couple of shovels and was well-prepared for fallen trees obstructing the streams.

Tee'itree, located on Marten Creek enroute to Tsuk'ǫǫ, is a spring muskrat hunting camp formerly used by Hamel Frank and many others during the 1950s and 1960s. This camp is named for the red-throated loon and literally means 'crying on the water'. It's situated in a clearing that can be reached from the south bank of Marten Creek next to a lake called Tee'itree Van, which is just a short distance by trail from Tsuk'ǫǫ. The lake is known for its abundant black ducks. Venetie people lived there seasonally in tents. According to Robert Frank, whitefish run out of Tee'itree Van in July and September. Residents would catch the whitefish in a fish trap. In July they would dry them, and in September they would freeze them.

What follows are some detailed excerpts from my field notes for the four-day boat trip:

> Day 1: Monday, June 9, 1997: At 3 p.m., after numerous delays, our four river boats were loaded up and ready to go. The boat drivers were Sonny Erick, Chief Allen Tritt, Ethel Simple's son Evert, and Jimmy Roberts. I was invited to be in Evert's boat. We were delayed about 15 minutes while waiting for elder Annie Christian, who was summoned and finally arrived at the landing in a pickup truck. Each riverboat was about 20 feet long, flat-bottomed, made of aluminum, and powered by a 25 to 40 h.p. outboard, with a lifter for going across shallow places.
>
> Shortly after shoving off around 3:30 p.m., Evert began having motor trouble, and we fell behind Sonny and Allen, but fortunately Sonny suspected problems and came back to check on us. It turned out to be a simple problem related to the way the gas line was hooked up, and we were soon on our way again. After the correction was made, I was asked to transfer to Sonny's boat, while one of Sonny's passengers, a young man named Duane, hopped from Sonny's boat into Evert's boat, to assist him should he have any further problems.
>
> In Sonny Erick's boat were his wife Judy, Judy's mother Ellen Henry, and myself. In Allen Tritt's boat were Abraham Henry Sr. (Judefy), Eunice William (Allen's sister), and several young children (most of whom are Allen's grandchildren). The youngest of these, a girl named Nicole, is only six. In Ethel's boat were Ethel, her son Evert, and five or six teenagers. In Jimmy's boat were Annie Christian and five or six more teenagers.
>
> About an hour's ride downriver, we hit a very powerful lightning and thunder storm, accompanied by huge drops of rain and small hail. Sonny finally pulled over to the shoreline and immediately built a fire, which he lit with gasoline. After about

ten minutes, he decided we should push on until we arrived at Earl Erick's cabin, known in Gwich'in as Earl Vizheh, on the east bank. We were soon joined there by Ethel's boat. The cabin was built about ten years ago (1985) as the base camp for a trapline used by Earl and Sonny. Sonny claims it was built "in a couple of days". We started a fire in the wood stove, but the smoke backed up because of a large gap between the stove opening and the bottom of the stovepipe. We waited out the storm for over three hours, drinking coffee made from river water, nibbling on cookies, and drying out our clothes.

When the rain finally let up, about 10:30 p.m., we saw Allen Tritt's boat go by. This led to a scramble to pack up all our gear and follow. All three boats held a rendezvous at the mouth of Marten Creek. There was speculation that the fourth boat, manned by Jimmy Roberts, may have turned back. No one imagined that the fourth boat had run into trouble. It was known that Jimmy never travels past a certain hour of the night, that it was his way to simply camp until morning and catch up the next day, so no one was too concerned.

It was not until four days later, upon our return, that we saw Jimmy's boat downriver from the village and realized something had seriously gone wrong. The story was that he had motor trouble, had to drift down and put up tents in the storm and spend the night. Luckily, the next morning someone else was returning on the river from Fort Yukon and rescued Annie and the kids, then went back to get Jimmy. The occupants of Jimmy's boat never made it to Tsuk'ǫǫ.

The boat drivers soon decided to head up Marten Creek (Tsuk'ǫǫ) a narrow clear-running stream about 40 feet wide at the mouth and narrowing to about 20 feet wide in its upper end. As daylight began to fade, the temperature dropped, and it began to get cold. But we continued for almost three more hours to Tee'itree, an old muskrat hunting camp lyrically named for the red-throated loon, lit. 'crying on the water'. Along the way we encountered two cow moose and their calves, a pair at a time. The second pair must have reappeared about seven times, crossing the land between meanders just quickly enough so that we could not outrun them. Sonny and Judy were both very cautious about getting too close to the cow, whom they feared could charge us and tip over the boat. Around every bend in the stream, we startled another pair of ducks. Clearly, this is a rich ecosystem teeming with wildlife.

At Tee'itree we pitched our tents in the open meadow and prepared a late supper of beef stew. Allen's boat brought in a freshly killed beaver and four ducks. We didn't turn in until 3:30 a.m.

Day 2: Tuesday, June 10: Most of us awoke around 9:30 or 10 a.m., but there were many sleepyheads, and no one was roused, so by the time everyone was up, had breakfast, and packed their gear it was 1 p.m. We proceeded up the creek until it became extremely narrow, nearly closed off by willows. We frequently ducked our heads to avoid the trees, only to come to a seeming dead end where the creek was blocked by two beaver dams.

Sonny was determined to get the boats up above the biggest of the beaver dams, and he and Allen and Duane put on hip waders and began to tear apart the dam. Meanwhile several of the teenagers put on their life vests and jumped into a pool of water just above the dam where the men were working. So while there was work there was also fun. In the meantime Judefy and Evert threw their rifles over their shoulders and walked off to scout ahead and see if they could find Tsuk'ǫǫ village. The village and the creek have the exact same name.

After the beaver dam had been cleared for an opening about ten feet across, Sonny made a plea for help to pull his boat up. I wanted to videotape the event but was needed for the pull. On our first try the boat hung up and refused to go over the hump, so we let it back down. Then we tugged again, and this time when the boat hung up Sonny jumped out onto the dam and helped pull it over. When Allen Tritt tried to do the same thing with his boat, however, it began to swamp from the front end. I think this was due to the fact that his boat had a lot more weight in it, largely due to a 55-gallon drum of gasoline. After the near swamping and sinking, Allen backed off and bailed the bottom with an empty coffee can for about an hour.

In the meantime, everyone began to pitch their tents and make camp right around the dam. Sonny and Judy went exploring upriver while the rest of us waited in suspense. Duane had a map, and with my GPS reading, it appeared to me that we had gone way past Tsuk'ǫǫ and were a long ways from our destination. But Allen Tritt laughed at my GPS findings, and it's a good thing no one believed me, for we were indeed very close to our destination. Tsuk'ǫǫ hour or so, Judefy and Evert came back and said they had found the village. Then Judy and Sonny returned, announcing that the old village and cemetery were only about a ten-minute boat ride away.

We made dinner and then headed up, heavily overloaded, to a landing near the cemetery. The boys began cutting saplings with their chain saws, but I did not take too active a part. I took another GPS reading and then drew a sketch map. I loaned my tape recorder to Judy Erick, and she began to interview her mother Ellen about family members who are buried there. As it turns out, three of Ellen's children, none of whom Judy remembers because they were all older than she, are buried here, side by side. Annie Roberts, Ellen's mother, died and was buried here in 1948. Seeing these graves again after 30 years was very touching to all. Everyone said they were doing all this for Ellen. Ethel and Judy, both in their 40s, had never been here before.

Other graves were identified enclosed in a wood fence surrounded by steel wire about four feet high. Another grave, surrounded by a wooden fence with cone-shaped corner cupolas, fell down while people were attempting to clean the surface inside of it. The pieces of the fence were piled up and left in a heap.

Sonny, the crew boss, and Allen, the chief, decided that we should build a peeled spruce rail around the entire graveyard, a task that turned out to be a two-day marathon. About thirty spruce trees were cut with a chain saw, peeled with axes, and carried up the hill. Post holes were dug for the railing. The women used butcher knives to cut away vegetation, and a rake to rebuild burial mounds. After about four hours, the women cooked a meal on the side of the hill in a big steel pot. The entree was duck soup, served with pilot bread. A big tub of strawberry Kool-Aid was prepared for the kids, while the adults drank coffee. The kids flaked out after a few hours, and Sonny gave them a little lecture about why they were here: the new fence was all about respect.

I helped out some but spent a fair amount of time taking photographs, videotaping, and plotting the location with the handheld Magellan GPS I had rented in Anchorage.

About 9 p.m. we packed up our gear and boarded Sonny's boat for the return trip to our camp at the beaver dam. The boat was overloaded, but by overloading and going slow, Sonny got everybody back in two trips. I went to bed at 11 p.m., but many of the teenagers stayed up until the wee hours. About 4 a.m. I heard rifle shots. The guys were shooting beavers.

Day 3: Wednesday, June 11: When I got up around 8:30 a.m. on Wednesday, the 11th, I heard someone whistling as he walked by my tent. The second time there was a voice announcing, "Hot coffee. Hot coffee." When I peeked out of the tent flap, I saw it was Judefy (Abraham Henry). I walked up to his tent and sat down and had a couple of cups of coffee with him. Since it was very quiet, I suggested doing an interview, and he allowed me to go get my tape recorder. The interview was quite good, but full of code-switching back and forth between English and Gwich'in, often in the same sentence. Judefy described an elaborate trail system connecting Venetie, Fort Yukon, Tsuk'ǫǫ, and Tee'itree.

After about an hour Judefy made breakfast, and I ate with him, downing pancakes and eggs. To my surprise, he brought along a collapsible picnic table, and it was very handy indeed. Judefy built his fire, as the Gwich'in always do, with trees laid parallel. The cooking was made easy by placing a rectangular piece of aluminum or tin from one side of a 5-gallon kerosene can directly on top of the fire. This piece of aluminum or tin made a level place for the coffee pot and the skillet.

I hung up some more of my wet clothes to dry and wandered over to the main camp, where there was a big tarp stretched out over an open fire. There I found the result of the 4 a.m. shooting: the carcasses of two beavers, a female with a yearling. These were butchered and pieces were roasted over the fire. I discovered that they really like the tail and the feet of the beaver. These are singed in the flames and then peeled. A big pot of beaver meat was prepared for taking back to the graveyard.

Things got off to a very slow start. The young people were very slow to get up, and again, no one roused them. Judy got up about noon, while Evert and Duane, the young men badly needed to work on the graveyard fence, slept until 2 p.m. We did not get underway for another half hour after that, despite the fact that most people were ready to go by 11 a.m. One reason that young people are allowed to sleep so late is that it is considered dangerous to wake up a person who is dreaming. Dreams, especially in young people, are thought to be part of the vision quest and are integral to the shamanistic experience. Ethel told me some of the girls were already bored and wanted to go back to Venetie. For two of them, this was their first camping trip, and most of them were listening to CD's through headphones.

We arrived at the Tsuk'ǫǫ graveyard again about 2:45 p.m. and immediately went back to work. This time I really pitched in and peeled logs, carried logs, held and measured railings, nailed rails to posts, and worked up a good sweat. Everyone seemed very impressed when I jumped in and dug a deep post hole. Digging holes seemed to be the job everyone wanted to avoid. We worked until about 5:30, stopped for a supper break, and then resumed work until we finished up at 8 p.m. I had my first taste of beaver tail, which was very tasty--kind of like a white fat or gelatin.

Ethel Simple prepared a little wooden plaque for her great-grandmother's grave. Shitsuu Ellen placed some small artificial flowers on the graves of her children and her mother--a very nice touch.

At 8 p.m. the men raised a large wooden cross Sonny Erick made with his chain saw. They all liked the idea of making one cross for all rather than a separate cross for each grave, and this saved us a fair amount of time. They also shortened the job by cutting longer rails. With longer rails, fewer holes had to be dug for fewer posts.

After raising the cross, everyone was called to gather round for a ceremony. Speeches were made by Allen Tritt, Sonny Erick, and Ellen Henry. Then they sang "Amazing Grace" and Chilig 18 from the Takudh Hymnal. While this was going on, I ran the video camera and took still shots of the entire group (Figure 3). Then the Henrys asked to have a separate family photo.

At this point I asked to be taken to the Tsuk'ǫǫ cabins--the old village--which for most was just an afterthought. Sonny was going to drop me off by myself, but I asked for someone to show me around, and Allen Tritt, the chief, kindly obliged. His grandson also tagged along. For me, this was one of the primary objectives, but all of my observations and photo-taking had to be crammed into little more than half an hour. I saw Ginnis Golen's cabin and cache. Down by the creek there was the remains of an old fish trap (da'anlee), and across the creek was one wall left standing from a cabin used by Daniel Flett. I also noted several other features. Tsuk'ǫǫ village lies on a large flat grassy meadow.

Around 8:30 p.m. Sonny came back to pick us up in his boat and take us back down to our camp at the beaver dam. The evening sun was still bright and everyone was anxious to get going, so we broke camp and packed up all our gear. Sonny was nervous about getting his boat back down over the dam, but it turned out to be a piece of cake. We loaded up quickly and set off down the creek, slowing up here and there to hunt ducks. It was sunny and the water was calm and very beautiful. We drove for almost exactly three hours, arriving at the mouth of Marten Creek (K'ǫǫ Gwitsik) at 12:30 a.m., again flushing ducks around virtually every bend. One difference we noted from our trip upstream was that the willows were blowing pollen on the creek, creating a sheet of white fluff that resembled snow. Most of us pitched our tents and turned in, but Ethel and Evert left with their boat at 3 a.m. to return directly to Venetie.

Day 4: Thursday, June 12 (summary): Allen and Judefy took off in their boat this morning for Venetie. Meanwhile I took Sonny and Judy's boat to their fish camp on the Yukon for a brief visit. Their camp is located on a big island where they have a fish wheel to catch and put up salmon in the early fall. Then after ascending the Teedriinjik we stopped briefly at Venetie Landing, K'ahtsik (aka Fish Camp), and Dachuu, three important historic sites where I took photos and notes based on Sonny's long experience with the area. The name K'ahtsik means 'at the confluence of the muddy and clear water.' Such places are good indicators of traditional subsistence sites because for some reason fish tend to concentrate there. We finally arrived at Venetie at 8 p.m., all very tired.

Tsuk'ǫǫ Graveyard Speeches

Transcript from video recorded by Craig Mishler on June 10, 1997. Edited by Craig Mishler. This is part of the closing ceremony after raising the large wooden cross. The original speeches are in English.

Allen Tritt: "This is our people who died long time ago--our great grandmother, grandfather that we never forgot. And you young people come here with us and look at us what we're doing, and in the future you're going to be like us. You guys are going to take over in no time, and remember that. You guys got to get together, work together like we do right here. It's going to belong to you. We got the Reservation. We're getting to Indian country. And you guys got to get along good and get together, work like this. This will never die, unless you don't do it. That's why I'm going to thank you people to be here with us. And remember that. We always respect for the people we care [about], that we never forgot."

John Erick Jr.: "Like I was telling earlier, talking to you guys a while ago about Ellen [Henry]. Her mother and her kids are buried here. This trip is making her happy. And that's what I told you kids, to be happy and work together. And she's really kind of grateful to come up here. She's been trying to come up here for thirty years, almost thirty years. She finally made it to the graveyard, and she's eighty-four year old. And you guys got to respect people like that, to help them as much as you can, to keep them strong."

Conversation in the Tsuk'ǫǫ Graveyard, June 10, 1997

Translated from the Gwich'in by Judy Erick, edited by Craig Mishler

From Ellen Henry [EH] tape #3, with Chief Allen Tritt [AT], Judy Erick [JE], Ethel Simple [ES], Eugina Erick [EE], Eunice Williams [EW], Abraham Henry [AH], and John Erick Jr. (Sonny Erick) [JEJ]

[Editor's Note: Shitsuu Ellen Henry is Judy Erick's mother. Abraham Henry is Judy's brother. John Erick Jr. is Judy's husband. Ethel Simple is Judy Erick's niece. Eugina Erick is John Erick Jr.'s niece. Eunice Williams is Allen Tritt's sister. The transcript which follows has been edited to eliminate digressions and preserve the essential dialogue.]

EH: I'll tell you. She [my mother, Sarah Roberts] said to me before she died, "My child, bury me at the end of my grandchildren's graves, for they are afraid to be here by themselves."

JE: Then who is in the first grave here? Patrick?

AT: No, William died first.

EH: Yes, William died first, then my child Madeline, then my little boy Patrick. and then my mother. That's the order they died in. She said for us to bury her at the end of the graves here.

JE: What about that big grave over there?

EH: Where?

JE: Whose children are they?

EH: Those are my Uncle Ned Robert's kids.

JE: What are their names?

EH: Margaret, Edna, and David. Allen, did you know that lot of others are buried here? Even one of Annie Christian's little children is buried here.

AT: Really?

EH: Also Elijah John's wife, Mary, is buried here.

AT: Yes.

EH: Her mother Shyaaghan Tsal ('Little Old Woman') is also buried here.

JE: Silas's [Silas John] wife, too?

EH: Yes, Silas's wife Lena is buried here.

AT: That one too?

EH: Yes. Down at Tee'itree near the crossing by the old houses, your grandmother Myrna [Myrna Roberts] was living there alone with her children when she [Lena] died there with her. She told me that she brought her children up here to tell people about her death, so they made a stretcher to bring her body up here. She told me that herself.

AT: Robert John is also buried here.

EH: Yes, Robert John is buried here; he's Henry John's oldest brother.

JE: Which one is his grave?

AT: I don't know.

EH: All of their graves are overgrown with brush.

AT: We got one there too. I think that must be your great grandma right there [spoken in English].

JE: Check around real good. She said there's more here than just these graves.

ES: Like this one right here. Where is it?

AT: That's one of them. Leave that one there! Don't move it [an old rotted cross]!

JE: Hey, don't move anything!

AT: Those will be our markers later . . .

EH: This one here is my mother's.

AT: Yes.

EH: These three [graves] are my children.

AT: Okay, this must be the space between them.

EH: Yes, there is a large space between all the graves. I remember my mother said to me before she died . . .

AT: Do you think that's Ned's grave over at the top of the hill?

EH: Hey, I'm trying to remember where they buried my uncle Ned.

AT: Moses [Sam] told me that it's at the top of the hill.

EH: Yes, that's my uncle Ned up there.

AT: He [Moses Sam] also said that Robert John was buried on the Venetie side.

EH: Really?

AT: Yes.

JE: Maybe that one way over there.

AT: I think it's about here.

EH: It's probably that one.

AT: Maybe they just didn't put a cross on it. Looks like there is a grave here but . . .

EH: Yes, was this [rotted cross] here?

ES: Yes, it was here.

JE: Ma, what year did she [Sarah Roberts] die?

EH: My mother died first, then Uncle Ned.

JE: What year?

EH: I don't remember what year. I was grieving so much back then that I didn't even watch the calendar or year.

JE: I thought you said 1948?

EH: Yes, in 1948. My children all died every month all in a row. I went through bad times.

AT: I remember when Ned was sick, and we knew he was going to die.

EH: My mother died and then Uncle Ned died.

AT: She died and when they were carrying her coffin by his house on the way here, he said, "Go by my doorway with her coffin so I can look at it," and they did.

EH: Yes, he [Uncle Ned] said he wanted to look at her sister-in-law's coffin for the last time. He told the people to bring her coffin by his doorway. [Translator's note: Ned was bedridden and couldn't make it to the graveyard.]

AT: Not long after that . . .

JE: Did he die not long after that?

EH: Yes, he died a short while [several days] later.

EH: I wish you all would cut down these big cottonwood trees. Did you say that Moses said this is Robert John's grave?

AT: He said it's on the Venetie side.

EH: This must be it then?

AT: That could be it.

EH: See, it's old. This is how they decorated crosses back then. Uncle Ned . . . right there.

JE: Who did these [decorated crosses]? Little Ginnis?

EH: Probably not . . . that Little Ginnis . . . Robert John died a long time ago. There's a grave here also, right, Allen? Is there a cross on it?

AT: It looks like there's a grave here. The ground caved in, look!

EH: Yes, you're right.

EW: Maybe it's Grandfather Ned, right?

EH: It [the cross] sure is rotten.

JEJ: There's a grave here. She's talking about forty years ago.

EH: It caved into the ground.

JE: Yes, it looks like a tall person.

EH: Yes, it does look like a tall person, see? We should mark each one with piled dirt.

EE: I wonder who that is, huh?

AT: Yes, we'll do that.

EH: I'm so happy that because of you all, I get to come back to my mother's and children's graves again. This must be Robert John's grave.

JEJ: [to EH] Don't step on a nail there!

ES: Robert John, who's he?

JE: Watch your step. There's a nail there.

EH: This is the way they used to decorate crosses and graves a long time ago.

JE: Are these [small graves] all children?

EH: Yes, but Uncle Ned's daughter Margaret was big--a big woman. Remember where we camped down at Tee'itree? We were living there when I remember Uncle Ned arrived. He said his daughter died the night before from hemorrhaging. My mother and them came up here. We stayed behind. And then Edna died. David too, but we weren't in this area.

JE: How big was this first one?

EH: William was just a little boy about this big [gestures].

JE: He was probably about five or six, huh?

EH: Yes. Patrick was smaller than him.

ES: This might be his grave marker?

EH: Maybe.

JE: Do you remember the day you came to his funeral?

EH: Yes. They were all buried here in a row with Mother in the back.

She wanted it that way. We'll re-mark their graves with [mounds of] dirt. I'm so happy right now, Judy. With God's help, I get to come to my mother's and children's graves.

JE: How many houses were on that hill?

EH: Jacob's house, Ginnis's house, Uncle Ned's, not far from there was Steven's. South of there was Grandpa Ch'eelil Viti' [see Ch'eelil Ti' in Chapter 6, Table 1], him and Grandma Ch'eelil Vahan. South of them were Henry John and [his wife] Sophie. None of those houses are there now.

AH: How do you translate "Ch'eelil Vahan" to English, anyway?

EH: Ch'eelil Vahan was the mother to Myrna and Sophie.

AH: It means, "Pulling something".

JE: Maybe "Mother of Sled Puller".

AH: [laughs] Is that what it means?

EH: Aunt Sophie once told me, Eunice. She said, "I was given the name 'Ch'eelil' because my father was always pulling lynx; that's how I got my name."

ES: Do you have any tissue paper, Ma? Is there tissue? Ma, I found one.

EH: This alpine berry's roots are sure hard to take out of the ground. They're long and I have to tear them out.

JE: How tall were trees back then?

EH: They were young spruce trees and young cottonwood trees. We could even see the graves from the village. Those tall spruce trees have grown up since then.

AH: All of this area was nothing but bare hills.

AT: Ever since I was told about drinking water near beaver dams I wouldn't drink it [changing the subject].

EH: You're not supposed to drink water near beaver dams. [Due to the risk of giardia.]

JEJ: But what's not safe to drink is the dead water near them.

AT: Dead water? Oh, it doesn't matter if the water is flowing by?

JE: What did people die from [changing the subject]?

EH: We don't know what people died from. They just got sick all of a sudden and died.

AH: They turned yellow and died. It was a bad disease.

JE: They now have medicine for that. It's [the disease] called yellow jaundice.

AH: I'm talking about the time when it happened. They all died right away.

EH: At that time, my little boy William was sick with us all the way from Venetie. Mother was at her cabin between here and Venetie. Your grandmother Mary and grandfather Elijah [Henry] and Nena were living at Vintinjir Tł'oo, you see? We passed them by dogteam from Venetie on our way to Tsuk'ǫǫ. Mother gave us muskrat skins and so did others on our way down. The snow was melted. There was only a small amount of snow on the trail, but when we arrived here, he died with us.

Coda

The above testimonies, both via the speeches and the extended conversation, do much to locate Gwich'in history in time and space. These moving testimonies help define a community shared by the living and the dead. It's important for those of us who are anthropologists to learn to be flexible with our research agendas. In this case, I learned that my personal goals of documenting the location and topographical features of these historic and cemetery sites were out of step with what the people I was working with were trying to achieve. Their sole purpose was to honor and pay respect to their ancestors. Once I realized this devotion, I sacrificed the completion of some things I would normally have done on my own, such as carefully measuring the log buildings and taking an inventory their contents. Yes, I took photographs and drew sketch maps of all of the obvious site features, but I also elicited sketch maps from two people who had lived at Tsuk'ǫǫ in the 1940s and 50s. Their sketch maps showed me where former Native cabins existed that have since burned down and also showed me how the sites of Tsuk'ǫǫ and Tee'itree were connected to each other by a trail system that led south to Fort Yukon and north to Venetie.

After helping the families fix up the graveyard and pay tribute to their deceased relatives, I found out that what I really wanted to learn about was not the material details of log house and cache construction and grave sites but the historical dramas that took place in and around them, such as the vivid and emotionally moving story of a dead woman's coffin being carried past a dying man's open doorway. Through oral interviews conducted in Gwich'in by Judy Erick and myself during and after the trip, a multitude of these little dramas have come to life and have become a part of the Tsuk'ǫǫ community's collective heritage. Unfortunately, transcripts of all these oral interviews, due to their great length, could not be included here.

While each ethnographic field trip such as this helps us to record many sites and stories, perhaps the best thing is that these trips themselves now become the raw material for narratives, the memories of which will be passed on to another generation.

Acknowledgments

An earlier much shorter draft of this essay was originally presented to the Alaska Anthropological Association Annual Meeting in 1998. I will forever be grateful to the Venetie community and to the Tritt, Henry, and Erick families for allowing me to participate in and help document their memorial.

Afterword

In the years since June, 1972, when I first started traveling to Gwich'in villages in rural Alaska, I've observed many changes that have affected their lives. Perhaps foremost are the dramatic life-changing advances in communication technology. In 1972 each village (except for Fort Yukon), only had one telephone, hooked up to a big satellite dish. All of the community's urgent health problems and air transportation needs were funneled through those single phones. In the 1980s village clinics acquired giant satellite dishes for medical communications. Local health aides were usually available, but they had only limited training for emergencies. The satellite dishes allowed health aides to receive advice and instruction from doctors.

I recall that the Venetie village phone was located in the home of Jessie Williams, the postmistress, and if we needed to charter a flight out of the village, we had to ask her to call a plane to come from Fort Yukon. Usually the only pilot available for charters was Cliff Fairchild based in Fort Yukon. Scheduled flights, referred to as the mail plane, only came in from Fairbanks on Mondays, Wednesdays, and Fridays, and charters were very expensive. There was another likeable option, however.

If a charter flight paid for by someone else came in to the village, we could ride back on it free of charge with the permission of the person who chartered it. So we had to be all packed up and ready at the airstrip when the charter landed in order to get on it. For a long time it was necessary to fly to Fort Yukon and change planes there in order to reach Venetie or Arctic Village. It was not until the late 1980s or early 1990s that daily nonstop flights became available, although today most communities receive at least two scheduled flights each day, seven days a week, from Wright Air. What made for more frequent daily flights was improved medical care. Individuals needing to go to the doctor in Fairbanks were able to fly free of charge, paid for by the Alaska Native Health Service or the Bureau of Indian Affairs.

Another thing that changed was radio and television. In 1972 people in the villages largely relied on Tundra Topics on KFAR-AM in Fairbanks and Trapline Chatter on KJNP-AM in North Pole to receive personal messages from friends and family. These radio messages were broadcast usually twice a day, in the morning and again in the evening, but Kenneth remembers that the evening messages came on KFAR at 9:20 pm and every household in Venetie would be eagerly listening.

People living in town would call the station and leave a message which was written down and then read over the air by a local disk jockey. The message could then be received even by people without electricity if they had a battery-powered radio. Of course, a lot of people eavesdropped out of curiosity, even if they were not expecting a message, to learn about who was having a birthday, who was coming in on the afternoon plane, who was being medevaced, or anything else that was going on in the private lives of their friends and neighbors. Today the widespread availability of the Internet in Gwich'in villages has all but eliminated the need for these radio services.

In 1972 there was no television at all in the villages. In 1973 the river flooded the old village in Venetie, forcing many residents to move up to higher ground. Funding grants for building new houses, both frame and log, made this move not only possible but practical. Venetie acquired electricity in the mid-1970s and private home phones in 1980. When I visited people in the old village down by the river during the 1970s, they were still using kerosene wick lamps or Coleman lamps fueled by white gas. Weekly movies, mostly westerns, were rented and flown in from Pictures, Incorporated in Anchorage and shown to the whole village in the community hall. The movie projector was powered by a noisy outdoor gasoline generator.

Fort Yukon had electricity as early as 1949, and in 1974 Fort Yukon finally received a local TV transmitter that went on the air for a few hours each day. The programming largely consisted of video tapes flown in from the public radio station in Fairbanks. Villagers quickly bought TVs and rooftop antennas, even though the programming was culturally irrelevant. Things like football games, classical music concerts, and commercials did not fit the Gwich'in subsistence lifestyle or their cultural heritage. The only programs with genuine appeal were wildlife documentaries, slapstick comedies, and John Wayne westerns.

Then there was a period during the 1980s and 1990s when people bought TVs along with VCRs. Home businesses offering video movie rentals sprang up and became highly popular. Jerry Frank remembers that the first rentals in Venetie were 8-track, followed by VHS, followed by DVD. Arctic Village did not get electricity until 1988, the year of the first big Gwich'in gathering, and electrification quickly brought about big changes in Gwich'in music. This was due in part to the efforts of Ben Boyd, a white guy who lived in the village and helped the Gilbert brothers (Gregory, Bobby, and Albert) start up a rock and roll band. Beatles songs soon became the rage, along with Santana's "Black Magic Woman."

The first television channels in Arctic Village came from a dish at the health clinic where two channels were broadcast to homes equipped with rabbit ear antennas. Then the first satellite TV dishes on private homes appeared in 1995. Today, of course, satellite dishes are mounted on virtually every roof, along with Internet service (see Fig. Af.1).

As local musicians were able to buy and use amplified instruments to play rock and roll music, there was a period of a couple of years, I remember, when Venetie had two dances at the same venue on the same night. Starting around 8 pm there would be fiddle music dances for the middle-aged and elderly. Then after the old folks finished their jigs and square dances around 11 pm, they were followed quickly by live bands playing rock and roll for the teens and young adults. Both dances were held in the same community hall. At first blush, I thought perhaps it was the beginning of the end for traditional Gwich'in fiddle music, but it didn't take very long for the fiddlers to amplify their instruments as well. Today the Gwich'in rock and roll craze has largely faded, with fiddle music bands thriving with the addition of drums, electric basses, and vocal microphones.

Fig. Af.1. Kenneth & Caroline Frank's satellite dishes in Arctic Village in 2013. The Spacenet dish on the side of the house was for internet and the one on the end of the roof was for television from the Dish Network. Photo by Craig Mishler.

Along with the entertainment value of mass media there has been a major downside to modern mass communications and transportation, as people's lives have been saturated with almost nothing but English language television. For many years the only Gwich'in language Alaskans could hear on the air was on KZPA-AM in Fort Yukon, Gwandak Public Broadcasting, which has only a low-powered 5KW signal. But starting in 2014, KRFF-FM in Fairbanks, The Voice of Denali, started broadcasting at 10,000 watts and is now heard on repeaters in 42 Interior villages. KTFF features a word of the day, which includes Gwich'in as well as many other Doyon Region languages, and features a program called Alaska Native Stories on weekday afternoons. The station also has a number of podcasts on the lives of Gwich'in elders that can be streamed from its web site.

The Canadian Gwich'in have also been quite active in radio due to the efforts of Ruth Carroll (now retired after 15 years) and William George Firth on CBC North in Inuvik. The local Fort McPherson station CBQM used to have music broadcasting and local news read in Gwich'in by elder Bertha Francis and other local volunteers, but she has sadly passed on. Today virtually all the station's programming comes from Radio One North in Inuvik, an affiliate of the CBC. And Old Crow fiddler Ben Charlie helps keep traditional Gwich'in dance music alive with his two-hour call-in radio show, Vuntat Njiik Nakaii, on CHON-FM in Whitehorse.

All of these mass media developments have greatly modified the Gwich'in social and cultural landscape. It is certainly tragic that a language which has flourished for hundreds or thousands of years could largely disappear in one or two generations. As one elder put it to me, "How come we're the last ones to speak our language?" One answer is that cumulative technological changes have ended the social isolation of Gwich'in communities, an isolation which allowed the language to flourish up until the mid-twentieth century. A very important book, *Our Whole Gwich'in Way of Life Has Changed / Gwich'in K'yuu Gwiidandài' Tthak Ejuk Gòonlih*, contains twenty-three Canadian Elders' testimonies about how their own lives have been transformed in the twentieth and twenty-first centuries (McCartney et al., 2020).

Few can deny that new technologies have improved the creature comforts of Gwich'in life in the modern world and have made villagers at least somewhat more secure economically. In a homeland defined by cold harsh winters, the rifle, the snow machine, the four-wheeler, and the outboard motor have all enhanced subsistence opportunities and made starvation a thing of the past.

Language Revitalization

The rise of village schools and residential schools where English is spoken exclusively have also contributed to devastating language loss. Kenneth Frank's experience is typical of the historical trauma encountered by his generation. Born in 1953 and raised in a family of eight children, Kenneth attended the BIA School in Venetie where he was physically punished by teachers for speaking his Native language. He was then sent away for two years to Wrangell Boarding School in Wrangell, Alaska, where he did not see his family from August to May. After that they sent him to secondary school at Chilocco Indian School in Chilocco, Oklahoma.

The Yukon Flats School District began hiring teachers and offering classes in Gwich'in during the late 1970s, and today it's being still taught by Paul Tritt Jr. in Beaver, Freda Joseph in Chalkyitsik, Virginia Peter in Fort Yukon, and Debbie Tritt-Kendi in Arctic Village. Apparently there is no formal instruction offered in either Circle or Venetie. And we were quite distressed to hear that Gwich'in is not taught at Birch Creek for the simple reason that Birch Creek (population of 35 in 2020) has no school and has not had one for the last twenty years!

On the Canadian side the Chief Zzeh Gittlit School in Old Crow, as well as the schools in Teetl'it Zheh (Fort McPherson), Tsiigehtshik, Aklavik, and Inuvik, all provide instruction in the language by indigenous educators. Florence Netro in Old Crow, Gladys Alexie in Teetl'it Zheh, Renie Koe in Tsiigehtshik, AnnaLee McCleod in Aklavik, and Annabelle Tetlichi in Inuvik are the instructors. Offerings vary from school to school, but the emphasis is on primary grades with a few classes taught at the secondary level.

From 2014-2019 Kenneth Frank was employed as a part-time Gwich'in language teacher at the Effie Kokrine Charter School in Fairbanks, but unfortunately that ended with the onset of the Covid-19 pandemic when the school closed down for an entire year. Gwich'in is now a severely endangered language, yet there are still many middle-aged adults working hard to revitalize it, providing advanced learning tools such as the suite of online courses developed by the Doyon Foundation and ably led by Gwich'in speaker Allan Hayton (see https://doyonfoundation.com/language/doyon-languages-online/). The Effie Kokrine school has reopened and students are now using the online course content and guided tutorials developed by Kenneth and Caroline Frank and others to teach themselves. This gives us all an abundance of hope because indigenous languages provide alternative ways of thinking and doing. They make the heart beat faster. They connect people spiritually. As the distinguished elder Trimble Gilbert says, "It's pretty hard to live without our language. We got to have it."

Fig. Af.2. Gwich'in immersion language class taught by Hishinlai' Peter and Lillian Garnett, summer, 2001, at the University of Alaska, Fairbanks. L to R, front row: Charleen Fisher, Hishinlai' Peter, Debbie Carroll, Dawn Jagow, Lillian Garnett. Back row: Mark Chapin, Amy Herbert, Jacqueline Joseph, Paul Williams Jr. Photo by Craig Mishler.

At the University of Alaska Fairbanks, Gwich'in has been taught for many years by Hishinlai Peter and Lillian Garnett and more recently by Sam Alexander of the Alaska Native Language Center. I was very lucky to be a student of Lillian and Hishinlai' in their immersion class taught during the summer of 2001 (see Fig. Af.2).

Several Gwich'in language summer workshops held for the purpose of revitalizing the language were held in Beaver (2011), Fort Yukon, and Anchorage (2014) during the decade between 2010-2019. Organizers include Rochelle Adams and Charleen Fisher of Beaver and Sam Alexander of Fort Yukon. Some of these weeklong workshops were sponsored by the Yukon Flats School District. The workshops brought together fluent speakers, language learners, and community leaders and included lots of storytelling and discussion. I was most fortunate to be able to participate in the Beaver and Anchorage workshops.

In March of 2021, Evon Peter and Hilda Johnson started the Tanan Ch'at'oh (Fairbanks Language Nest) project, an immersion program for urban preschool children, but it only lasted for about one year. In recent years, Gwich'in speakers and language learners are increasingly using the Internet a lot to communicate, now an essential tool for language revitalization. Facebook groups such as Diiginjik K'yaa Ch'at'oh, Gwich'in Language, and #SpeakGwichinToMe are all important social media channels, although they largely rely on language literacy more than speaking skills.

One luminous initiative which has had solid success is the Molly of Denali children's series on PBS, which has been partly written and co-produced by Gwich'in activists Princess Daazhraii Johnson and Rochelle Adams. Molly is 10-year-old fictional animated creation of a Gwich'in adolescent and the first popular culture role model for Alaska Native girls. Molly speaks some Gwich'in, primarily greetings and leave-takings, but the primary emphasis is on her traditional values, feelings, and behavior. This mindful, entertaining, and educational series began in 2019 and is now in its third season. It received a Peabody Award in 2020.

Another recent project co-directed by Princess and by Alisha Carlson is the short film *Diiyeghan Nąįį Taii Tr'eedaa* ('We Will Walk the Trail of Our Ancestors'), a 2022 documentary filmed entirely in Gwich'in that builds on the theme of reciprocity. The lead roles in this film are played by Alisha and her grandfather, the Rev. Trimble Gilbert of Arctic Village.

On Facebook, a new Gwich'in revitalization group, "Venetie, Alaska (Chandalar Village)", has been started by Patrick Semple, the son of Margo and Gary Simple. This marvelous private site features historic photos, video interviews, and streaming video podcasts by Patrick and Gary, as they reminisce, sing and play their guitars, practice their subsistence lifestyle, and adlib about what's going on socially and culturally in their local community and beyond. Now in its second year, it's a lively multimedia experience shared daily by over 1200 members.

So what will the future bring? One time many years ago when I asked Judy Erick for a book title suggestion, she came up with T'aih k'iighai' gwarandaii. 'We go on living because of our strength.' One thing we know is that the Gwich'in continually strengthen each other. They deeply love their culture and their language. They have joy in their lives. They are historically conscious, they are resilient, they are politically savvy, and they will always find ways to protect themselves, their subsistence resources, their water, and their homeland. Propelled into modern life while also consulting their elders, they have learned how to adapt and survive, and there is a solidarity and a majesty in that struggle.

Appendix A:
Ch'oozhįį Western Gwich'in Kinship Terms

Compiled by Craig Mishler and Kenneth Frank

Possessive Prefixes	
my	shi-, sha-, shee-, shoo-
our	dii-
your (singular)	ni-, na-, nii-, nee-
your (plural)	nakhwo-, nakhwee-
his or her	vi-, va-, vee-, voo-
their	goo-
somebody's	ch'a-, ch'i-

Consanguinals	**Terms of Address (first person possessive)**
me, myself	shii
mother	ne'ęę or mama or amaa; shahan (reference)
father	ti'yąą or abaa or baba; shiti' (reference)
daughter**	shichi' (male speaker) or shiyeetsi' (female speaker)
son**	shidinji' (male speaker) or shizhuu (female speaker)
grandchild°	shichuii'/shikyuii' (male speaker) or shicheii'/ shitseii (female speaker)
children	tr'iinin naii
siblings	khaihłok ch'araat'ok (reference)
old and yo male siblings	shachaa nąįį (reference)
old and yo female siblings	shijuu nąįį (reference)
youngest sibling	khąįįts'ą' (reference)
older sis	sheejii
older sis's dau or son	shuu (address) or shahoo (reference)

younger sis	shijuu
younger sis's dau or son	shuu (address) or shahoo (reference)*
older bro	shoondee
older bro's dau	shuu (address) or shahoo (reference)
older bro's son	shuu (address) or shahoo (reference)
younger bro	shachaa
younger bro's dau	shuu (address) or shahoo (reference)
youngest bro's son	shizhi'* (address or reference, male teasing)
mo's sis	sheek'aii
mo's sis's or bro's dau	sheejii (older), shijuu (younger)
mo's sis's or bro's son	shoondee (older), shachaa (younger)
mo's bro	shee'ii
mo's mo	shitsuu
mo's fa	shitsii
fa's sis	shitsuu (for respect, same as fa's mo)
fa's sis's or fa's bro's dau	sheejii (older), shijuu (younger)
fa's sis's or fa's bro's son	shoondee (older), shachaa (younger)
fa's bro*	shitii
fa's mo	shitsuu
fa's fa	shitsii
stepfather	ti'yąą
stepmother	sheek'aii
godfather	shiti' giiyiłtsaii (reference)
godmother	shahan giiyiłtsaii (reference)

Affines	**Terms of Address (first person possessive)**
husband	shakai'
husband's mo (mo-in-law)	ne'ęę or shitsuu
husband's fa (fa-in-law)	ti'yąą or shitsii
husband's older or yo bro	shagwhaii
husband's older or yo sis	shagwhaii
sis-in-law*#	shagwhaii
bro-in-law*#	shąą (male to male speaking) or shaghwaii (male to female or f to m)
in-law	Note: shąą may be used for any distant male and shaghwaii for any distant female in-law

	and of same generation or older generation.
dau-in-law	shiyeh'at (female speaking) or gwiyeh'at (reference), or shichi' (male speaking) (KF)
son-in-law (female speaking)	shichi' kai' (male speaking) or sheedeenyaa
mo's bro's wife	shaghwaii
mo's sis's husband	shąą (male speaking) or shaghwaii (female)
fa's bro's wife	shaghwaii
fa's sis's husband	shąą (male speaking) or shaghwaii (female)
wife	sha'at (address) or shitr'injaa (reference)
wife's mo (mo-in-law)	shootr'i'
wife's fa (fa-in-law)	shiyehghan
wife's older or yo bro	shąą
wife's older or yo sis	shaghwaii
wife's sis's dau	shaghwaii
wife's sis's son	shąą
wife's bro's son	shąą
wife's bro's dau	shaghwaii

Other Common Terms

all our ancestors	nakhwotsii nąįį (lit. all your ancestors)
the generation before us	diiyehghan nąįį
my generation	diik'yaa nąįį (lit. all our brothers and sisters)
my parents	shiyehghan
my family	shizheh k'aa
my relative	shalak (address)
all my living relatives	shalak nąįį (address), diidaazhii nąįį (reference, lit. all our living relatives)
my coastal people partner	shitłįh (address)
my mother's side	ne'ee ts'ąįį
my father's side	ti'yaa ts'ąįį

Other Special Relations (terms of address)

sweetheart (m. or f.)	sha'oodee
partner	shaadhidii/nihłaatr'aadii
friend	shijyaa, jya', shijya'
friends	shijyaa nąįį
wife's other husband*	shah'oo (used humorously between married male friends)
widow	kheezhii (reference)
his nephew	vivyuu (reference)
mother of (personal name)	vinh
orphan	chiitee

Key to Symbols

**No special terms are used for adopted sons or daughters, but they will sometimes say dink'iłthat ('I raised him or her')

°These split terms reflect regional dialect differences. Shichuii' and shicheii' are used by speakers from Arctic Village and Venetie while shikyuii' and shitseii are favored by residents of Fort Yukon.

*Joking relationships

#Just as in English, one term suffices for sister-in-law and another for brother-in-law, even though they each represent different kinds of relationships. In other words "shagwhaii" can be used for either my wife's sister or for my brother's wife. And "shąą" can be used for either my wife's brother or my sister's husband.

Additional Notes

These notes were taken from telephone conversations between Kenneth and Craig over the years.

December 11, 1998: Kin terms are different not only between men and women but also between clans. That is, if someone is Ch'itsyaa, he or she will use different terms than if he or she is Naantsąįį. Those who are Tinjiraatsyaa (in the middle, married into their own clan) might call you just about anything, even though it is inappropriate. They might use the word for brother-in-law (shąą) instead of the word for uncle (shitii), or the word for grandpa (shitsii) in place of father-in-law (shiyehghan).

There was formerly a good deal of humor expressed in kin terms between the clans. There was no end to the teasing that went on. For example, the elder Treenahtsyah (Trimble Gilbert's great grandmother) used to call Johnny Frank and all his brothers, "shakai'" (my husband). In turn, Johnny and his brothers would tease her back with something else. More about Treenahtsyah can be found in the *Neerihiinjìk* story, "Sarah and the Old Women" (Mishler 2001).

February 1, 2000: When clan affiliation takes over, a new set of rules apply. If two people have a common clan affiliation (i.e. if both are Ch'itsyaa or both are Naantsąįį) but are too distantly related to use terms of address, the younger person will address the man who is his or her senior by one generation as "shee'ii" (my mother's brother). And the older man will address the younger person as "shuu" (my sister's child). If two people have a common clan affiliation but are distant, the younger person will address the woman who is his or her senior by one generation as "sheek'aii" (my mother's sister) and the older woman will address the younger person as "shuu" (my sister's child).

If two men of the same generation have a common clan affiliation but are distant, they will call each other "shoondee" or "shachaa" (my older brother or my younger brother). If two women have a common clan affiliation but are of the same generation, they will address each other as "shee'ii" or "shijuu" (my elder sister or my younger sister). If a man and a woman of the same generation have a common clan affiliation but are distant the man will address the woman as "shee'ii" or "shijuu" and the woman will address the man as "shoondee" or "shachaa." Most of the kin terms specific to the Ch'itsyaa and Nantsąįį clans have been lost.

In-laws who are very distant and whose clan identities are unknown are simply referred to as shalak (my relative).

November 9, 2022: Gwich'in speakers have a very different notion of the English term "cousin." In fact it would be fair to say that there are no such thing as cousins in Gwich'in. What are "cousins" in English are equivalent to "brother" (shoondee and shachaa) and "sister" (sheejii and shijuu) in Gwich'in, with a distinction made between those older and younger than the speaker. However, "nephew" and "niece" are conflated to shuu (address) or shahoo (reference) for both bro's son or daughter and for sister's son or daughter. As with grandchild, gender is not distinguished.

November 11, 2022: Even in our traditional stories about animals, kinship terms of address pop up from time to time. For instance, in one story Wolverine calls Vasaagihdzak "shą̨ą̨" (my brother-in-law), which most listeners find surprising and rather comical. In another story, the willow tree calls Vasaagihdzak "shee'ii" (my mother's brother), and in yet another tale Raven calls Brown Bear "shee'ii."

Appendix B:
-Nyaa Verb Stem Paradigm: Gwich'in Verbs of Saying

In Old Crow and Ft. McPherson dialects -nyaa becomes –nuu
Compiled by Craig Mishler and Kenneth Frank

-nyaa I, he, or she says or said; they say or said; but nyaa can also be used by itself at the end of a sentence to make a declarative statement, to underscore and emphasize what precedes it. The closest gloss for the sentence ending nyaa would be 'that's how it is'. The examples below are in rough alphabetical order. N = book reference followed by page # for *Neerihiinjìk: We Traveled from Place to Place: The Gwich'in Stories of Johnny and Sarah Frank.*

dadhohnyaa	You all be quiet! (plural)
daihnyaa t'ihnyaa gaanandaii?	you know what I mean?
danąhnyaa	he told us, he said to us
didhiinyaa	Be quiet! (singular)
deegwaahnyaa	it just became quiet, you could hear a pin drop
jyaa diinyaa	that's what you said, you said it
jyaa diinyaa ǫ'	you said that
jyaa dihnyaa	I say or I'm saying this
jyaa diinya'	I said that
jyaa dagoogahnyaa	that's what they said to them
jyaa danąhnyaa	that's what he told us
jyaa diginyaa	that what they're saying
dagavahnyaa	he told them
dagavaihnyaa	I told them
deenyaa?	what did he say?
dee'in digiiyahnyaa?	what do they say he's doing?
deegwinyaa?	what's up? what's going on?
deeginyaa?	what are they saying?
deihnyaa gaanandaii?	do you know what I'm saying?

deiinyaa t'iinyaa?	what do you mean?
deenyaa t'inyaa	what is he saying? what does he mean?
deiinyaa?	what are you saying?
deihnyaa ganandaii	do you know what I'm saying?
diigahnyaa	they told us
diinahnyaa	he or she told us
diinoiinyaa	have mercy on us [as in a prayer]
diirahnyaa	that's what they [our ancestors] told us
jyaa dohnyaa	that's what you're saying
gahnyaa	he calls it [a name] N126
gavahnyaa	he told them
gavaihnyaa	I told them
giiyahnyaa	so they said, that's what they said about him or her, that's what they're telling him or her, that's what they call him, her, or it
ginyaa or ginyaa ǫ'	that's what they say, they say
ginyaa googahnyaa	they say that's what they said
ginyaa ji'	if they say...
giyuunyaa	they thought...
gok'aiirinyaa	we're defending them
vak'aihnyaa	I'm defending him or her
googahnyaa	they say, that's what they say, that's what's been said
goorahnyaa	that's what they said about them, they say about them
goovahnyaa	that's what he or she said to them, that's what he or she said about them
goovaihnyaa	I said to them
govoiihnyaa	that's what I think of them
gwinyaaso	they say, it is said
gwinyaa shagwandak	tell me what they're saying (news, gossip)
juu t'aiinyaa?	who are you talking about?
jyaa diigahnyaa	that's what they told us
jyaa digwinyaa	hearsay, what people are saying
jyaa dihnyaa or jyaa dih	that's what I'm saying [dih is an abbreviation of dihnyaa]
jyaa digwiinya'	we said it, that's what we said
jyaa diinahnyaa	that's what he said to us

jyaa diigahnyaa	that's what they said to us
jyaa doiinya' noihnyaa	I want you to say this to him or her
jyaa googahnyaa	that's what they told them
jyaa gwinyaa	that's what they're saying
jyaa reh ginyaa	that's really what everybody says
jyaa nihłaraanyaa	we're telling each other
jyaa nyaa	that's what he or she said
jyaa varahnyàa	that's what they said or we said about him or her
jyaa varahnyaa	that's what they say or we say to him or her
jyaa vaihnya'	I told him or her
jyaa vahaihjyaa	I'm going to tell him or her (future tense)
jyaa vaihnyaa	I told him that, that's what I told him
naihnyaa	I told you
nahnyaa	he or she told you
nagahnyaa	they told you N332
nakhwahnyaa	he told you all N602
noihnyaa	I thought you...
nyaa yahnyaa	he meant what he said
oiihnyaa	I thought...
shagahnyaa	they told me
shaiinyaa	you told me, you said to me (as in the love song "Goodbye shaiinyaa")
shahnyaa	he or she told me (name of the daughter of Shahnyaati', famous trading chief)
sharahnyaa	they told me
t'avaiinyaa	you said that to him or her
t'avaihnyaa	I said it to him or her,
t'agavahnyaa	he or she said that to them
t'agavaihnyaa	I said that to them.
t'agahnyaa	that's what or who they're talking about
aii lee t'agwaiinyaa?	are you saying that?
t'agwaihnyaa	I said it, what I'm talking about, what I'm saying N168, N326
t'agwaih	(a shortened form of t'agwaihnyaa)
t'agwahnyaa	he said it, he talked about it, he meant to say, he told
t'agwarahnyaa	we call it, that's where we're talking about
t'agogwahnyaa	that's what they're saying about that N188, N574

t'agoorahnyaa	that's what we say about them
t'ahnyaa	he or she told or said to [direct object] e.g.
shiti' t'ahnyaa	'he told my father'
aii t'aihnyaa	that's what I meant, that's what I'm talking about [may be abbreviated as aii t'aih]
t'anałagaanyaa	they had an exchange of words, they argued
t'arahnyaa	as they would say, so it's said, what they were talking about, what they mean
aii t'arahnyaa	that's what it is
t'arahnyaa Gwich'in o'	I think maybe it is
t'aragwahnyaa	that's how the story goes
t'ashagahnyaa	I've been told
t'iyahnyaa	he/she told him/her N24, N666
t'iginyaa	they're saying that
jyaa nyaa t'iginyaa	that's what they're saying
t'igiinya'	they said
t'igwinyaa	it is said, so it's been said
t'igahnyaa	what they're talking about
t'igiyahnyaa	they said about him or her
t'igiiyah'in goorahnyaa	that's what they say about that
t'inyaa	he or she's saying
t'inyaa łee	that's what he's saying
t'iinyaa	you're saying that, you're right
łyaa t'iinyaa	you're absolutely right
t'ihnyaa/ t'iihnyaa	I'm saying, I'm talking about [may also be ab breviated as t'ih]
chan t'iinyaa	say that again
varahnyaa	they say, we say
nyaa varahnyaa	he or she said, they say
vaihnyaa	I said to him or her, I asked him or her for something, I told him or her, I named
vaiinyaa	ask him for something (an object) [imperative]
veihnyaa	I'm giving him or her advice (a warning)
veenyaa	he's giving him or her advice (a warning)
veiinya'	I gave him or her advice (a warning)
vaiinyaa	you referred to it a little while ago N560
yahnyaa	he or she told him or her

Appendix C:
Discography of Gwich'in Fiddle Music

(Except where otherwise noted, all recordings are self-produced and privately released compact disks. Many are no longer available for retail sale.)

Compiled by Craig Mishler

Colin Adjun, *Fiddler of the Arctic* (1981) lp record and cassette
CBC Northern Service Broadcast Recording
-------. *Dusty the Leader* (n.d.), cassette only
Box 286, Kugluktuk, NU X0B 0E0
cmadjun@qiniq.com
-------. *Beluga Waters* (1997) CD and cassette
Spiritwalker Productions, 5101 54 St, Yellowknife, NT, X1A1W6 (867) 873-3912
Noel Andre, *Lonesome Indian* (2010)
Spiritwalker Productions, 5101 54 St, Yellowknife, NT, X1A1W6 (867) 873-3912
Allan Benjamin, *Gwitchin Fiddleman* (2001) cassette only
Box 7, Old Crow, Y.T. Y0B 1N0 (867) 966-3172 Also on Facebook.
-------. *Didee & Didoo* (2010).
Boyd Benjamin, *Home Sweet Home* (2011)
The Flying Gwitch'in Fiddler (2013).
Home Sweet Home: Fire on the Ice (2016)
Available from Boyd at Box 31464, Whitehorse, Yukon Y1A 6K8
boydbenjamin.com Also on Facebook.
Ben Charlie, *Ben Chuck: Old Crow Fiddler* (2002)
25-5 Klondike Road, Whitehorse, Y.T. Y1A 3L7 Broadcasts a music show on CHON-FM Whitehorse, weekday afternoons. Also on Facebook.
e-mail: benchuck@nnby.com

Brennan Firth, *Iitsii Adahłii* (2013)
℅ Betty Vittrekwa-Firth, Box 351, Fort McPherson, NT X0E 0J0. Can be ordered online from Amazon.com. gwichinbrennan@gmail.com

-------. *Teetl'it Gwich'in* (2016)

Harold Frost, *Vuntut Gwitchin Fiddler* (2001)
Box 55, Old Crow, Y.T. Y0B 1N0

Trimble and Gregory Gilbert, *Neets'aii Gwich'in Fiddlers* (2001) also on cassette.
Box 22006, Arctic Village, AK 99722

Trimble Gilbert Maple Sugar. In: *Centrum Fiddle Tunes Archives, Vol. 1: 20th Anniversary Festival Sampler.*
Centrum, Box 1158, Port Townsend, WA 98368.

Victor Modeste, *Mackenzie River Rambler* (2010)
Spiritwalker Productions, 5101 54 St, Yellowknife, NT, X1A1W6 (867) 873-3912

Charlie Peter, *Music of the Alaskan Kutchin [Gwich'in] Indians* (1974) vinyl lp and CD. Edited with liner notes by Craig Mishler, Smithsonian Folkways Records FE4070. May be previewed and ordered online at: https://folkways.si.edu/music-of-the-gwichin-indians-of-alaska/american-indian/album/smithsonian

Dennis Wayne Thompson, *Gwich'in Pride* (2003)
Limited edition. Ft. McPherson. Also on Facebook.

Bill Stevens Discography

Long Playing Vinyl Record Album:
Bill Stevens: Yukon Fiddle Favorites (1982)

Cassette Tapes:
Athabascan Old-Time Fiddling Festival (anthology, 1983)
Fairbanks: Institute of Alaska Native Arts.
Bill Stevens: Yukon Fiddler (1984) out of print but reissued: see Down River Blues below.

The Metal That Sings: 1984 Athabascan Old-Time Fiddling Festival (anthology, 1985) Fairbanks: Institute of Alaska Native Arts. Track 3: "Over the Waves".

Compact Discs:

Bill Stevens: Alaska Gwich'in Fiddler (1995)

Bill Stevens: Alaska Gwich'in Fiddler Plays Favorite Hymns (1997) also on cassette.

Gwich'in Athabascan Fiddle Music (1999) also on cassette, with liner notes by Craig Mishler.

Grey Eagle (2002; limited reissue 2011) Reissue includes previously unreleased tunes "Danny Boy" and "Uncle Joe").

19th Annual Athabascan Fiddlers Festival, Vol. 1 (anthology, 2002) Fairbanks: Athabascan Fiddlers Association. Includes "Jig Tune" and "Blue Moon of Kenucky" (with Frances Williams).

19th Annual Athabascan Fiddlers Festival, Vol. 2 (anthology, 2002) Fairbanks: Athabascan Fiddlers Association. Includes "Downriver Boogie" and "Don't Tell Me What to Do" (with Mike and Daisy Demientieff).

Fiddlin' Through the Years: A Collection of Old-time Fiddle Favorites (2005).

Indian Pete and the Band of Brothers: Native American Soldier (2006). Bill appears as sideman for Pete Peter on "Eagle Island Blues".

Down River Blues (2008) Reissue of 1984 sessions with singer-guitar player Artie Joseph, includes additional tracks.

CD Anthologies

Athabascan Fiddlers Live 1994: Old Time Fiddle Tunes (anthology, 1995) Includes many fiddlers. Produced by Bill Stevens and Tony Scott Pearce. Fairbanks: Athabascan Fiddlers Association.

Athabascan Fiddle Favorites: Vols. 1 and 2 (anthologies) Includes Gwich'in fiddlers as well as others.Produced by Dixie Alexander. Directed by Bill Stevens and Tony Scott Pearce Fairbanks: Athabascan Fiddlers Association.

The Wood That Sings: Indian Fiddle Music of the Americas (anthology, 1997). Washington, D.C. National Museum of the American Indian, Smithsonian Institution, Smithsonian Folkways SF 40472.

19th Annual Athabascan Fiddlers Festival, Vols. 1-3 (anthologies, 2002, CDs only) Fairbanks: Athabascan Fiddlers Association. Includes many fiddlers.

Songs & Stories of the Arctic Neets'aii Gwich'in: A Message To The World (anthology, 2020, CD and streaming) Produced by Barrett Martin, Sunyata Records. Contains five fiddle tunes by Brennan Firth and short speeches by several elders.

Videos

Fairbanks Fiddle Festival (1988) Whitehorse, Yukon: Northern Native Broadcasting. Includes many fiddlers. Northern Native Broadcasting, Whitehorse, Yukon, YT (867) 668-6629 or nnby@yknet.yk.ca

Athabascan Old-Time Fiddling Festival (1998) Fairbanks: Athabascan Fiddlers Association. Includes many fiddlers.

References

Note: Source material for this book is derived from several manuscript collections. These are abbreviated below as: NAC = Records of the Church Missionary Society of London (Correspondence), Microfilm MG 17 B2. National Archives of Canada, 395 Wellington Street, Ottawa, Ontario K1A 0N3. AEPRL = Journals of Robert McDonald, Microfilm P 340, MS 4001. Archives of the Ecclesiastical Province of Rupert's Land, Manitoba Provincial Archives, 200 Vaughan Street, Winnipeg, Manitoba R3C 1T5. ADOMI = Archives Deschâtelets, Oblates of Marie Immaculate, 175 Rue Main, Ottawa, Ontario, Canada K1S 1C3. EDAUA = Collection of the Episcopal Diocese of Alaska, University of Alaska, Rasmuson Library, Fairbanks, Alaska 99775.

To the best of my knowledge, Missions, O.M.I., which contains the first-hand accounts of Oblate missionaries seems to be available in Canada only at the Archives Deschâtelets in Ottawa. Similarly, The Church Missionary Intelligencer, which contains first-hand accounts of Anglican missionaries in the service of the Church Missionary Society, can only be found in Canada at the Leonard Library, Wycliffe College, Toronto.

Abeita, Luci. 1980. Largest Native Land Conveyance Ever. *The Council* (monthly newsletter of the Tanana Chiefs Conference), February, p 3.

Abel, Sarah Chitze. 1993. Interviewed by Adeline Charlie. Interpreted by Alice Frost. pp. 6-11. Rampart House: *Stories Told by Our Elders.* Yukon Territory: Students at Ts'ek Gehtr'oonatun Zzeh College.

Adams, Laura Parmalee. n.d. Up to Zero Typescript, chapters 25-27. Includes lengthy excerpt of letter received from John Fredson dated December, 1943. Archives of the Jessie DuPont Library, University of the South, Sewanee, Tennessee.

Alaska Boundary Tribunal. 1903. *Appendix to the Case of the United States Before the Tribunal Convened at London.* Washington, D.C.: U.S. Government Printing Office.

Alexander, Virginia and Clarence Alexander 2005 *Gwich'in to English Dictionary.* Fort Yukon: Privately published by the authors.

References

Alexander, Clarence. 2011. Speech made at Diiginjik K'yaa Eegaaraa'ee: We Are Learning Our Language, Visioning Session. Gwich'in Language Workshop, Cruikshank School, Beaver, Alaska, May 24.

American Folklife Center. 1923. AFC 2000/007: Edward Sapir/Kutchin Cylinder Recordings. Audio recordings of John Fredson by Edward Sapir at Camp Red Cloud, Pennsylvania. Tape transfers of original wax cylinder recordings are held at the Archives of Traditional Music. Library of Congress, Washington, D.C.

Anglican Church Records, Yukon Diocese. 1922. Parish Register. Box 38, Folder 1. Yukon Territorial Archives, Whitehorse.

Andrews, Elizabeth F. 1977. *Report on the cultural resources of the Doyon region, central Alaska.* 2 vols. Fairbanks: University of Alaska, Anthropology and Historic Preservation, Cooperative Park Studies Unit.

Anonymous. 1910. Untitled news item. *The Tanana Leader.* June 2, p. 4.

Anonymous. 1911. Untitled news item. *The Dawson News.* August 22.

Anonymous. 1925. *Alaska Churchman*, Vol 19(2) April, p. 8.

Anonymous. 1945. Obituary for John Fredson. *The Alaska Churchman.* September, p 9.

Anonymous. 1981. Gerald Fitzgerald, Mapmaker for the U.S. Geological Survey (obituary). *The Washington Post,* February 27.

Anonymous. 1996. 5th Gwich'in Gathering. *Indian Life* 17(3):15ff.

Arndt, Katherine. 1996. *Dynamics of the Fur Trade on the Middle Yukon River, Alaska, 1839 to 1868.* Ph.D. dissertation, University of Alaska, Fairbanks. Ann Arbor: UMI.

Atwood, Margaret. 1970. *Lobsticks: Lobstick, A Spruce Tree Trimmed of all but the Top Branches* [volume of 12 poems]. Guelph, Ont: Alive Press.

Bakker, Peter. 1996. Broken Slavey and Jargon Loucheux: A first exploration. pp. 317-320. In Ernst Håkon Jahr and Ingvild Broch, eds., *Language Contact in the Arctic: Northern Pidgins and Contact Languages.* Berlin and New York: Mouton de Gruyter.

_____. 1997. *A Language of Our Own: the Genesis of Michif, the Mixed Cree-French Language of the Canadian Métis.* New York: Oxford University Press.

Ballantyne, Michael. 1848. *Hudson's Bay, or, Every-day life in the wilds of North America : during six years' residence in the territories of the honourable Hudson's Bay Company.* Edinburgh: W. Blackwood. Excerpts of the journal and photos of lobsticks may be accessed at: www.mhs.mb.ca/docs/pageant/14/ballantynejourney.shtml

Basso, Keith H. 1979. *Portraits of "The Whiteman": Linguistic play and cultural symbols among the western Apache.* New York: Cambridge University Press.

Bauman, Richard. Verbal Art as Performance. *American Anthropologist* 77 (1975) 290-311.

Beairsto, Shelagh Marie. 1999. Dinjii Kat Chih Ahaa: Gwich'in Notions of Leadership. M.Ed. Thesis, Univ. of Manitoba, 1999.

Beardy, Flora and Robert Coutts, eds. 1996. *Voices from Hudson Bay: Cree Stories from York Factory.* Montreal and Kingston: McGill-Queen's University Press.

Beaudry, Nicole. 1997. The Challenges of Human Relationships in Ethnographic Inquiry: Examples from Arctic and Subarctic Fieldwork. pp. 63-83. In G. F. Barz and T.J. Cooley, eds., *Shadows in the Field: New Perspectives for Fieldwork in Ethnomusicology.* New York: Oxford University Press.

Beck, Max. 1997. Interview with Craig Mishler in Eagle City, July 11, 1997.

Bennett, Margaret. 1989. *The Last Stronghold: Scotch Gaelic Traditions in Newfoundland.* St. John's: Breakwater Books.

Black, George. 1913. Letter to Dr. Alfred Thompson, M.P., November 12. Government file: Rampart House, Royal Canadian Mounted Police, 1913. Yukon Territorial Archives, Whitehorse.

Bergsland, Knut. Aleut Dialects of Atka and Attu. *Transactions of the American Philosophical Society* N. S. 49:1-128. Philadelphia, 1959.

Blondin, George. 2006. *Trail of the Spirit.* Edmonton: NeWest Press.

Boas, Franz and George Hunt. Kwakiutl Texts. *Memoirs of the American Museum of Natural History* 5. New York 1905.

Boas, Franz. The Eskimo of Baffin Land and Hudson Bay. *Bulletin of the American Museum of Natural History* 15. New York 1901-1907.

_____. 1972. Professional Correspondence Wilmington, Delaware: Scholarly Resources. Microfilm of original letters deposited at the American Philosophical Library, Philadelphia.

Bompas, William Carpenter. 1867. Annual Letter to the Secretaries, Church Missionary Society, December 9, from Fort Chippewyan. Rupert's Land Provincial Archives, Mss. 4001. Winnipeg.

Boon, Thomas C.B. 1965. William West Kirkby, First Anglican Missionary to the Loucheux. *The Beaver* 295(Spring):36-43.

Brooks, Alfred H. 1898. Journal of a Trip to Alaska in 1898. Unpublished field notes. *U.S. Geological Survey*, Technical Data Unit, Anchorage.

_____. 1900. A Reconnaissance in the Tanana and White River Basins, Alaska, in 1898. U.S. *Geological Survey Annual Report* 20, Vol. 7 (pp.425-494).

Brown, Carolyn S. 1987. *The Tall Tale in American Folklore and Literature.* Knoxville: The University of Tennessee Press.

Brown, Jennifer S.H. 1980. *Strangers in Blood: Fur Trade Company Families in Indian Country.* Vancouver: University of British Columbia Press.

_____. 1983. Women as Centre and Symbol in the Emergence of Métis Communities. *The Canadian Journal of Native Studies* 3(1): 39-46.

_____. 1988. A Parcel of Upstart Scotchmen. *The Beaver* 68(1):4-11.

Bruce, Robert Sr. 1993. Interviewed by Laurence Charlie. pp. 51-56. *Rampart House: Stories Told by Our Elders.* Yukon Territory: Students at Ts'ek Gehtr'oonatun Zzeh College.

Burch, Ernest S. Jr. and Craig Mishler. 1995. The Di'hą̱į̱ Gwich'in: Mystery People of Northern Alaska. *Arctic Anthropology* 32(1):147-172.

Bureau of the Census. 1900. Twelfth Census of the United States, Northern District, Alaska. Household enumeration sheet for Gens de Large River. U.S. Department of Commerce.

_____. 1910-1920. Thirteenth and Fourteenth Censuses of the United States. Household Enumeration sheets for Eagle Native Village. U.S. Department of Commerce.

_____. 1920-1950. Fourteenth through Seventeenth Censuses of the United States, Alaska. Household enumeration sheets for Chandalar Village [Venetie] and Circle Village. U.S. Department of Commerce.

_____. 1930. Fifteenth Census of the United States. Fourth Judicial District, Alaska. Household Enumeration sheets for Arctic Village. U.S. Department of Commerce.

_____. 1940. Sixteenth Census of the United States. Chandalar District, Alaska. Household Enumeration sheets for Christian Village. U.S. Department of Commerce.

Bureau of Indian Affairs. 1939. Alaska Village Census Rolls. Record Group 75. Microfilm Roll 12: Circle. U.S. National Archives, Seattle.

Burke, Clara Heinz. 1961. *Doctor Hap*. New York: Coward McCann.

Burke, Grafton. 1921. Letter to John Wood, September 12. Typescript. Episcopal Church Archives, Austin, Texas.

_____. 1923. Northward the Course of the Kingdom. *Spirit of Missions* 88(3): 171-74.

_____. 1925. Fire, Flood, and Flu on the Yukon. *Spirit of Missions*, December, pp 754-56.

Burlington Free Press. 1869. Life in Alaska. p. 3. April 6. Orig. *Harper's Magazine.*

Cadzow, Dan. 1892-1939. Daniel Cadzow Fonds. Yukon Territorial Archives, Whitehorse.

_____. 1896-1920. Dan Cadzow papers. Rasmuson Library. Archives of the University of Alaska, Fairbanks.

_____. 1910. Letter to Bishop Stringer from Rampart House, September 10. Isaac O. Stringer Papers. Genreal Synod Archives, Anglican Church of Canada, Toronto.

Cameron, Agnes Deans. 1909. *The New North: Being Some Account of a Woman's Journey through Canada to the Arctic.* New York: D. Appleton.

Cairnes, D.D. 1914. *The Yukon-Alaska International Boundary, between Porcupine and Yukon Rivers.* Geological Survey of Canada Memoir 67, Ottawa.

Cashman, Edward. 1900. Subreport of Edward Cashman. pp. 161-169. In W.R. Abercrombie, Alaska, 1899: *Copper River Exploring Expedition, Alaska, 1899*. Washington, D.C.

Cass, Elizabeth. 1959. Some Observations on the Loucheux Indians. Typescript summary of an interview with Peter Lord at Old Crow, *Y.T.*, tape # 3. Ethnology Division Archives, National Museums of Canada, Ottawa.

Caulfield, Rick. 1983. *Gwich'in Athabaskan Place Names of the Upper Yukon-Porcupine Region, Alaska: A Preliminary Report.* Technical Paper Number No. 83, with maps. Juneau: Alaska Dept. of Fish and Game, Division of Subsistence.

CBC North. 2017. Folk band seeks Gwich'in songwriter's family to solve copyright conundrum. https://www.cbc.ca/news/canada/north/gwichin-love-song-goodbye-shaanyuu-copyright-1.4016249

Champagne, Joseph-Étienne. 1943. First Attempts at the Evangelization of Alaska. *Les Études Oblates* II: 15-22.

Chapman, John Wight. 1914. W. *Ten'a Texts and Tales.* Leyden: E.J. Brill.

Charlie, Charlie Peter. 1997. Interviewed by Craig Mishler in Fairbanks, November 14.

Clark, Annette McFayden. 1970. Koyukon Athapascan Ceremonialism. *Western Canadian Journal of Anthropology* 2:80-88.

Cline, Mike. 1966. Huslia's Hole Hunters. *Alaska Sportsman* 32:30-33.

Clouston, Jo Storer. 1912. Orkney Surnames. In: Alfred W. Johnston and Amy Johnston, eds., *Old-Lore Miscellany of Orkney, Shetland, Caithness, and Sutherland.* Vol. V. London: King's College.

Coates, Kenneth. 1982. Furs Along the Yukon: Hudson's Bay Company—Native Trade in the Yukon River Basin, 1830-1893. *BC Studies* 55:51-78.

Cohen, Stan. 1996. *Yukon River Steamboats: A Pictorial History.* Missoula: Pictorial Histories Publishing Co.

Cole, Douglas and Ira Chain. 1990. *An Iron Hand Upon the People: the Law Against the Potlatch on the Northwest Coast.* Seattle: University of Washington Press.

Cook, Eung-Do. 2004. *A Grammar of Dëne Sųłiné (Chipewyan).* Algonquian and Iroquoian Linguistics - Special Athabaskan Number, Memoir 17. Winnipeg: Algonquian and Iroquoian Linguistics.

Coudert, J.L. and Le Chevalier, J. 1955. About the First Evangelization of Alaska. *Missions des Oblats* 82(288):371-393.

Craig, J.D. 1912. Letter to Rev. I.O. Stringer, September 4. Anglican Church Records, Yukon Diocese. Box 9, Folder 13, Correspondence.

Cunningham, Keith. 1992. *American Indians' Kitchen-Table Stories.* Little Rock: August House.

Dall, William H. 1870. *Alaska and Its Resources.* Boston: Lee and Shepard.

_____. 1898. Travels on the Yukon and in the Yukon Territory in 1866-1868. pp. 2-242. *The Yukon Territory.* London: Downey & Co., 1898. Reprinted by AMS Press, New York, 1975.

Dauenhauer, Richard. 1976. *Riddle and Poetry Handbook.* Anchorage: Alaska Native Education Board.

Davis, Richard, ed. 1996. *Lobsticks and Stone Cairns: Human Landmarks in the Arctic.* Calgary: University of Calgary Press.

de Laguna, Frederica. 1969. The Atna of the Copper River, Alaska: The World of Men and Animals. *Folk* 11/12:17-26.

_____. 1994. Letter to Craig Mishler, August 11.

_____. 1999. *Travels Among the Dena: Exploring Alaska's Yukon Valley.* Seattle: University of Washington Press.

de Reuse, Willem. 2009. *Hän Athabascan Tales and Narratives told by Louise Paul.* Unpublished mss.

Dementieff, Laverne. 2021. On Deg Xinag. Language Journeys, Speaker Series. Video interview with Allan Hayton. Morris Thompson Cultural and Visitors Center. https://www.morristhompsoncenter.org/language-journeys-laverne-demientieff-on-deg-xinag/

Demientieff, Martha. 1974. Taped interview with Lucinda Corey, November 7. Unpublished transcript in "Alaskan Folklore" class project. Craig Mishler Papers. Consortium Library, University of Alaska Anchorage.

References

Dixon, Roland B. Maidu Texts. *Publications of the American Ethnological Society* 4. New York 1912.

Dorion, Leah Marie. 2014. *My First Métis Lobstick.* Saskatoon Gabriel Lamont Institute.

Dorson, Richard. 1982. *Man and Beast in American Comic Legend.* Bloomington: Indiana University Press.

Drane, Frederick. 1955. Letter to Arthur Chitty, n.d. Typescript Archives of the Jessie DuPont Library, University of the South, Sewanee, Tennessee.

Dremeaux, Lillie. 2003. *Slavey Jargon and the presence of French loanwords in Northern Athabascan.* Senior thesis, Swarthmore College. Available for online download at: https://www.swarthmore.edu/linguistics/linguistics-tri-college-class-2004

Duchaussois, P. 1923. *Mid Snow and Ice: The Apostles of the North-West.* London: Burns, Oates, & Washbourne.

Duchaussois, R.P. 1921 *Aux Glaces Polaires.* Ville la Salle: Noviciat de Marie Immaculée.

Easton, Norm. 2007. "King George Got Diarrhea": the Yukon-Alaska Boundary Survey, Bill Rupe, and the Scottie Creek Dineh. *Alaska Journal of Anthropology* 5(1):95-118.

Elford, Leon W. and Marjorie Elford (comp.) c. 1981. *English-Chipewyan Dictionary.* Prince Albert: Northern Canada Evangelical Mission.

Episcopal Church. 1899-1972. Episcopal Church Diocese of Alaska. Fort Yukon Parish Registers. Microfilm. University of Alaska Polar Regions and Archives, Rasmuson Library, Fairbanks.

Espinola, Judith. 1974. The Nature, Function, and Performance of Indirect Discourse in Prose Fiction. *Speech Monographs* 41(3):193-204.

Farneski, Anna. 1998. A Gathering for the People's Sake: the Gwich'in Indian Nation Unites to Face Threats to its Future. *Heartland Magazine, Fairbanks Daily News-Miner,* Vol. 5 No. 26 (June 26), 8ff.

Firth, John. 1920. *Reminiscences of An Orkney Parish.* Stromness: Orkney Natural History Society. Reprinted 1974.

Fisher, Robin. 1977. *Context and Conflict: Indian-European Relations in British Columbia, 1774-1890.* Vancouver: University of British Columbia Press.

Fitzgerald, Gerald. 1927. Date Book for 1927. Unpublished field notebook in the possession of Gerald Fitzgerald's daughter, Patricia Aubin, Gaithersburg, MD.

_____. 1951. *Surveying and Mapping in Alaska.* U.S. Geological Survey, Circular 101. Washington, DC.

Frank, Dan. 1995. Personal communication with Craig Mishler, in Venetie.

Frank, Kenneth. 1997. Personal communication with Craig Mishler on January 1 in Arctic Village.

_____. 2000. Personal communication with Craig Mishler, July 30.

Frank, Kenneth and Craig Mishler. 2001. Frank Family Tree. In Craig Mishler, ed., *Neerihiinjìk: We Traveled From Place to Place. The Gwich'in Stories of Johnny and Sarah Frank.* 2nd ed. Fairbanks: University of Alaska Native Language Center.

Fredson, John. 1921-30. Correspondence with John W. Wood. Approx. 20 letters, Mss. Episcopal Church Archives, Austin, Texas.

_____. 1926-34. Four letters, Mss. Archives of the Jessie DuPont Library, University of the South, Sewanee, Tennessee.

_____. 1929. Wild Melodies from the Arctic. *The Etude* 47(4): 271.

_____. 1938-45. Correspondence with Alaska Territorial School Board: letters, reports, accounts, personal employment history. Stored in Episcopal Mission House, Venetie. Microfilmed in part by the Archives of the University of Alaska, Rasmuson Library, Fairbanks.

_____. 1939. Letter to Charles Hawkesworth, Office of Indian Affairs, Juneau, November 22. RG 75, Box 220, Bureau of Indian Affairs. National Archives, Seattle.

_____. 1982. Vashrąįį K'oo Gwats'ą' Tr'ahaa'òo: A Trip to Arctic Village. Pp. 40-49. In J. McGary, ed., *John Fredson Edward Sapir Hàa Googwandak/Stories Told by John Fredson to Edward Sapir.* Alaska Native Language Center, University of Alaska Fairbanks.

_____. 1982. Fort Yukon. pp. 22-29. In Jane McGary, ed., *John Fredson Edward Sapir Hàa Googwandak: Stories Told by John Fredson to Edward Sapir.* Fairbanks: Alaska Native Language Center, University of Alaska.

Fredson, John and Edward Sapir. 1923. Kutchin Texts and Translations. Typescript. Ethnology Division Archives, National Museum of History, Ottawa.

Frost, Stephen Sr. 1993. Interviewed by Shelagh Beairsto. pp. 19-25. *Rampart House: Stories Told by Our Elders.* Yukon Territory: Students at Ts'ek Gehtr'oonatun Zzeh College.

Gascon, Fr. 1863. Letter to Bishop Taché. Typescript. ADOMI.

Gibson, Walter. 1974. *Hoyle's Modern Encyclopedia of Card Games.* Garden City, NY: Doubleday.

Gilbert, Trimble. 1983. Personal communication with Craig Mishler, May 26, in Fairbanks.

_____. 1989. Ties Between the Natives of Arctic Village and Northern Yukon. Pp. 227-230. In *Borderlands: 1989 Heritage Conference, June 2nd-4th, 1989.* Whitehorse: Yukon Historical and Museums Association, Yukon College, Alaska Historical Society, and the University of Victoria. Copy at University of Alaska Anchorage Consortium Library.

Gilles-Mousseau, R.P. 1946. L'affaire d'Alaska. *Études Oblates* 5(3):161-175.

Goddard, Pliny Earle. 1911. Jicarilla Apache Texts. *Anthropological Papers of the American Museum of Natural History* 8. New York.

_____. 1917. Beaver Texts. *Anthropological Papers of the American Museum of Natural History* 10, Pts. 5 and 6. New York.

Goffman, Erving. 1974. *Frame Analysis: An Essay on the Organization of Human Experience.* New York: Harper Colophon Books.

Grant, George M. 1873. *Ocean to Ocean: Sandford Fleming's Expedition Through Canada in 1872.* Toronto: James Campbell & Son.

Gregor, Reverend Walter. 1881. *The Folk-Lore of the North-East of Scotland.* London: the Folk-Lore Society.

Grollier, Henri. 1860. Letter to Mgr. Taché, July 20. English typescript. ADOMI.

_____. 1860. Letter to Mgr. Taché from Fort Norman, July 20. Archive of St. Boniface, Winnipeg. Typescript, 26 pp.

Gross, Lawrence W., ed. *Native American Rhetoric*. Albuquerque: University of New Mexico Press.

Grider, Margaretta. 1927. Letter to John W. Wood, October 8. Includes excerpt of a letter from John Fredson received several days earlier. Episcopal Church Archives, Austin, Texas.

Gruening, Ernest. 1968. *The State of Alaska*. New York: Random House.

Gubser, Nicholas. 1965. *The Nunamiut Eskimos: Hunters of Caribou*. New Haven: Yale University Press.

Guédon, Marie-Françoise. 1974. *People of Tetlin, Why Are You Singing?* Ottawa: National Museums of Canada, Ethnology Division Paper No. 9.

Hadleigh-West, Frederick. 1964. *The Netsi Kutchin: An Essay in Human Ecology*. Ph.D. dissertation, Louisiana State University. Ann Arbor: University Microfilms.

Hall, Edward S., Jr. 1975. *The Eskimo Storyteller*. Knoxville: University of Tennessee Press.

Hallowell, A. Irving. 1926. Bear Ceremonialism in the Northern Hemisphere. *American Anthropologist* 28:1-175.

Hardisty, William L. 1852a. Fort Yukon Post Journal for March 16. B.240a/5/Folio13. Hudson's Bay Company Archives, Winnipeg.

_____. 1852b. Letter to James Anderson, November 5. B.200/b/28. HBCA, Winnipeg.

_____. 1855. Fort Yukon Post Journal for November 22. B.240a/8/Folio 38. HBCA, Winnipeg.

_____. 1857. Letter to Sir George Simpson from Fort Youcon, November 10. D.5/45, fos. 262-264; also Microfilm 3M114. HBCA, Winnipeg.

_____. 1867. The Loucheux Indians. pp. 311-320. In "Notes on the Tinneh or Chepewyan Indians of British and Russian America." *Annual Report of the Smithsonian Institution for 1866*. Washington, D.C.

_____. 1872. The Loucheux Indians. *Report of the Smithsonian Institution for 1866*. Washington, D.C.: U.S. Govt. Printing Office.

Hayes, Charles Willard. 1892. An Expedition Through the Yukon District. *National Geographic Magazine* 4:117-162.

Hawkesworth, Charles. 1939. Letter to John Fredson, Venetie, December 21. RG 75, Box 220, Bureau of Indian Affairs. National Archives, Seattle.

Heine, Michael, Alestine Andre, Ingrid Kritsch, and Alma Cardinal. 2007. *Gwichya Gwich'in Googwandak: The History and Stories of the Gwichya Gwich'in as told by the Elders of Tsiigehtshik.* Rev. ed. Tsiigehtshik and Fort McPherson: Gwich'in Social and Cultural Institute. Available online for download at: https://gwichin.ca/publications/gwichya-gwichin-googwandak

Hennigh, Lawrence. 1966. Control of Incest in Eskimo Folktales. *Journal of American Folklore* 79 (312):365-369.

Herbert, Belle. 1982. *Shandaa: In My Lifetime*. Ed. by William Pfisterer. Fairbanks: Alaska Native Language Center.

Hess, Bill. 2010. Wasilla, Alaska by 300. . .and then some: the Blog. http://wasillaalaskaby300.squarespace.com/journal/2010/8/5/on-the-day-that-her-brother-was-honored-daisy-stevens-sponso.html

Hirshberg, Diane B., Douglas Cost, and Edward Alexander. 2023. Adaptation Isn't Just for the Tundra: Rethinking Teaching and Schooling in Alaska's Arctic. pp. 9-24. In: *Education, Equity, and Inclusion: Teaching and Learning for a Sustainable North*. Cham, Switzerland: Springer Polar Sciences (Open Access).

Hoijer, Harry. 1938. *Chiricahua and Mescalero Apache Texts*. Chicago: University of Chicago Press.

Hole, Christina. 1976. *British Folk Customs*. London: Hutchinson and Company.

Holloway, J. Michael. 2014. *Dreaming Bears: A Gwich'in Indian Storyteller, a Southern Doctor, a Wild Corner of Alaska*. Kenmore, WA: Epicenter Press.

Holtved, Erik. 1951. *The Polar Eskimos: Language and Folklore* 1 (Texts) (Meddelelser om Grønland 152). Copenhagen.

Hulen, David. 1988. Far-flung Kutchin People Gather in Arctic Village. *Anchorage Daily News*. June 13, Pp. A-1ff.

Hunter, James. 1859. Exploratory Mission Voyage to Mackenzie River Districts: Archdeacon Hunter's Journal. *Church Missionary Intelligencer.* October, November, and December. 228-240;264-266; 280-285.

Hymes, Dell. 1975. Breakthrough Into Performance. pp. 11-74. In: Goldstein, K. and Ben-Amos, D. (eds.). *Folklore: Performance and Communication.* The Hague: De Gruyter.

_____. Discovering Oral Performance and Measured Verse in American Indian Narrative. In: *New Literary History* 8(3):431-457, 1977.

Ikuta, Hiroko. 2011. Embodied Knowledge, Relations with the Environment, and Political Negotiation: St. Lawrence Island Yupik and Iñupiaq Dance in Alaska. *Arctic Anthropology* 48(1):54-65.

Inoue, Toshiaki. 2004. The Gwich'in Gathering: The Subsistence Tradition in Their Modern Life and the Gathering against Oil Development by the Gwich'in Athabascan. *Senri Ethnological Studies* 66:183-204.

International Boundary Commission. 1918. *Joint Report Upon the Survey and Demarcation of the International Boundary Between the U.S. and Canada Along the 141st Meridian From the Arctic Ocean to Mt. St. Elias.* Washington, D.C.: U.S. Department of State.

Jacobs, Melville. 1959. *The Content and Style of an Oral Literature.* Chicago: University of Chicago Press.

_____. 1972. Areal Spread of Indian Oral Genre Features in the Northwest States. In: *Journal of the Folklore Institute* 9(1):10-17.

Jakobson, Roman. 1971. Shifters, Verbal Categories, and the Russian Verb. pp. 130-147. In: *Roman Jakobson Selected Writings* 2. The Hague: De Gruyter Mouton.

James, Sarah. 2005. In the Footsteps of the Ancestors: "I Am Caribou People." *Parabola* 30(2).

Jetté, Julius and Eliza Jones. 2000. *Koyukon Athabaskan Dictionary.* Ed. by James Kari. Fairbanks: Alaska Native Language Center, University of Alaska.

Jetté, Julius. 1908-1909. On Ten'a Folklore. *Journal of the Royal Anthropological Institute* 38:298-367; 39:460-505.

_____. 1911. On the Superstitions of the Ten'a [Koyukon] Indians. *Anthropos* 6:95-108, 241-259, 602-615, 699-723.

_____. 1913. Riddles of the Ten'a [Koyukon] Indians. *Anthropos* 8:181-201, 630-651.

John, Daniel. Audio recording by Craig Mishler, GW1044 (1973). Alaska Native Language Archive, available online at: https://www.uaf.edu/anla/record.php?identifier=GWI044

_____. 1973. Sam Peter stories recorded by Craig Mishler, March 30. Alaska Native Language Archives, University of Alaska Fairbanks. KU972Mi1986. See tape Daniel_John-01_sideA.wav. Also Daniel John tape GW1044 side B.

John, Elijah. 1980. Interview taped in Gwich'in by Craig Mishler at Fort Yukon, August 16.

_____. 1983. Interview with the author in Fort Yukon, Alaska, March 5.

John, Peter. 1991. *The First Christmas Tree: Ts'eba Tthadda.* Transcribed by James Kari and translated by Paul George. Fairbanks: Alaska Native Language Center.

Johnson, Ben. 2021. The History of Hogmanay. (https://www.historic-uk.com/HistoryUK/HistoryofScotland/The-History-of-Hogmanay/)

Johnston, Alfred W. and Amy Johnston, eds. 1907-08. *Orkney & Shetland Miscellany.* Vol. I. London: the Viking Club.

Johnston, Sam. 2016. *Four Tlingit Stories.* Transcribed and translated by Jeff Leer. Whitehorse.

Jones, Eliza and Chief Henry. 1976. *Koyukon Riddles: Kooltsaah Ts'in'.* Fairbanks: University of Alaska Native Language Center.

Jones, Eliza, ed. 1979. *The Stories That Chief Henry Told: Chief Henry Yugh Noholnigee.* Fairbanks: University of Alaska Native Language Center.

Jones, Strachan. 1867. The Kutchin Tribes. pp. 320-327. In "Notes on the Tinneh or Chepewyan Indians of British and Russian America." *Annual Report of the Smithsonian Institution for 1866.* Washington, D.C.

Jones, William. 1917. Objiwa Texts. ed. T. Michelson. *Publications of the American Ethnological Society* 7, Pt. 1. New York.

Kalifornsky, Peter. 1977. *Kahnuht'ana Qenaga*. ed. James Kari. Fairbanks: Alaska Native Language Center.

Kari, James, ed. 1980. *Kich'ighi: Dena'ina Riddles*. Anchorage: University of Alaska National Bilingual Materials Development Center.

_____. 2010. *Ahtna Travel Narratives: A Demonstration of Shared Geographic Knowledge Among Alaska Athabascans*. Fairbanks: University of Alaska Press.

Kari, James and Adeline Peter Raboff. 2011. *Compilation of Yukon Flats Athabascan Place Names for Stevens Village, Beaver, Birch Creek and Fort Yukon*. Report for the U.S. Fish and Wildlife Service, 2011.

Kennecott, Robert. 1859. Journal. In James A. James, ed., *The First Scientific Exploration of Russian America and the Purchase of Alaska*. Evanston and Chicago: Northwestern University Press, 1942.

_____. 1860a. Letter to Lucy Hunter Baird from Mackenzies River above Fort Simpson, August 21. pp. 78-80. In Debra Lindsay, ed., *Modern Beginnings of Subarctic Ornithology: Correspondence to the Smithsonian Institution*. Winnipeg: Manitoba Record Society, 1991.

_____. 1860b. Letter to Lucy Hunter Baird from Ft. Youkon, Youkon River, December 18. pp. 93-95. In Debra Lindsay, ed., *Modern Beginnings*.

_____. 1860c. Letter to Spencer Baird from Youkon, December 18. pp. 96-104. In Debra Lindsay, ed., *Modern Beginnings*.

_____. 1862. Letter to Spencer Baird from The Grove Cook Co., Illinois, October 29th. pp. 139-141. In Debra Lindsay, ed., *Modern Beginnings*.

_____. 1942. Journal. In James A. James, ed., *The First Scientific Exploration of Russian America and the Purchase of Alaska*. Evanston and Chicago: Northwestern University Press. Orig. 1859.

Kirkby, W.W. 1860. Letter to the Church Missionary Society, June 20. NAC.

_____. 1861a. Letter to the Church Missionary Society, May 17. NAC.

_____. 1861b. Annual Report to the Church Missionary Society, November 30. NAC.

_____. 1861c. Journal. NAC.

_____. 1862. Annual Report to the Church Missionary Society, November 29. NAC.

_____. 1863. The Indians on the Youcon. In H. Hind, *Explorations in the Interior of the Labrador Peninsula. Vol. I.* London: Longman, Green, et al.

_____. 1872. A Journey to the Youcan, Russian America. pp. 416-420. *Smithsonian Institution Annual Report for 1864.* Washington, D.C.

_____. 1942. Robert Kennicott Journal. In James A. James, ed., *The First Scientific Exploration of Russian America and the Purchase of Alaska.* Evanston and Chicago: Northwestern University Press. Orig. 1859.

Krauss, Michael and Victor Golla. 1981. Northern Athabaskan Languages. In *Handbook of North American Indians, Vol. 6, The Subarctic*, ed. June Helm, pp. 67-85. Washington: The Smithsonian Institution.

Krauss, Michael. 1983. Notes on Slavey Jargon in Gwich'in. Based on interview with Katherine Peter, August 17. Mss. KU962K 1982. Alaska Native Language Archive, University of Alaska, Fairbanks.

_____. 1988. Letter to Craig Mishler from Fairbanks, Alaska, April 11.

Laverdure, Patline and Ida Rose Allard. 1983. *The Michif Dictionary: Turtle Mountain Chippewa Cree.* Ed. by John Crawford. Winnipeg: Pemmican Publications.

LeClaire, Nancy and George Cardinal. 1998. *Alberta Elders' Cree Dictionary.* Ed. by Earle Waugh. Edmonton: University of Alberta Press.

Lederman, Anne. 2001/2002. Native and Métis Fiddling: Portrait of a People. *Fiddler Magazine* 8 (No. 4): 4-11.

Leechman, Douglas. 1950. Loucheux Tales. *Journal of American Folklore* 63(248):158-162.

_____. 1952. Folk-lore of the Vanta Kutchin. *Bulletin* No. 126:76-93. Ottawa: National Museum of Canada.

_____. 1954. The Vanta Kutchin. *Bulletin* No. 130, A.S. No. 33. Ottawa: National Museum of Canada.

Lewes, John Lee. 1899. Letter to the Governor, Chief Factors, and Chief Traders, from Fort Simpson, November 17, 1842. pp. 25-26. In Otto Klotz, ed., *Certain Correspondence of the Foreign Office and of the Hudson's Bay Company: copied from original documents.* Ottawa: Government Printing Bureau.

Li, Fang Kuei and Scollon, Ronald. 1976. Chipewyan Texts. *Institute of History and Philology Academia Sinica Special Publications* 71. Nanking/ Taipei Taiwan.

Li, Fang-Kuei. 1946. Chipewyan. In Harry Hoijer, ed., *Linguistic Structures of Native America.* pp. 398-423. Viking Fund Publications in Anthropology 6. New York: The Viking Fund.

Lindow, John. 1974. A Note on the Sources of Redundancy in Oral Epic. *Journal of American Folklore* 87(346): 365-369.

Lindsey, Kelsey. 2017. Unhealthy air in rural Alaska homes targeted in tribal program. *Alaska Dispatch News*, August 7, pp. A1ff.

Lysyk, Kenneth, Edith Bohmer, and Willard Phelps. 1977. *Alaska Highway Pipeline Inquiry.* Ottawa: Dept. of Indian Affairs and Northern Development.

Loola, William. 1894. Letter to Thomas Canham, November 21. Box 1, Envelope C. Archbishop Thomas Henry Canham Papers, General Synod Archives, Anglican Church of Canada, Toronto.

Loovers, Jan Peter Laurens. 2011. Making Lobsticks: Marking Histories with Teetł'it Gwich'in. pp. 190-197. In John P. Ziker and Florian Stammler, eds., *Histories from the North: Environments, Movements, and Narratives.* Boise: Department of Anthropology, Boise State University.

_____. 2016. Making Lobsticks: Traveling Trails with Teetł'it Gwich'in. *Sibirica* 15(1):41-63.

Lowie, Robert. 1960. *Crow Texts.* Berkeley & Los Angeles: University of California Press.

_____. 1983. *The Crow Indians.* Lincoln & London: University of Nebraska Press. Orig. 1935.

M'Lot, Maria. 2002. *Kâ Isinâkwâk Askîy: Using Cree knowledge to perceive and describe the landscape of the Wapuksk National Park Area.* M.A. thesis, University of Manitoba Natural Resources Institute. Access online at: https://mspace.lib.umanitoba.ca/items/2f4058ba-bca9-4648-940b-2de62cb42be5

Mackenzie, Alexander. 1966. *Voyages from Montreal on the River St. Laurence.* Ann Arbor: University Microfilms. Orig. 1801.

MacNeish, June Helm. 1954. Contemporary Folk Beliefs of a Slave Indian Band. *Journal of American Folklore* 67:185-198.

Mackenzie, Clara Childs. 1985. *Wolf Smeller (Zhoh Gwats'an).* Anchorage: Alaska Pacific University Press.

MacLeod, Margaret Arnett. 1953. Red River New Year. *The Beaver.* Outfit 284, December. pp. 43-47.

Mair, Charles. 1908. *Through the MacKenzie Basin: A Narrative of the Athabasca and Peace River Treaty Expedition of 1899.* Toronto: William Briggs. Access online at: https://www.gutenberg.org/ebooks/12569

Malcolm, Sarah. 1975. Taped interview in Eagle Village on August 15 with Craig Mishler. Transcript in Craig Mishler Papers, Consortium Library, Anchorage.

Martin, Richard. 1983. Personal communication with Craig Mishler, May 23, in Fairbanks.

_____. 1993. *K'aiiroondak: Behind the Willows.* Ed. by William Pfisterer. Fairbanks: University of Alaska Press.

Mason, Michael H. 1924. *The Arctic Forests.* Hodder and Stoughton Ltd., London.

Massie, Merle. 2012. The lobstick: our next national symbol? *The Globe and Mail,* October 25.

Matesi, Joseph. 2016. *Gwich'in Athabascan Place Names. Steese National Conservation Area, Draanjik River, and Porcupine River.* Fairbanks: Alaska Native Language Center.

McAllister, David. 1964. Riddles and Other Verbal Play Among the Comanches. *Journal of American Folklore* 77:251-257.

McCartney, Leslie and the Gwich'in Tribal Council. 2020. *Our Whole Gwich'in Way of Life Has Changed/Gwich'in K'yuu Gwiidandài' Tthak Ejuk Gòonlih.* Edmonton: University of Alberta Press.

McClellan, Catherine. 1975. *My Old People Say: An Ethnographic Survey of Southern Yukon Territory.* 2 vols. Ottawa: National Museums of Canada Publications in Ethnology No. 6.

_____. 1987. *Part of the Land, Part of the Water: A History of the Yukon Indians.* Vancouver and Toronto: Douglas & McIntyre.

McDonald, Robert. 1862. Letter to the Church Missionary Society, August 20. NAC.

_____. 1863a. Letter to the Church Missionary Society, June 1. Microfilm Reel MG 17 B2, NAC.

_____. 1863b. Journal entries for April 24 and July 31, 1863b. Mss. 4001, AEPRL.

_____. 1863b. Journal. AEPRL.

_____. 1863c. Letter to the Church Missionary Society, June 24. NAC.

_____. 1864. Letter to the Church Missionary Society, June 25. Microfilm Reel MG 17 B2, NAC.

_____. 1865. Journal. AEPRL.

_____. 1866. Journal, April 21. AEPRL.

_____. 1866-75. Journals. Microfilm copy at the NAC.

_____. 1868. Journal. AEPRL.

_____. 1875. Annual Letter to the Church Missionary Society, January 25. NAC.

_____. 1893. Journal. April 20. Microfilm P 340, MS 4001. AEPRL.

_____. 1889. *Chilig Takudh Tshah Zit: Hymns in Takudh Language.* 2nd ed. Society for Promoting Christian Knowledge, London.

_____. 1900. Journal. December 31. Microfilm P 340, MS 4001. AEPRL.

McGary, Mary Jane. 1984. Gwich'in Gwandak. M.A. Thesis, University of Alaska Fairbanks. Access online at: https://www.uaf.edu/anla/record.php?identifier=KU978M1984

McGary, Mary Jane (ed.) 1982. *Edward Sapir John Fredson Hàa Googwandak: Stories Told by John Fredson to Edward Sapir*. Fairbanks: Alaska Native Language Center, University of Alaska.

McGrath, J.E. 1893. The Boundary South of Fort Yukon, *National Geographic* IV (February 8): 181-188.

McKennan, Robert A. 1933. Letter of April 20 to Dr. J.B. Mertie. Robert McKennan Collection, Baker Library, Dartmouth College, Hanover, NH.

_____. 1959. *The Upper Tanana Indians.* New Haven: Yale University Publications in Anthropology No. 55.

_____. 1965. *The Chandalar Kutchin.* Arctic Institute of North America, Montreal.

_____. 1965. Loche's Potlatch. pp. 128-129. *The Chandalar Kutchin.* Montreal: Arctic Institute of North America.

Mendenhall, T.C., J.E. McGrath, and J. Henry Turner. 1893. The Alaskan Boundary Survey. *National Geographic Magazine* IV:177-197.

Mendenhall, Walter C. 1898. Reconnaissances from Resurrection Bay to the Tanana River. NoteBook No.1. Unpublished field notes. U.S. Geological Survey, Technical Data Unit, Anchorage.

_____. 1900. A Reconnaissance from Resurrection Bay to the Tanana River, Alaska, in 1898. *U.S. Geological Survey*, 20th Annual Report, Part 7:265-340.

Mendenhall, Walter C., and F.C. Schrader. 1903a. Copper Deposits of the Wrangell Mountain Region, Alaska. *USGS Bulletin* No. 213: 141-148.

_____. 1903b. The Mineral Resources of the Mount Wrangell District, Alaska. *USGS Professional Paper* No. 15. Washington, DC.

Mercier, François Xavier. 1983. *Recollections of the Youkon District, 1868-1885.* Ed. and transl. by Linda Finn Yarborough. Alaska Historical Commission, Juneau.

Merriam, Allan P. 1972. Anthropology and the Dance. pp. 9-27. In Tamara Comstock, ed., *New Dimensions in Dance Research: Anthropology and Dance—The American Indian: The Proceedings of the Third Conference on Research in Dance.* New York: CORD.

Mertie, Evelyn. 1982. *Thirty Summers and a Winter.*, Mineral Industry Research Laboratory, School of Mineral Industry, University of Alaska, Fairbanks.

Mertie, J. B., Jr. 1925. Geology and Gold Placers of the Chandalar District. *U.S. Geological Survey Bulletin* 773E, pp. 215-263.

_____. 1928. Preliminary Report on the Sheenjek River District. *U.S. Geological Survey Bulletin* 797C, pp. 99-123.

_____. 1930. The Chandalar-Sheenjek District, Alaska. *U.S. Geological Survey Bulletin* 810B, pp. 87-139.

_____. 1933. Letters of April 25, May 2, and May 25 to Robert McKennan. Robert McKennan Collection, Baker Library, Dartmouth College, Hanover, NH.

_____. 1978. Oral history interview. Interviewed by Dick Tagg, U.S. Geological Survey, Menlo Park, California, April 8. Transcript located in the office of the Chief Geologist, U.S. Geological Survey, Reston, VA.

Mishler, Craig. 1973. Unpublished field notes and recording session with Daniel John in Chalkytsik, March 30. See Alaska Native Language Archive. Recording GW1044. Also UAA Archives, Craig Mishler papers. Series 1: Research and writing files. Subseries 1d: Gwich'in research files; 1940-2021, Box 5, Folder 3.

_____. 1974. Producer and editor. *Music of the Alaskan Kutchin [Gwich'in] Indians.* Lp and compact disc with liner notes. FE 4070. Washington, D.C.: Folkways Records, Smithsonian Institution.

_____. 1983. Taped interviews with Abraham Luke, July 11 in Delta Junction and July 27 in Dot Lake, Alaska.

_____. 1981. "He Said, They Say": the Uses of Reporting Speech in Native American Folk Narrative. *Fabula* 22(3-4):239-249.

_____. 1982. John Fredson: A Biographical Sketch. In J. McGary, ed., *John Fredson Edward Sapir Hàa Googwandak/Stories Told by John Fredson to Edward Sapir*. pp. 10-20. Alaska Native Language Center, University of Alaska, Fairbanks.

_____. 1983. Mizhur, Monsieur? A Gwich'in Card Game. Paper presented to the American Folklore Society Annual Meeting, Nashville, TN. See Chapter 14 below.

_____. 1986. Audio cassette tape recording of the Gwich'in Naming Ceremony for Katrina Frank, held at the Athabascan Old-Time Fiddling Festival, Fairbanks, Alaska. 30 minutes. Author's private collection.

_____. 1990. Missionaries in Collision: Anglicans and Oblates Among the Gwich'in, 1861-1865. *Arctic* 43(2):121-126. See Chapter 1 above. Original available for online download at:http://pubs.aina.ucalgary.ca/arctic/Arctic43-2-121.pdf

_____. 1993. *The Crooked Stovepipe: Athapaskan Fiddle Music and Square Dancing in Northeast Alaska and Northwest Canada.* Urbana: University of Illinois Press.

_____. 1999. Native Village of Venetie Tribal Government Historic Preservation Plan and Site Inventory: Final Report. National Park Service Grant Number: 02-97-NA-0237.

_____.(ed.) 2001. *Neerihiinjìk: We Traveled From Place to Place: The Gwich'in Stories of Johnny and Sarah Frank.* 2nd edition with CD. Fairbanks: Alaska Native Language Center, University of Alaska.

_____. 2010. Video tape recording of Gwich'in Naming Ceremony for Daisy Stevens' grandchildren, held at the Gwich'in Gathering in Fort Yukon. Author's private collection.

_____. 2012. Collaborating with the Tiger: The Evolution of an Essay. *Arctic Anthropology* 49(2): 188-193.

_____. 2013. *The Blind Man and the Loon: the Story of a Tale.* Lincoln and London: University of Nebraska Press.

_____. 2023. Guide to the Craig Mishler Papers. Anchorage Consortium Library Archives: https://archives.consortiumlibrary.org/collections/specialcollections/hmc-1300/

Mishler, Craig and Kenneth Frank. 2020. *Dinjii Vadzaih Dhidlit: The Man Who Became a Caribou.* 2nd ed. Hanover, N.H.: IPI Press.

_____. 2021. Shriniinlii 'Fix It': The Grease Mechanics of Translating Gwich'in. pp. 461-478. In: *Indigenous Languages and the Promise of Archives.* Ed. by Adrianna Link, Abigail Shelton, and Patrick Spero. University of Nebraska Press, Lincoln.

Mishler, Craig, Kenneth Frank, and Allan Hayton. 2014. Collaborating in Gwich'in on the Web: Khahłok Gwiti'it'agwarah'in. In: *Working Papers in Athabaskan (Dene) Languages*, 2013. Vol. 12, pp. 22-29. Fairbanks: Alaska Native Language Center.

Mishler, Craig and William Simeone. 2004. *Han: People of the River, Hän Hwëch'in.* Fairbanks: University of Alaska Press.

_____. 2006. *Tanana and Chandalar: the Alaska Field Journals of Robert A. McKennan.* Fairbanks: University of Alaska Press.

Mitchell, William 'Billy'. 1982. *The Opening of Alaska, 1901-1903.* Ed. by Lyman Woodman. Anchorage: Cook Inlet Historical Society.

Monaghan, Pat. 1977. Nuchalawoyya Diary. *Alaska Magazine* Vol. XLIII, Number 6, pp, 26-27ff.

Moore, Patrick. 1999. *Dene Gudeji: Kaska Narratives.* Watson Lake, Y.T.: Kaska Tribal Council.

Morehead, Albert, Richard Frey, and Geoffrey Mott-Smith. 1964. *The New Complete Hoyle.* Garden City, N.Y.: Doubleday & Co.

Morgan, Lewis Henry. 1997. *Systems of Consanguinity and Affinity of the Human Family.* Lincoln: University of Nebraska Press. Reprint of 1871 edition.

Morgan, Lewis Henry. 1959. *The Indian Journals, 1859-62.* Ed. by Leslie A. White. Ann Arbor: University of Michigan Press.

Murray, Alexander Hunter. 1847-1848. Fort Yukon Post Journal, 1847-48. B.240a/1/Folios 25, 26B, and 34D. HBCA, Winnipeg.

_____. 1848. Youcon Journal No. 1, entries for January 1 and November 24. B240a/2/Fo.14, HBCA, Winnipeg.

Nelson, Richard. 1973. *Hunters of the Northern Forest.* Chicago: University of Chicago Press.

_____. 1983. *Make Prayers to the Raven.* Chicago: University of Chicago Press.

Netro, Hannah. 1993. Interviewed by Shelagh Beairsto. Interpreted by Alice Frost. pp. 12-18. *Rampart House: Stories Told by Our Elders.* Yukon Territory: Students at Ts'ek Gehtr'oonatun Zzeh College.

_____. 2000. Tape VG 2000-4-13. Vuntut Gwitchin First Nation Oral History Collection, Old Crow.

Netro, Joe. 1980. *A Book of Indian Legends and Storys from Old Crow, Yukon Territory.* n.p. Copy at University of Alaska Consortium Library, Anchorage.

Northern Native Broadcasting. 1989. *Needaa: Gwich'in Niin Tsyaa.* Season 3, Show 22. Videotape, 58 minutes. Whitehorse.

Nute, Grace Lee, ed. 1954. Journey for Frances. *The Beaver* Outfit 285 (Summer): 12-18.

Orth, Donald. 1971. *Dictionary of Alaska Place Names.* USGS Professional Paper 567. Washington, DC.

Osgood, Cornelius. 1936. *Contributions to the Ethnography of the Kutchin.* New Haven: Yale University Publications in Anthropology No. 14.

_____. 1959. *Ingalik Mental Culture.* New Haven: Yale University Publications in Anthropology No. 56.

Overstreet, William, and Robert Chapman. 1982. Memorial to John Beaver Mertie Jr., 1888-1980. *Geological Society of America Memorials,* Vol. XII:1-8.

Patchen, Pauline. 1946. Report on Field Visit, June 17-19, 1946. Alaska Department of Public Welfare. RG 107, Series 51. Alaska State Archives, Juneau.

Payment, Diane. 2003. Marie Fisher Gaudet (1843-1914): 'la Providence du fort Good Hope'. Access online at: https://ecclectica.brandonu.ca/issues/2003/2/gaudet.html

Pearce, Tony Scott. 1985. Musical Characteristics of Tanana Athabascan Dance Songs. Unpublished M.A. thesis, University of Alaska, Fairbanks.

Peake, F.A. 1975. Robert McDonald (1829-1913): The Great Unknown Missionary of the Northwest. *Journal of the Canadian Church Historical Society* XVII(3):54-72.

Peter, Katherine. 1974-1979. Transcripts and translations of Elijah John's stories recorded by Craig Mishler. KU973P1974z. Downloadable as a PDF file. Alaska Native Language Archive, University of Alaska Fairbanks.

_____. 1978. *Deenaadai' Gwich'in Oozhri' (Traditional Gwich'in Names).* Introduction by Jane McGary. Fairbanks: Alaska Native Language Center.

_____. 1979. *Dinjii Zhuh Ginjik Nagwan Tr'iłtsaii: Gwich'in Junior Dictionary.* Anchorage: National Bilingual Materials Development Center.

_____. 1992. *Neets'ąįį Gwindaii: Living in the Chandalar Country.* Fairbanks: Alaska Native Language Center.

Peter, Moses. 1974. Audio recording by Craig Mishler, ANLC1057 (1974). Alaska Native Language Archive, available online at: https://www.uaf.edu/anla/record.php?identifier=ANLC1057.

Peterson, Jacqueline and Jennifer S.H. Brown, eds. 1985. *The New Peoples: Being and Becoming Métis in North America.* Winnipeg: University of Manitoba Press.

Petitot, Émile. 1887. *Traditions indiennes du Canada nord-ouest.* Cinquième partie: Traditions des Dené Tchippewayans. Alençon.

_____. 1889. *Quinze ans sous le Cercle Polaire.* Paris: E. Dentu.

_____. 1891. *Autour du Grand Lac des Esclaves.* Paris: A. Savine. Available online at: http://www.canadiana.org/ECO/ItemRecord/11181?id=49434ab4871a8854

Pike, Warburton. 1896. *Through the Subarctic Forest.* New York: Edward Arnold.

Podruchny, Carolyn. 2006. *Making the Voyageur World.* Lincoln and London: University of Nebraska Press.

Porter, Robert P. 1893. *Report on the Population and Resources of Alaska, Eleventh Census, 1890.* Washington, D.C.

Rainey, Froelich. 1947. *The Whale Hunters of Tigara.* Anthropological Papers of the American Museum of Natural History 41, Pt. 2. New York.

Rasmussen, Knud. 1932. *Intellectual Culture of the Copper Eskimos.* Report of the Fifth Thule Expedition, 1921-24, 9. Copenhagen.

Raspe, Rudolf Erich. 1902. *The Adventures of Baron Muchausen.* New York: Thomas Y. Crowell. Available online via Google Books. Orig. 1795.

Rausch, R. A. 1953. On the Status of Some Arctic Mammals. *Arctic* 6:91-147.

Remington, C.H. [Copper River Joe] 1939. *A Golden Cross? On Trails from the Valdez Glacier.* Los Angeles: White-Thompson.

Rice, Keren. 2007. Personal communications with Craig Mishler.

Robert, Myra. 1979. Taped interview with Craig Mishler , May 15, in Venetie.

_____. 1980. Taped interview with Craig Mishler, April 5. Translated from the Gwich'in by Moses P. Gabriel.

Roberts, Irene. 2011. Interview in Fairbanks on July 24 with Craig Mishler. Written notes.

Roberts, Jeannette. 1975. Nuchalawoyya. *Theata* Vol. III. pp. 21-22. Fairbanks: University of Alaska Student Orientation Services.

Roberts, Malcolm 'Sandy'. 1973. Taped interview with Craig Mishler at Circle, Alaska. March 26. Author's private collection.

Rooth, Anna Birgitta. 1971. The Alaska Expedition 1966. Lund, Sweden: *Acta Universitatis Ludensis*, Sectio1(14).

Sackett, John. 1972. The History of the Stick Dance. *Tundra Times*, March 15, page 2.

Sahlins, Marshall. 2022. *The New Science of the Enchanted Universe: An Anthropology of Most of Humanity*. Princeton, N.J.: Princeton University Press.

Salmon, David. 2007. Personal communication with Craig Mishler, in Fairbanks, March 16.

Sam family. 2001. Draft obituary for Moses Sam Sr., typescript prepared for newspaper publication. Courtesy of Patrick Semple.

Sam, Moses. 1996. Interview in Arctic Village on May 29 with Craig Mishler. Alaska Native Language Archive, University of Alaska Fairbanks. KU972Mi1998. Tape#11Moses-Sam01_SideB.wav

Samarin, William J. 1996. Arctic origin and domestic development of Chinook Jargon. pp. 321-329. In Ernst Håkon Jahr and Ingvild Broch, eds., *Language Contact in the Arctic: Northern Pidgins and Contact Languages*. Mouton de Gruyter: Berlin and New York.

Sapir, Edward. 1924. Personal Names among the Sarcee Indians. *American Anthropologist,* New Series, Vol. 26, No. 1. (Jan. - Mar.) pp. 108-119.

Sapir, Edward and Morris Swadesh. 1939. *Nootka Texts*. Philadelphia: University of Pennsylvania Press.

Sapir, Edward and Harry Hoijer. 1942. *Navaho Texts.* Iowa City: Linguistic Society of America.

Satterlee, Capers n.d. Man at Thirteen. Unpublished typescript courtesy of Mrs. Florence Martin, Spartanburg, N.C.

Schieffelin, Edward. 1883. Photo album. James Wickersham Collection. Image #ASL-P277-017-034. Alaska Historical Library, Juneau. Digital print may be viewed online at https://vilda.alaska.edu/digital/collection/cdmg21/id/917/rec/1 Also see the Huntington Library, San Marino, California: https://hdl.huntington.org/digital/collection/p15150coll2/id/9397

Schneider, William S. 1976. *Beaver, Alaska: The Story of a Multi-Ethnic Community.* Ph.D. dissertation, Bryn Mawr College. Ann Arbor: University Microfilms.

Scollon, Ronald and Suzanne B.K. 1979. *Linguistic Convergence: an Ethnography of Communication at Fort Chipewyan, Alberta*. New York: Academic Press.

Scott, J. Karen. 1994. The Use of Talking Circles as Part of the Therapeutic Milieu: A Conversation With Alice Modig. In Sharon K. Araji, Ed. *Society: An Alaskan Perspective*. Dubuque, IA: Kendall/Hunt. Orig. in *The Canadian Nurse/L'Infirmier Canadienne* 87 No. 6 (1991).

Scott, S. Osborne and D.A. Mulligan. 1951. The Red River Dialect. *The Beaver* Outfit 282: 42-45.

Séguin, Jean. 1862a. Letter to Fr. Mouchette, from Peel River, July 20. *Missions O.M.I.*, 1866, pp. 233-250.

_____. 1862b. Letter to Bishop Taché, July 22, from Peel River. Typescript. ADOMI.

_____. 1862c. Letter to Bishop Fabre from Fort Yukon, October 20. Typescript. ADOMI. Original in French. Quote translated by Mishler.

_____. 1862d. Letter to Frs. Faraud and Moulin from Fort Yukon, October 20. Typescript. ADOMI. Original in French.

_____. 1862e. Letter to Bishop Faraud and Fr. Moulin, October 20. Typescript. ADOMI.

_____. 1863a. Letter to his parents, June 2. Typescript. ADOMI.

_____. 1863b. Letter to Bishop Taché. Mission St. Jean, Fort Yukon, July 27. Typescript. ADOMI.

Shipley, Nan. 1967. Anne and Alexander Murray. *The Beaver* Outfit 298: 33-37.

Seton, Ernest Thompson. 1911. *The Arctic Prairies: A Canoe–Journey of 2,000 Miles in Search of the Caribou Being the Account of a Voyage to the Region North of Aylmer Lake*. New York: Charles Scribner's Sons.

Simpson, George. 1832. Colin Campbell. 'Character Book' for 2nd Class Officers. A.34/2, Folio 16, No. 17. Microfilm 423. HBCA.

Sherzer, Joel. 2002. *Speech Play and Verbal Art.* Austin: University of Texas Press.

Skinner, Alanson. 1916. Plains Cree Tales. *Journal of American Folklore* 29 (113): 341-367.

Sloan, Delores 1982 Interview with the Institute of Alaska Native Arts. *IANA Newsletter*, November-December, p. 5.

Slobodin, Richard. 1964. The Subarctic Métis as Products and Agents of Culture Contact. *Arctic Anthropology* 2(2): 50-55.

_____. 1966. *Métis of the Mackenzie District.* Ottawa: Canadian Research Centre for Anthropology, Saint-Paul University.

_____. 1981. Kutchin. In *Handbook of North American Indians, Vol. 6, The Subarctic*, ed. June Helm, pp. 514-532. Washington: The Smithsonian Institution.

Smetzer, Mary Beth. 2007. Athabascan chief laid to rest. October 16. *Fairbanks Daily News-Miner.*

Smith, George H. 1961. Kon-Ta-Kyah, Hermon Alumnus. *Mount Hermon Alumni News* 62(1): pp. 14ff with photos.

_____. 1962. Letter to Arthur Chitty, February 26. Typescript. Archives of the Jessie DuPont Library, University of the South, Sewanee, Tennessee.

Smith, Philip S., and Gerald Fitzgerald. 1933. Letter of January 3 to Robert McKennan. Robert McKennan Collection, Baker Library, Dartmouth College, Hanover, NH.

Solomon, Hannah P. 1985. Interview on February 14. Tape H90-06-69, Rasmuson Library, Oral History Collection. University of Alaska, Fairbanks.

Stefansson, Vihjalmur. 1909. The Eskimo Trade Jargon of Herschel Island. *American Anthropologist* n.s. 11(2): 217-232.

Stern, Pamela. 2013. *Historical Dictionary of the Inuit.* 2nd ed. Lanham, Md: Scarecrow Press.

Stevens, Bill. 2013. *Ch'adzaa Aghwaa: He Carries the Dance: The Life and Times of Gwich'in Fiddler Bill Stevens.* Ed. by Craig Mishler, Maryanne Allan, and James Kari. Fairbanks: Alaska Native Knowledge Network, University of Alaska Fairbanks.

Stevens, Daisy. 1994. Gwich'in Gather at Old Crow. *The Council,* Vol. 19 No. 6 (Aug/Sept), 5.

Stewart, Ethel G. 1955. *Fort McPherson and the Peel River Area.* Unpublished M.A. thesis, Queen's University, Kingston, Ontario.

Stringer, Isaac O. 1909. Diary. General Synod Archives, Anglican Church of Canada, Toronto.

_____. 1912. Diary for August. Microfilm, Reel 4. Isaac O. Stringer Collection, Yukon Territorial Archives, Whitehorse.

Stuck, Hudson. 1905. Letter to Mr. Wood from Fort Yukon, February 6. Episcopal Church Archives, Austin, Texas.

_____. 1905-1918. Journals. 10 vols, Mss. Archives of the Episcopal Diocese of Alaska, Fairbanks. Microfilmed by the Archives of the University of Alaska, Rasmuson Library, Fairbanks.

_____. 1914. *Ten Thousand Miles with a Dog Sled.* New York: Charles Scribner's Sons.

_____. 1977. *The Ascent of Denali*. Seattle: the Mountaineers. Reprint of 1914 original, based on 1913 journal deposited at the American Geographic Society Library, New York. Includes journal kept by Walter Harper.

Swanton, John. 1905. Haida Texts and Myths: Skidegate Dialect. *Bulletin of the Bureau of American Ethnology* 29. Washington.

Szasz, Margaret (ed.) 1994. *Between Indian and White Worlds: The Cultural Broker.* Norman: University of Oklahoma Press.

Tedlock, Dennis. 1972. On the Translation of Style in Oral Narrative. pp. 114-133. In: Bauman, Richard and Paredes, Américo (eds.). *Towards New Perspectives in Folklore*. Austin: University of Texas Press.

Thomas, Kenny Sr. 2005. *Crow Is My Boss: Taatsą́ą' Shaa K'exalthet: The Oral Life History of a Tanacross Athabaskan Elder*. Ed. by Craig Mishler. Norman: University of Oklahoma Press.

_____. 2010. Interview recorded by Craig Mishler in Tok, Alaska, October 11, 2010.

Toelken, Barre. 1969. The 'Pretty Languages' of Yellowman: Genre, Mode, and Texture in Navajo Coyote Narratives. *Genre* 2(3):211-235.

Tritt, Abel. 1979. Taped interview with Craig Mishler, May 18, in Arctic Village.

Tritt, Albert n.d. Journal. Unpublished Mss. in Gwich'in and in English. University of Alaska Archives, Rasmuson Library, Fairbanks.

Tritt, Lincoln. 1988a. Letter to Craig Mishler, May 13, from Arctic Village.

_____. 1988b. Memorandum to Invited Participants, May 27, from Arctic Village.

Tritt-Frank, Caroline. 1989. *Nich'itsal Dzehgak Oozhįį.* Fairbanks: Yukon Flats School District and the Alaska Native Language Center.

Turner, J. Henry. 1893. The Boundary North of Fort Yukon. *National Geographic* IV:189-197.

Turner, Victor. 1977. *The Ritual Process: Structure and Anti-Structure.* Ithaca: Cornell University Press.

U.S. Department of the Interior. 1940a. Corporate Charter of the Native Village of Venetie, Alaska. Washington: U.S. Govt. Printing Office.

_____. 1940b. Constitution and By-Laws of the Native Village of Venetie, Alaska. Washington: U.S. Govt. Printing Office.

Van Bibber, Dan. 1989. Dan Van Bibber. pp. 20-25. *In Their Honour.* Whitehorse: Ya Sa To Communications Society.

Vološinov, V. N. 1971. Reported Speech. pp. 149-175. In: Matejka, Ladislav and Pomorska, Krystyna (eds.). *Readings in Russian Poetics: Formalist and Structuralist Views*. Cambridge, Mass.

Wagner, Günter. 1931. Yuchi Tales. *Publications of the American Ethnological Society* 8. New York.

Wagner, Roy. 2016. *The Invention of Culture*. 2nd ed. Chicago and London: University of Chicago Press. Orig. 1975.

Wallis, Mae. 1976. Interview with Craig Mishler in Fort Yukon, June 20. Audio recording available via the Alaska Native Language Archive, digitized cassette tape Side A. See https://www.uaf.edu/anla/record.php?identifier=KU972Mi1986

Webb, Melody. 1993. *The Last Frontier: A History of the Yukon Basin of Canada and Alaska.* Lincoln: University of Nebraska Press. Orig. 1985.

Wesbrook, Mary E. 1969. A Venture into Ethnohistory: The Journals of Rev. V.C. Sim, Pioneer Missionary on the Yukon. *Polar Notes* 9:34-45.

Whymper, Frederick. 1869. *Travel and Adventure in the Territory of Alaska.* New York: Harper Brothers.

Wood, John W. 1921. Letter to Grafton Burke, February 1. Typescript. Episcopal Church Archives, Austin, Texas.

_____. 1921-30. Correspondence with John Fredson. Approx. 20 letters, typescript. Episcopal Church Archives, Austin, Texas.

Wooden, Leonidas. 1900. Letter from Fort Yukon, January 16. Episcopal Church Archives, Austin, Texas.

_____. 1901. Letter to Rev. Joshua Kimber from Fort Yukon, Alaska, July 13. Episcopal Church Archives, Austin, Texas.

_____. 1902. Letter to Rev. Joshua Kimber, January 2. Episcopal Church Archives, Austin, Texas.

_____. 1904. Letter to Rev. Joshua Kimber, January 8. Episcopal Church Archives, Austin, Texas.

Woods, Lizzie. 1905-09. Letters to John W. Wood, Mss. Episcopal Church Archives, Austin, Texas.

Wright, T.G.A. 1911. The Venerable Robert McDonald. Typescript based on an oral interview with McDonald. EDAUA.

Wymper, Frederick. 1868. *Travel and Adventure in the Territory of Alaska.* London: John Murray. Reprinted by Readex Microprint, 1966.

Ye Sa To Communications Society. 1989. *In Their Honour*. Whitehorse.

Index

Index

Index

O

P

Q

R